PHOTOGRAPHY

HISTORY · ART · TECHNIQUE

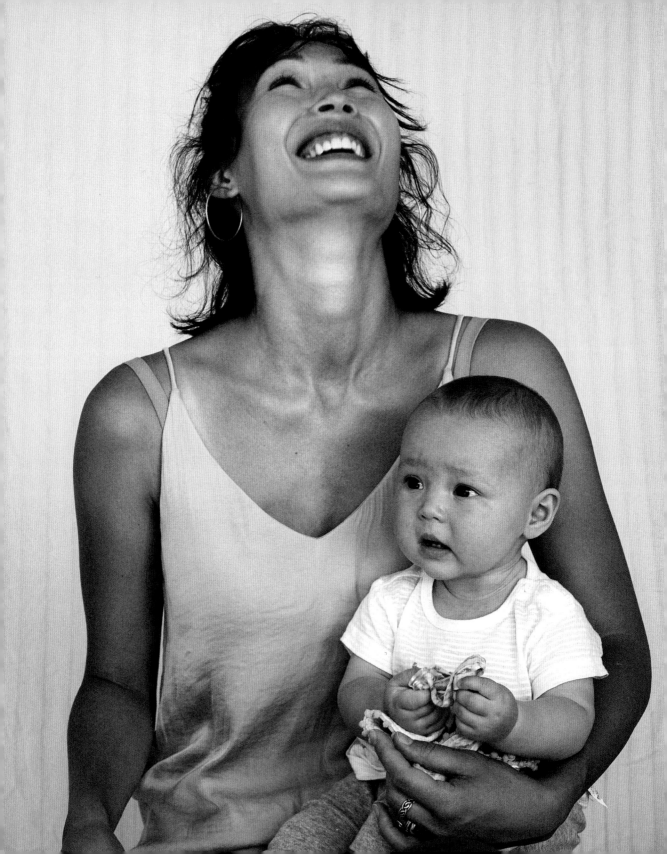

PHOTOGRAPHY

HISTORY · ART · TECHNIQUE

TOM ANG

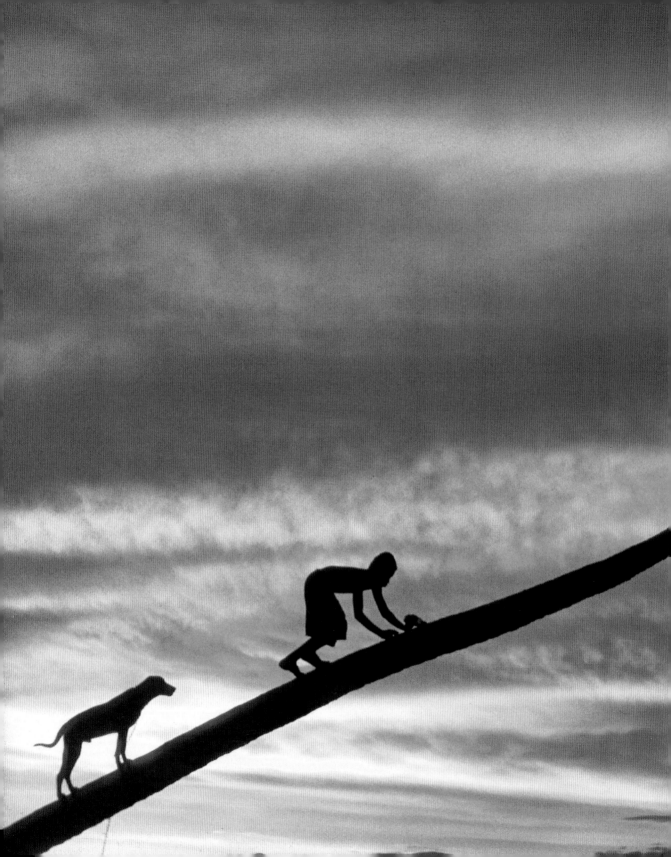

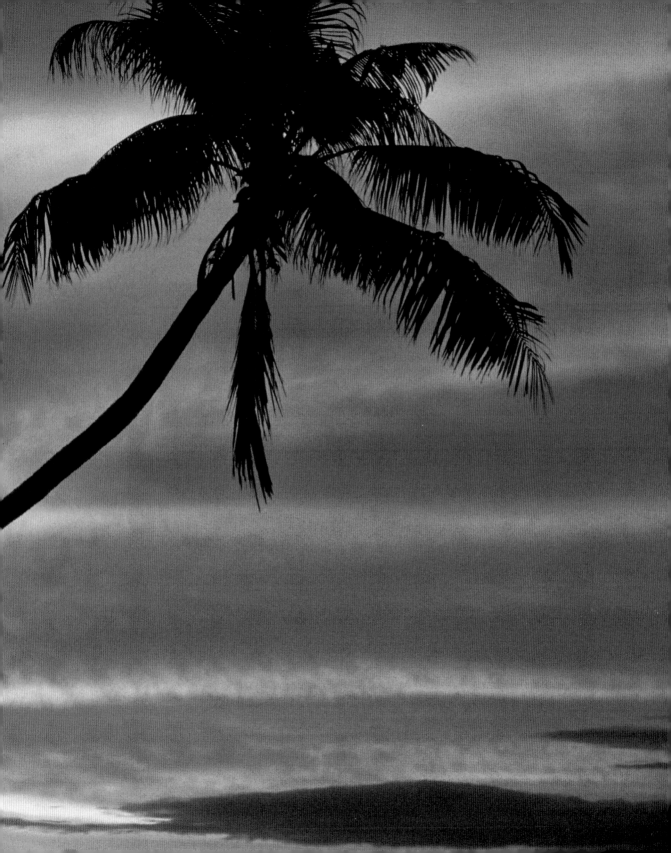

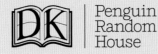

This book is dedicated to those who have taught me photography

Designed, edited, and project managed
for DK by Dynamo Limited

DK DELHI

Art Editor	Anita Yadav, Pushpak Tyagi
Senior DTP Designer	Neeraj Bhatia
DTP Designers	Anita Yadav, Mohd. Rizwan, Vikram Singh
Pre-production Managers	Balwant Singh, Sunil Sharma
Production Manager	Pankaj Sharma
Project Picture Research	Deepak Negi
Jacket Designer	Tanya Mehrotra
Jacket DTP Designer	Rakesh Kumar
Jackets Editorial Coordinator	Priyanka Sharma
Managing Jackets Editor	Saloni Singh

DK LONDON

Senior Editor	Chauney Dunford
Senior Art Editor	Nicola Rodway
Managing Editor	Gareth Jones
Senior Managing Art Editor	Lee Griffiths
Pre-production Producer	Jacqueline Street
Senior Producer	Rachel Ng
Jacket Designer	Surabhi Wadhwa-Gandhi
Jacket Editor	Emma Dawson
Jacket Design Development Manager	Sophia MTT
Publisher	Liz Wheeler
Publishing Director	Jonathan Metcalf
Art Director	Karen Self

First published in Great Britain in 2005 as
Eyewitness Companions Photography.
The revised edition published in 2019 by
Dorling Kindersley, 80 Strand, London, WC2R 0RL

Copyright © 2005, 2019 Dorling Kindersley Limited
A Penguin Random House Company
2 4 6 8 10 9 7 5 3 1
001–312777–Sept/2019

All rights reserved. No part of this publication may be
reproduced, stored in a retrieval system, or transmitted
in any form or by any means, electronic, mechanical,
photocopying, recording, or otherwise, without the prior
written permission of the copyright owner.

A CIP catalogue record for this book is
available from the British Library.
ISBN: 978-0-2413-6360-7

Printed in China.

A WORLD OF IDEAS:
SEE ALL THERE IS TO KNOW

www.dk.com

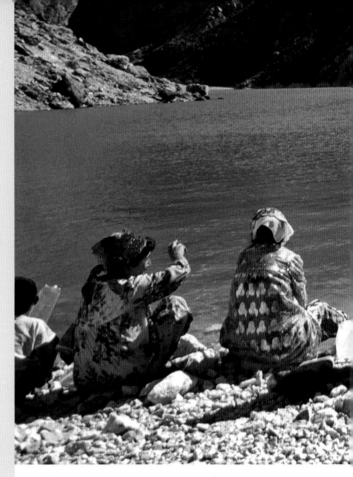

Contents

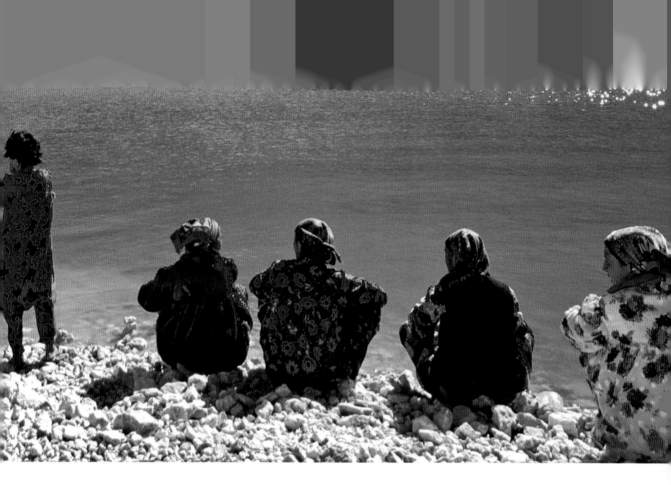

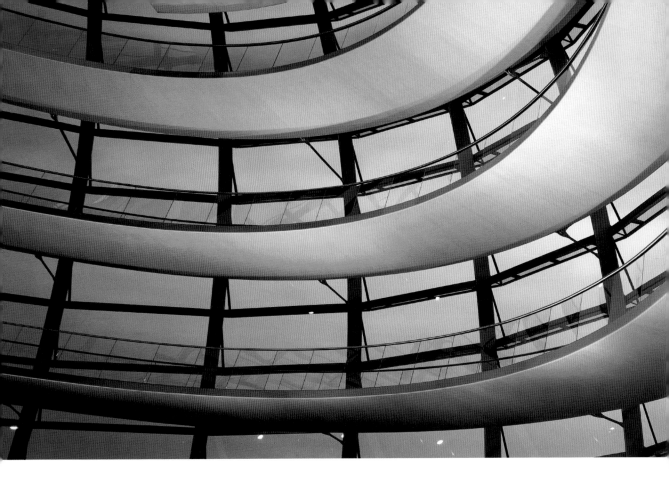

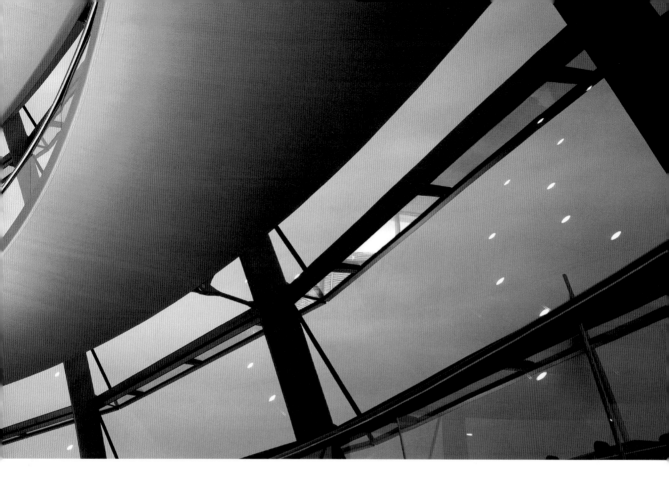

It is well known that photography means "writing with light". However, that is an understatement on a scale equal to saying that literature is simply "writing with a pen". Photography means so much more than that. To contemplate the true extent of its social reach and cultural impact is awe-inspiring.

Photography is inextricably interwoven into modern life. Photographs are all around us, we see them everywhere, and, since cameras have become an essential feature of mobile phones, billions of people around the planet are snapping images several times a day. But photography is not just about pictures. Much of modern technology, such as the creation of integrated circuits and microchips, use photographic masks in their manufacture.

At the same time, the power of photography to shape our lives is as strong as ever. A single photograph – such as the shot of missiles being deployed in Cuba in 1962 – can take the world to the brink of war. An image can create worldwide notoriety. Consider the celebrities over the years whose misbehaviour with each other have kept the paparazzi busy and readers entertained.

Born out of the Victorian era's obsession with the mechanization of all activities, photography was – and still is – the product of a triumvirate of art, science, and technology. The tremendous advances made by digital photography, for example, relied on the bedrock of imaging sciences that were developed for interstellar observation and satellite surveillance.

>> **Working with light**
This image is not just about children on their way to church for their first communion. It is a joyous celebration of the power of light.

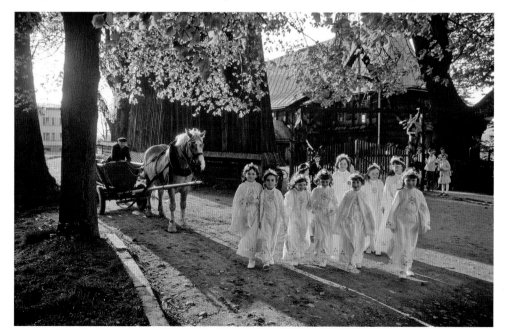

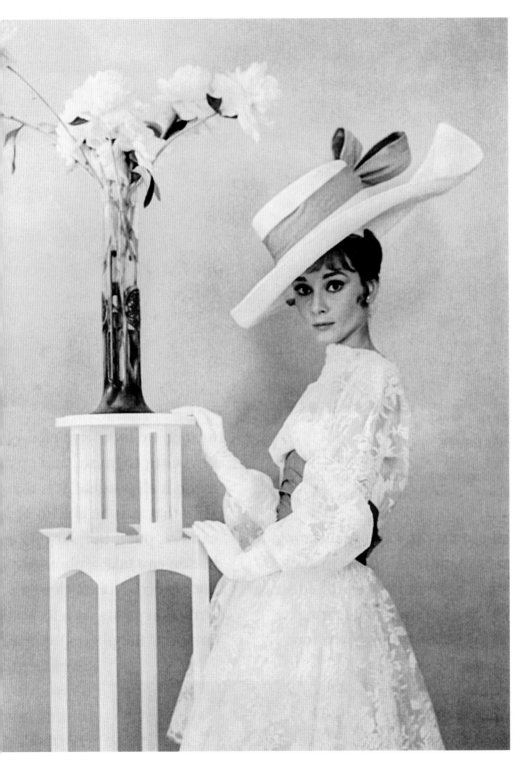

《 Consummate art
Photography can
preserve ephemeral
gestures and beauty
forever, as in this
timeless image of
Audrey Hepburn
by Cecil Beaton.

>> **Flower power**
At once a literal representation of the power of a flower against armed forces, this image was also a rallying point for anti-Vietnam war protests.

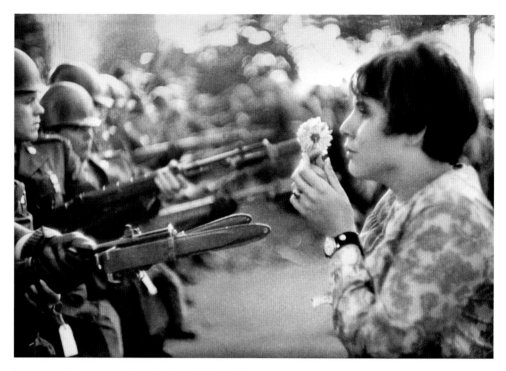

>> **Illustrating another world**
Images taken from space appear so perfect and stunning, some people find it hard believe they are genuine.

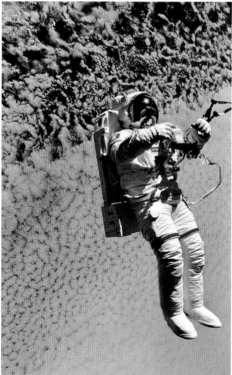

Photography has taught us so much. From the telescopic images of the far reaches of the universe to the microscopic images of the intricacies of nature, photography has opened our eyes to the beauty of our own and other worlds, showing us things that were previously beyond human vision. Photographs can capture meaningful memories, or be distorted to abet deceit. They can be used to seduce, or insult, and are capable of bringing great joy or sorrow. Furthermore, photographs can communicate highly complicated realities: images of disease or injury are sent routinely to specialists for diagnosis, while forensics teams rely on photographs to record vital evidence.

We admire and value photography because of its ability to inspire individual vision, and are awed by its capacity to change universal

>> **A universal language**
Images can be understood in any language or culture, like this joyful picture of dancers outside a jazz club taken by Malian photographer Malick Sidibe (1935–2016).

perception. For the former, we must give credit to the physicists, chemists, and engineers who made it all possible: it is thanks to their skills that anyone able to pick up a camera, put it to their eye, and press a button can take a photograph. Skill is not needed. Nonetheless, photography's attraction grows with its ability to empower the photographer. A small investment in learning is rewarded with rich returns. It is enormously satisfying to produce an image that matches your original vision and communicates that vision to others. It is little wonder that making photography is one of the world's favourite pastimes; and a career in photography is an aspiration nurtured by millions. Photography's capacity for immediate impact and honesty of presentation gives it the power to enhance our understanding of situations, and influence our opinions. This is because of the primacy of visual perception: we depend on sight more than on any other sense for our survival.

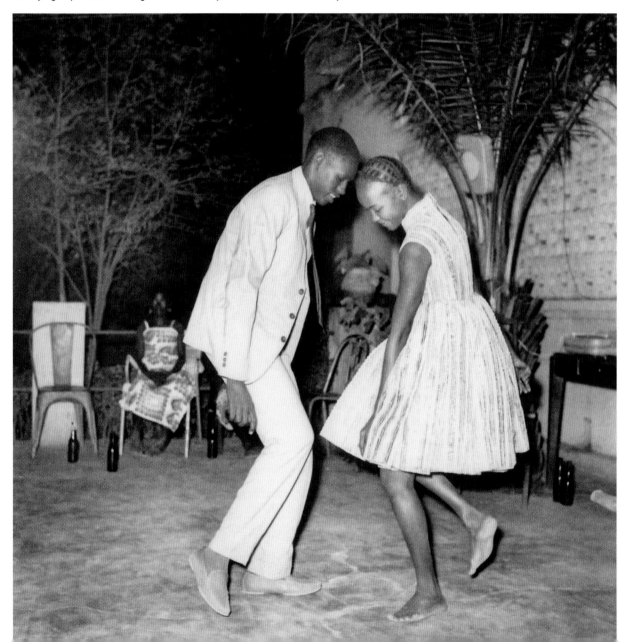

As a result, a photograph can convey almost any human emotion, even complicated interpersonal tensions, in an instant. As a result, pictures dominate international communication. Greater than being worth a thousand words, an image can be understood in a thousand languages.

While you may not agree with philosopher and cultural theorist Paul Virilio (1932–2018) that photographs are a virus on the planet, it is true that the typical city-dweller is bombarded by photographs every waking moment of his or her life. From the carefully chosen print that adorns the bedroom wall, to the pictures of happy, healthy friends and families engulfing our social media streams; from the gritty images in our newspapers to the glossy images in the junk mail; from the advertising posters along the roads, and in the stations selling products and lifestyles, to the celebrity portraits and paparazzi shots that fill countless magazines, we simply cannot escape from photographs.

It could be argued that advertising photography is the medium that powers many industries. Scenic views of exotic locations whet our appetites for travel, while seductive and sophisticated images arouse our desire to own a particular make of car or kitchen. It is photography that largely informs and influences our choices as consumers. The capacity to cause change is one of photography's most alluring characteristics. For decades it was the needling probe of humanity, retarding reckless war-mongering, shocking the world into action over famine, and revealing abuses in strife-torn areas. It can also inspire us to push ourselves further. Pictures of acts of heroism

◻ Fashioning styles
It is hard to imagine how modern fashion could have developed without the help of photography. No other medium can depict so clearly while suggesting much else.

» Every moment
Billions of people carry a camera with them all the time in the form of smartphones. We can record every moment of our lives from dawn to dusk, capturing expressions, colourful lighting and treasured moments.

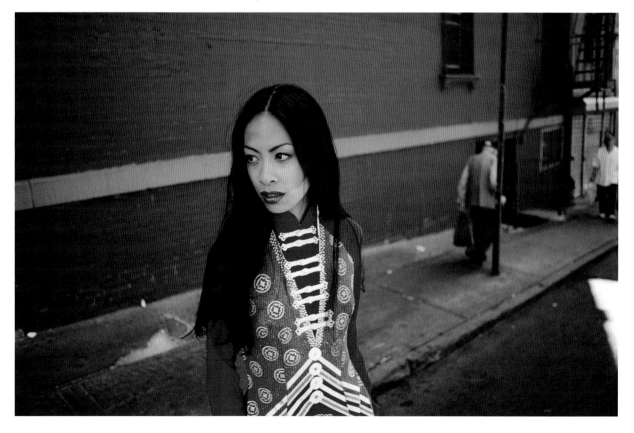

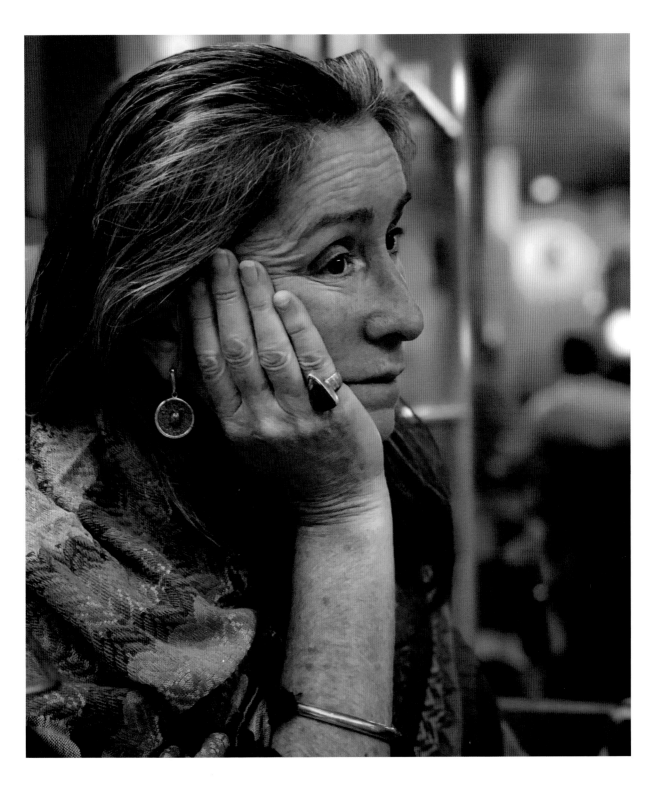

or courage – such as students being rescued from flooded caves – show us what we are capable of and give us something to aspire to.

This book is a tribute to those photographers who have changed the world, both through their vision and through their committed, sometimes painful pursuit of truth and beauty. It celebrates the great, the good, the terrifying, and the glorious.

The emotional span of photography is as wide as any person can experience. I hope that when reading the book you will be awed, troubled, and inspired by turn. At the same time, the book offers you a resource: how to equip for and improve your own photography, and to learn more. Above all, I hope that this book will open your eyes to see beneath the surface of the photograph, and look behind the image to reach the truths within.

Natural vision
Our vision of the natural world has been shaped by stunning images made by skilled, and sometimes extremely brave, photographers, such as this award-winning shot of sharks, taken by Doug Perrine.

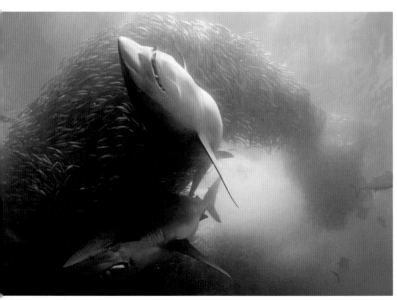

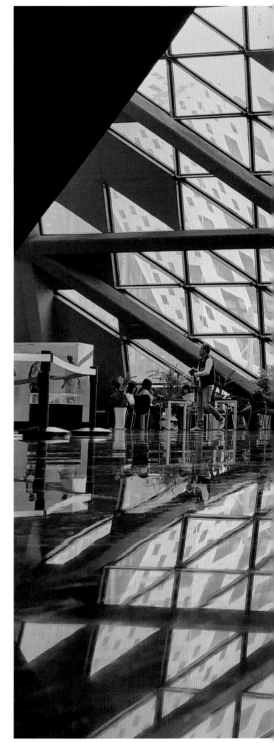

Unique views
Photography has given us new ways to see the world. The geometric shapes and reflections in modern airport spaces can offer an abstract take on the everyday.

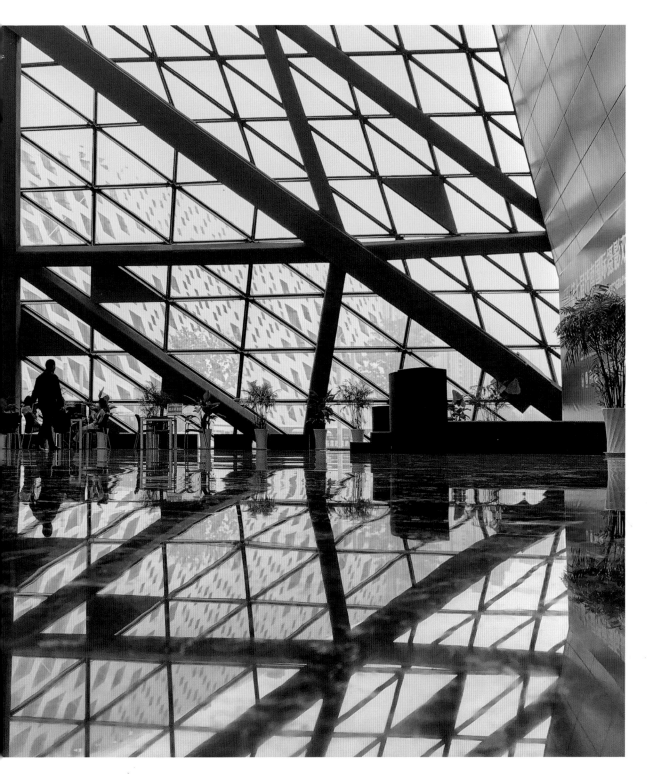

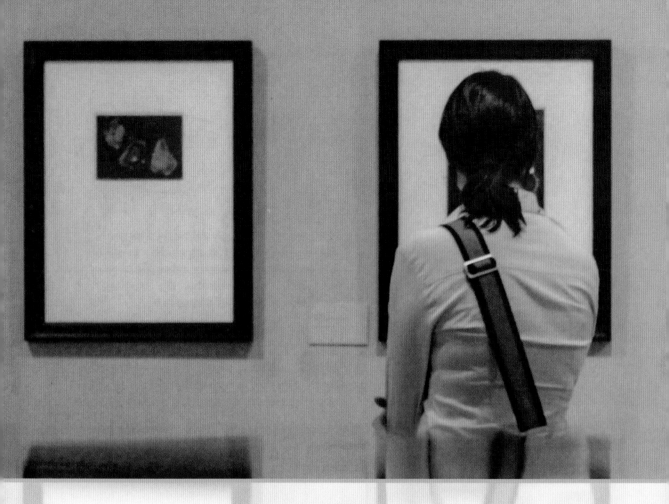

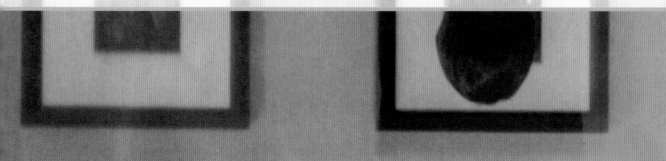

GALLERY OF
PHOTOGRAPHERS

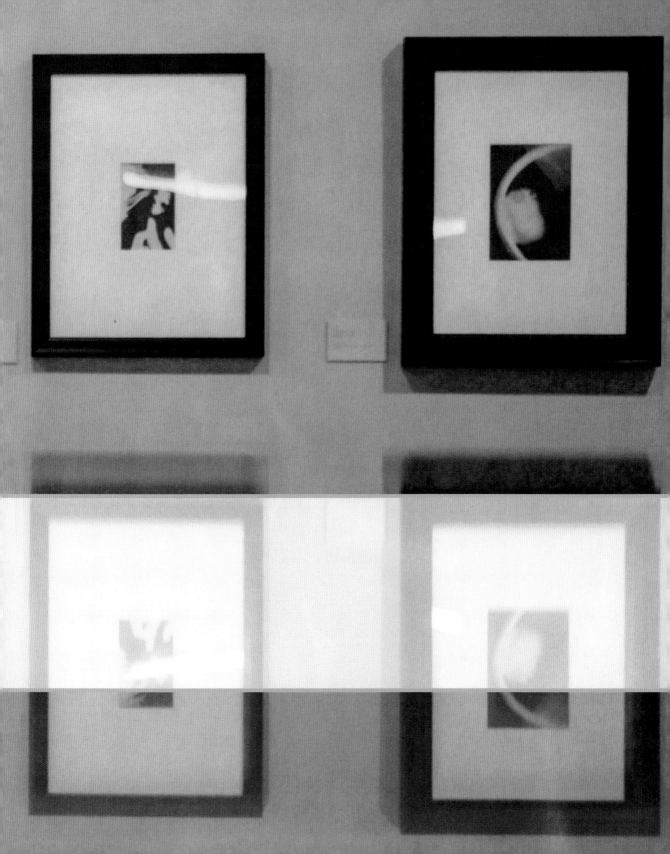

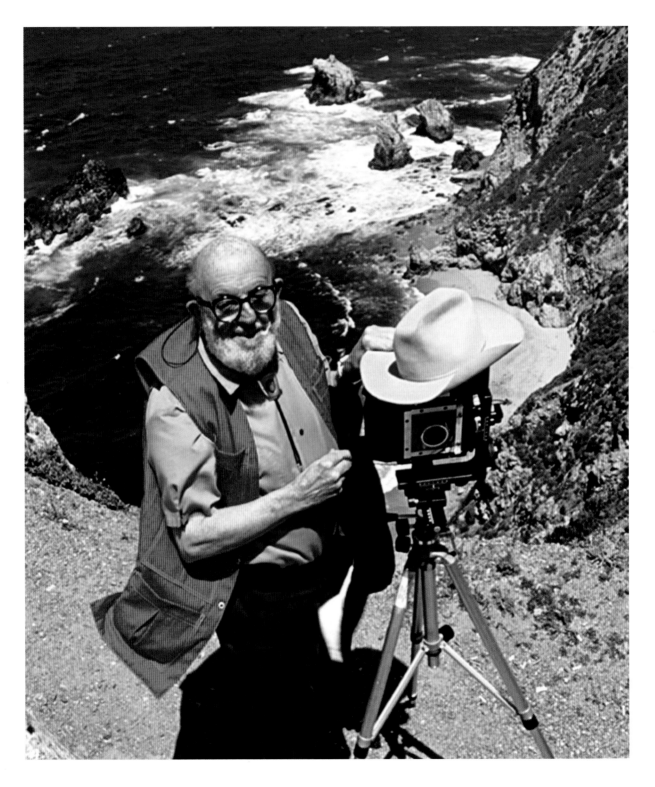

The greatest photographers have challenged and expanded our visual horizons. They have taught us to see the world in a different way, and how better to appreciate and understand it. As photographers we can learn so much from these artists who inspire us to seek excellence in our own work.

The shining beacons in the history of photography are those creative and technical geniuses whose work demonstrates not only a total control over their medium, but also combines clarity of vision, determination, invention, and a receptiveness to new ideas. Much, though not all, of the history of photographic output is written by the originators of the art, and their work continues to inspire all who follow them.

However, one of the great appeals of photography is shared with other arts such as music and theatre: one does not need to be an original creator to enjoy photography, work professionally, and even win great acclaim. The vast majority of published and exhibited photography is in fact the work of the elaborators – superlative artists who were often inspired to take up photography by the originators, and who have themselves become great artists in their own right. Most photographers create their own images through the exploration and exploitation of the work of photographic pioneers. Indeed, part of the creative struggle for many photographers is to find an individual style or to make their own distinctive mark which is different and sets them apart from those who inspired them.

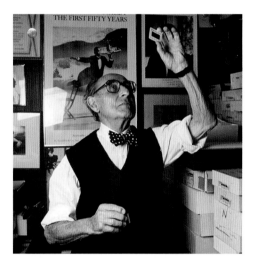

<< **Alfred Eisenstaedt**
Eisenstaedt is considered by many to be the father of photojournalism (see p.42).

This gallery of photographers celebrates both those who have defined and beaten new paths – whether artistic, conceptual, or technical – and also those photographers who have taken well-trodden paths to a new level of creativity or expertise.

Some have circumnavigated the globe many times in pursuit of grandiose photographic projects. Others have literally put their life on the line and endured hardships and physical violence in order to use their photography to act as an advocate for the dispossessed or vulnerable.

Yet others have ventured no farther than their city limits, leading self-contained lives. And while some have concentrated all their energy on the same subject for their entire career, you will also find photographic polymaths who work comfortably from the documentary to the commercial, from landscapes to still-life.

<< **Ansel Adams**
This acclaimed landscape photographer recorded some of the most beautiful places on the planet (see p.24).

The artists on the following pages demonstrate that there are many paths to photographic greatness. However, if there is one trait that great photographers share, it is that time and again they show themselves to be humble and accepting of their chosen subjects. There is re-invention and renewal in every imitation. In photography, what matters most is not believing in yourself, but believing in the integrity of your subject.

In a world that is swarming with images, the power of a truly great photograph to become rooted in the memory is a magical and admirable thing – the image's greatness defined by its time in history, and its synthesis of form, light, and, of course, its momentary significance. The photograph is a physical, tangible link to one moment in history, a point of revelation, and artistic birth. Whatever the subject, a great photograph requires one fundamental thing: that a photographer – fully aware, highly skilled, and suitably equipped to preserve the image for posterity – was present at the crucial moment.

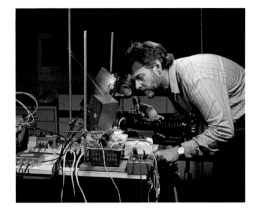

⌃ Stephen Dalton
Dalton uses cutting-edge technology and high-speed photography to shoot the natural world (*see p.40*).

» Margaret Bourke-White
This intrepid photojournalist would go to extraordinary lengths to get her picture, and here she shows no fear while working high on the Chrysler Building, New York (*see p.33*).

⌄ Eve Arnold
Arnold was revered for her documentary images – especially her film stills. Working on a film set required her to work unobtrusively yet quickly to capture telling moments (*see p.28*).

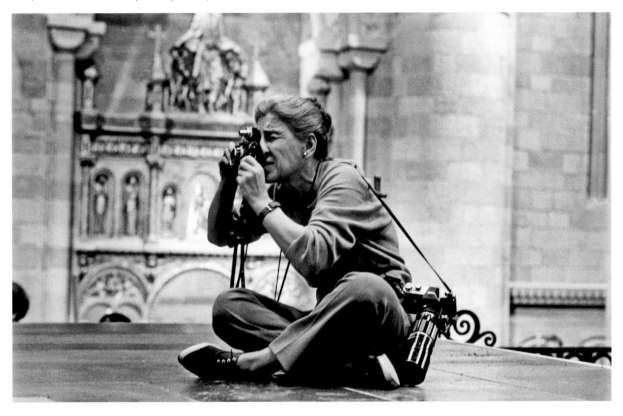

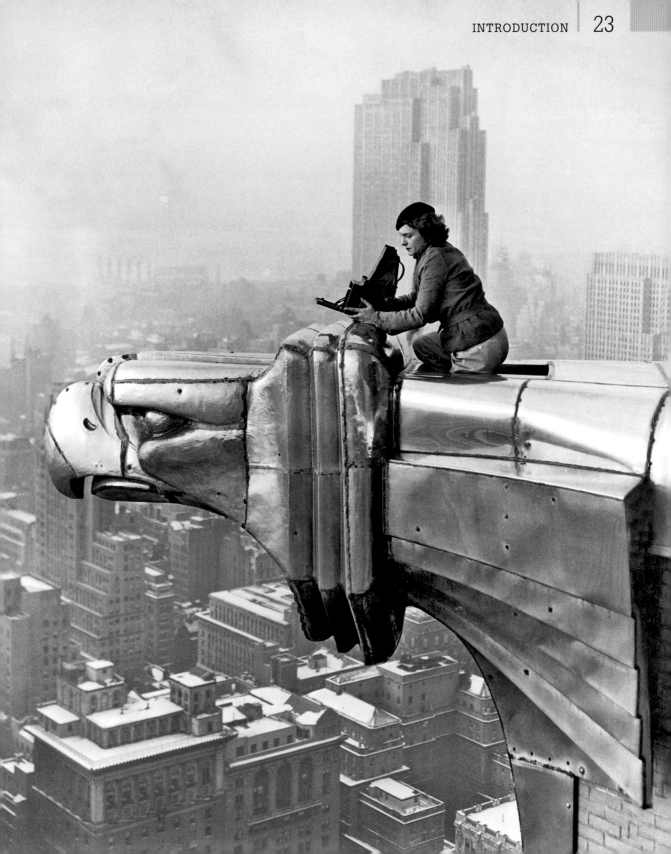

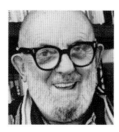

Ansel Adams

AMERICAN 1902–1984

Best known for the matchless monumentality of his landscape photography, Ansel Adams was a versatile photographer, who was widely influential. He had a flawless command of photographic technique.

›› CAREER HIGHLIGHTS

1916	Takes his first photographs of Yosemite National Park, California
1927	First portfolio *Parmelian, Prints of the High Sierras* published
1931	One-man show at Smithsonian Institute, Washington D.C.
1935	*Making a Photograph*, first in a classic series of books, published
1948	Awarded the Guggenheim Fellowship
1960	*Portfolio 3: Yosemite Valley* published

As Adams said "You don't take a photograph, you make it." The most enduring examples of his contribution to photography are his richly detailed, pin-sharp, and exquisitely lit landscapes – almost all of them created on large-format film. Thanks to the impact of his landscape works, which exulted in and celebrated the beauty of the American wilderness, Adams' photography entered the political sphere, playing a part in the conservation movement in the USA.

Adams was influenced by the pictorialist and precisionist ideals of contemporary photographers, such as Paul Strand and Edward Weston. He contributed to the development of the Zone System (*see opposite*), which has influenced generations of photographers at both professional and amateur levels throughout the world.

A prolific photographer, Adams also founded a gallery in Yosemite National Park, set up an academic department for photography in San Francisco, and helped to establish the photography department at the Museum of Modern Art in New York. His many books have become classics.

›› Aspens, Northern New Mexico
One of his most celebrated images, seeing this print in the original in order to appreciate the delicate spectrum of silvery tones should be part of every photographer's education.

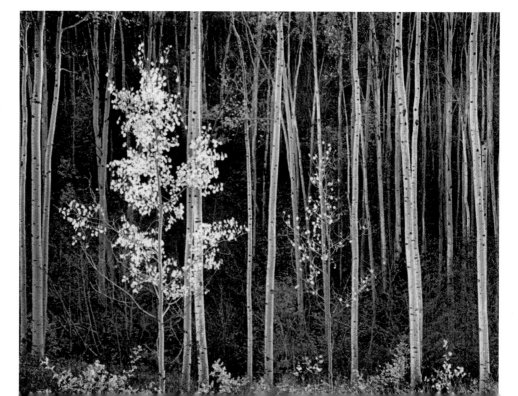

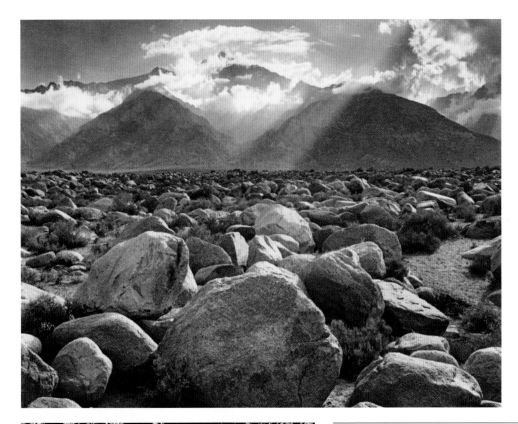

‹‹ Mount Williamson, from Manzanar, California
Exploiting an extensive depth of field created by using camera movements, Adams captures a distant sunburst while keeping the foreground rocks sharply detailed.

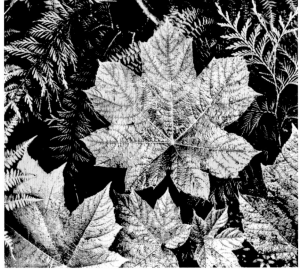

⌃ Leaves, Glacier National Park
Even when working close up, Adams succeeds in conveying the monumental. He achieves this through strong composition and by ensuring all major elements are sharply detailed.

›› ZONE SYSTEM

The Zone System helps the photographer to translate a scene into the photographic medium. It is a three-stage process – of previsualization, exposure, and development – based on analyzing the scene according to a scale of ten zones of brightness ranging from deep shadow to bright highlight. Previsualization is the technique of picturing the desired result before a photograph is taken: by doing this against the range of brightness, the best camera exposure for the film can be set. The film is developed to compensate for the range of zones in the scene in order to produce a desired contrast. The print is then made, trying to match the result to the previsualized image. With the rise of miniature formats and automatic exposure, the Zone System has retreated into a niche.

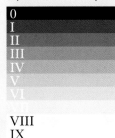

‹‹ Zone system scale
This system divides the brightness spectrum into 10 equally spaced steps, each one a stop apart. Zone V is the crucial middle grey – tanned skin, grass in the sun and so on.

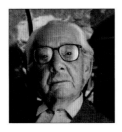

Manuel Álvarez Bravo

MEXICAN 1902– 2002

Combining Mexican and European influences, Álvarez Bravo's work straddles surrealist and documentary styles. His images – described by Nobel laureate Octavio Paz as "realities in rotation" – can be read on several levels.

》 CAREER HIGHLIGHTS

1930	Teaches at San Carlos Academy
1943	Starts work as stills photographer for films
1975	Awarded the Guggenheim Fellowship
1984	Awarded Victor & Erna Hasselblad Prize

A self-taught photographer, Álvarez Bravo was a child at the time of the Mexican Revolution of 1910. He began working professionally for the journal *Mexican Folkways* in 1928, documenting Mexican cultural history. Bravo's style arose from the traditions and myths of *mestizo* Mexico – the blend of indigenous Indian with Spanish – but was also influenced by ideas brought from Europe by visiting photographers, such as Cartier-Bresson (*see pp.38–39*). His work gave a poetic vision of modern Mexico, validating it as an emerging nation. His centenary in 2002 as Mexico's greatest living photographer was a cause for national celebration.

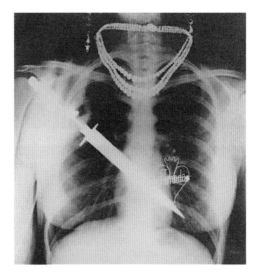

⌃ X-ray Photograph
One of the earliest pioneers of using the x-ray for art photography, here Álvarez Bravo offers a teasingly pseudo-scientific and objective treatment of the theme of murderous love.

》 Invented Landscape from Fifteen Photographs
A common theme for surrealists was the interplay between the man-made and the natural. In this image the shadows do all the suggesting and none of the explaining.

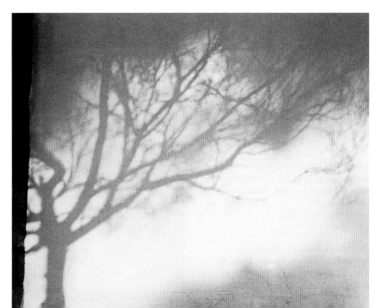

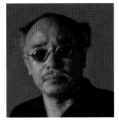

Nobuyoshi Araki

JAPANESE 1940–

One of Japan's most controversial photographers, Nobuyoshi Araki's work crosses from observation of modern Japan to pornography, and back. His snapshot style is unashamedly voyeuristic and widely influential.

›› CAREER HIGHLIGHTS

1971	*Sentimental Journey* published
1989	*Tokyo Nude* published
2008	Awarded Austrian Decoration for Science and Art

After years in advertising, Araki turned his observant eye to women – particularly those working in nightclubs, and as prostitutes. Celebrated for holding up a mirror to the moral ambiguities of Japanese society, Araki has been subjected to the attention of censors unwilling, or unable, to distinguish documentary photos from pornography.

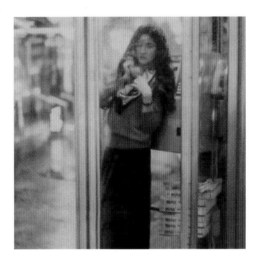

« Telephone Booth from *Tokyo Nostalgia* Even when seen individually, Araki's images hint at narrative. At the same time, we cannot tell if the image is candid or not.

Diane Arbus

AMERICAN 1923–1971

The powerful images of Diane Arbus haunt the viewer like no other; they are a benchmark of unflinching honesty in portraiture. Yet she said "A photograph is a secret about a secret. The more it tells you the less you know."

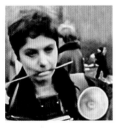

☑ A Young Man in Curlers Arbus's portrait at first appears uncompromising, but reveals itself to be tender and sympathetic of the subject's defiant unease.

›› CAREER HIGHLIGHTS

1960	First pictures published in *Esquire* magazine
1963	Awarded the Guggenheim Fellowship (and then again in 1966)
1967	Exhibits at Museum of Modern Art, New York

Having developed an excellent reputation as a fashion stylist helping out her husband, fashion photographer Allan Arbus, Diane Arbus only began photographing in her mid-30s. A successful career in advertising and fashion followed. Arbus was one of the first photographers to use on-camera flash balanced with daylight in her portraiture. One of the hallmarks of her work, it helps to flatten and make the light artificial, bringing the subject unfettered and unflatteringly to the fore.

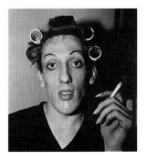

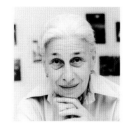

Eve Arnold

AMERICAN 1912–2012

At the top of her profession for more than 50 years, Eve Arnold's approach to documentary photography was self-effacing almost to a fault. Her work tells everything about the subject and nothing about the photographer.

Arnold's rapid rise made her a legend among photographers. After just six weeks of study with the famously hard-to-please Alexey Brodovitch, then art director at *Harper's Bazaar*, she was given her first commission for the magazine. Within three years, she had been approached by the equally fastidious Magnum agency and was made a full member in 1955 – the first woman to be admitted. While her work took her all over the world – most notably to China, working for *LIFE* and *The Sunday Times Magazine* – she is best known for her work on film sets. By winning the trust of those she worked with, Arnold achieved a special intimacy with stars such as Marilyn Monroe and Joan Crawford. She brought the genre of production stills to a standard that few, if any, have since attained.

CAREER HIGHLIGHTS

1986	Won Krasna-Krausz Book Award for *In Retrospect*
1995	Awarded Master Photographer by International Center of Photography
2009	*Eve Arnold's People* published

⊠ **Cowboy, Inner Mongolian Steppes, China**
This image displays Arnold's fine instincts for magazine photography. The composition reveals atmosphere and suggested movement, yet it still has ample space for titles or text.

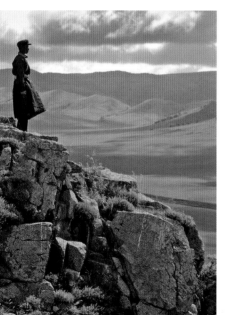

⊠ **Anthony Quinn and Anna Karina**
The stars relaxing on the set of *The Magus* in 1976 are depicted in documentary style. This is a revealing image that conveys the charisma and charm of the actors.

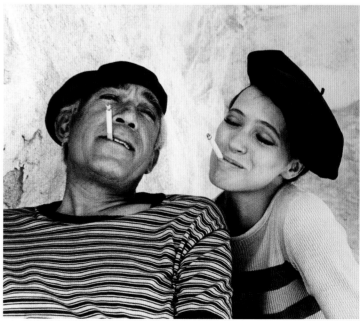

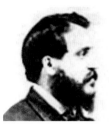

Felice Beato

BRITISH C.1825–1906/8

One of the great pioneers of travel photography, Felice Beato was a tireless documentarist whose importance is only now being recognized. His views of Japan provide a unique record of the country in the 1860s and 70s.

Temples, Nagasaki
This road of temples at Nagasaki with the Kazagashira mountains behind shows Beato's artistic and documentary style.

》 CAREER HIGHLIGHTS

1856	Exhibits photographs in London of the Battle of Balaclava
1863	Starts photographing in Yokohama
1878	Photographs in Burma

Born in Italy but naturalized British, Beato was incorrigibly restless throughout his life. He recorded the aftermath of the Crimean War in the Mediterranean and went on to document the Indian Mutiny of 1858. In 1863 he moved to Japan, where he spent 14 years photographing daily life. He eventually settled in Burma.

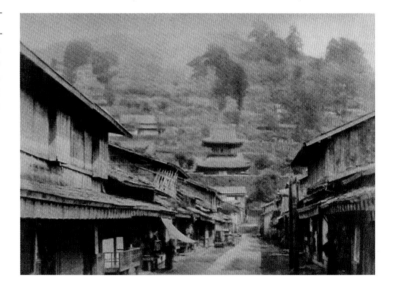

Karl Blossfeldt

GERMAN 1865–1932

An untrained and amateur photographer who used his photography to teach art students about natural forms, Karl Blossfeldt celebrated nature's beauty, creating a unique body of work of matchless consistency.

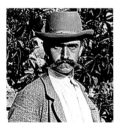

Young Shoots
Working at magnifications of nearly 30 times life-size, Blossfeldt stunned the art world with the beauty of the forms he revealed.

》 CAREER HIGHLIGHTS

1898	Starts teaching at Kunstgewerbemuseum, Berlin
1928	*Uniformen der Kunst* published
1932	*Wundergarten der Natur* published

In 1890 Blossfeldt began to cast models of botanical specimens and photograph plants. Treating the plant as a "totally artistic and architectural structure", his photographs grew into a collection of thousands of botanical studies. He explained: "Since only simple forms lend themselves to graphic representation, I cannot make use of lush flowers."

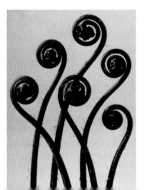

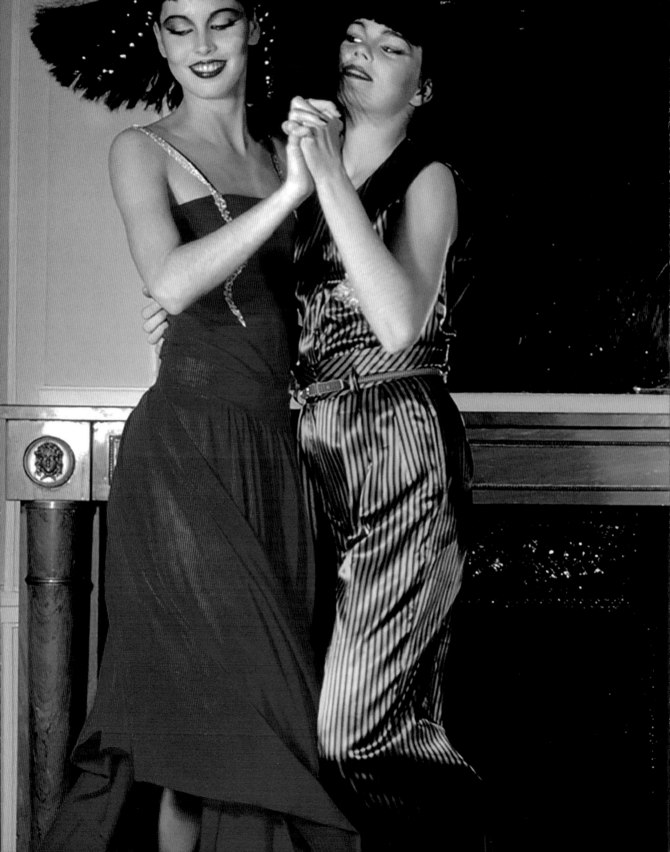

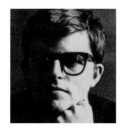

Guy Bourdin

FRENCH 1928–1991

One of the most accomplished fashion photographers of his generation, Guy Bourdin gained notoriety through images that were considered shocking at the time. Today, his work appears light-heartedly stylish and polished.

First exhibited as a fine artist, Bourdin's surrealist and elegantly anarchic images soon caught the attention of *Vogue* magazine. He insisted his photographs be viewed in their intended context and for the following 33 years, his work was never seen outside the pages of fashion magazines. The first solo photographic exhibition of his work was shown only 10 years after his death, but throughout his career he continued exhibiting his drawings. From the mid-1970s he worked on advertising campaigns, most notably for Miyake, Jourdan, and Chanel. Bourdin had a reputation as a hard taskmaster, testing the endurance of his models to the limit. Indeed, violence – expressed as shocking colours and contrasts – is never far from the narrative of his pictures.

» Charles Jourdan, Spring 1978
Bourdin's advertising work set new standards for its knowing, artistically self-referential wit. Here, a Polaroid proof displaces the main image creating a tension between picture planes.

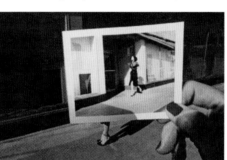

» CAREER HIGHLIGHTS

1952	Exhibits at Galerie 29, Paris
1955	Starts photographing for *Vogue*
1975	Photographs campaign for fashion designer Issey Miyake
1988	Receives Infinity Award, International Center of Photography

» Charles Jourdan, Summer 1977
Bourdin's mastery of composition is evident in this image. Despite its numerous interlocking elements and elaborate lighting, the viewer's gaze is still led straight to the shoes.

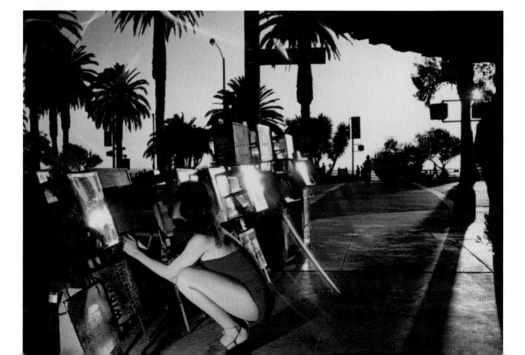

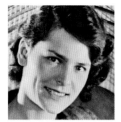

Margaret Bourke-White

AMERICAN 1904–1981

Epitomizing the notion of an uncompromising photojournalist, Bourke-White went to extreme measures to get a picture. A technical virtuoso, she could work in the toughest conditions, and still bring back flawless images.

In 1929, two years after graduating from Cornell University, Bourke-White landed a staff job as an industrial photographer for *Fortune* magazine, then became one of the founding staffers on *LIFE* magazine, where she worked for the rest of her career. Bourke-White was infamously aggressive in pursuit of both assignments and pictures, once saying: "If you banish fear, nothing terribly bad can happen to you." In the 1930s, she photographed in the Soviet Union and her work provided an early record of the emerging nation.

Bourke-White's tenacity was demonstrated when she met Mahatma Ghandi. Before agreeing to pose for photographs next to a spinning wheel, he requested she learn to spin. She duly did and got her picture.

» CAREER HIGHLIGHTS

1936	Becomes photographer for *LIFE*
1937	Takes images for Erskine Caldwell's book *You Have Seen Their Faces*
1945	Photographs General Patton's visit to the Buchenwald camp

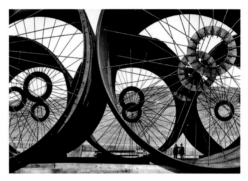

« Construction of Fort Peck Dam
Bourke-White's early industrial photographs, such as this shot of giant pipes used to divert the Missouri River, combined visual sophistication and technical prowess.

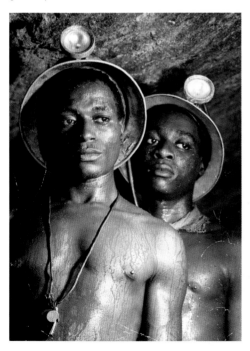

« Gold miners, Robinson Deep
Despite the harsh conditions, Bourke-White used a large-format camera to deliver this technically perfect and powerful image of miners working deep underground.

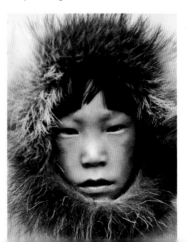

« Eskimo, Canada
This shows Bourke-White's later, sparse approach to photography. Characteristically, she chose to cover this story in the depths of winter, eschewing the comforts of working in summer.

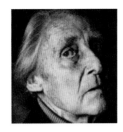

Bill Brandt

BRITISH 1904–1983

The subjects of Bill Brandt's photography seem to speak clearly and with directness through the print. Given his status as a master of photography, Brandt's output was surprisingly small, but much of his work remains iconic.

⊠ Afternoon and Evening
Even Brandt's fashion photography – here of a model in evening dress, published in *Picture Post* in 1951 – has menacing undertones: the shadows appear to close in on the model.

Born into wealth and privilege in Germany, Brandt turned to photography while studying architecture. His time as assistant to Man Ray (*see p.60*) laid the foundations for a non-purist attitude to the photographic process, and a surrealist streak that was to characterize his work.

On settling in Britain in 1931, he worked as a documentary photographer, motivated by a combination of humanist and left-wing ideals, while also making use of actors and models.

After World War II, he became disillusioned with documentary work and turned to nudes, portraiture, and abstracts. Brandt's series of nudes in landscapes, exploiting the projection distortion effects of a wide-angle lens used closeup, were shocking at the time, their references to the works of Picasso and Henry Moore notwithstanding. His understanding of light and form found eloquent expression in print, making him one of the most widely collected of photographers.

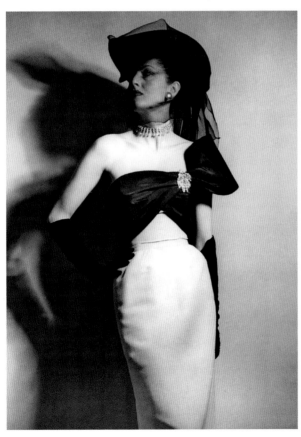

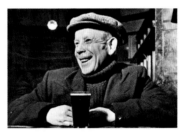

« Man in Pub, London
Brandt regularly used models in his work. This shot of a man in a pub illustrated a 1946 *Picture Post* essay titled *The Doomed East End*, which covered post-war rebuilding in London.

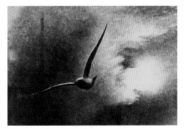

« Fog, London Bridge
Brandt's reportage of London, like this image of a gull soaring over the Thames, defined the image of the city as dreary and fog-bound.

》 CAREER HIGHLIGHTS

1929	Assists photographer Man Ray
1936	*The English at Home* published
1951	*Literary Britain* published
1961	*Perspective of Nudes* published
1983	Curates *The Land* exhibition at Victoria and Albert Museum, London

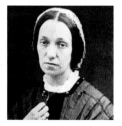

Julia Margaret Cameron

BRITISH 1815–1879

It was her eye for the intimate and the intensity of her portraiture that made Julia Margaret Cameron unique. With a productive period of just 14 years, her career is the shortest of any world-class photographer.

⟫ CAREER HIGHLIGHTS

1863	Receives first camera as gift
1865	First exhibitions
1867	Exhibits in Paris
1868	Exhibits in London
1874	Illustrates Alfred Lord Tennyson's *Idylls of the King*

Cameron could be regarded as the patron saint of amateur photography. She photographed out of love, although in her case it bordered on obsession. She was given her first camera by her daughters when she was 48 years old. Unfettered by niceties, she made family, servants, and visitors to her home – including luminaries such as historian Thomas Carlyle – pose for her to create portraits or romantic tableaux. She coaxed an extraordinary intensity of emotion from her subjects, creating images with a defined sense of style, working her sitters to the limit. Alfred Tennyson allegedly left the poet Henry Longfellow with the warning, "Do whatever she tells you. I shall return soon and see what is left of you."

Working in the dim, soft light she favoured, Cameron used glass plates requiring exposures that often lasted several minutes. The photography establishment were, she reported, "manifestly unjust" in their criticism of her work, but by the 1870s her prints were in great demand. Cameron left Britain for Ceylon (now Sri Lanka) in 1877, and all but gave up photography. Her modern reputation has been assured by her inclusion in Alfred Stieglitz's *Camera Work* magazine in the early 1900s.

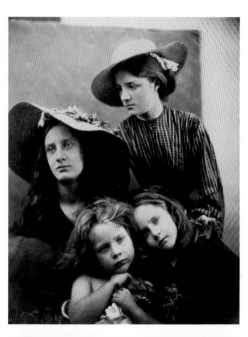

《 Summer Days
This image shows that Cameron was an early master of the group photo. The grace and poise of her groupings is remarkable given the lengthy preparations and long exposures needed.

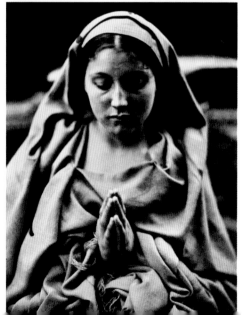

《 St Agnes
This tableaux of the martyred saint combined classical themes with a covert Victorian sensuality, mirroring the tension in John Keats contemporaneous poem, *The Eve of St Agnes*.

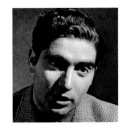

Robert Capa

HUNGARIAN 1913–1954

The photojournalist as hero, Robert Capa characterized the notion of the swashbuckling photographer who braved bullets with a winning grin, always getting his picture with an uncanny ability to be in the right place at the right time.

Born André Friedman, Robert Capa studied political science in Berlin in the early 1930s, during which time he took his first published photograph, of Trotsky. With the rise of Hitler, he was forced to move to Paris where he invented the persona of the "famous American photographer Robert Capa" in order to justify charging a premium rate. He moved through the heady high-art circles of pre-war Paris, meeting luminaries such as Ernest Hemingway and Pablo Picasso, and influential photographers such as Henri Cartier-Bresson (*see pp.38–39*).

His coverage of the Spanish Civil War (1936–39) is justly hailed as a perfect example of rounded, passionate, and humanist photojournalism, producing the iconic image of a soldier at the moment of his death. His technique was shorn of inessentials, powered by his dictum "If your pictures aren't good enough, you're not close enough", and was shaped by the Leica camera's abilities and limitations. Despite his derring-do reputation, he loathed war, confessing once that "It's not always easy to stand aside and be unable to do anything except record the sufferings around one", and fervently hoped to be "unemployed as a war photographer till the end of my life."

Besides his images, one of his lasting contributions to photography was the founding of photographic agency Magnum (with Polish photojournalist David "Chim" Seymour, Frenchman Henri Cartier-Bresson, the Briton George Rodger, and American William Vandivert). The agency's combination of hard-nosed commercialism and humanist idealism bears Capa's mark.

⟫ CAREER HIGHLIGHTS

1936	Photographs Spanish Civil War
1938	Portfolio published in *Picture Post*
1942	Hired by *Collier's Weekly*
1943	Hired by *LIFE* magazine
1947	Co-founds the Magnum picture agency

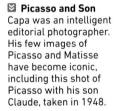

⊠ Picasso and Son
Capa was an intelligent editorial photographer. His few images of Picasso and Matisse have become iconic, including this shot of Picasso with his son Claude, taken in 1948.

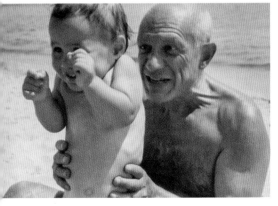

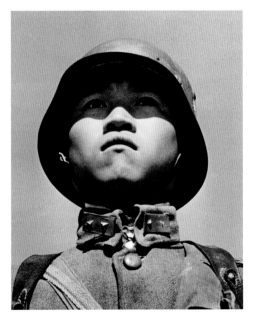

⟫ Chinese Teenage Soldier
Capa photographed this teenage soldier in Hankow (now Wuhan) in China in 1938. The low perspective mocks the threatening nature of the soldier, whose youth is all too obvious.

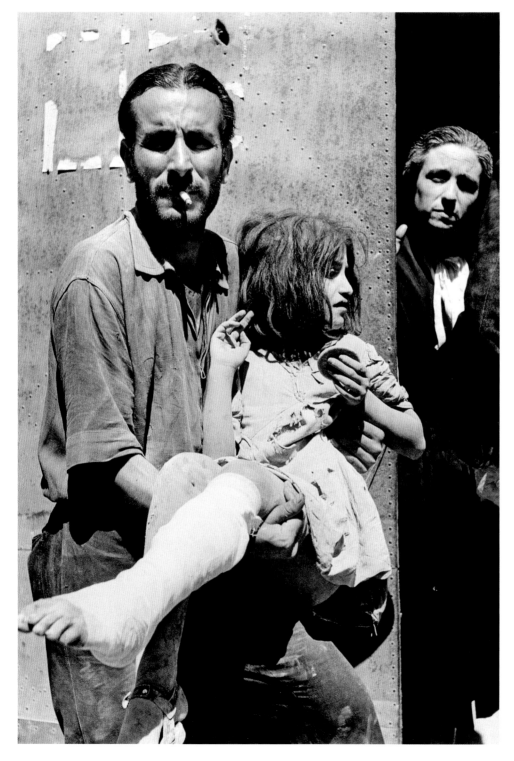

« The Battle of Troina, 1943
Capa's interest was in exploring the human side of war. His genius lay in his innate ability to capture people's emotions. This moving image, taken during World War II in the aftermath of the American bombing of the German-held town of Troina in Sicily, draws in the viewer by clearly depicting the fear, anger, and pain of the three subjects.

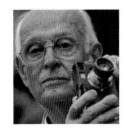

Henri Cartier-Bresson

FRENCH 1908–2004

The greatest inspiration to countless photographers, Cartier-Bresson was an elusive person and yet one of the most approachable photographers. His work is a perfect union of the intellectual and the humanist.

Inspired by Hungarian photojournalist Martin Munkacsi's vivacious image of black youths running into the sea, Cartier-Bresson forsook his art studies and took up photography. He was passionate about his work and would prowl the streets of Paris with his camera from morning until night, as his prolific output testifies. Much of Cartier-Bresson's greatest work was produced in a few productive years during the 1930s. Blessed with determination (and good luck), he covered the Spanish Civil War, escaped from the Nazis, worked for the French Resistance, and then went on to film the liberation of Paris and its return to French hands in 1944.

After World War II, Cartier-Bresson helped found the Magnum photographic agency, remaining its father-figure and best-known photographer throughout its early years – itself a remarkable achievement. His own words that "no one thing is independent of another...one thing rhymes with another, and light gives them shape", explain the philosophy behind his photography more clearly than volumes of analysis ever could.

⟫ CAREER HIGHLIGHTS

1935	Studies film with photographer Paul Strand; assists film-maker Jean Renoir
1937	Makes documentary film of Spanish Civil War
1947	Co-founds the Magnum agency
1952	Exhibits major retrospective *Decisive Moment* in the Louvre, Paris
1973	Menil Foundation of Houston commissioned to edit his life's work
2003	Retrospective at Bibliothèque Nationale de France, Paris

▼ **Hyères, France**
Even without the perfectly positioned cyclist, the lines of the stairs, railing, and road would form a pleasing composition. An optical illusion makes the cyclist seem smaller than reality.

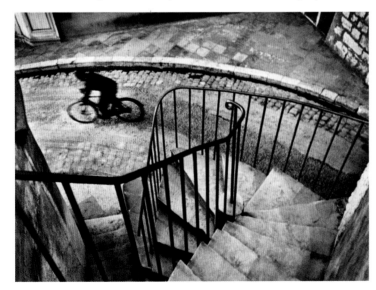

▼ **Balthus with his Wife and Daughter**
This seemingly informal family shot of the artist Balthus shows Cartier-Bresson's compositional sophistication. Balthus's gaze separates him from the women and their source of amusement, which lies out of frame.

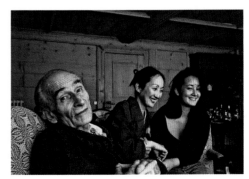

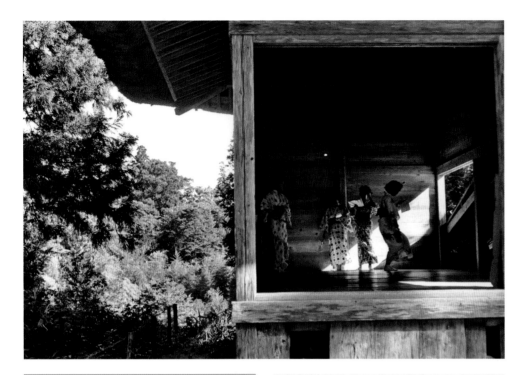

《 Japan, 1965
Photographing the rehearsal of a Noh play from the side rather than the front, Cartier-Bresson demonstrates lateral thinking. The frame of the rehearsal room encloses the artificial dramatic world, while the pine trees reflect the *kagami-ita* (painting of a pine tree) used as a backdrop.

》 STANDARDIZING THE LENS

Although Cartier-Bresson did use various focal lengths, the vast majority of his work was "taken" (his word) through a 50mm lens. Only by paring back his equipment to the barest minimum could he work the camera like a "sketchbook, an instrument of intuition and spontaneity, the master of the instant which, in visual terms, questions and decides simultaneously."

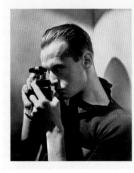

《 Viewfinder
An early portrait of Cartier-Bresson shows him looking through a universal viewfinder attached to his favoured Leica camera. The viewfinder shows fields of view for different lenses.

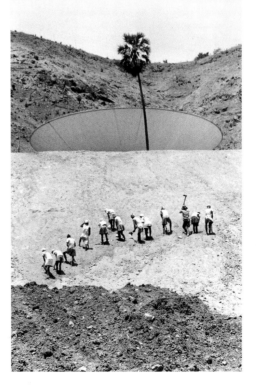

》 Atomic Energy Plant in India, 1997
Cartier-Bresson's later work lost none of its ability to surprise. The three planes of this image shift and incline at different angles, rendering it more unsettling the closer it is examined.

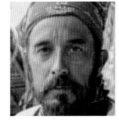

Valdir Cruz

BRAZILIAN 1954–

The images of Valdir Cruz reveal that documentary photography, when carried out with simplicity, conviction, and purpose, still retains the power to plead the case of the under-represented and dispossessed.

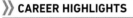
Irokai-teri, Venezuela, 1997
Cruz did not use artifice or clever camera angles to achieve this image; instead he allowed the children's naturally graceful poses and dignified expressions to speak for themselves.

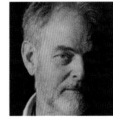

⟩⟩ CAREER HIGHLIGHTS

1996	Exhibits at Fotofest, Houston; awarded the Guggenheim Fellowship
2003	*Faces of the Rainforest* published
2017	*Presences* published

Turning to professional photography in his late 30s while he was living in New York, Cruz rediscovered his Brazilian roots and so found a focus for his work. His images helped publicize the plight of the remote, threatened tribes of the Brazilian rainforest. Cruz's approach was deceptively naive, straightforward, and free of visual gimmickry.

Stephen Dalton

BRITISH 1937–

Taking high-speed nature photography to new heights by using technical invention and artistic vision, Dalton reveals the beauty of the natural world by capturing movements that are too quick for the human eye to see.

European Tree Frog
The beauty of the frog's leap is perfectly revealed with three stroboscopic flashes exposed on 35mm colour film.

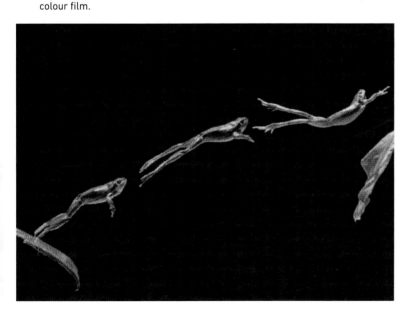

While high-speed photography is nothing new – Harold Edgerton photographed bullets in flight in the 1930s – Dalton used the techniques on unpredictable live subjects, tiny insects such as moths, bees, and wasps, as well as birds. This requires flash exposures of 1/25,000 of a second or shorter, of extremely high power, with responsive switching devices. Although mainly shot in the studio, his work has brought a new beauty and realism to this type of photography.

⟩⟩ CAREER HIGHLIGHTS

1970	Starts high-speed photography work
1975	*Borne on the Wind* published
1978	Becomes Honorary Fellow of the Royal Photographic Society
1999	*Secret Worlds* published

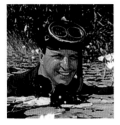

David Doubilet

AMERICAN 1946–

Visual awareness and technical prowess have made David Doubilet the greatest of underwater photographers. His work has inspired many to explore the wonders of the marine world and influenced the style of nature films.

☑ **Slick Swimmers**
Breathtaking composition and clarity of detail, the hallmark features of Doubilet's work, are evident in this image. Subtle lighting and careful use of flash focus the viewer's gaze.

Having taken up snorkelling at a very young age, Doubilet was only 12 years old when he began to scuba dive, and just 13 when he started photographing underwater using a Brownie camera wrapped in a watertight bag. By 1972, at the age of 26, he was working regularly for *National Geographic*, and has since completed over 75 assignments for the magazine.

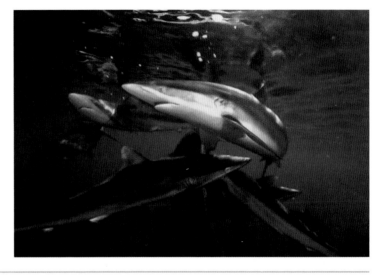

》 CAREER HIGHLIGHTS

1989	*Light in the Sea* published
1992	*Pacific: an Undersea Journey* published
1999	*Water Light Time* published
2005	Founding member of the International League of Conservation Photographers

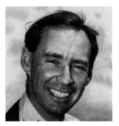

Max Dupain

AUSTRALIAN 1911–1992

The most important documentary photographer of Australian life and architecture, Max Dupain left a finely crafted legacy of photographs, producing iconic work with a uniquely Australasian "voice".

☑ **Sunbaker, 1937**
This, Dupain's signature image, rose quickly to iconic status. With its stark composition, Dupain exploits a tension between the ambiguous position of the body – the person could be injured – with its bronzed physical perfection.

》 CAREER HIGHLIGHTS

1934	Starts working professionally
1948	*Max Dupain Photographs* published
1975	Retrospective at Australian Centre of Photography, Sydney
1982	Receives an OBE

Influenced by Modernism, Dupain fused a love and understanding of his country with a minimalist style of photography, often using the harsh lighting conditions that he regularly encountered in Australia to his advantage. In the course of a long career, he moved comfortably between architectural, industrial, and portrait photography, working both commercially and as a documentary photographer.

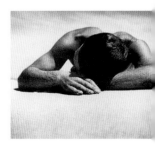

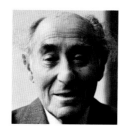

Alfred Eisenstaedt

GERMAN 1898–1995

Considered by many to be the father of photojournalism and the greatest of photographers, Alfred Eisenstaedt was above all a consummate professional who retained his modesty, as well as his capacity to be amazed by life.

Throughout a long career spent mostly in the top ranks of photojournalism, Eisenstaedt was sparing in his use of equipment, frequently only working with one camera. This, and the ability to disappear into the background, made him a master of candid photography. He contributed some 2,500 stories to *LIFE* magazine, and nearly 90 covers. Less well known is the fact that Eisenstaedt pioneered the celebrity profile, giving publicity shots the respectability of the picture essay. His down-to-earth approach is exemplified by his advice that "the most important thing is not clicking the shutter, it is clicking with the subject."

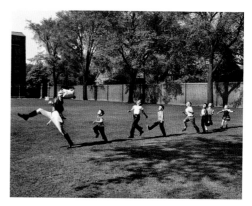

⌃ Drum Major, Ann Arbor, 1950
This photograph of children imitating a drum major during his practice is one of Eisenstaedt's best-loved images. It shows his knack of being in the right place at the right time.

« Sophia Loren
The formal presentation of the room, characteristic of an architectural photograph, is thrown awry by the relaxed figure on the bed.

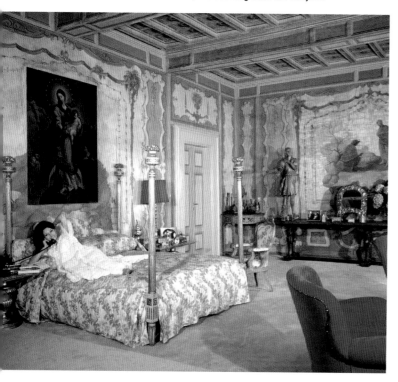

⟩⟩ CAREER HIGHLIGHTS

1927	Sells first photograph
1935	Buys Rolleiflex; emigrates to USA
1954	Exhibits at George Eastman House, Rochester, New York
1966	*Witness to Our Time* published
1971	*Photojournalism* published
1981	*Germany* published
1989	Receives National Medal of the Arts

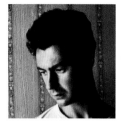

Elliott Erwitt

AMERICAN 1928–

With a rare ability to capture a fleeting moment, Elliott Erwitt's work ranks him unequivocally among photography's greats. It demonstrates photojournalism of the highest order of observation, prediction, and timing.

Erwitt studied photography during World War II, serving as a photographer in Germany and France before continuing with film studies. By the 1960s he was gaining a reputation as the funny man of photography, sealed in 1974 with his book on dogs *Son of Bitch*, which remains unchallenged as the most humorous photography book ever published. While continuing his work as a stills photographer, Erwitt started making films in the 1970s. He is a sensitive documentarist and highly successful advertising photographer, with a reputation for having a deceptively laid-back approach. He advises "Keep working, because as you go through the process...things begin to happen."

» New York City, 1953
This warmly intimate image of Erwitt's family was taken early in his career. Already, his eye for richly subtle composition and the emotionally charged moment is evident.

» St Tropez, France, 1968
Erwitt's classic study of the seafront blends a sharp eye for the mildly surreal with a warm humanity. His images incite laughter not in mockery but from sharing the absurdities of life.

» CAREER HIGHLIGHTS

1954	Joins Magnum
1971	Films *Beauty Knows No Pain*
1977	Films documentary *Glassmakers of Herat, Afghanistan*
2002	Awarded the Royal Photographic Society's Centenary Medal and an honorary fellowship
2011	Given the International Center of Photography's Infinity Award for Lifetime Achievement

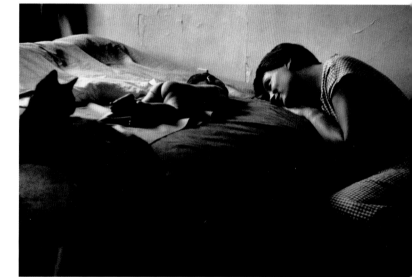

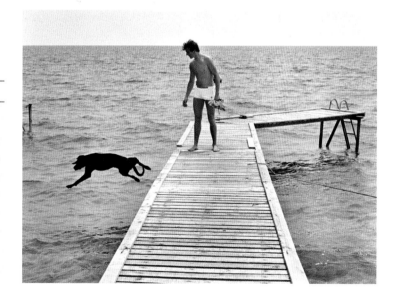

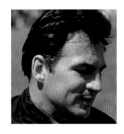

Ernst Haas

AUSTRIAN 1921–1986

The most articulate of photographers – both in words and images – Ernst Haas taught us virtually everything we know about using colour in photography. He was a technical pioneer with a painter's eye.

A dropout from medical school who took up painting, Haas was 26 before he found his calling. When he did, he was unstoppable. His first picture essay – of the homecoming of soldiers to his native Vienna in 1947 – was a stunning debut: nearly every shot on the first roll of film was publishable. It led to an invitation to join the photographic agency Magnum, and another to work for *LIFE* magazine.

》 IMAGES OF MOTION

By using very slow (12 ASA) colour film in indoor arenas, Haas was exploring new territory. Low light called for long exposures, which smears the moving image over a single frame, thus depicting motion in a way inaccessible to any other medium. Haas used a viewfinder camera so that he could watch the action during the exposure (it is blacked out in an SLR camera). This helped him control the otherwise highly unpredictable results.

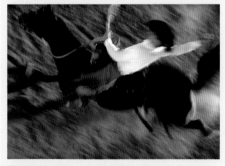

⬢ Bronco Rider, California, 1957

With the very-fast-moving action of a bronco rider, only the very shortest of exposure times will freeze action. Conversely, a moderately short exposure time – 1/8 or 1/4 of a second – will be sufficient to induce a blurred image. A longer exposure time could render the image unintelligible. Here, Haas exposed generously while keeping the outlines of the subject clear.

While working in the USA, Haas was captivated by the colours of New Mexico and gave up black-and-white photography to use only Kodachrome and Leica equipment. He went on to discover blurred motion photography while shooting a rodeo in light deemed useless by other photographers.

Haas travelled throughout the world and many of his picture essays still set standards for photographers today. A recipient of an honour almost each year of his professional life, Haas proclaimed: "The limitations of photography are in yourself, for what we see is only what we are." A fine source for photographic *bon mots*, his genius is perhaps best defined by his rhetorical question: "If the beautiful were not in us, how would we ever recognize it?"

》 Doge's Palace, Venice, 1955

To make this photograph, Haas worked in the most unpromising lighting conditions to deliver a timelessly elegant image.

》 CAREER HIGHLIGHTS

1943	Studies photography at Graphischen Lehr- und Versuchsanstalt, Vienna
1945	Photographs for American Red Cross
1953	*Magic Images of New York* published in *LIFE*
1962	Has retrospective at Museum of Modern Art, New York
1962	The film, *The Art of Seeing* is made
1971	*The Creation* published
1975	*In America* published
1986	Wins Hasselblad award

Mandala Mudra Prayer Beads, India, 1974
Combining a harmonious composition of colours with informative content, this image, shows a monk's mandala mudra symbol of enlightenment expressed through the hands.

Raindrop on Leaf
In a development of the traditional still-life aesthetic, Haas delved deep into detail to compose deceptively simple images of plants. These have become some of his best-known and most widely published works.

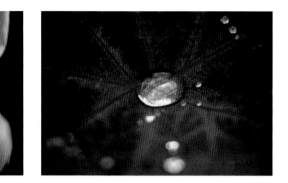

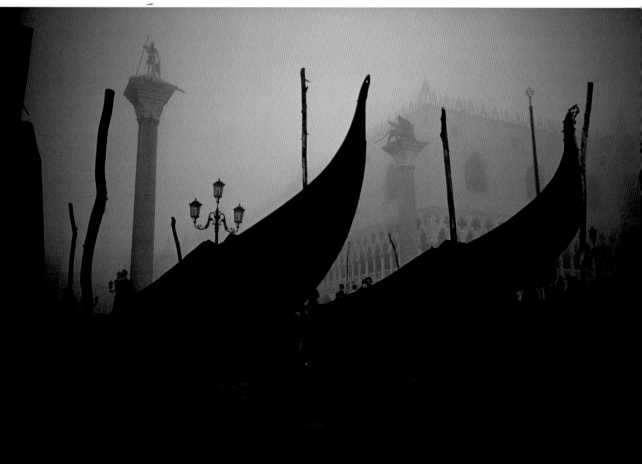

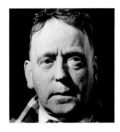

John Heartfield

GERMAN 1891–1968

Powered by political passion and using a subversive Dadaism all of his own, John Heartfield's photomontages remain powerful and barbed. His images demonstrate an acute sensitivity and a sardonic humour.

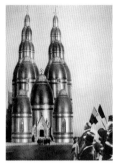

Born Helmut Herzfeld, Heartfield initially led a career as an artist and in the interwar years he became increasingly rebellious. Under the influence of Dadaism, he found a channel, through photomontage, for his protest at the Weimar Republic and the rise of the Nazi party.

◄ We Pray to the Power of the Bomb
Heartfield's 1934 photomontage of artillery shells at different scales made to look like a cathedral was shockingly striking in its time.

›› CAREER HIGHLIGHTS

1920	Organizes First International Dada Fair, Berlin
1940	*One Man's War Against Hitler* exhibition, London
1954	Elected to Deutsche Akademie der Künste

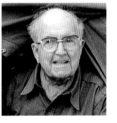

Eric Hosking

BRITISH 1909–1991

As the founding father of modern nature photography, Eric Hosking was a technical innovator. His dedication to wildlife preservation led the way for using photography for conservation campaigning.

◙ Barn Owl
This celebrated image of a barn owl caught in midflight with a vole hanging from its beak is the most widely published nature photograph from the 1950s.

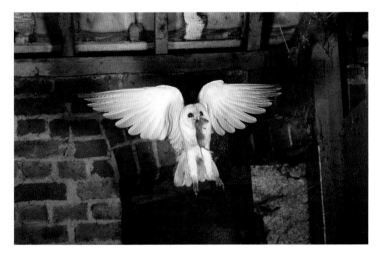

Through a deep respect for wildlife, together with infinite patience and meticulous technical skills, Hosking compiled the first comprehensive library of bird images. An expert in bird behaviour, he was one of the first to use colour film – Kodachrome – for natural history photography. In 1948 he was also the first photographer to use electronic flash to capture birds in flight.

›› CAREER HIGHLIGHTS

1929	Embarks on nature photography career
1944	*Birds of the Day* published
1955	*Birds* published

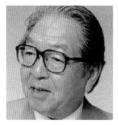

Eikoh Hosoe

JAPANESE 1933–

The work of Eikoh Hosoe is rich with significance, as art object, as investigation into sexual separateness, as representation of identity anxiety, even as symbolist theatre, but all his images have a powerful impact.

Hosoe's images appear at first merely to be nude or tableaux studies, but the totality of his work reveals a preoccupation with identity. His widely acclaimed books reveal a sure touch in picking collaborators. The legendary writer Yukio Mishima was the subject of his darkly erotic images in the book *Barakei (Ordeal by Roses)*. Hosoe revealingly said: "The photographer who wields [the camera] well can depict what lies unseen in his memory."

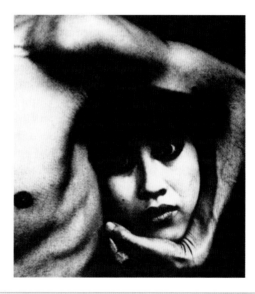

◁ Manwoman from Man and Woman
Hosoe's work dramatically combines allegory with dance and theatre, as in this image from his collaboration with the dancer Tatsumi Hijikata.

≫ CAREER HIGHLIGHTS

1960	*Man and Woman* published
1963	*Barakei (Ordeal by Roses)* published
2003	Awarded the Royal Photographic Society's Special 150th Anniversary Medal and an honorary fellowship

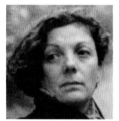

Graciela Iturbide

MEXICAN 1942–

Imbued with an insider's understanding, Graciela Iturbide's photographs of her native Mexico expose the shallowness of mainstream travel photography that is motivated only by the stunning image.

▽ Mujer Angel (Angel Woman)
This incongruous image of a woman in a rocky landscape carrying a portable radio poses more questions than it actually answers.

An apprenticeship with Manuel Alvarez Bravo (*see p.26*) inspired Iturbide to document Mexico's indigenous peoples. One of her most famous photo essays focuses on the matriarchal values of the Zapotec Indians. Her work examines the tensions between native and modern cultures, Catholicism, and pre-Hispanic beliefs. It has a nascent discomfort, as if constantly in search of resolution.

≫ CAREER HIGHLIGHTS

1990	Exhibits at MoMA, San Francisco
1996	*Images of the Spirit* published
2013	Retrospective held at Tate Modern, London

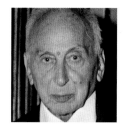

André Kertész

HUNGARIAN 1894–1985

Master of the epigrammatic composition, André Kertész delighted in the poetry of the street, exposing the elegance of chance occurrences. Henri Cartier-Bresson admitted "Whatever we have done, Kertész did it first."

Kertész was one of the first to master the Leica camera and to recognize its potential. He moved in the circles of interwar Paris's artistic elite, where his spontaneous approach to photography was a revelation for the time, influencing Brassaï, Capa (*see pp.36–7*), and Cartier-Bresson (*see pp.38–9*). After emigrating to the USA, he became a successful editorial photographer for Condé Nast magazines, but he is best known for his timeless and quietly stylish personal work.

》 Hal Sherman Performing Mid-air Splits
With a whimsicality rare in photography, Kertész caught the dancer and comic Hal Sherman performing. For this work, the Leica's precise shutter release was indispensable.

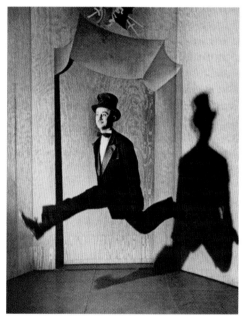

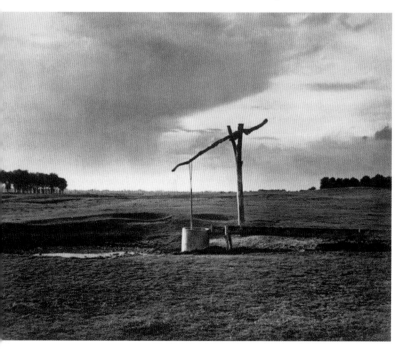

》 CAREER HIGHLIGHTS

1917	First photograph published: *Erkedes Ujsag (Interesting Newspaper)*, Budapest
1936	Works for Keystone Studios, New York
1962	Wins Gold Medal, Venice Biennale
1975	Awarded the Guggenheim Fellowship

《 Well in Puszta, Hungary
Kertész's early documentary work in his home country forms a remarkable collection. This image wraps a sign of poverty – the well – in sunshine to make a lightly ironic comment.

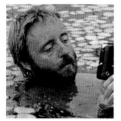

Frans Lanting

DUTCH 1951–

One of the most stylish and innovative of nature photographers, Lanting's sensitive photographic approach is guided by his training in environmental science. He has given the public a deeper understanding of wildlife.

Abandoning a career in environmental studies in 1980, Lanting combined his love of photography and the natural world. Approaching his assignments with scientific thoroughness, he spends weeks with his subjects getting to know them. He has pioneered the wide-angle, closeup view of animals simply by learning how to get closer to them than anyone else. For him, success in nature photography is "part science, part expedition skills, and part human relations skills". An ambassador for the World Wide Fund for Nature, Lanting's mission is to use his photography to champion local and global conservation efforts.

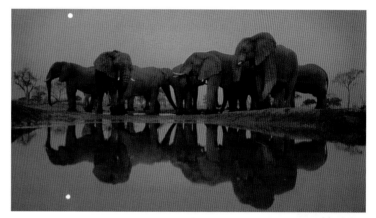

African Elephants
Slow-moving elephants allow Lanting to use a long exposure, enabling him to record colours that low light renders invisible to the naked eye.

》 FLASH IN THE FIELD

One of Lanting's contributions to nature photography is his skilful use of flash balanced with existing light. The colouring of light that he achieves can bring out incredibly accurate detail. Elaborate set-ups are required to avoid results that look artificial, so Lanting travels with six or more portable flash units, stands, and soft-boxes (to soften the lighting).

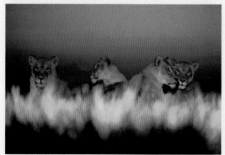

African Lions
Lanting's inventive use of flash is well illustrated in this picture, taken in Botswana. The lower part of flash coverage has illuminated the out-of-focus grasses in the foreground, making them glow like a fire.

》 CAREER HIGHLIGHTS

1985	Starts working for *National Geographic* magazine
1988	Wins World Press Photo award
1991	Wins BBC Wildlife Photographer of the Year award
1994	*Okavango, Africa's Last Eden* published
1995	Wins Kodak Fotokalender Preis
1997	*Eye to Eye, Intimate Encounters With the Animal World* published
2000	*Jungles* published
2006	*LIFE, A Journey Through Time* published
2017	*Into Africa* published

Giant Water Lilies
Judicious use of electronic flash lighting balanced with a long exposure for the low light bring out the stillness of this pond.

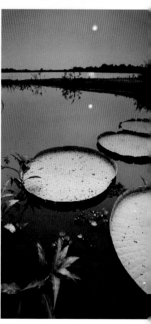

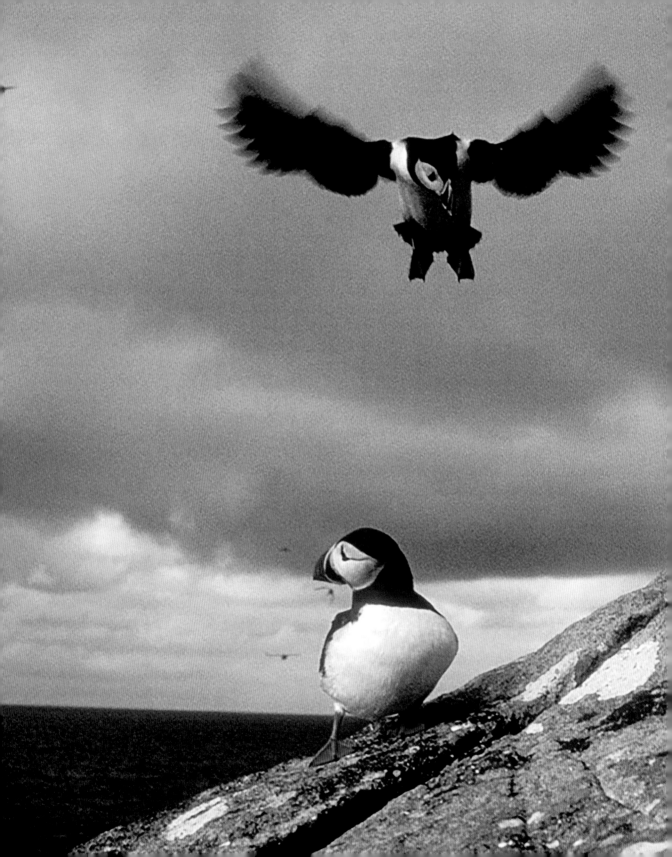

Frans Lanting
Deep knowledge of animal behaviour
enables Lanting to make stunning
photographs seemingly without effort.
This picture of a group of puffins gathering
off the coast of Scotland is perfectly timed
and full of character.

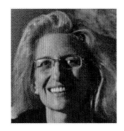

Annie Leibovitz

AMERICAN 1947–

Annie Leibovitz's whole-person portraiture – a highly evolved style of posing with precision lighting and staging – has never lost its ability to surprise. A remarkable number of her photographs have become modern icons.

⟫ CAREER HIGHLIGHTS

1971	Graduates in Fine Arts from San Francisco Art Institute
1973	Chief photographer for *Rolling Stone* magazine
1983	First contributing photographer to *Vanity Fair* magazine
1984	Wins Photographer of the Year award
1991	Retrospective at the National Portrait Gallery in Washington
2009	Awarded the International Center of Photography's Infinity Award for lifetime achievement and the Royal Photographic Society's Centenary Medal

While her professional origins as a rock-band photographer will occasionally resurface mischievously in her images, Leibovitz is best known for her elaborate celebrity portraits, which are essentially modern tableaux. Using complex lighting – often flash balanced with daylight in outdoor locations – and theatrical settings, yet still allowing herself to respond to the spur of the moment, Leibovitz contrives to hide all technical artifice while making the subject the main focus of the image. At best, her work reaches below the surface and captures something of the subject's inner self.

Leibovitz's style of photography is ideal for her most influential showcase, *Vanity Fair* magazine, as her images serve to iconize the subjects with the photographer's own editorial comment, their brilliance often overshadowing the accompanying feature articles themselves.

Her outlook is revealed in her own words: "I'm pretty used to people not liking having their picture taken...if you do...I worry about you." In 2007, the Brooklyn Museum, New York, honoured her with a major retrospective that toured the USA, Europe, and Asia.

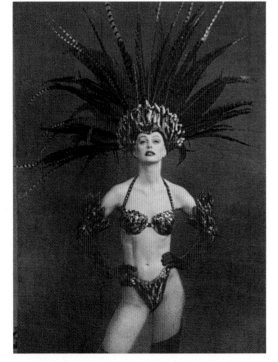

《 Akke Alama
Leibovitz shows the dancer Akke Alama in a bold, flaunting pose. The intrusion of the edge of the background paper enhances the sense of theatrical artifice.

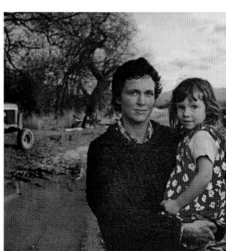

《 Trini Campbell
Leibovitz's portrait of mother and child, from her *Women* series, is typical of her treatment of "ordinary" people. The image is shorn of glamour in contrast to her "celebrity" images.

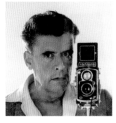

Herbert List

GERMAN 1903–1975

A man of contradictions, Herbert List was a coffee merchant turned photojournalist. He was a perfectionist, whose enduring images are hedonistic celebrations in a style that is both avant-garde yet formalist.

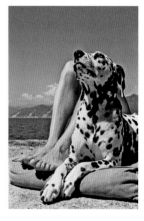

The turning point in List's ordered life as a Hamburg merchant was his meeting with German photographer Andreas Feininger in 1929, which led him into photography. He started with experiments in surrealism and other avant-garde ideas, concentrating on the male figure in a spirit influenced by the *Jugendbewegung* movement, which extolled a romantic vision of youth. While Europe erupted into full-scale war, he photographed boys amongst the ruined temples of Greece, exploring surrealist interpretations of classical Hellenic ideals.

Forced to return to Germany, where he was drafted to design maps for the army, he photographed the ruins of Munich at the end of the war. An associate member of Magnum from 1951, he was sufficiently wealthy to refuse assignments, funding his own projects that were published in *LIFE*, *Picture Post*, and other magazines. Since the 1920s, List had been collecting drawings, and by 1965 he had given up active photography to concentrate on curating what had become one of the world's most important private collections.

▲ **Man and Dog, Portofino**
This relaxed seaside shot is one of List's best known images thanks to its arch sensuality and perfect composition.

» CAREER HIGHLIGHTS

1929	Starts to photograph
1933	Exhibition at Galerie du Chasseurs des Images, Paris
1936	Works for *Verve* and *Vogue* magazines
1951	Joins Magnum
1953	*Licht über Hellas* published
1958	*Caribia* published
1965	Gives up photography to curate own Old Master drawings collection

» **Torremolinos**
List's portrait of young men under a reed roof combines formalist elements (graphic lines of light and shadow) and surreal elements (the viewpoint and the pose) with homoeroticism.

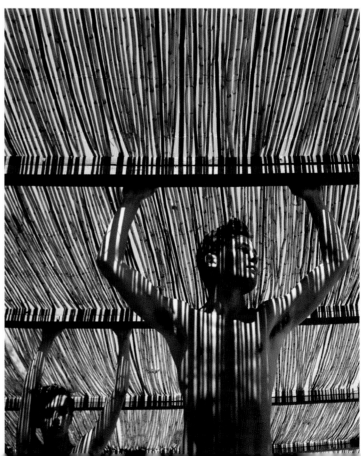

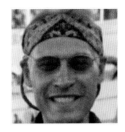

Leo Mason

BRITISH 1952–

A love of sport and adventure permeates all of Leo Mason's images. He has embraced new technology, from the super-telephoto lens to the remote control, to push the artistic limits of sports photography.

One of the first to photograph sports with a creative vision that extended beyond the actual event to abstract shape and colour, Mason started his career in advertising before turning to sports photography. His intelligent questing style – always in search of a different and surprising view – was so striking that in 1975, only one year after changing tack, he joined the *Observer* magazine as chief sports photographer. He explains: "From the beginning, I hunted alone, always looking for a personal statement of a particular sport or athlete...always prepared to try anything...in an attempt to create an image that might... encapsulate the beauty and grace of sport. I try to be the 'eye' for the viewer who could not be present."

» CAREER HIGHLIGHTS

1981	Exhibition at Shelly Gallery, London
1984	Wins Colour Portfolio sports photographer of the year
1993	Exhibition at Icon Gallery, London

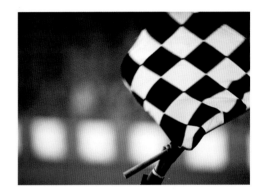

» Chequered Flag
Mason has used a long focal length set to a wide aperture to throw the background out of focus to counterpoint the blurred row of rectangles against the black and white of the flag.

» Crew Race
Capturing the movement of many oarsmen in this image is technically simple in principle, but difficult in practice. The length of exposure must be timed perfectly so that it is blurred enough but not too much. Photographic skill and knowledge of the sport are needed.

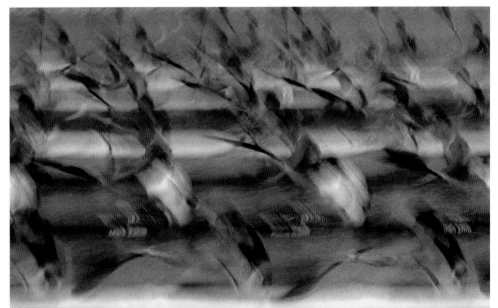

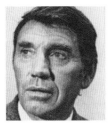

Don McCullin

BRITISH 1935–

Anguished and articulate, in words as well as images, McCullin's work reveals his compassionate vision and his innate ability to uncover dignity in utter desperation, giving a voice to those who suffer.

Having learned how to use a camera in the Royal Air Force, McCullin's photographic break came early in his career, when his pictures of a street gang, later linked with the murder of a policeman, were published in the *Observer* newspaper. This led quickly to war assignments for the leading British Sunday newspapers. Taking enormous risks, he soon achieved his ambition to be known as a photographer. While best known for his war images (most notably from the Congo, Vietnam, and Cambodia), McCullin's work at home on the underclass of British society, his haunting landscapes, and darkly luminous still-lifes are all part of the man and his photography. Through his autobiographical accounts, we know more about his anxieties and pains than those of any other photographer. He once said that "when human beings are suffering, they tend to look up, as if hoping for salvation. And that's when I press the button." Since the 1980s McCullin has documented the people and landscapes of remote parts of India, Indonesia, and Africa. However, in 2015 he visited northern Iraq to capture the struggle between the Kurds and ISIS in Syria and Turkey.

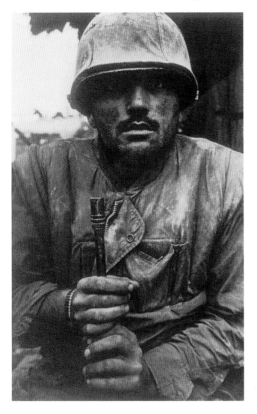

⟩⟩ CAREER HIGHLIGHTS

1953	Becomes photo assistant in RAF
1959	Pictures published in the *Observer*
1964	First assignment covering the civil war in Cyprus for the *Observer*
1980	Has retrospective at Victoria and Albert Museum, London
1993	Awarded CBE; honorary doctorate from University of Bradford; Dr Erich Salomon Preis
2007	Awarded Royal Photographic Society's Centenary Medal
2017	Knighted for services to photography
2019	Major retrospective at Tate Britain, London

⟨⟨ Shell-shocked Soldier, 1968
McCullin's lasting legacy is his face-to-face depiction of the pain of war. The haunting strength of this image is matched by McCullin's written account about this marine in Vietnam.

⌄ Funeral, Zambia
Shown in Christian Aid's *Cold Heaven* exhibition, this image records the funeral of an AIDS victim. Like the best of McCullin's work, deeper layers are revealed with repeated viewing.

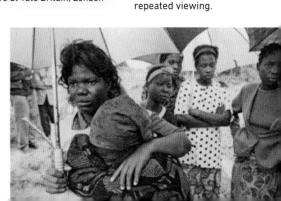

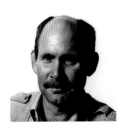

Steve McCurry

AMERICAN 1950–

A photographic craftsman with the instincts of a journalist, Steve McCurry's work appears to be carried on waves of serendipity, uncovering the humanity in even the most extreme situations of war and privation.

McCurry is the consummate photojournalist with a knack of being in the right place at the right time. Working in locations such as India, Pakistan, and Afghanistan, which suit his colour-rich style, he produced some of the late-20th century's iconic images, in particular the mesmerizing portrait of an Afghan girl, which first appeared on the cover of *National Geographic*. His stories tend to have a humanist slant and his images speak convincingly of his personal involvement with the subjects. With a willingness to engage in their lives, if only briefly, he is rewarded by a clear sense of humanity in his work. He once explained: "If you wait...the soul would drift up into view."

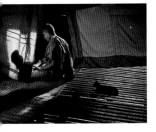

⏶ Buddhist Monk Studying, 1998
Tact and faultless technique are evident in this study made in Aranyaprathet, Thailand. With an almost palpable heat and silence, the image's ability to make you feel you are there is a perfect example of great travel photography.

》 CAREER HIGHLIGHTS

1984	Wins four World Press Photo prizes
1988	*Monsoon* published
1999	*Portraits* published
2005	Awarded honorary fellowship of Royal Geographical Society

》 THE POWER OF THE IMAGE

This image from McCurry's book *Monsoon* reveals that photography can sometimes have unexpected results. McCurry spotted this man wading through the floodwaters carrying his ruined sewing machine. When the picture appeared on the cover of *National Geographic*, the machine manufacturers sent the man a new one.

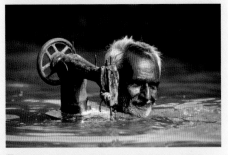

⏶ Indian Tailor with Sewing Machine, 1983
Despite the adverse conditions this man is smiling: this speaks as much for the power of the camera as McCurry's rapport with his subjects.

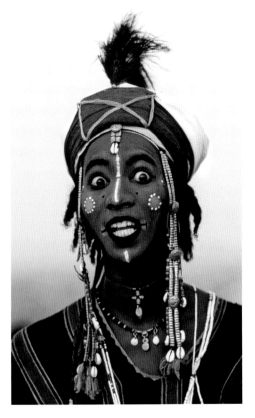

⏶ Tahoua, Niger, 1986
McCurry's travel portraiture is characterized by the subject's strong eye contact. This image shows an elaborately decorated woman.

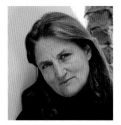

Susan Meiselas

AMERICAN 1948–

One of the leading exponents of photojournalism, Susan Meiselas is renowned for her uncompromising documentary style. She shows enormous physical courage and patient tenacity in her work.

Meiselas began her career as a photography teacher, but turned a corner when she met photojournalist Gilles Peress, who guided her towards membership of Magnum with her study of showgirls and strippers. At the age of 30, she travelled to Nicaragua where – with a mixture of naive foolhardiness and genuine courage – she documented the civil war. Her coverage has become the best record extant of the internecine conflicts.

Gaining a taste for such work, Meiselas went on to cover the civil war in El Salvador. In 1997 she curated a photographic history of Kurdistan that resulted in a pioneering website. Subsequent projects have combined photography, video, first-hand testimonies, and original artworks. Active in her espousal of the underprivileged, she says of her work that it is "about bearing witness to an indigenous people who face extinction".

⟩⟩ CAREER HIGHLIGHTS

1976	*Carnival Strippers* published
1979	Awarded the Robert Capa Gold Medal
1981	*Nicaragua* published
1997	*Kurdistan: In the Shadow of History* published
2018	Major retrospective held at San Francisco Museum of Modern Art

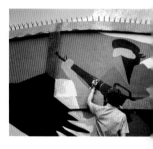

Managua, Nicaragua, 1979
This colourful mural could have made a great travel photograph. But the menacing subject matter shows its true meaning.

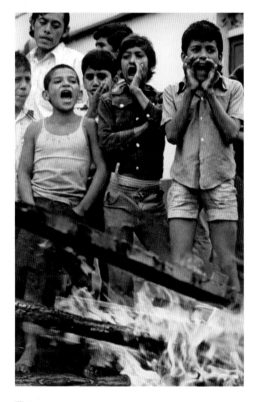

⌃ **Matagalpa, Nicaragua, 1978**
Meiselas positioned herself amongst the protagonists to capture this image of children shouting at the National Guard.

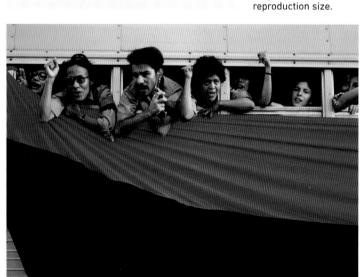

Managua, Nicaragua, 1979
This image shows photojournalism and spot-news photography at their best. It is symbolic, strongly composed, and ideal for use in magazines in any reproduction size.

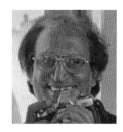

Raghu Rai

INDIAN 1942–

Powered by perceptive intelligence and a profound love of his country, Raghu Rai's pictures often ask more questions than they answer. His work shows a rare mastery of both black-and-white and colour photojournalism.

As a photographer, Rai has concentrated on the single subject of India all his working life. This approach has enabled him to examine his homeland and its people at leisure, lovingly, and with the greatest of subtlety. At the same time, Rai's technique is classically minimal. Most of the time, he uses a wide-angle lens and a 35mm camera, and occasionally a panoramic camera. He has worked as both a photography director and a photographer, and is equally at home working in black and white and in colour.

Widely exhibited and published, Rai's work includes coverage of major figures, such as Indira Gandhi and Mother Theresa. He describes photography as "an intense passion" and his pictures reflect his deep emotional response to his subjects. His most famous work explores the aftermath of the 1984 Bhopal mass poisoning when the Union Carbide chemical factory leaked, killing thousands of people. His book on Bhopal, *Exposure: Portrait of a Corporate Crime*, demonstrates the enduring nature of visual investigation when technical virtuosity is combined with a need to say something passionately. Rai confesses: "I am always exploring... If I relax I am bound to miss some great photo opportunities... There are thousands of themes left."

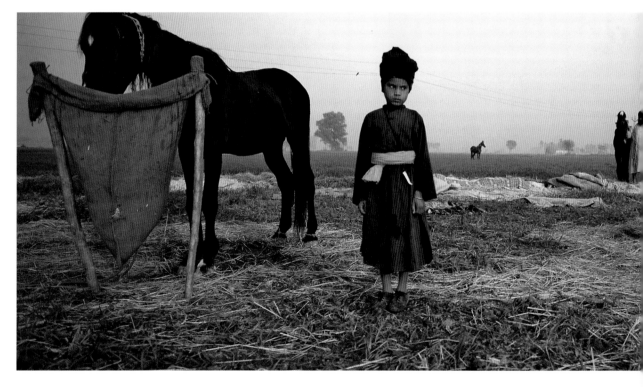

》 CAREER HIGHLIGHTS

1965	Photographs for *The Statesman*
1974	*A Life in the Day of Indira Gandhi* published
1977	Has retrospective at National Gallery of Modern Art, Delhi
1982	Director of Photography, *India Today*
1993	Wins Photographer of the Year, USA
1996	*Mother Theresa* published
2002	*Exposure: Portrait of a Corporate Crime* published
2015	*Picturing Time* published

☑ Nihang at Amritsar
Rai's portrait of a young Nihang in a camp at Amritsar uses a panoramic camera to locate his subject in a composition of elegantly static forms. The boy, who belongs to the Guru Gobind Singh – the tenth Guru's army – wears a typical blue Sikh dress.

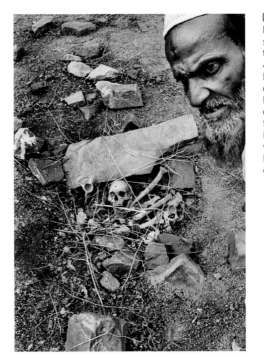

◀ Cemetery, Bhopal
Mohammed Aziz is shown returning to the cemetery where 4,000 people were buried in the first days after the 1984 Bhopal disaster. Rai depicts his subject from an unusual angle: it confronts the living with the dead in a hauntingly powerful composition.

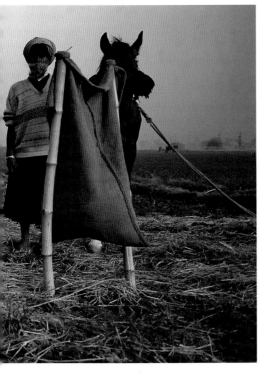

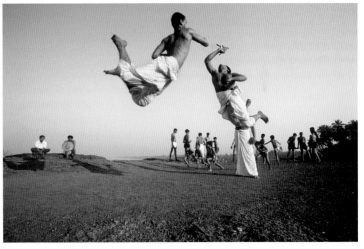

⌃ Kalarippayat Demonstration
Two masters of the Indian martial art of Kalarippayat – a precursor of the better-known martial arts of the Far East – demonstrate their agility during a mock fight. Rai locates himself low and deep in the action.

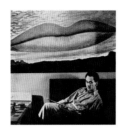

Man Ray

AMERICAN 1890–1976

Remarkable for its technical range, intelligence, and wit, Man Ray's work shows a penchant for experimentation. Yet photography for him was as an adjunct to his art. He once said, "I photograph what I do not wish to paint."

Emmanuel Radnitsky started his career as a draughtsman in 1912, but was soon drawn to the emerging art movements of Europe. Changing his name to Man Ray on his marriage in 1914, he also initiated a change in artistic direction. Although his work is often associated with the artistic developments of Paris from the 1920s to the 1950s – Ray lived in the city from 1921 until his death – his first major influence was the visionary American photographer, publisher, and gallery director Alfred Stieglitz (*see p.63*).

By 1923, Ray had received numerous commissions from leading fashion magazines of the time, and had become an established photographer.

Almost as famous for his assistants, who included photographers Berenice Abbott and Lee Miller, Ray was a prolific experimentalist both with the camera and in the darkroom. His mischievous working principle was "to do what one is not supposed to do" and his work conferred respectability to darkroom curiosities, such as the Sabattier Effect and photograms.

》 Jacqueline Goddard as a Nun
Goddard (neé Barsotti) was one of Ray's favourite models. The Sabattier Effect used on the print disguises the nun's habit, turning it into a cubist-like form.

》 CAREER HIGHLIGHTS

1915	Buys a camera to photograph his paintings. First one-man show at the Daniel Gallery, New York
1920	Collaborates with artist Marcel Duchamp
1925	Photographs for French and American editions of *Vogue*
1928	Films *L'Etoile de Mer* (*The Star of the Sea*)
1967	*Salute to Man Ray* exhibition at the American Center, Paris

⊻ Rayograph 19
This image was made using the rayograph technique in which objects are placed on photographic paper and exposed to light.

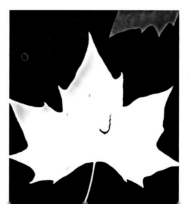

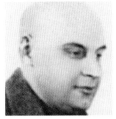

Alexandr Rodchenko

RUSSIAN 1891–1956

It was Alexandr Rodchenko's injunction "to take several different shots of a subject from different points of view... as if one examined it in the round" that has guided photographers and cinematographers ever since.

A painter, graphic designer, and sculptor, Rodchenko took to photography in his early 30s, and quickly realized that the camera's ability to look at objects from any angle made it the mechanical equivalent of the human eye. This fitted well with his Constructivist ideals, leading him to declare that "In order to educate Man to a new longing, everyday objects must be shown with totally unexpected perspectives."

》 CAREER HIGHLIGHTS

1915	First Suprematist works
1923	Photographs appear in *LEF* magazine
1932	Photographs sports and parades

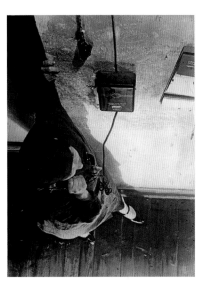

《 At the Telephone, 1928 Rodchenko's search for unusual viewpoints not only reveals fresh perspectives, it also conceals the ordinary, forcing the obvious underground.

Sebastião Salgado

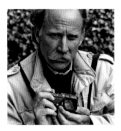

BRAZILIAN 1944–

A magisterial presence in the world of photojournalism, Sebastião Salgado has turned the picture essay into the picture magnum opus, composing vast edifices of imagery around themes of the disadvantaged masses.

☑ Doctor's Waiting Room, Chad Salgado's images are often masterpieces of composition. There is an almost painterly quality about the figures in this doctor's waiting area.

》 CAREER HIGHLIGHTS

1990	*Uncertain Grace* published
2000	*The Children* published
2013	*Genesis* published
2015	*The Scent of a Dream* published

With a doctorate in economics, Salgado approaches his photography with the thoroughness of a disciplined academic. The intelligence of his picture-making – exclusively in 35mm black-and-white film – is evident in the craftsmanship of every image. As a UNICEF special representative, he campaigns to save the Brazilian rainforest.

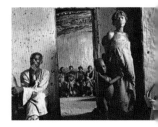

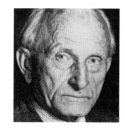

August Sander

GERMAN 1876–1964

An advocate of photography's power to document, August Sander was made famous by his monumental portraiture project. This rich and vastly influential work has inspired artists, filmmakers, and photographers alike.

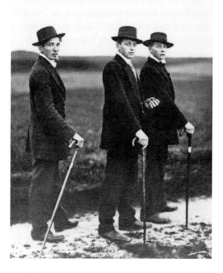

》 Young Farmers, 1914
In this celebrated portrait, the dapper young men appear too polite to refuse to pose, but are clearly impatient to keep going.

》 CAREER HIGHLIGHTS

1925	Starts *People of the 20th Century*
1929	*Face of our Time* published
1952	Inclusion of works into MoMA collection

Although Sander produced significant work in architecture and landscape, he is best known for his lifelong project *People of the 20th Century*. This was a series of portraits that he took to document German society. His heterogeneous depiction of the German nation clashed with Nazi ideology and the plates for his book *Face of our Time* were seized and destroyed.

⊠ Maude Callen, Midwife, 1951
Smith's work fused rich editorial content with strong composition. Here a midwife in rural North Carolina teaches colleagues how to examine babies for abnormalities.

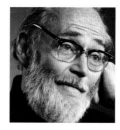

William Eugene Smith

AMERICAN 1918–1978

Inspirational in his ability to speak through a narrative spun from superbly crafted images, William Eugene Smith perfected the picture essay genre and brought photojournalism to new heights of artistry.

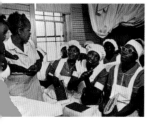

An early starter, Smith sold photographs to newspapers while still in his mid-teens. He was the archetypal humanist who once asked: "What use is having a great depth of field, if there is not an adequate depth of feeling?" His 1956 picture essay on Pittsburgh, USA, is a pinnacle of the genre. This laid the foundation for his major work in Minamata, Japan, which gave rise to many iconic images.

》 CAREER HIGHLIGHTS

1939	Works for *LIFE*
1957	Joins Magnum
1971	Photographs in Minamata, Japan

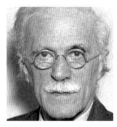

Alfred Stieglitz

AMERICAN 1864–1946

A measure of the greatness of Alfred Stieglitz is that no one can decide which of his contributions to photography is the greater: his own work or his influence, as editor and gallery director, on the course of American photography.

Born in the USA but educated in Germany, Stieglitz considered himself wholly American, yet he was instrumental in bringing European influences across the Atlantic. A tireless campaigner for modern photography, he poured money and monumental energy into publishing projects and exhibitions. Nonetheless, he concentrated on fine art towards the end of his life. His legendary, painstakingly produced magazine *Camera Work* was as important for the painters it published as for the photographers. While full of praise for the objective clarity of Edward Weston's work (*see p.93*), his own images were sentimentally pictorialist, ranging from romanticized urban views to the tender eroticism of his Georgia O'Keeffe studies. His credo is evident from a letter in which he writes "No school, no church, is as good a teacher as the eye understandingly seeing what's before it."

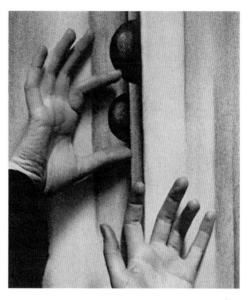

Georgia O'Keeffe: A Portrait
Stieglitz photographed his wife, artist Georgia O'Keeffe, with a rich visual vocabulary that was emotive and celebratory. Even here, a study of her hands is sketched with sexual innuendo.

» CAMERA WORK

Published irregularly by Stieglitz between 1903 and 1917, *Camera Work* was an influential showcase for Stieglitz's circle of leading painters, writers, and photographers. All but ignored on its publication, the magazine has had an enormous influence on 20th-century art practice, and has become the art magazine by which others are judged.

» CAREER HIGHLIGHTS

1902	Founds Photo-Secession group
1903	First issue of *Camera Work* published
1905	Founds Photo-Secession Gallery

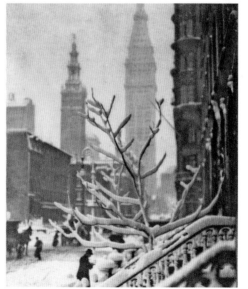

Two Towers – New York, 1911
While championing the crisp modernity of photographers such as Weston and Strand, Stieglitz also produced dreamy cityscapes, such as this snowy scene.

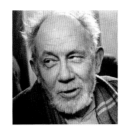

Josef Sudek

CZECH 1896–1976

For a photographer to gain the sobriquet "Poet of Prague", in a city replete with artistic genius, is remarkable. For Josef Sudek to do so with an oeuvre founded in his garden shed and with subjects within its vicinity is an inspiration.

Sudek was unable to continue his career as a bookbinder when he lost his arm in World War I. Having taken up photography some years earlier, he began to take it more seriously on his return from the war. Sudek's photography found its truest expression in work created at his modest home and in Prague. Despite his disability, he used large format cameras almost exclusively. He worked patiently: some themes occupied him for as long as ten years. In addition to documenting subjects such as the reconstruction of Prague's St Vitus's Cathedral, he published eight books, which are full of quiet studies of light, hinted-at forms, and deserted spaces in which he seems to breathe life into the inanimate.

» CAREER HIGHLIGHTS

1927	Works in his garden studio in Prague
1933	First one-man exhibition
1961	First photographer to receive Artist of Merit Award
1974	Has retrospective at George Eastman House, Rochester, UK

☑ Glasses and Eggs
Sudek made many extraordinary still-lifes of ordinary objects. They range from the sharply detailed to the softly atmospheric.

» Melnick Chateau, 1957
This is one of 284 panoramas of Prague and its surrounding countryside that made up Sudek's monograph *Panoramic Prague*.

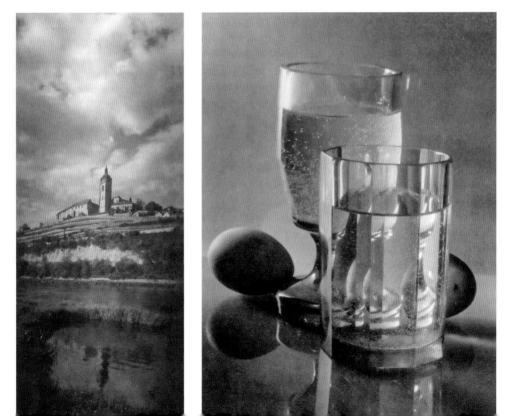

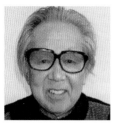

Shoji Ueda

JAPANESE 1913–2000

Seeming to inhabit a parallel universe, Ueda's images are full of emptiness and space – implied and manifest. Using understatement and suggestion, his work is celebrated as a response to photography that is truly Japanese.

Starting conventionally by attending photography school, opening a studio, and establishing a local photography group, Ueda's career was interrupted by World War II, but resumed in 1946. His best-known work centres on the extensive sand dunes of Tottori in western Japan, and shows Surrealist tendencies (he has said that Renée Magritte was an inspiration) as well as a Zen-motivated preoccupation with form. Ueda amply demonstrates that the subtle variations and linear forms of sand dunes make superb backgrounds. Working in black and white, Ueda left some 60,000 prints to the photography museum in Kishimoto, which was founded in his name in 1995.

❯❯ CAREER HIGHLIGHTS

1951	Exhibits in Ginza, Tokyo
1960	Exhibits in Museum of Modern Art, New York
1975	Teaches photography at Kyushu Sangyo University
1983	Has retrospective at Tokyo State Gallery

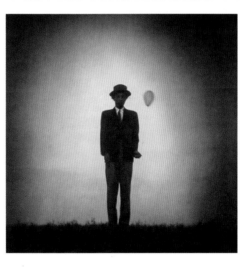

《 Self-Portrait with Balloon
This early self-portrait from 1948, is both a tribute to Magritte and a question about the nature of reality. Where exactly is the balloon?

No Title, Sand Dunes
Ueda's image is singular in its exploration of the photographic possibilities of these sand dunes in western Japan.

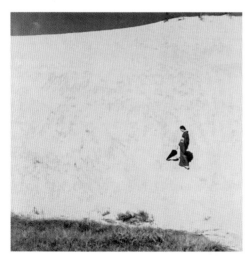

《 No Title, Sand Dunes
This innovative photograph is a carefully staged tableaux. Ueda uses the photographic illusion of space to create visual confusion.

THE STORY OF
PHOTOGRAPHY

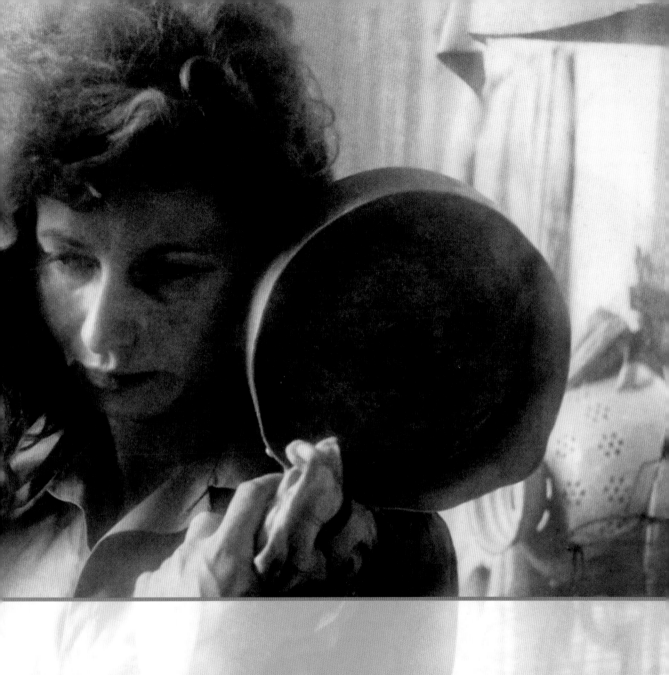

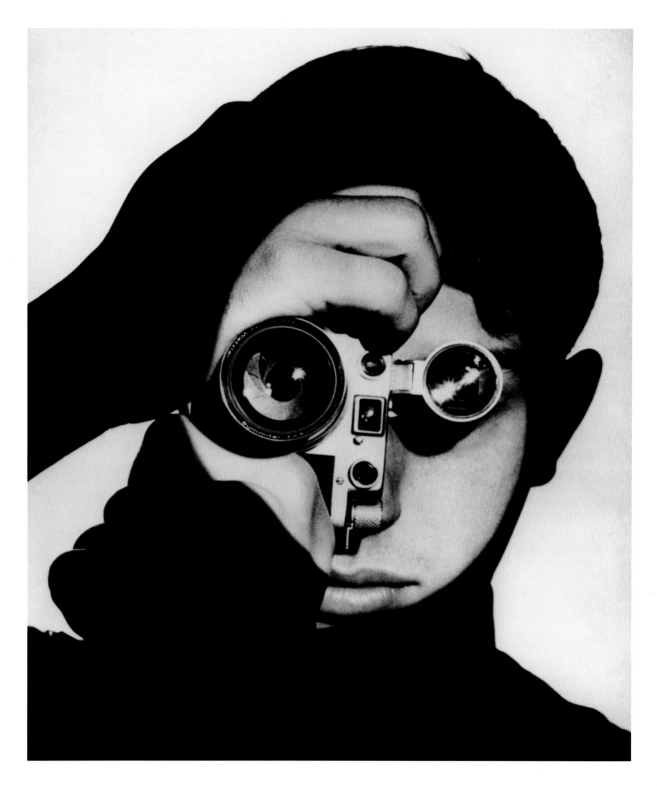

Photography arose from the work of artists, scientists, and technologists in the 19th century, and has grown to become a medium that touches every part of human activity. From the earliest black-and-white prints to the latest digital images, photography has the power to challenge, inspire, inform, and amuse.

Photography is a multi-faceted medium, and its history is made up of the interweaving of three major strands. The artistic movements that influenced and were influenced by photography gave it an identity separate from the other visual arts. Cultural exchanges between photography and society, which had a lasting effect in newspapers and magazines, have broadened public knowledge and understanding of issues and events. And technological developments, such as the explosion in digital image capture and manipulation in the late 1990s, have enabled photographers to continue to break new ground.

A variety of art movements have institutionalized a diverse range of artistic practices in photography. The effect of Dadaism on photography in the 1920s was to inspire the creation of images tinged with an iconoclastic mischievousness and wit. This was in marked contrast to the brooding, introspective style of photography motivated by Post-Modernist insecurities. And that was different again from Secessionist responses – all grain and grief – to the shiny objectivity of Modernism.

Like the phases of a personal history, different aspects of photography vary in importance at different stages of its development. The early impact of photography was entirely restricted to the wealthy, leisured classes. The cost of materials such as silver, and hand-made optical equipment, was far too high to allow the average person to take advantage of the new technology. As a result, the social influence of photography at that time was arguably negligible. Once photography became industrialized in the 20th century, it was able to reach the mass market,

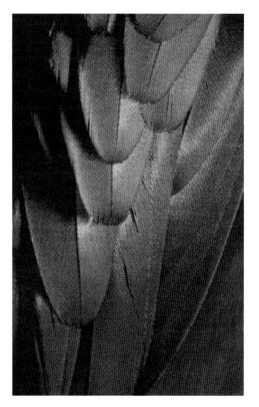

◰ **Green-winged Macaw**
This image by Stephen Dalton (*see p.40*) shows the fine detail and vivid colours that can be captured by high-quality lenses.

◰ **Andreas Feininger portrait, 1950s**
Feininger's iconic portrait of Dennis Stock portrays the photographic eye as intensely scrutinising and slightly threatening.

becoming accessible to all but the poorest and most disadvantaged. Its influence on social awareness and debate grew to be all-powerful (until television became the primary medium of mass communication). Documentary photography was increasingly used as a means of campaigning, and became an influential tool in lobbying for change.

From the early use of the camera obscura as a drawing aid to the discovery of the first photo-sensitive compound, new technology has been at the forefront of artistic creativity. The arrival of roll film and miniature cameras in the early 20th century freed photographers from the studio and heralded a new age of photojournalism, documentary reporting, and candid photography. Similarly revolutionary was the introduction of colour. This brought new challenges – both artistic and technical – while allowing photographers to cover subjects with greater realism. As technology continued to march on, long focal-length, large-aperture lenses revolutionized nature and sports photography by greatly extending the optical reach of cameras.

More recently, the emergence of computer technology has democratized photography. Even people with little interest in photography can take pictures instantly on their mobile-phone cameras, and then share them via the internet. On a larger scale, satellite imaging has given us new insights into the universe and our planet.

☑ Me and Cat, 1932
This image was made by superimposing two photographs – a self-portrait by Wanda Wulz and an image of her cat.

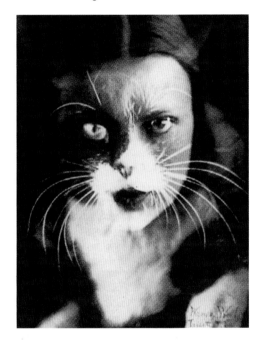

Photography in the 21st century is more widespread and diverse than at any other time in its history. Modern photographers are in an enviable position – the interplay of artistic, cultural, and technological influences are perfect for creativity and innovation.

☑ The changing face of portraiture
Changing trends can be seen in a Victorian calling card, a 1940s fashion picture, and a modern-day digitally enhanced image.

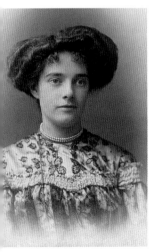

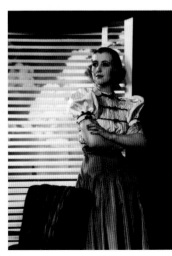

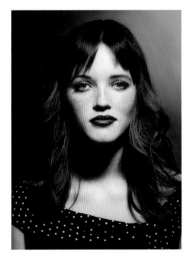

» Satellite imaging
This false-colour image of Lake Carnegie in Western Australia was taken by NASA's Landsat satellite in 1999.

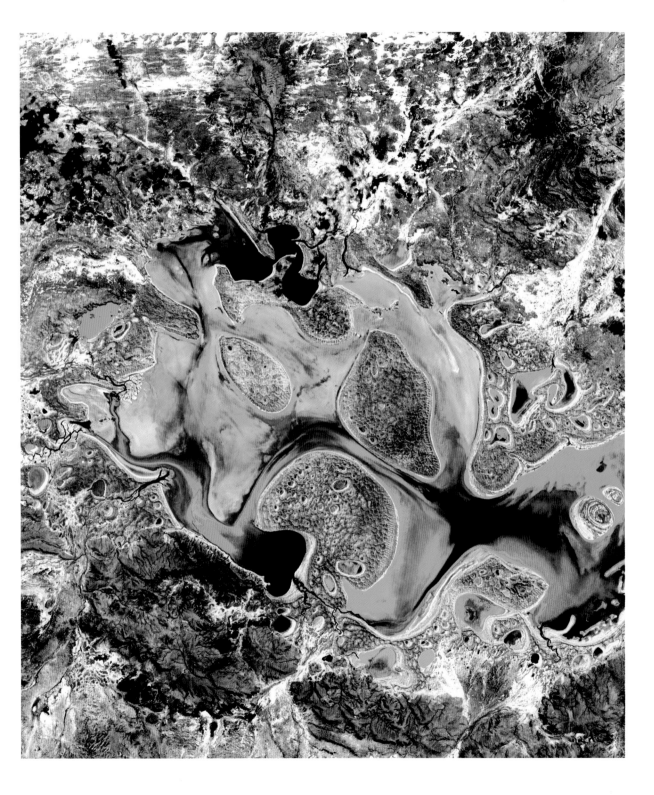

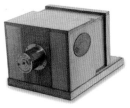

⌃ Giroux Daguerreotype camera
The first type of camera to be placed on public sale, this model was made in 1839 in Paris.

The dawn of photography (1820–60)

Working with light was well understood as early as the 5th century BC, when the first experiments using the principle of the camera obscura were recorded. Building on this principle, Joseph Nicephore Niépce (1765–1833) created the first photograph, but it was his associate Louis Daguerre (1787–1851) who invented the world's first widely used photographic process, known as the daguerreotype.

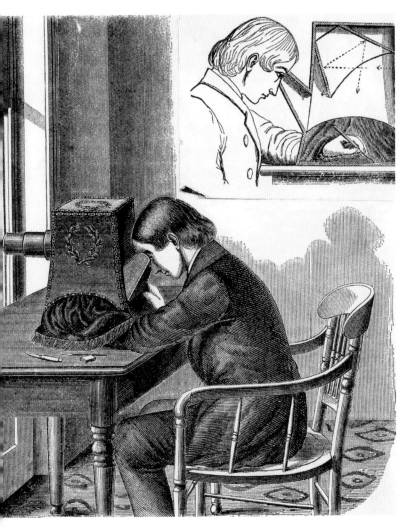

Camera obscura

The camera obscura (Latin for "darkened chamber") was a building block in the development of the camera. It is a box with a hole in one side through which light enters and projects onto the opposite side, creating an upside-down image of the scene. In about 1826 Niépce used a camera obscura to project light onto a glass plate coated with light-sensitive bitumen to capture the view from his window. It was the first photographic image but the process involved an eight-hour exposure, and the image soon lost contrast.

Daguerreotype

Fellow Frenchman Louis Jacques Mandé Daguerre was a set designer and showman. He created a show called a Diorama, in which painted scenes of up to 20m (66ft) in width were illuminated to create a visual spectacle. He created many of these scenes using a camera obscura, and began to experiment with ways of fixing the image without having to trace and paint it. By 1837 he had created fairly successful images, with the considerable help of Niépce, who sadly died before his contribution to the partnership was acknowledged. They created small images with exquisite metallic tonality and surprisingly sharp detail. Daguerre named his process the daguerreotype, and demonstrated his invention to the public in 1839.

《 Table-top camera obscura
This Victorian woodcut shows a camera obscura – a forerunner of the first cameras – being used as a drawing aid by an artist.

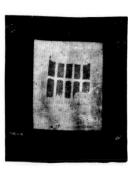

Latticed Window
(with the Camera Obscura)
August 1835

When first made, the squares
of glass about 200 in number
could be counted, with help
of a lens.

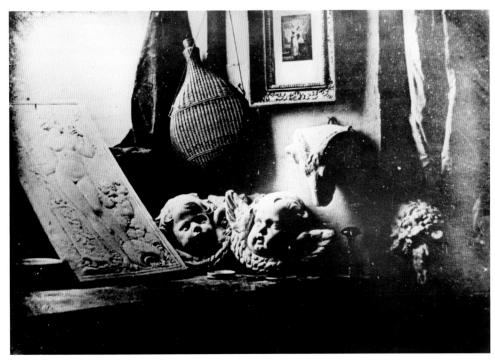

« Fox Talbot's negative
Made in the summer of 1835, the first negative ever created was surprisingly detailed despite its postage stamp size. Fox Talbot notes that it is possible to make out the 200 individual squares in the latticed window.

« Daguerreotype image, 1837
This image was captured with the daguerreotype method, a positive-only photographic process that allowed no further reprints of the original.

Calotype process

At about the same time others were attempting to create a permanent record of an image. In Britain, William Fox Talbot (1800–77) had been experimenting with semi-transparent paper sensitized in a chemical solution to make a negative, from which he then made a positive print. He announced his calotype process in 1841. The British claim to have truly invented photography, since Fox Talbot's was the first negative-positive process from which any number of prints could be made from a negative. The disadvantage of this method was that the exposure time was often as long as an hour.

Patenting the process

By the mid-1800s, inventors recognized the power of patents, and both Daguerre and Fox Talbot were determined to profit from the inventions that had cost them time and money to develop. With commendable generosity and vision, the French government bought the rights to the daguerreotype and put them into the public domain. As a result, daguerrotype portrait studios soon started opening all over Europe and the Americas.

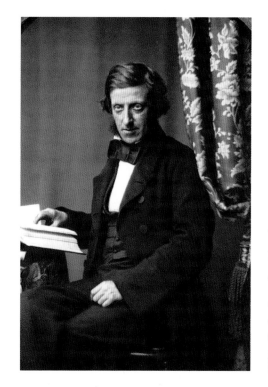

» Frederick
Scott Archer
A hero of early
photography, Archer
put his invention in
the public arena,
but died in poverty.

Improving processes

In its early days, photography was a technical handicraft, albeit one easily mastered by the dedicated amateur. In part due to Fox Talbot's firm hold on the use of the calotype process, and in part because of its inability to record detail, many photographers were driven to search for other techniques. Often they concealed new discoveries for fear of giving away an advantage to competitors. For instance, it is thought that Louis Daguerre kept his use of especially large aperture lenses secret.

By the 1850s, the basic principles of photography were understood: the initial image was captured by exposing paper sensitized with silver salts to light. The resulting image was "latent" (invisible to the naked eye), but could be developed into a visible negative when processed in an alkaline developer. The image had to be "fixed" by washing away the silver salts that were not developed as their presence would fade the image. Light-sensitive paper was then placed under the negative and exposed to light. Further processing produced a positive print.

The wet collodion process

The first competition to Fox Talbot's calotype process was the wet collodion process, invented by Frederick Scott Archer (1813–57). It had one key advantage over the calotype process – it used large sturdy glass plates to produce beautifully clear images. The size of the print was limited only by the size of the plate. However, its big drawback was that it had to be "worked in the wet", by dipping the glass plates, just before exposure and in the dark, in a sensitizing solution of silver nitrate. Exposure then took place while the plates were still damp. Processing of the image followed immediately afterwards.

In heart-warming contrast to the greed of his fellows, Archer placed his invention in the public arena in 1851. However, it was another year before photographers were able to take advantage of the technique, as Fox Talbot tried to claim that his patent covered Archer's invention. Nonetheless, wet collodion cameras swept calotypes and daguerreotypes out of photographic studios within a few years.

» **EARLY WAR IMAGES**

The Crimean War (1853–56) was the first military conflict to be photographed, but even then it was subject to censorship. Pictures of the battlefield and the dead were not permitted. Instead, we have pictures of soldiers posing for the camera. The wet collodion process made war photography possible. Even though the apparatus had to be transported in a large wagon, it did liberate photographers from the confines of the studio.

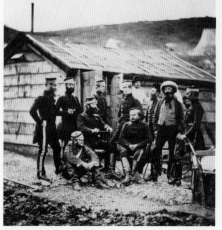

« **Group of Soldiers in the Crimean War (1855)**
British photographer Roger Fenton (1819–69) was restricted to taking formal group photographs behind the lines in the Crimean War, due to the cumbersome photographic apparatus of the wet collodion process.

The rise of the portrait

The relatively instant and painless creation of a print that bore full human likeness caught the Victorian public's imagination, and the direction that popular photography first took surprised its inventors. People were not the most obvious subjects for photography, because it was hard for live subjects to keep sufficiently still for the long exposures (two or more minutes) that were needed to produce the images. But a few minutes of immobility were nothing compared to the hours of sitting required for a portrait painter.

Far more important, however, was the fact that the mechanized nature of the photographic process meant that portraiture was no longer the preserve of the wealthy. Creating an accurate record of a person's appearance – formerly the domain of the skilled painter – was now all but automatic. As a result, the earliest photographers, studios, and accessories all focused on portraiture.

In France it became popular to leave a calling card printed with the owner's likeness. When Queen Victoria adopted the practice, the craze spread quickly throughout Britain. The demand for these

cartes de visite could only be met by production-line methods, which meant that portraiture was the first area of photography to be mass-produced. Calling-card cameras were developed in the 1860s, and soon models were available with four or more lenses, which took four or more pictures at a time. Mass printing and card-trimming facilities sprang up in major cities around the world.

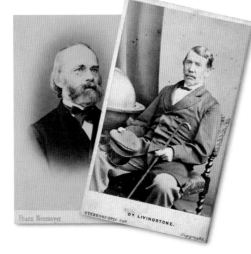

◀ Miniature portraits
These calling cards show Scottish explorer David Livingstone and German botanist von Naegeli, and were popular in the late 19th century.

▼ Portrait studio
This image shows a sitter posing for a portrait at Fox Talbot's studio in Reading, Berkshire, in around 1840.

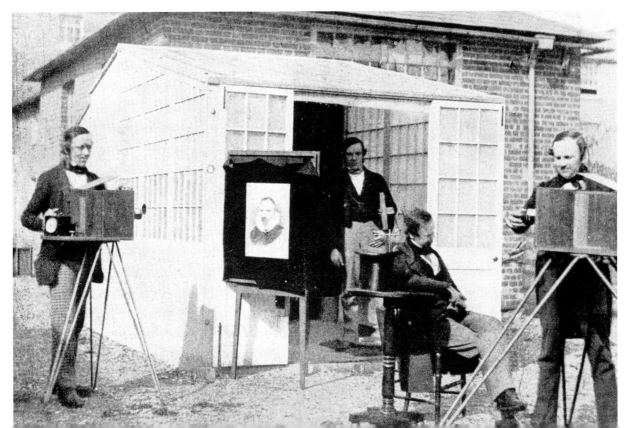

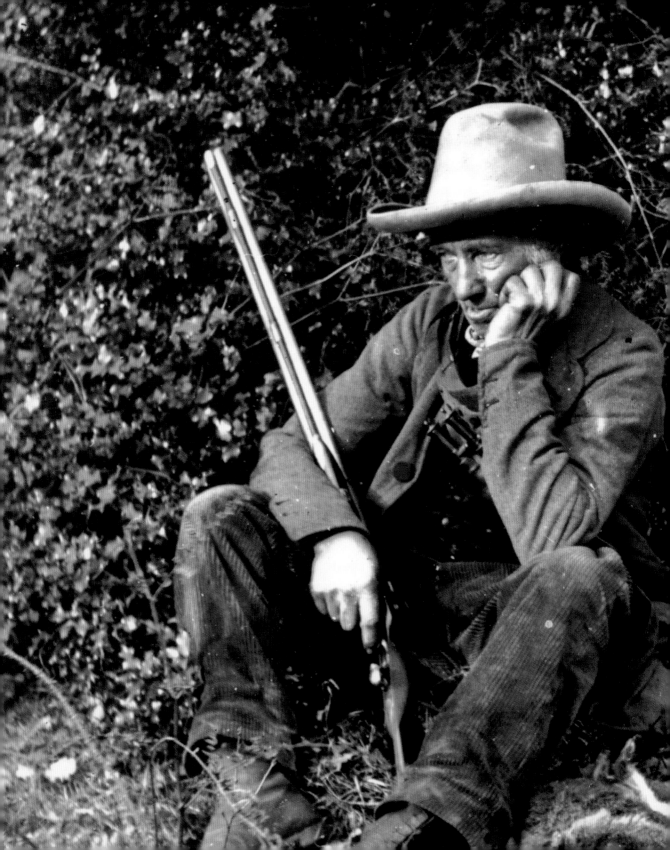

Pot shot
This carefully posed picture of a hunter with his catch of rabbits and birds was made by William Grundy, active in the 1850s and 1860s. He was best known for stereoscopic images.

Commanding the medium (1860–90)

In step with their growing command of the medium, photographers began to diversify and split into camps with opposing artistic ideologies. Soon, photographers were able to extend their visual language by using colour. Techniques were also invented to analyze motion, helping to establish the value of photography as a scientific tool.

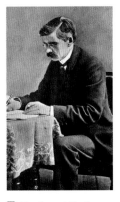

⌃ **Ferdinand Hurter**
Hurter (1844–94) invented the actinograph, an early type of exposure meter, with Vero Driffield (1848–1915).

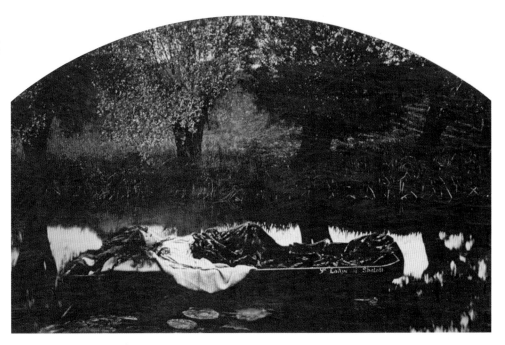

⟫ **Henry Peach Robinson's** *Lady of Shalott* (1882)
To illustrate Tennyson's poem, Robinson used multiple exposures and collaged elements. The photograph resembles Millais' painting *Ophelia*.

Innovation

The growing mass-production of photographs meant that what had started out as a handicraft evolved into an industrial discipline focused on quality control. There was a further scramble to make money from patents, and scientists, recognizing the commercial potential, began to experiment with photography. At the forefront of research were Vero Charles Driffield and Ferdinand Hurter, who laid the foundation for sensitometry – the study of photographic responses to light – and the accurate measurement of film speed. In 1890 they published the "characteristic curve", a graph showing a light-sensitive material's response to light and processing. The curve is still used today, even in digital photography.

An artistic approach

From the rather defeatist declaration "from today, painting is dead" (attributed to the French painter Paul Delaroche [1797–1856], on seeing a daguerreotype for the first time) to the clichéd sneer "but is it art?", relations between photography and art have always been strained. Nonetheless, it was not long before photographers started to

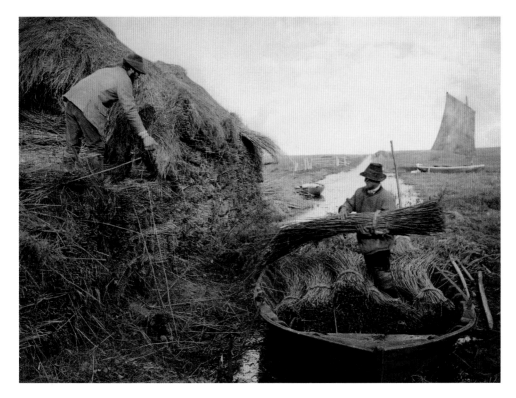

◀ **Pictorialist representation**
Peter Henry Emerson's espousal of the natural led him to depict rural scenes in a light that conveyed the beauty but hid the hardships. This image entitled *Ricking the Reed*, taken in Britain in around 1886, is a good example.

imitate artists, and artists started toying with cameras (if only in private).

As photographers began to pursue an artistic direction, they soon found themselves divided in their aims and techniques. Some chose to imitate fine art directly, partly due to the inherent need for static poses, and the similarities between the portrait and painting studio. Their work sought to out-do fine artists, and was often costumed elaborately, lit in *chiaroscuro* with strong contrast between light and dark, and pregnant with literary references. Oscar Gustav Rejlander (1813–75), Julia Margaret Cameron (*see p.35*), and Henry Peach Robinson (1830–1901) embraced this approach. This period also saw the inception of photographic perfectionism – the ambition to create the perfect negative and the perfect print. This required meticulous, studio-based techniques, and posed subjects. In reality it was an attempt to establish a photographic élite.

In contrast to the approach of fine-art practitioners, some photographers exploited the improving ability of the medium to capture the spontaneous occurrences of everyday life. They wanted to photograph the people, life, and light of their world in a natural context, without manipulation or artifice. Their ideology was that photography did not need to refer to classical works, but should be an art form in its own right. The most vociferous proponent of this style was Peter Henry Emerson (1856–1936), who published books and gave lectures on the subject. Ironically, he renounced photography as an art form in 1900, complaining that new technology produced images that "look like the photograph of a painting...it is hand work, and not photography."

◀ **Fine-art portrait**
A portrait of an unknown woman, taken by Swedish photographer Oscar Gustav Rejlander in London in around 1870.

» **Hand-coloured daguerreotype image**
This image was made for stereoscopic viewing by Antoine Claudet, which, when seen through a special viewer, appeared as a single 3D image.

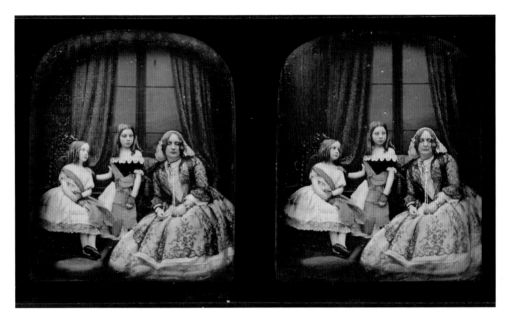

The birth of colour

Barely had the water dried off the first prints before photographers began to clamour for a way to record in colour. The first method was to apply colour by hand. Painters who had felt sidelined by the explosion in popularity of portrait photography found their fine art skills back in demand. The images were small and delicate, and some surviving examples are exquisite portrait miniatures.

The work of Louis Ducos du Hauron (1837–1920) provided important developments in the search for a photographic method of recording colour. Building on the earlier findings of physicists Thomas Young and James Clerk Maxwell, who published papers on light and colour theory, he developed the "trichrome" theory of colour photography in 1869, which used filters to separate red, green, and blue light in three separate exposures. Predating practical equipment and techniques by decades, Ducos du Hauron's work also included schemes of subtractive and additive colour mixing.

Early travel photography

As the quality of equipment and materials improved and processes became easier to manage, photographers could travel further afield. Some scoured the world for pictures that were eagerly consumed by a public keen to learn about distant lands. For instance, William Henry Jackson hauled huge cameras – some large enough to expose

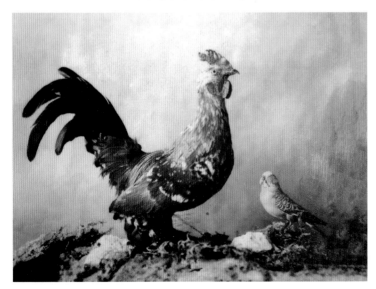

« **Additive-colour image**
After exposure, Ducos du Hauron's three colour negatives were each used to make an engraved colour plate, which was used to make a print. This laid the foundation for the mass-printing process that is still in use today.

20 x 24-inch glass plates – into the Wild West of his native America, creating many revelatory landscape images. It was his pictures that inspired the US government to create national parks.

Capturing movement

By the 1870s, the technology existed to allow exposures in small fractions of a second. This was crucial to the work of Eadweard Muybridge (1830–1904), who was trying to prove that a galloping horse raises all four feet off the ground at once. To do this he used a battery of cameras activated by tripwires to photograph a fast-moving horse. This inspired the 11-volume work *Animal Locomotion*. Muybridge realized that his sequential images could represent movement. In 1879 he invented the Zoopraxiscope, a spinning drum with a sequence of pictures inside. When the images were viewed through a hole they gave the impression of continuous movement.

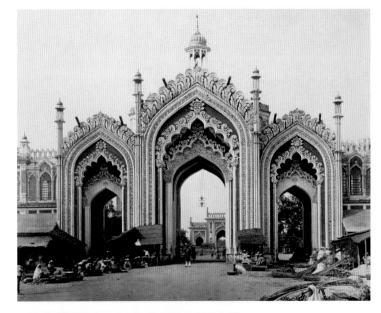

⌃ **Early travel picture**
This image shows the gateway of the Hoospinad Bazaar in Lucknow, India, photographed by Samuel Bourne (1834–1912) in around 1860.

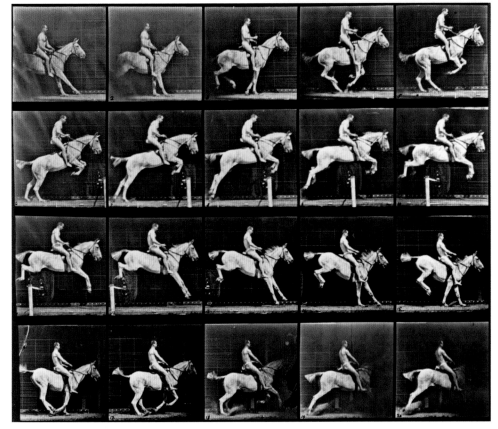

≪ **High-speed sequence**
This photographic sequence of a rider jumping a hurdle on a horse formed part of Eadweard Muybridge's *Animal Locomotion* project.

Ambulance Wagon in the Desert
Timothy O'Sullivan (1840–82) made this study in the Carson Desert, Nevada, in 1867 while working on the Geological Exploration of the Fortieth Parallel.

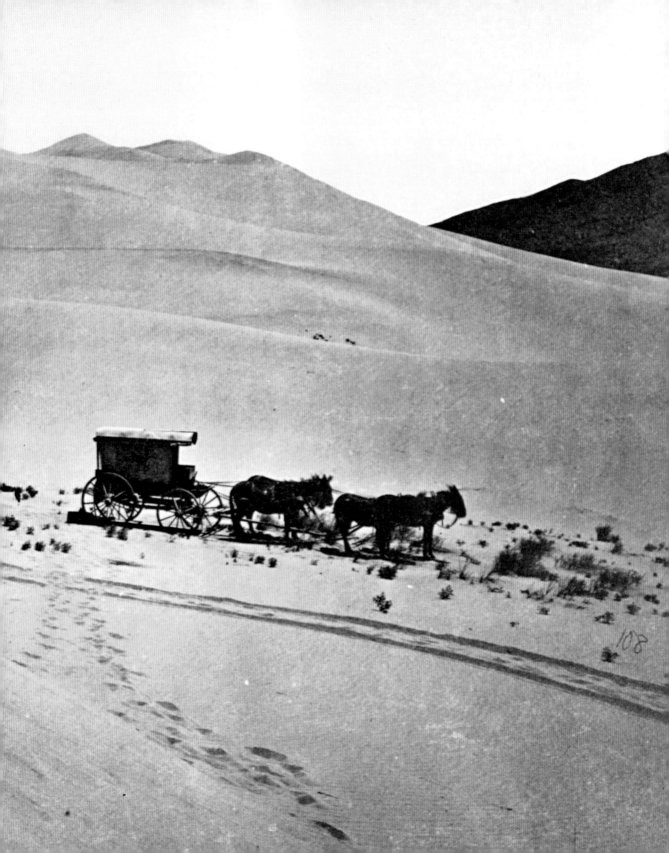

Expanding horizons (1890–1920)

The late-19th and early-20th centuries saw photography reach the mass market. Audiences were attracted by magic lantern shows and easy-to-use cameras were widely available. Technological advances enabled photographers to explore an increasingly wide range of styles, from candid and investigative photography, to humour and fashion.

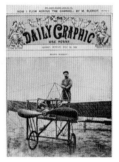

⏫ Illustrated news
The front cover of the illustrated newspaper the *Daily Graphic*, published in London, in 1909.

Illustrated newspapers

In the 1890s, the use of pictures of any sort in newspapers was a source of lively debate. Photographs first appeared in newspapers as woodcuts or engravings, but following experiments by the *Daily Graphic* in 1880, these artist-mediated processes were replaced by the photo-mechanical process of half-toning. Initially rejected as unintellectual, the use of occasional images grew into fully illustrated reportage. Documentary photography was in use from 1890, and by 1919, the use of photography in newspapers was routine.

Projecting the image

Enabling a crowd of people to see the same picture at the same time was an important stage in the development of photography. The magic lantern was invented in the mid-17th century, but it was not until the Victorian era that it became a popular source of education and entertainment for large audiences. Images were produced as prints made on glass, known as "positives", which allowed light to pass through. A gas or oil lamp with multiple wicks produced light that was collected by a mirror and light-gathering box, and reflected onto the slide. A focusing lens projected the image onto a white wall or screen. At the turn of the 19th century, this method of projection was the public's main source of visual information on foreign lands, and even on aspects of life in their own country, such as architecture. The magic lantern laid the foundation for the slide projector and photographic enlargers.

⏬ Magic lantern projector
An image placed on a transparent plate between a light source and a lens projects a sharp image onto a flat surface. Modern projectors still adhere to the same principles of this oil-fired lantern of 1895.

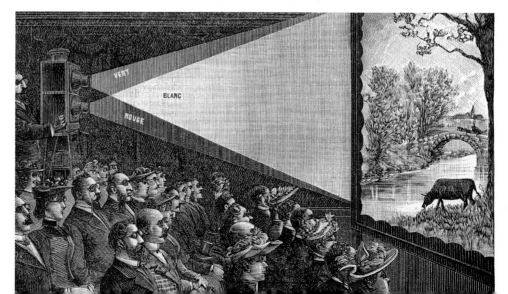

Cameras for the masses

George Eastman (1854–1932) of Rochester, New York was one of the many people to take up photography as a hobby in the late 19th century. However, it was still an expensive pastime that required cumbersome equipment and complicated techniques, so Eastman began to experiment with ways of making the process simpler and more affordable.

Fortunately, the technology existed to enable Eastman to conduct his experiments and realize this ambition. He developed and marketed dry plates coated with gelatin, before applying the same gelatin coating to celluloid film rather than glass plates. This led to the creation of the first roll-film, which Eastman used in a pre-loaded camera, the "Kodak", in 1888. Users returned the camera for the exposed film to be processed and the camera was returned to the user with a new film.

Eastman's success was partly due to his inspirational marketing ideas, including the slogan "You press the button, we do the rest", which accompanied the release of the Kodak. It was cheap to manufacture, easy to use, and gave good results. However, at US$25, the first mass-produced camera was still a luxury item. But it was immensely popular and it democratized photography for the first time.

One of Eastman's most successful cameras was the Box Brownie (named after Frank Brownell, its designer). Launched in 1900, it was made of

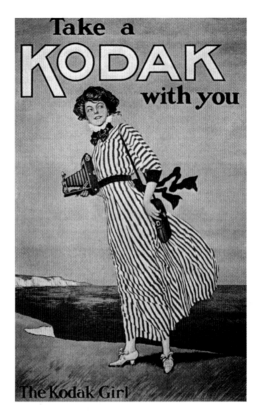

◀ **Kodak advertising**
George Eastman had a great skill in coining slogans and product names, such as the meaningless "Kodak", chosen because Eastman liked the letter "K" and wanted a unique word.

cardboard and wood, and cost only US$1. By the time Eastman died (taking his own life in 1932 and leaving the final message "My work is done – why wait?") Kodak was one of the best-known brand names in the world.

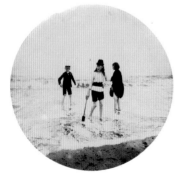

▲ **Early Kodak image**
This seaside scene was taken by an unknown photographer at the end of the 19th century, probably on the Kodak No.1 camera, which produced circular images.

❯❯ PHOTOGRAPHIC HUMOUR

By 1900, technological and economic advances meant that people from all walks of life could take "snapshots" of their lives and activities. The first artist of the snapshot was Jacques Henri Lartigue (1894–1986). His best-known images show his acute observation and sense of humour.

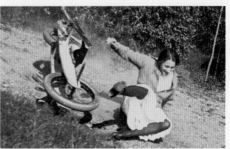

◀ **The Fall**
This image was taken by Lartigue in 1913, ten years after he received his first camera. His images are taken off-the-cuff, and often dramatize the ordinary.

Improving colour

While the Kodak and Box Brownie cameras had made photography available to the masses, enthusiasts were still searching for innovations and improvements. Even so, it took 35 years from Du Hauron's initial work on trichrome colour photography (*see p.80*) before an industrial method of recording colour images on a large scale was developed.

The autochrome process arrived in 1904. It was invented by the industrious French brothers Auguste (1862–1954) and Louis (1864–1948) Lumière, who discovered the technique while refining their method of cinematography, which they had invented in 1895. Starch grains extracted from potatoes were coloured with red, green, and blue dye, then scattered on a glass plate. A light-sensitive bromo-iodide silver emulsion was applied to the plate, and the film was exposed through the coloured grains. It could be viewed as a positive transparency after processing, and gave luminous images with wide tonal gradation. At its height, output reached a million plates a year, despite the laborious production methods. War photographers such as Jean-Baptiste Tournassoud (1866–1951) even took autochrome plates at the frontline in World War I, bringing back colour images that have a clarity and realism rarely seen in pictures of the conflict.

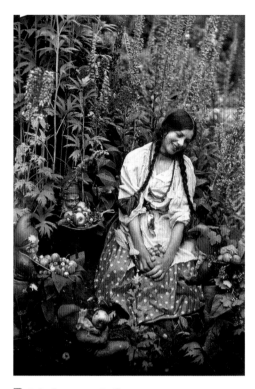

⌂ **Autochrome portrait**
Old Familiar Flowers, taken by Mrs G.A. Barton in 1919, shows how the soft pastel colours of autochrome transparencies lent themselves well to portraits, giving accurate skin tones.

» **The Lumière brothers**
Louis and Auguste Lumière tried many substances for carrying red, green, and blue dyes for their autochrome process, before settling on potato starch granules.

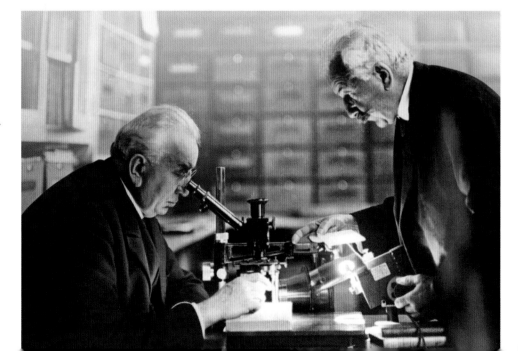

The power of the image

As early as the 1850s, photographs had been used for ideological and political aims. Herbert Ingram (1811–60), MP for Boston, Lincolnshire, from 1856, used the *Illustrated London News* to publicize Liberal reformist ideals. After his death, the publication continued to use photographs to highlight social welfare issues, such as factory conditions, child labour, and poverty.

In the 1890s, the ability to capture raw, irrefutable images led to the emergence of documentary photography as a discipline in its own right. In New York, a Danish immigrant named Jacob Riis (1849–1914), who worked as a crime reporter for the *New York Tribune*, began campaigning on behalf of the city's slum residents. His photographs – only intended as a record of poverty – have matured into a body of work that has had a lasting influence on modern-day documentary photographers.

Paul Martin (1864–1942) took candid photographs of Victorian London using a "Facile", a hand-held camera disguised as a large parcel. Best known for his 1895–96 series *London by Gaslight*, Martin's studies of daily life and poverty were derided by the photography establishment, which felt that "a plate demanded a noble subject – a cathedral or a mountain".

Lewis Hine (1874–1940), also appalled by the poverty of New York's immigrant underclass, began work as an investigative photographer for the National Child Labour Committee in 1908. Hine often hid his large Graflex camera in a lunch-box, in order to gain access to areas that photographers were prevented from visiting.

⟫ EARLY FASHION PHOTOGRAPHY

As a medium, photography has a natural tendency to turn the ugly into the beautiful. But it was not until photographs could be published in mass-distribution media such as newspapers that its power to glamorize was realized. The trend continues to this very day – fashion is inextricably linked with fashion photography.

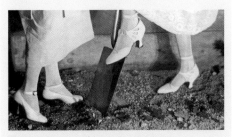

⌃ Feet Wearing High Heel Shoes
Taken in 1919 by the Frenchman Baron de Meyer, this image is one of the first examples of the use of photography to sell fashion.

⌄ Investigative photography
This portrait of a 10-year old cotton-spinner in New England, taken in 1910, was one of many taken by Lewis Hine that forced the US government to reform child labour legislation.

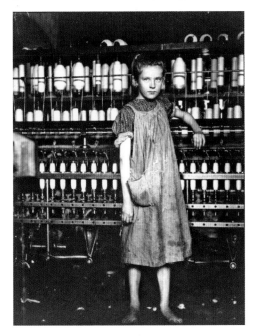

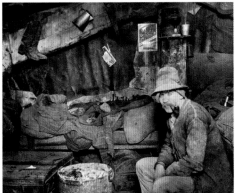

⟪ Exposing poverty
This image of a junk man's living quarters in a New York tenement house was taken by Jacob Riis in 1891, and supported his campaign to improve living conditions of the poor.

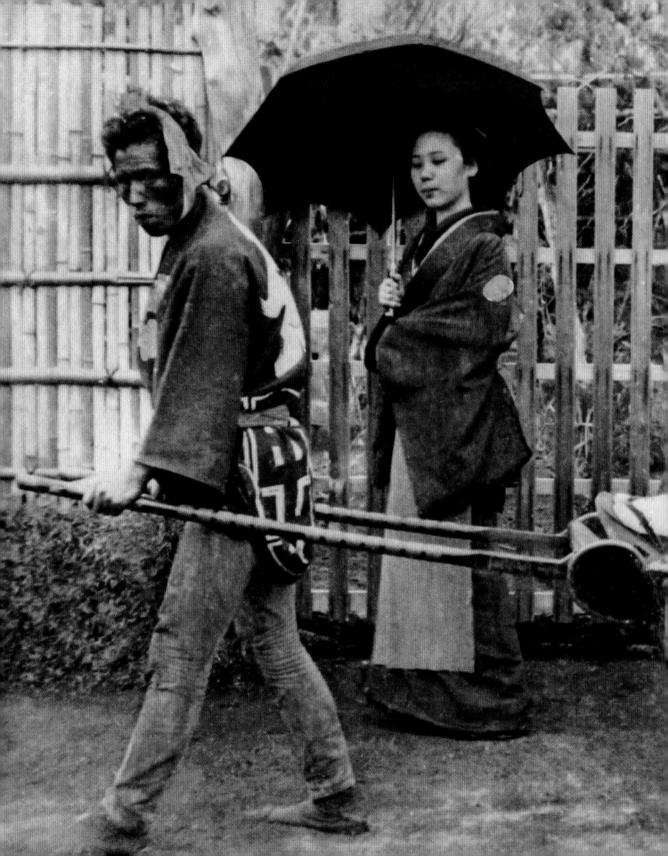

Hand-coloured Study
This unidentified hand-coloured picture was taken between 1900 and 1920. The intense red shades of light areas suggest that the colouring was intended to be artistic rather than realistic.

Awareness and vision (1920–50)

As photography became less expensive and more widely available, a diverse range of people found their voice in the visual image. Propagandists and social reformers alike used photography to spread their message. Artists, too, were quick to take advantage of new equipment, and used innovative techniques to push the boundaries of self-expression.

A revolution in equipment

The 1920s saw the introduction of 35mm film, one of the most important inventions in the development of photography. From 1911 to 1913, German designer Oskar Barnack (1879–1936) had worked on cutting 70mm-wide ciné film in half to create 35mm film. Regarded as tiny at the time, the resulting 24 x 36mm frame needed enlargement, which meant that any defects were also magnified, making precision manufacturing and high-quality lenses necessary.

People were sceptical about the practicality of 35mm film. As a result, the first compact camera, produced in 1924, was the German Ermanox, which used 60mm roll film. It was equipped with a large-aperture lens, which made it possible for photographers to work indoors using only the available light as the light-source. The success of the Ermanox prompted production of the Leica in 1925. More compact and easier to use than the Ermanox, it soon became the essential tool for photojournalism.

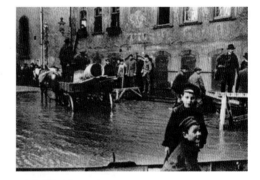

⬇ **Early 60mm Ermanox image**
Erich Salomon, who took this picture of Marlene Dietrich in 1929, was the first to master using the Ermanox for candid shots.

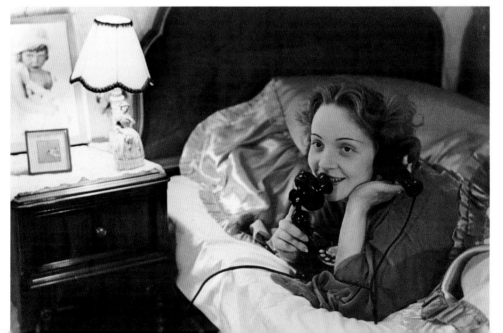

⬆ **Early 35mm Leica image**
Oskar Barnack, the inventor of the Leica, was an accomplished photographer. The very first rolls of film taken using his camera, including this image from the early 1920s, show him taking full advantage of the mobility it afforded.

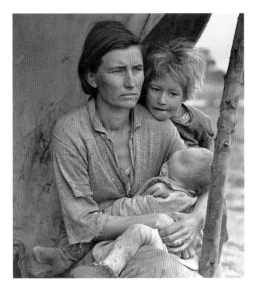

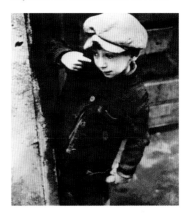

FSA documentary image
One of the most famous images in the Farm Security Administration series was a portrait of this migrant worker and her children, taken by Dorothea Lange in 1936 at a camp in Nipomo, California.

Nazi propaganda
Taken in 1939 in Berlin, this image of women exercising in the Bräuteschule (school for brides) is typical of propaganda of the Nazi regime.

Exposing the truth
Roman Vishniac often posed as a peddler to avoid arrest. He photographed this emaciated Polish boy after the Nazi invasion of 1939.

Photography and propaganda

The use of photography as a powerful means of conveying a political point of view flourished. Never before had the world been so closely scrutinized. One of the most celebrated documentary exercises was the photography commissioned in the 1930s by the sociologist Roy Stryker, at the US government's Farm Security Administration (FSA), which was set up to help the rural economy after the Depression. Stryker selected a team of photographers that included Ben Shahn, Walker Evans, Dorothea Lange, and Carl Mydans. Their work was (and still is) widely exhibited and published, surpassing its original purpose.

At this time amateur photography had become so widespread that in Germany it was exploited for political ends by the Propaganda Ministry run by Joseph Goebbels. Photographs reinforcing the concept of the Aryan German family – happy, healthy, strong – were used for propaganda purposes. This was achieved by encouraging amateurs to photograph their lives and produce attractive images of themselves.

But the Aryan ideal was not the only side of the story – Russian-born Jew Roman Vishniac (1897–1990), a distinguished scientist and art historian, photographed the plight of the Jews in Western Europe between 1933 and 1939. He is best known for his images of the Warsaw ghetto.

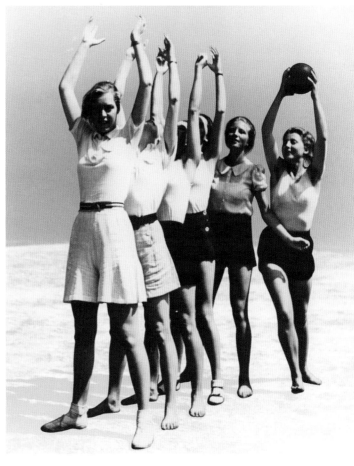

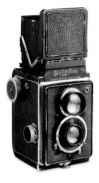

New camera designs

In response to Leica's success and the acceptance of its "ultra-miniature" format, and in part because Leica had secured the patent around its design, manufacturers sought new ways to design cameras. This led to the development of the single-lens reflex (SLR), in which a mirror in the light-path of the lens reflected the image

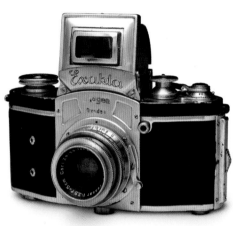

onto a focusing screen. Just as the picture was about to be taken, the mirror flipped out of the way before the shutter closed so that what was seen was captured on film. The first 35mm SLR camera to be produced was probably the Kine Exakta in April 1936, although the Russian Sport may have been released a year earlier.

A separate evolutionary line was the twin-lens reflex (TLR) camera. Mechanically simpler than the SLR, its operation was almost silent. It used medium-format roll-film to produce high-quality images. Favoured by professionals, it was quick to use and could be precisely focused.

However, the early SLRs and TLRs shared a defect; the image was reversed left-to-right. This was corrected by a 1948 SLR camera that used a pentaprism, which folded the light-path to rectify the image.

⊼ **Twin-lens reflex camera**
The Rolleiflex from Rollei (1929) was one of the first TLR cameras.

≫ **Single-lens reflex camera**
The Kine Exakta was the first production single-lens reflex camera for 35mm format. It offered a range of interchangeable lenses.

Artistic development

In Europe in the 1920s, the increasing influence of modernistic thinking and the rebellion against the philosophical thought and artistic forms of the

≫ **Eliezer Lissitzky's *Runner in the City***
This superimposed image was taken in 1930 by Lissitzky, a Russian artist, architect, teacher, and designer who worked with photomontages.

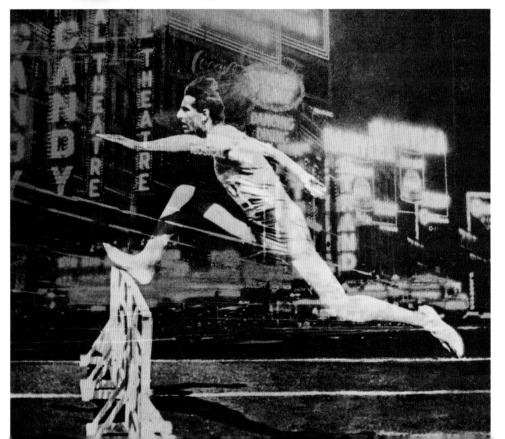

19th century, led to a flowering of art movements. Of these, Dadaism and Surrealism – both of which sought inspiration from the subjective and the unconscious – had the greatest impact on photography, since the directness of the medium suited their radical agenda. This is perhaps most evident in the work of Man Ray (*see p.60*).

It was also at this point that the photographic technology of films and lenses reached a level sufficient for photographers to truly explore the limits of their vision. This can be seen in the faultless technical quality of the work of photographers Ansel Adams (*see pp.24–5*), Paul Strand, and Edward Weston. Such was their concentration on nature that the usually taciturn Henri Cartier-Bresson (*see pp.38–9*) is reported to have exclaimed "The world is going to pieces and people like Adams and Weston are photographing rocks!" Despite such derision, Adams, Weston, and other photographers formed Group f/64 (misleadingly named after an aperture setting that cannot produce the sharpest image) in 1932, with the aim of achieving the perfect print.

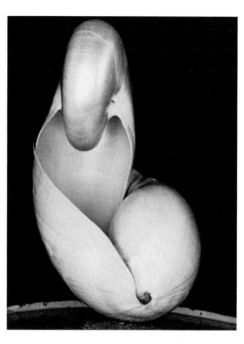

≪ **Edward Weston's**
The Shell
Weston and his associates often took close-ups of objects like seashells, vegetables, and rocks, which are now revered for their timeless quality.

Instant photography

In 1944 American Edwin Land (1909–91) experimented with the technique of combining developing-fluid and fixing-fluid in the same solution. By using an innovative process that caused silver to migrate from one layer (the film) through a thin gel to another layer (the print), he invented the peel-apart photograph. His first Model 95 Polaroid camera was sold in 1948. Colour polaroids were introduced in 1963 and by 1972 the peel-apart design was replaced by a single print the size of a postcard.

≫ **Land's
Polaroid Camera**
The camera design was as ingenious as the instant prints themselves. With precision rollers, complicated paper paths, and paper engineering, they were processing labs as well as cameras.

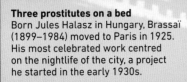

Three prostitutes on a bed
Born Jules Halasz in Hungary, Brassaï
(1899–1984) moved to Paris in 1925.
His most celebrated work centred
on the nightlife of the city, a project
he started in the early 1930s.

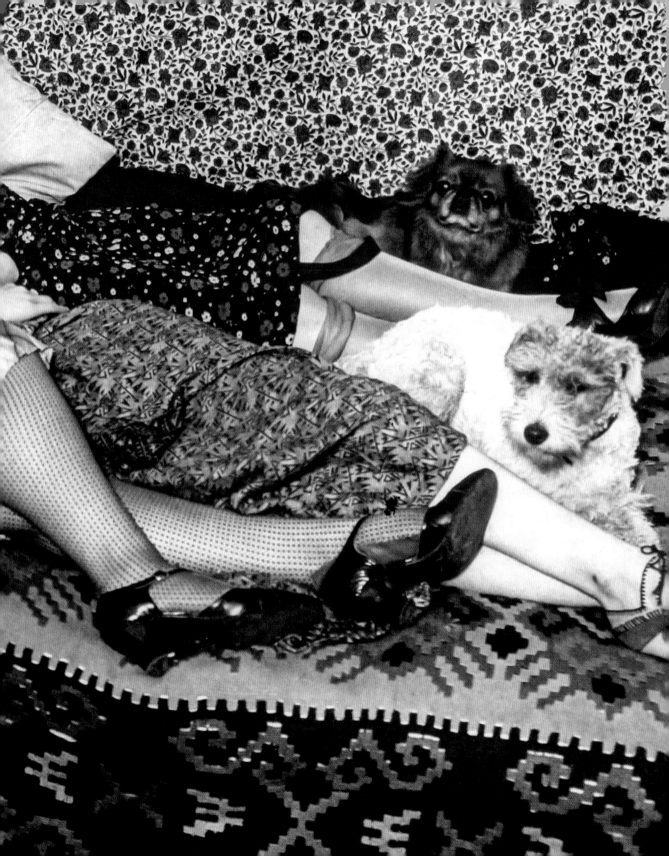

Innovations and rebellions (1950–70)

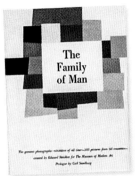

As a war-weary world took stock, a mix of cynicism and reformist energy gripped photographers. Using the highly mobile Leica camera, photojournalists worked undercover to reveal stories that would otherwise have gone unreported. Meanwhile, a revolution in fashion photography was at the forefront of the style rebellion of the late 1960s.

⏶ **The Family of Man**
Possibly the most successful photographic exhibition ever, its catalogue was also an immensely successful publication that remained in print for over 50 years.

⏷ **Visiting The Family of Man**
For many visitors, drawn by the humanist spirit of the images, this was their first contact with exhibition-quality photographs.

Family of Man exhibition

Central to the humanist impact on photographic practice was the 1955 exhibition *The Family of Man*, curated by Edward Steichen (1879–1973). A vast and ambitious project, it contained 503 images from 273 photographers around the world. The aim of the exhibition was to show that "the art of photography is a dynamic process of giving form to ideas and of explaining man to man." The exhibition proved that photography was the premier means of communication of the age. During its eight-year tour it travelled to 37 international centres, drawing nearly 10 million visitors.

The era of the photojournalist

The public appetite for news magazines, which grew during World War II, did not wane in peacetime. The circulation of the UK magazine

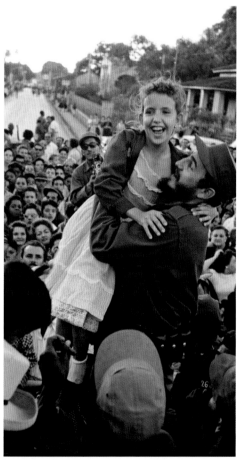

⏶ **Fidel Castro**
Burt Glinn's image of Castro being mobbed by crowds on his triumphant journey to Havana, Cuba in 1959, shows a perfect coordination of news event with the human moment.

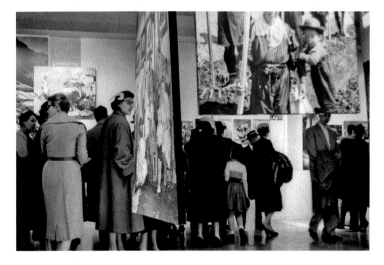

Picture Post (already one million during the war) rose by 30 per cent in the following years. The period from 1950 to 1970 saw the peak of magazine publishing, from consumer fashion titles such as *Harper's Bazaar* and *Vogue*, to natural and social history titles such as *National Geographic*, and news magazines such as *Time*, *LIFE*, and *Paris Match*. At its height, *LIFE* had a circulation of 30 million.

By the 1950s, photojournalists were being sent around the world to cover news stories and events, and were increasingly seen as newsworthy in their own right. Their adventurous and seemingly glamorous lives were often the subject of news features and articles.

Magazine photographers such as Don McCullin *(see p.55)*, Margaret Bourke-White *(see p.33)*, and Irving Penn (1917–2009) were in great and constant demand. As the post-war depression set in, photographers sought to give impetus to the reconstruction of devastated towns and ravaged economies by laying injustices bare. This was also the period in which the picture essay reached an apogee, with photographers such as Henri Cartier-Bresson *(see pp.38–9)*, William Eugene Smith *(see p.62)*, Bruce Davidson (1933–), Robert Frank (1924–), and William Klein (1928–) producing eloquent series of pictures.

Reaching into the dark

The new breed of world-travelling photojournalist needed a source of lighting that was as mobile as a 35mm camera. The answer was to come from the work of American physicist Harold Edgerton (1903–90), who conducted investigations into making an exposure so brief that it would capture movements such as the flight of a bullet. One of his insights – that the exposure must last only as long as the accompanying flash of artificial light – formed the foundation for all flash photography. His investigations led to the invention of the stroboscope, which provided enormous amounts of light for just a fraction of a second. In the process, he created the basis for the portable electronic flash-gun. Edgerton's work during the 1950s and 1960s produced numerous classic photographs, from bullets tearing through playing cards to athletes frozen in motion. His images caught the public imagination, showing that a great scientist can produce great art.

⟫ EARLY IMAGE MANIPULATION

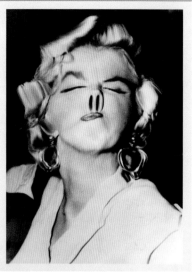

Weegee was born Assher Fellig in 1899 in the Ukraine. After emigrating to the USA in 1909, he found work as a newspaper photographer. He adopted the name Weegee, from the "Ouija" divination board, in tribute to his uncanny intuition. In 1948 he started to experiment with image distortions, which became a full-time occupation by the late 1950s. He used a variety of techniques, including printing through curved glass, boiling negatives to distort them, and photographing through ash-trays.

⟫ Marilyn Monroe
This image is from a series from 1963. The pictures were made by shooting through a plastic lens that gave different distortions as it was moved.

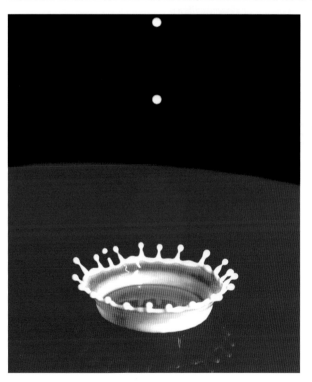

⌃ **Harold Edgerton's** *Milkdrop Coronet*
This image, taken in 1957, captures the beauty of the moment in a way that the human eye could never appreciate. The flash exposure would have been 1/50,000 of a second or less.

New frontiers

Today it is taken for granted that major events are recorded on film for posterity. In the 1960s, deep-sea diver Jacques Cousteau (1910–97) revealed the astonishing variety of life beneath the waves by working with Harold Edgerton to perfect the lighting systems that were required to film in a world previously unseen by a mass audience. But amazingly, when the race to be the first in space was won by the Soviet Union in 1961, photographing this momentous achievement was not deemed a priority. The first pictures from space were actually shot with a camera smuggled on board the 1962 Mercury flight by astronaut John Glenn. The impact of these images persuaded NASA to commission specially modified cameras from Linhof, Nikon, and Hasselblad.

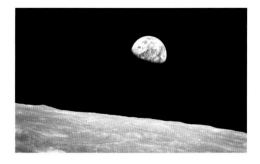

⌃ **Photography in space**
This is the view of the Earth-rise that greeted the Apollo 8 astronauts as they came from behind the moon in 1968.

Fashion photography

Closer to home, photography was undergoing a revolution, as fashion photography became increasingly influential. London in the Swinging Sixties was a fashion hotspot, and as a result British photographers such as David Bailey (1938–) and Terence Donovan (1936–96) became household names, and their images made fashion photography both prestigious and infamous. Newspapers and magazines reflected this trend, with clothes, fashion designers, and fashion photographers becoming newsworthy. The era's spirit of liberation was reflected in the work of Helmut Newton (1920–2004) and Guy Bourdin (*see p.32*), who used sexuality as a selling tool.

⟫ **Underwater lighting**
Filmed with Harold Edgerton's underwater lighting, the undersea pioneer Jacques Cousteau explores the seabed in 1969.

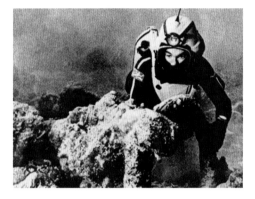

⟫ **Fashion shoot**
This image of the model Jean Shrimpton and photographer David Bailey was taken by an assistant in a studio in Paris in 1963.

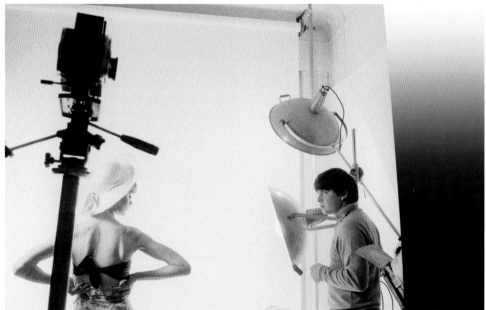

Meanwhile, the burgeoning careers of high-society photographers Lord Snowdon (1930–2017) and Lord Lichfield showed that photography had reached across society, gaining Establishment respectability while being embraced by counter-cultural, iconoclastic youth.

The Vietnam War

Far from the frivolities of fashion, the Vietnam War drew hundreds of photographers to document its death, destruction, and moral decrepitude. The US armed forces welcomed journalists and photographers, believing that the coverage would help the war effort. Numerous careers were made (and some sadly ended) by the war, including those of Britons Larry Burrows (1926–71) and Don McCullin (*see p.55*), and Americans Eddie Adams (1933–2004) and Catherine LeRoy (1944–2006).

Perhaps the most stunning proof of the power of photography as a documentary medium was the testimony of two rolls of film taken by amateur photographer Ronald Haeberle. Recording the massacre by US troops of up to 500 civilians at My Lai, his pictures provided concrete evidence that shocked the world. It is widely accepted that this, along with a handful of other key photographs that brought home the chaos of Vietnam, was instrumental in turning American and international opinion against the war, leading to the withdrawal of US troops.

⊠ Massacre at My Lai
Among the most notorious of Vietnam photographs is Ronald Haeberle's coverage of the My Lai massacre, including this image of an old man taken moments before he was shot by US soldiers.

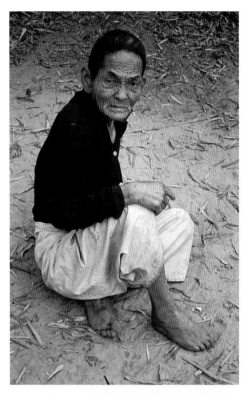

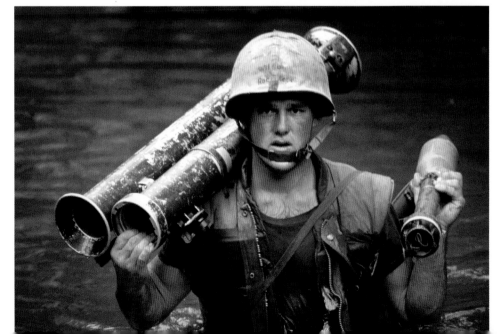

◀ Portrait of war
Larry Burrows's coverage of the Vietnam War is regarded as the most comprehensive and understanding. This image, taken in 1966, shows PFC Philip Wilson carrying a rocket launcher across a stream in the demilitarized zone. Twelve days later, he was killed in action.

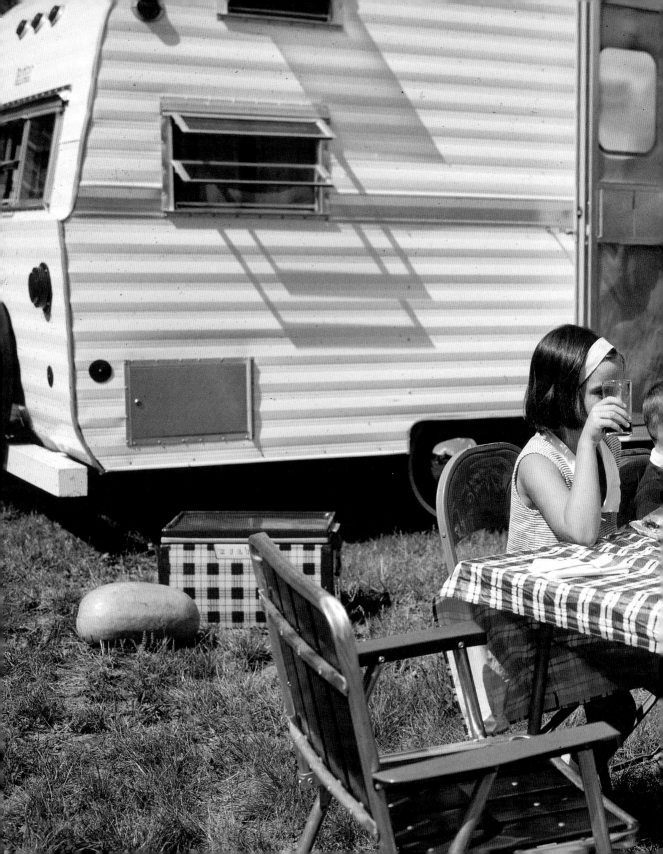

Family in the Sun
While colour photography revealed the horrors of war in Southeast Asia, back in the United States it was the essential tool for advertising products and promoting lifestyles.

Divergences (1970–90)

As developments in technology broadened the scope of photography, photographers grew more confident in their own prowess. This led to more fluid methods of photography and a blurring of traditional categories, as snapshots became fine art, and fashion borrowed from documentary. Photographic technology increased our understanding of ourselves and our universe.

New colour photography

A new wave of topographical photography arose during the 1970s. In a reaction against the aesthetics of Ansel Adams, Edward Weston, and the rest of the Group f/64 (see p.93), it valued the ephemera and artefacts of everyday life but was driven, above all, by an obsession with colour. Chief amongst the innovators was American William Eggleston (1939–). His images monumentalized the trivial – a street-sign, a shoe, or a child's tricycle – and were widely imitated. Others such as Americans Stephen Shore (1947–), Richard Misrach (1949–), and Joel Sternfeld (1944–) used large-format cameras to take images that gloried in the grubby – street corners, empty swimming pools, and parking lots – almost in deliberate mockery of the meticulous methods and natural subject-matter of the early visionaries.

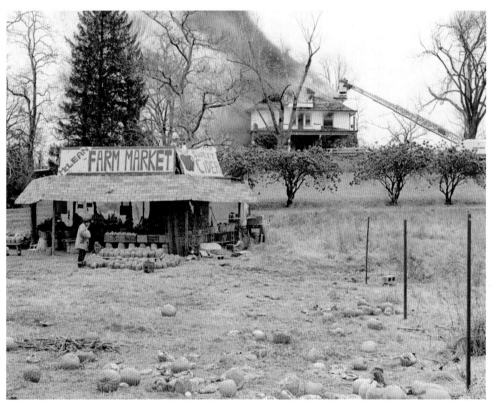

» **Awareness and vision**
Joel Sternfeld combined acute observation with a fine sense of composition. Here, a fireman buys pumpkins while his colleagues tackle a fire.

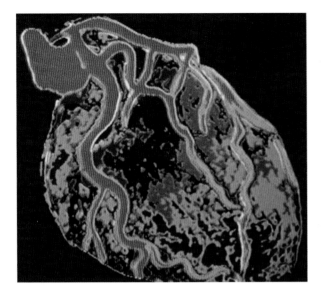

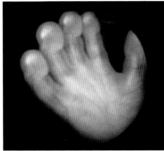

Early image manipulation
Howard Sochurek pioneered digital manipulation. He brought scientific images, such as this picture of a heart, to public notice through his use of colour.

Medical breakthroughs
An example of a photographic tool extending the reaches of science, this image of a 3-month old human foetus was taken with an endoscope – a long tube with a lens at the end.

The rise of imaging

Elsewhere, digital technology began to have an impact on how images were used. In 1970, Howard Sochurek, a photographer with *LIFE* and *National Geographic*, rescued a computer being thrown out by NASA and used it to digitally manipulate images. Coming some 20 years before the development of Adobe Photoshop,

Sochurek's work was visionary but too far advanced for the technology available. He had to photograph the results of his manipulations on a television screen because it was not possible to print them out to sufficiently high quality. He showed the possibilities, but the world had to wait until 1990 for computing and software to catch up.

Through digital images, our ability to see and record the world was extended by making visible the previously invisible processes of nature. For example, NASA's Landsat satellites revealed massive land forms, along with continental-scale patterns of weather. And in medicine, endoscopes allowed us to see inside the womb.

ELECTRONIC ADVANCES

The growing popularity of photography fuelled innovation from manufacturers. Electronic circuits were increasingly used for camera functions, enabling features such as auto-exposure to be added at low cost. Digital techniques also powered enormous advances in lens design – for the first time, it was possible for a zoom lens to match the performance of a single-focal length lens.

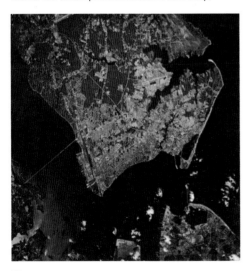

Landsat view
Images of the Earth taken by satellite remote-sensing were highly accurate yet artificial in their colours. They opened the way to an acceptance of the digitally enhanced image.

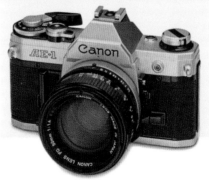

Canon AE1
Introduced in 1976, this mid-market camera was the first to use a micro-processor to control many of its functions. Its internal modular design greatly simplified assembly.

» **Time and Stern magazines**
By the 1980s, pop groups could push current affairs off the covers of news magazines. The strongest growth in circulation was seen in celebrity publications.

⌄ **Celebrity photography**
The subject of this photograph, Princess Diana, became the world's most photographed "celebrity". Her popularity as a subject for the paparazzi led indirectly to her death in 1997.

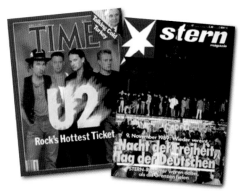

The growth of celebrity

Television was gaining ground at the expense of current affairs magazines such as *LIFE*, *Stern*, and *Paris Match*. While the once-mighty titles dwindled, others developed to satisfy a growing preoccupation with celebrity. And to feed the hunger for pictures of film, television, and pop stars came a new breed of photographer: the paparazzo.

Named after *Paparazzo*, the news photographer in Fellini's film *La Dolce Vita*, the paparazzo was immune to weather or insult, tirelessly tenacious, extremely mobile, and a photographer whose subject-matter was not the person, but celebrity itself. While hints of the paparazzi approach can be seen in the work of editorial photographers such as Alfred Eisenstaedt (*see p.42*), Dirck Halstead, and Harry Benson, they did work within a framework of consent. In contrast, the paparazzi disregarded both permission or privacy. And they were helped by very long focal-length lenses (600mm and larger) with high-quality fast film and rapid motor-drives that allowed dozens of shots to be taken in sequence.

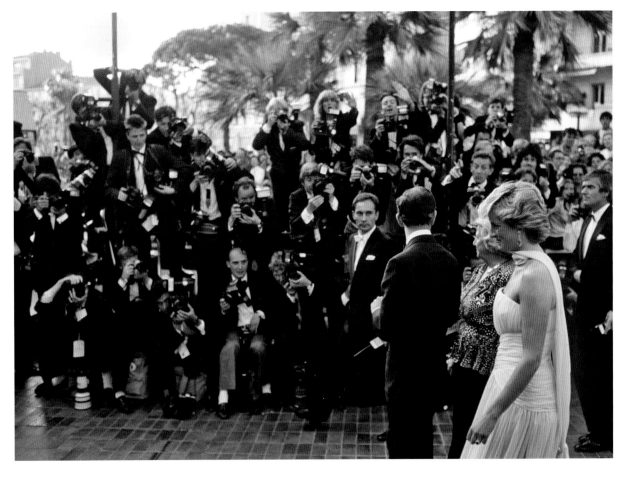

Advertising sophistication

A high point in photographic history was the successful partnership of photography with a wave of creativity in the advertising world. Innovative campaigns that used clever visual puns and brilliant photography, such as those for Dunhill, Smirnoff, and Ferguson, led the world in sophisticated art direction. These campaigns relied on the skill and input of versatile photographers such as John Claridge and Steve Cavalier, who, in their turn, relied on skilled technicians to painstakingly blend, colour, and manipulate images by hand.

Changing face of portraiture

The capture of the human likeness was one of the first trends in photography. The whole of photographic history can be written through portraiture – changes in portrait styles directly reflect the technological and artistic preferences of the time. In the 1980s and 1990s a loss of confidence at the heart of photography – symptomatic of cynicism at the heart of society – can be seen in portraiture's increasingly self-questioning style. This crisis of direction and identity is seen clearly in the work of Cindy Sherman (1954–), whose message is that portraits can tell you nothing about someone, since the appearance of the subject (in Sherman's case, herself) can vary considerably when photographed

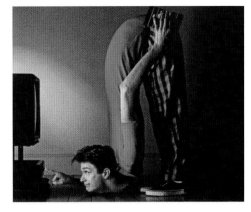

« Bendy man advert
This 1987 advertisement for Ferguson by Steve Cavalier was achieved by combining three transparencies blended into a seamless and stunningly convincing image.

in different styles. At the same time, the growing use of image manipulation raised questions about photography's veracity.

Holography

The invention of the laser in 1960 had made it possible to create a fully three-dimensional image – the hologram. Early holograms were used to simulate precious artefacts for display. The images appeared solid and were dimensionally perfect representations of the objects. By the 1970s and early 1980s holograms were all the rage, with large-scale versions appearing as exhibits in art galleries and smaller versions being worn as jewellery. However, the technology for creating them was cumbersome, and live objects could be holographed only with the most sophisticated lasers. In-fighting among the pioneers inhibited its development. As an art-form it blossomed and died within ten years, but continues in more prosaic forms as rainbow holograms on credit cards and novelty toys.

⌄ Video stills self-portrait
Cindy Sherman appropriates the visual characteristics of a video to create this self-portrait as a nameless character in an untitled video film, caught as a video stills grab.

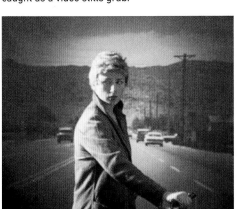

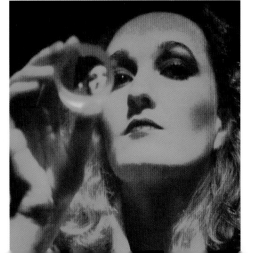

« Holographic image
The artist Edwina Orr created a hologram of herself in 1982 by using an extremely powerful and brief blast of laser light.

Model wearing Christian Lacroix
Hybrid styles of photography
proliferated in the 1980s. This fashion
image taken in Paris in 1987 by Abbas
(1944–2018) reflects the documentary
roots of the photographer.

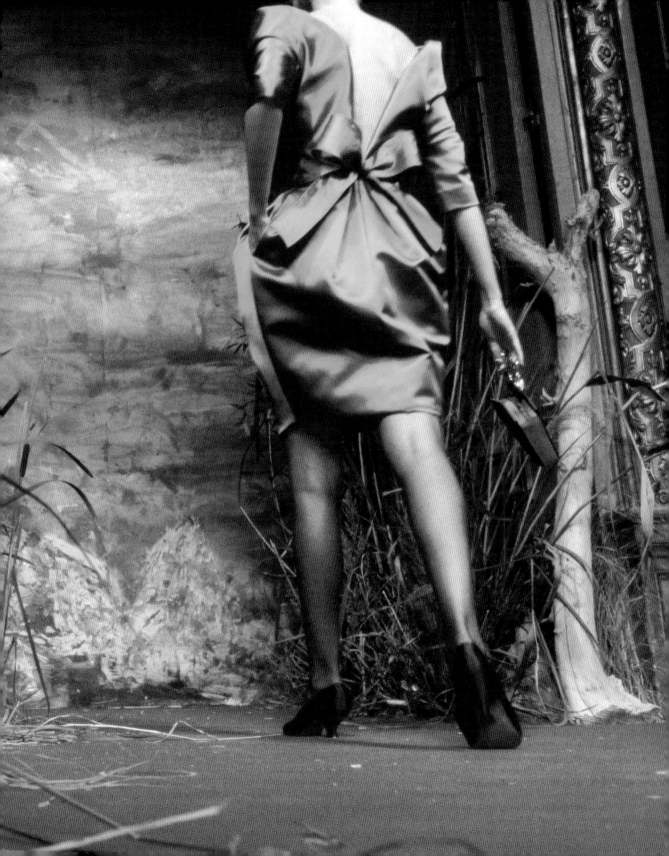

The digital revolution (1990–)

The launch in 1990 of the digital-imaging program Adobe Photoshop was a milestone in photographic technology, and sparked an explosion in image manipulation and digital photography. Meanwhile, the widespread availability of digital cameras, video, and the internet led to a challenge to film-based photography, and a blurring of the line between professional and amateur.

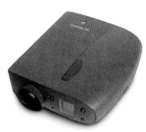

⊼ **Apple Quicktake 100**
This was one of the first consumer digital cameras costing under £600 (US$999) with a 640 x 480 pixel image.

⊻ **Creativity in news photography**
The public's familiarity with sophisticated and imaginative images allowed news photographers greater creative freedom.

New technology
In 1990, Kodak launched the DCS-100 digital camera, the first professional model to come on the market. It featured a sensor of what was then a staggering 1.3 megapixels, housed in a Nikon F3 body, and had 200MB of memory. A separate unit with a black-and-white monitor and a hard disk could be connected for reviewing and storing images. The camera with accessories weighed a back-breaking 25kg (55lb) and cost £18,500 (US$30,000 at 1990 exchange rates). Four years later, Apple launched its first digital camera, the Quicktake 100. Its relatively low cost of £600 (US$999) meant that the convenience of digital photography began to outweigh reservations about low image quality. In 1994, Photoshop version 3 offered the ability to work in layers, which meant that images could be superimposed and individually adjusted. Such was the pace of development that by 2004 digital cameras were able to exceed 35mm film in image quality.

Online access
The growth and accessibility of the world wide web revolutionized the way images were viewed, used, and sold, by enabling a single image to be seen by millions of people simultaneously. The original resides on the owner's computer, and can be accessed by anyone visiting their website. For the first time, photography was wholly democratized. Not only did access become unlimited by distance, it was unrestricted by time zones, opening hours, or publication cycles. No longer did photographers need middle men to publish their images on a national – or even international – scale. The number of web pages containing photographs grew from some 30 million in 2000 to more than 100 million just four years later. Almost overnight, internet users became the largest producers and consumers of images.

New colour photojournalism
By the 1990s, black-and-white photography was a niche activity, practised by die-hard enthusiasts and a handful of photojournalists whose work was seen on exhibition walls or sold as fine-art prints. The medium of photojournalism was colour – preferably lots of it and as violently bright as possible. Briton Chris Steele-Perkins (1947–), American Alex Webb (1952–), and Belgian Harry Gruyaert (1941–) were at the fore of this new style. Artistically, photographers exploited the limitations

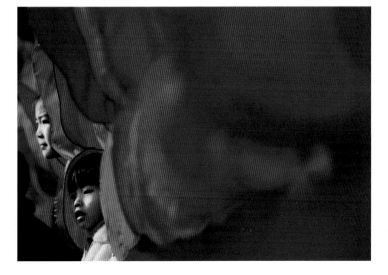

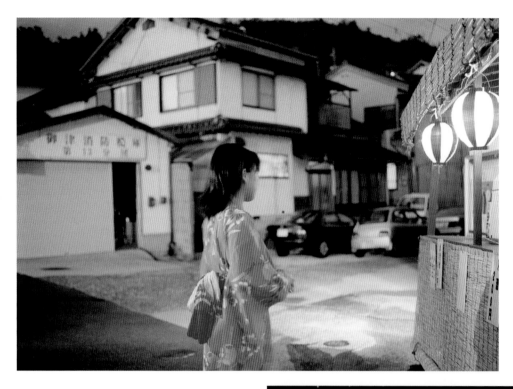

《 **Colour photojournalism**
Chris Steele-Perkins took this image in 2000 in Japan. It is characteristic of his pictorial style, which refers obliquely, rather than directly.

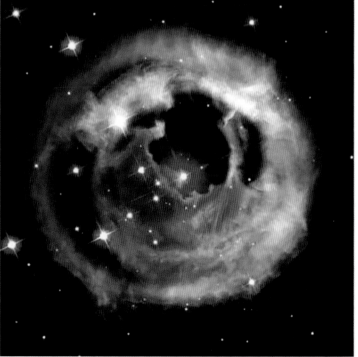

Hubble image, 2004
A burst of light and cloud of circumstellar dust surround a star 20,000 light years away, captured by Hubble's Advanced Camera for Surveys.

of slide film – particularly its tendency to turn shadows black – to project an emotional response onto the subject. Their photographs feature pure colours and solid blacks, and use colour for its expressive, emotive force rather than for its descriptive capacity.

Probing deepest space

The reach of colour photography achieved intergalactic proportions with the launch of the Hubble telescope in 1990. The first optical telescope to orbit the Earth above the atmospheric clutter that obscures the light of stars, the reflecting telescope could capture distant details with incredible clarity. However, the first images were disappointing due to miscalculations in the telescope's optics. In 1993, Hubble was repaired by astronauts while still in orbit, and by the end of the year stunning images of stars thousands of light years away were beamed back to Earth. Its performance surpassed all expectations and reached the near-theoretical limits of what was possible.

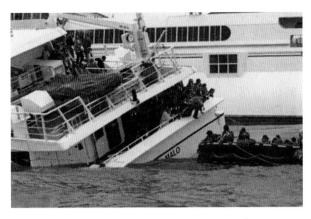

◄◄ **Amateur news photograph**
The sinking of the St Malo ferry off the coast of Jersey in 1995 was captured on film by holidaymakers. Most newspapers used amateur pictures in their coverage.

Amateur press photography

The availability of high-quality equipment to the general public has led to a subtle restructuring of professional practices. Some areas, such as travel photography for picture libraries, are actually dominated by hard-working amateur photographers. News pictures are also increasingly provided by non-professionals. Being more numerous, they are more likely to be on the spot when an incident occurs than the lone photojournalist, and are often carrying professional-standard equipment. Many of the images of the devastating tsunami disaster in southeast Asia in late 2004 that appeared in the media were taken by holidaymakers.

Freedom of the press

Professional photographers, especially those working in war zones, are battling against restrictions on their freedom to report. Ever since World War II, the armed forces and journalists have tried to find ways to work together. Politicians and army commanders encourage positive press and are extremely wary of negative coverage of operations that might lead to criticism from a public increasingly tired of war. Recently, the practice of "embedding" journalists into a service unit was introduced, intended to prevent free-roaming reportage. However, it emerged that soldiers were allowing photographers access to events – both behind and at the battle-front – that they would never have seen had they been reporting on their own.

Yet, as photographers clamour to exercise their freedom, at times they also fail to act sensitively or responsibly towards those they report on. Tales of photographers waiting for the moment of death of a starving child or of photojournalists instructing rioting youths to throw stones to order have damaged the public's trust of journalists.

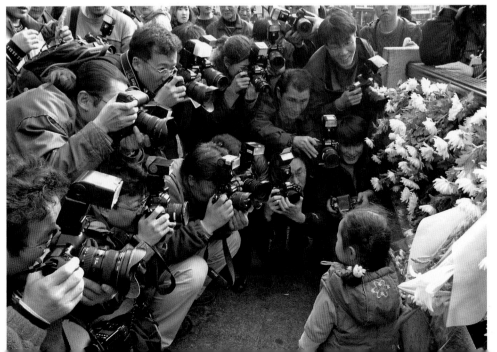

» **Press intrusion**
A child laying a flower at a memorial of a subway disaster in Daegu, South Korea, 2003, is upset by a crowd of photographers.

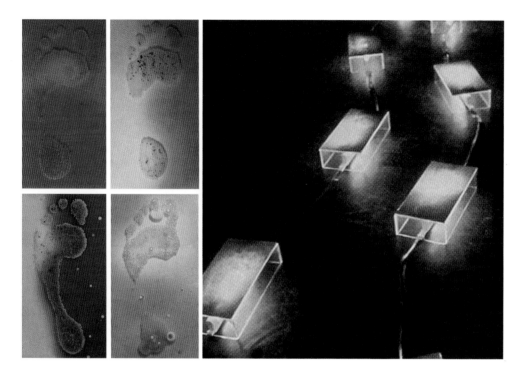

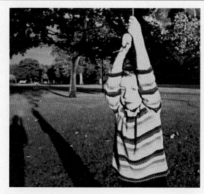

《 Heather Barnett's Footprints
Ingeniously bridging science and art to uncover new ways of depiction, Heather Barnett has used culturing techniques to image her feet for this installation, representing them as organically growing footprints.

Diversities of image

The breadth that photography now comprises has expanded to include a variety of technology and uses, from creating photo-etched templates for electronic micro-circuitry to speed-trap cameras and surveillance imaging. At the same time, artists such as Heather Barnett have explored the use of scientific imaging to expand the language of artistic vision.

Today, digital photography has put imaging into the hands of anyone with a computer, and their images can reach all round the world. As digital cameras and mobile phone cameras proliferate in hundreds of millions, the time has come when more images could be taken in a single year than in the rest of the history of photography put together.

》 MOBILE PHONE CAMERAS

In the process of fighting its corner in the competitive mobile phone market, Nokia, the Finnish phone company, accidentally became the world's largest supplier of cameras. These phones – whose camera functions are contained in a thumbnail-sized unit – produced higher quality images than the first digital cameras. Hundreds of millions of mobile phones are sold each year, but Nokia's market dominance has now been surpassed by manufacturers such as Samsung, Huawei, and Apple.

《 Fred Pulling Branch
This image was taken on a camera phone by the photographer Harry Borden (1965–), for the Nokia Fonetography competition.

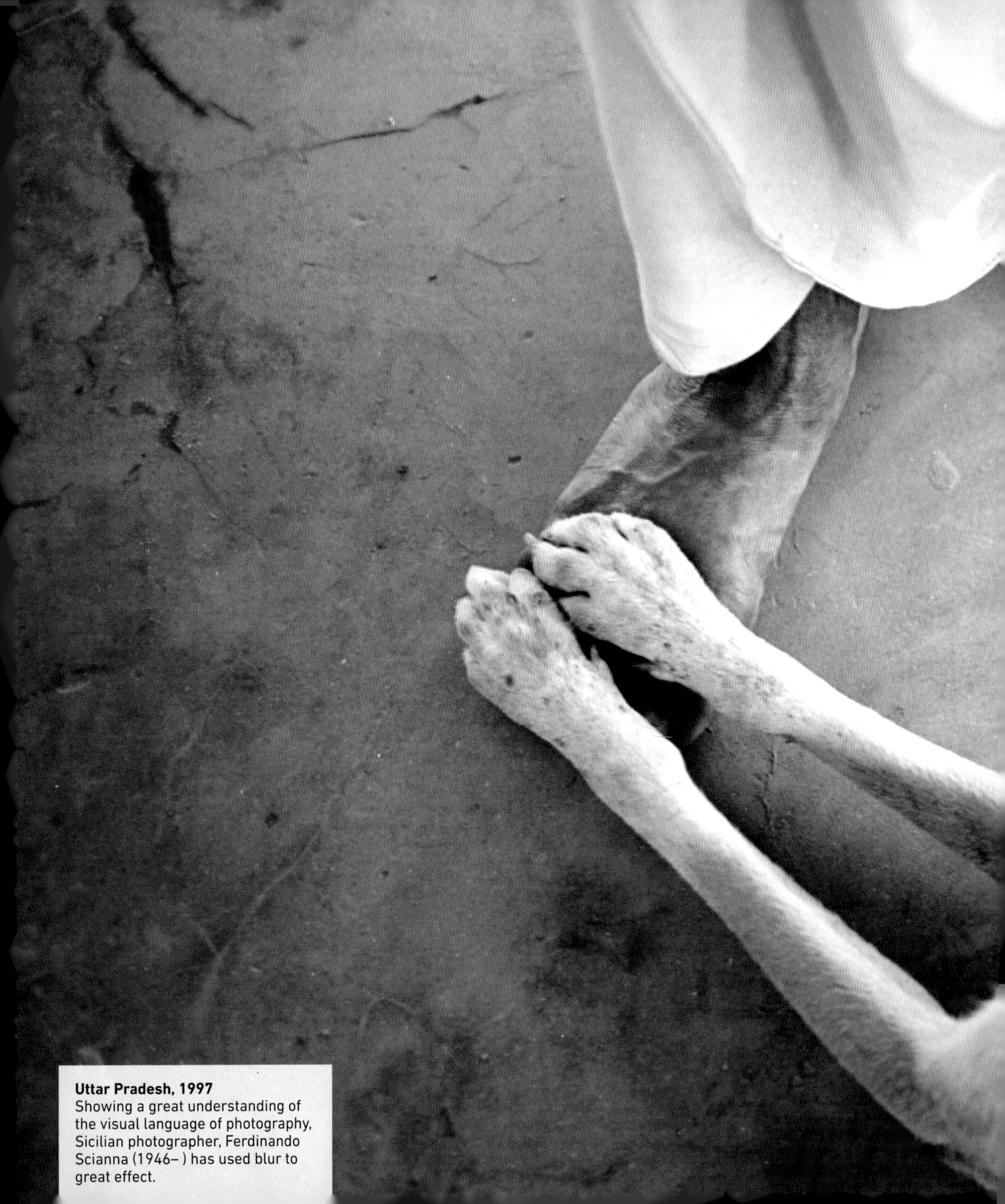

Uttar Pradesh, 1997
Showing a great understanding of the visual language of photography, Sicilian photographer, Ferdinando Scianna (1946–) has used blur to great effect.

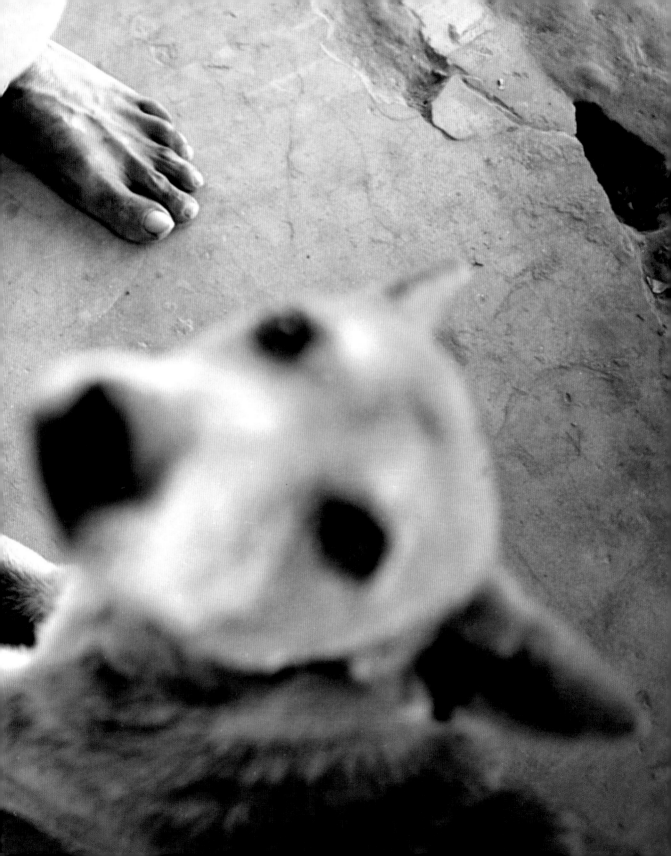

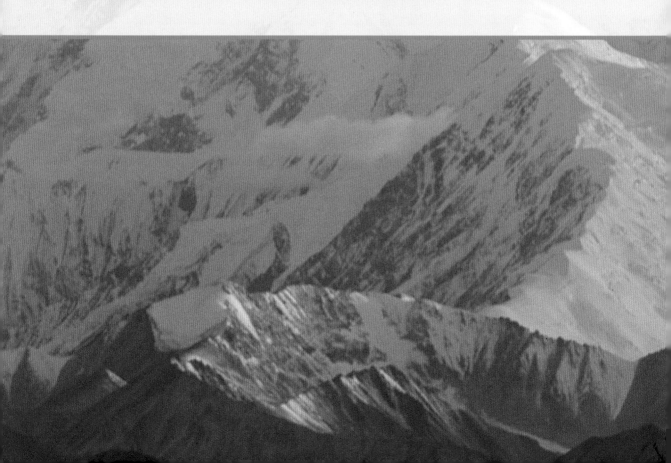

PHOTOGRAPHIC TOOLS

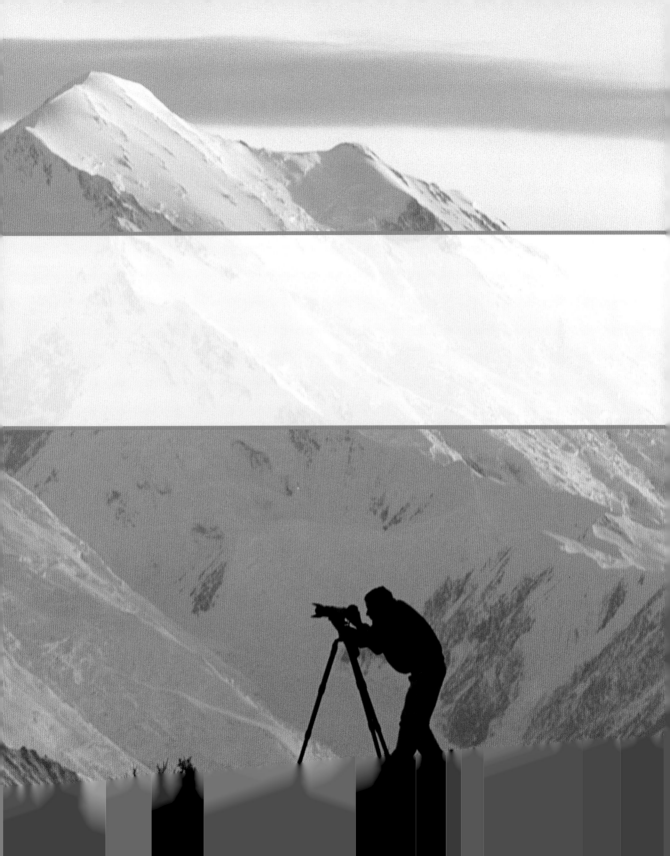

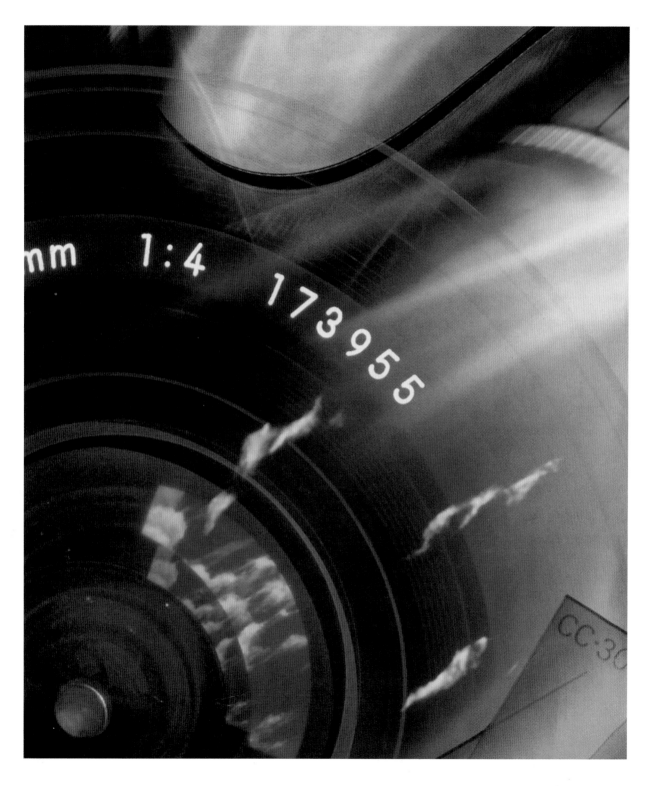

The basic tool of photography – from the earliest days of silver salts to digital – remains the camera. Every imaging system depends on protecting a light-capturing element from the outside. Exposure then opens it up to light, and it is at that magical, transcendent moment that the photographic process begins.

While the principle of controlling the access of light to a recording medium has remained unchanged, today's cameras – all high-tech precision instruments – could not be more different from their early counterparts.

The first models were essentially large, empty, boxes. Given a modicum of skill, early enthusiasts could build their own. But a modern camera is not only small, it is incredibly densely packed. Just about every cubic millimetre is crammed with electronic circuitry, optical, mechanical, and power-management components. And while the first cameras allowed the operator only to uncover and focus the lens, modern cameras offer a profusion of buttons, dials, and displays on their bodies.

Most modern cameras require such high precision and delicacy in assembly that even the most skilled hands can no longer be relied on to assemble one. Many camera components are so delicate that only computer-controlled machinery can handle them without causing damage. The next time you hold even an entry-level camera, remember that it has been built with more finesse, and uses more intricate parts, than the most finely crafted Fabergé egg.

Cameras were formerly optical-mechanical devices – combining lenses and fine machinery. In digital cameras, almost all of the mechanics have been replaced by electronics or electrical parts. In smartphone cameras, there may even be no moving parts at all. Nonetheless, the vast majority of the famous images we know and love were created on film-using cameras, rather than digital. Even today, some die-hard photographers still insist on film-using mechanical cameras. However, digital imaging is now overwhelmingly the dominant form of photography.

The rise of digital photography since the beginning of the 21st century has decimated old industries, created new leaders, and transformed the practice of photography from top to bottom. It has blurred the distinction between amateur and

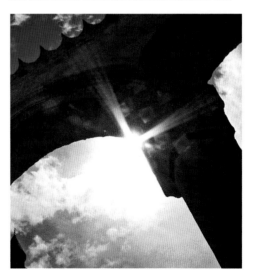

◀ Lenses
Modern lenses can record detail with great fidelity of colour and sharpness as well as freedom from distortion. There is something to suit every budget and requirement.

◀ Controlling light
Cameras are primarily concerned with controlling and using light to create the desired image.

>> **Wide-angle views**
Wide-angle lenses allow the photographer to capture a greater depth of field, so are popular for photographing the natural world.

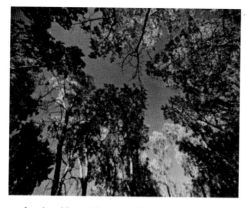

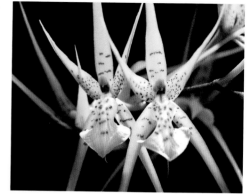

^ **Close-up views**
Formerly the province of enthusiasts, close-up photography is now possible with any digital or smartphone camera.

professional by putting superlative technical quality into equipment affordable to many amateurs. From the capture of images to their manipulation and worldwide distribution, our computers and smartphones hold tremendous digital imaging power.

Digital photography also requires new dimensions of skill. Modern photographers must master not only photographic techniques, but also be competent using computers, imaging software, and navigating the internet. However, technology has not completely superseded darkroom work: film processing and fine printing with an enlarger remain highly fulfilling creative activities.

One of the joys of photography is that it really does have something for everyone. You can snap photos on a smartphone and share them with just your friends and family, or with millions around the world. You can use an "auto-everything" compact camera or master top-grade equipment to match your interests and ambitions. This chapter will guide you through the myriad choices available, from simple to high-end cameras, to accessories, lenses, and software.

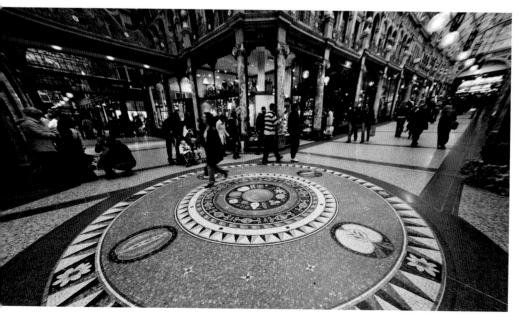

<< **Panoramic shots**
Views which take in more than the eye can see are one of photography's contributions to how we see the world. The panorama is an artificiality created image by a special camera or lens.

>> **Photography on the move**
Today's photographer relies on a sophisticated range of tools, but such modern, lightweight equipment would have been beyond the dreams of early photographers.

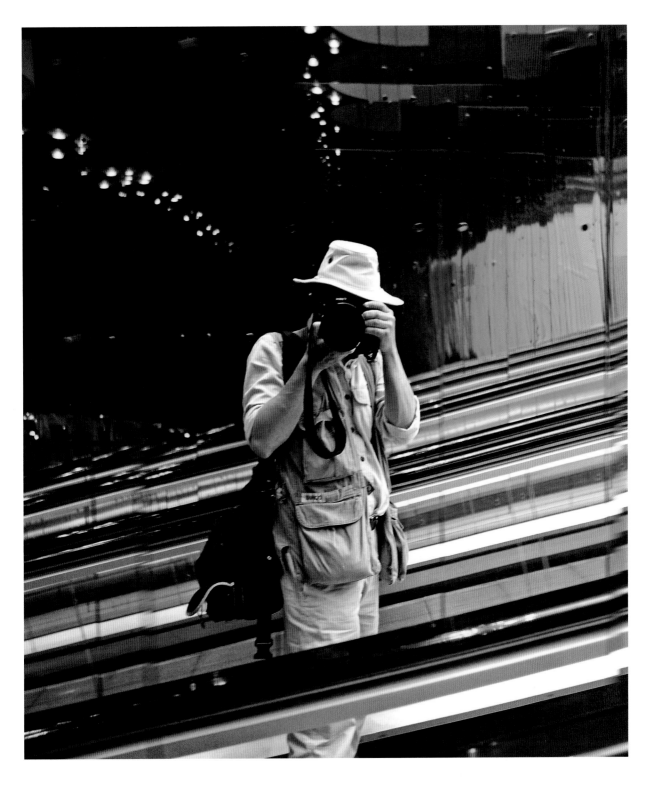

The camera

The photographic industry toiled for over a century to master the entire photographic process, from creating capable equipment to refining every stage after recording the image. While modern photography is dominated by digital cameras, the advantages of film-using cameras remain: they require no computers or software, and the cost-to-quality ratio is unbeatable. And with film-using cameras now cheaper than ever, there has even been a resurgence in photography based on film and darkroom work. In contrast, cameras in smartphones can effortlessly deliver impressive image quality.

Types of camera

The most common type of camera is that installed in smartphones. These are extremely compact, using tiny lenses and sensors. Digital cameras come in many different types to cater for a wide range of uses (*see p.122-7*). The latest digital cameras offer the most accessories and biggest choice of lenses (*see pp.134-5*). Film-using cameras are the least common, with very few in production, but there is a large supply of used equipment available.

Features of a typical camera

With increasingly sophisticated features, such as built-in zoom lenses and special effects, all digital cameras allow the photographer to exert extensive creative control.

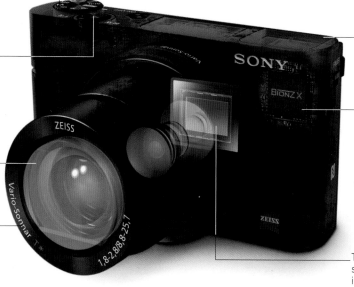

The mode dial sets exposure and various automatic modes of operation, such as video, panorama, etc.

The viewfinder shows exactly what is framed by the lens and also shows the effect of exposure, colour balance, and aperture

The shutter release button can be partially depressed to initiate a series of functions, from autofocus to exposure measurement

A zoom lens may be permanently attached or interchangeable

The lens may retract into the camera for compactness

The image processor focuses the lens, and turns digital data into images

The sensor or film surface captures the image for processing

Optical viewfinder

» SENSOR SIZE AND QUALITY

As a general principle, the larger the image sensor that captures the image, the better the image quality technically possible. Modern cameras balance quality sufficient for professional use with sensors sized to work with compact cameras and lenses. Tiny sensors used in smartphones are sufficient where there is a good level of light. Larger sensors of APS-C or "full-format" size (24 x 36mm) can record great detail and a wide range of brightness, and also perform well in poor light.

Digital cameras

Modern models are engineered to give high-quality results reliably in all kinds of lighting conditions. Most camera can be configured to suit a range of users thanks to the numerous functions and options they offer. Today, the quality available ranges from the high to extremely high.

⌃ Panasonic Lumix DMC-GX80
Featuring a 17.3 x 13mm, 16.8 MB sensor, this camera takes high-quality images suitable for most amateur needs.

Interchangeable lens

Smartphone cameras

Today, the quality of a camera on a mobile device can help sell the phone. Many use two or more lenses to provide zoom and other features. Image quality may be suitable for many professional uses. These cameras are also useful for capturing video footage, thanks to their large screens, and can reach quality standards once thought impossible.

Flash unit

Multiple lenses

» Smarter photography
Capable of capturing high-quality images and video, smartphone cameras offer a level of versatility and convenience unmatched by other types of camera.

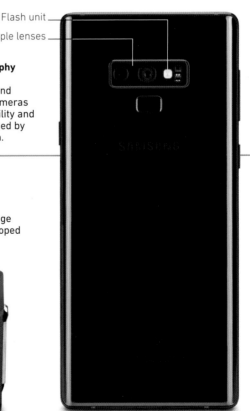

Film-using cameras

In the search for a different kind of imagery, film-using cameras have returned from near-extinction and are growing in popularity. Few cameras are produced new, but there is a large pool of used cameras available, some offering the highest quality at affordable prices. Inexpensive plastic cameras are also becoming more popular.

⌄ Holga 120FN
A basic yet quirky choice, this cheap range of cameras has developed a cult-like following.

Film winding knob

Plastic lens for "toy" camera effect

Digital cameras

The modern, autofocus, auto-exposure digital camera offers excellent value photography – highly accessible, it can also deliver quality capable of meeting the highest demands. There are three basic designs. The simplest is the compact camera, which uses a permanently attached lens with the screen on the back of the camera serving as the viewfinder. Bridge cameras combine versatile functions and a fixed lens, while system cameras use interchangeable lenses. One type of system camera is mirrorless and more compact than the SLR type, which uses a mirror assembly for viewing.

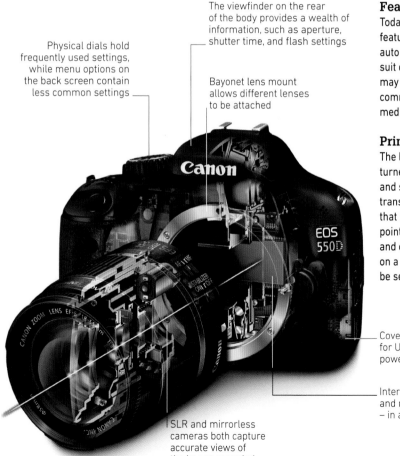

The viewfinder on the rear of the body provides a wealth of information, such as aperture, shutter time, and flash settings

Physical dials hold frequently used settings, while menu options on the back screen contain less common settings

Bayonet lens mount allows different lenses to be attached

SLR and mirrorless cameras both capture accurate views of the image recorded by any attached lens

Covers protect connectors for USB, HDMI, sound, power, and so on

Internal motors charge the shutter and move the mirror – if present – in and out of position

Features of a digital camera
Today's digital cameras are packed with features, including auto-exposure modes, auto white balance, and autofocus modes to suit different subjects. Basic image manipulation may be possible in some models. Wireless communications for file transfer and social media connections may also be included.

Principles of digital cameras
The light focused by the lens onto the sensor is turned into electrical signals. These are digitized and sent to an image-processing unit that translates the data into colour information that is, in turn, constructed into an image. At this point, the image may undergo further processing and compression before it is sent to be stored on a memory card. Alternatively, the image may be sent straight to a memory card in its raw form.

» THE DIGITAL SENSOR

If you use the LCD screen of a digital camera to frame a picture, you are effectively viewing the image through the same lens that takes the image (as with an SLR camera, see pp.127). The lens projects the image onto a sensor, which sends the image data to be viewed on an LCD screen. However, unlike film-using cameras, which employ a very limited range of film sizes, digital cameras use many different sizes of sensor. The vast majority are less than one quarter of the size of 35mm film. One effect of this is that depth of field increases, which can limit your creative control.

» How a digital file is made
Creating a digital image is an entirely different process to capturing one on film.

Light is reflected from the subject

The image is focused on to the camera's sensor

The image is stored on a memory card or chip

The image is converted into a digital signal

The sensor is a grid of light-sensitive pixels – each creates an electrical signal

Performance

In practice, what matters is not a camera's feature count, but its performance. Are colours recorded precisely? Does the camera set the exposure consistently and correctly? Is focus accurate? Is the image sharp enough without being overly so? That is, does the image preserve details without exaggerating edges? These are the most important questions to consider before buying a digital camera. Try to examine sample images to get a good idea of what is available. Check digital photography websites or online reviews. Many allow you to download sample images at full resolution for you to examine. Consult major retail sites to read reviews by users of the equipment to learn about others' evaluations.

Pixel count and image quality

The pixel count (also called "resolution") is the number of picture elements on the imaging sensor that capture an image and set the upper limit of what a camera can achieve. The majority of digital cameras and many smartphone cameras count at least 12 megapixels (12 million pixels or 12MP), which is more than enough for most uses. This means that when choosing a camera, factors other than pixel count will be more important, such as how easy it is to use and whether its other specifications, such as zoom lens features and viewfinder type, meet your needs. The quality of the optics is also key. A good lens on an 8MP camera can give better results than a 12MP model with an inferior lens.

Memory cards and capacity

Use the memory card type and reputable brand that is recommended for your camera. For best performance, particularly for high-resolution cameras and for future-proofing your purchase, use cards rated with high speeds, such as UHS Speed Class 3. High speed is essential if you wish to record video at ultra-high definition. Choose a card capacity that comfortably holds no more than a few days' worth of photography. Failure of a card with very big capacity could mean the loss of a large number of images. It is best to format cards in the camera in which they are used.

» CARD CAPACITY (NUMBER OF JPEGS – APPROX)

Card size	2GB	4GB	8GB	16GB	32GB	64GB	128GB	256GB
8 Megapixel / 1MB file	715	1420	2800	5700	11400	22850	45000	91000
12 Megapixel / 3MB file	475	950	1900	3700	7700	15000	29000	60000
16 Megapixel / 4MB file	360	720	1450	2900	5800	12100	24500	48000
24 Megapixel / 7MB file	240	480	900	1900	3900	7700	15000	29000

Cameras for different activities

Digital cameras are hugely versatile because they are easily set up to meet different needs – you can set them to be fully automatic, so you do not need to know anything about photography to obtain useable images. Or you can set many models to full manual control. Different types of camera have different strengths. If you want absolutely the best quality, you may need a larger camera and a larger budget. If you want the most compact camera, you will have to sacrifice some quality or features.

Lightweight photography

Although some models are so compact that they easily fit in a pocket, there is nothing lightweight about their performance. Compact digital cameras can capture panoramas, video, and stills that are suitable for every subject, from children to pets, parties, holidays, and travel – all with minimal technical fuss or experience needed.

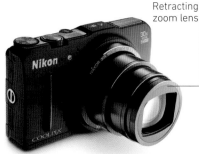

Retracting zoom lens

⌄ Panoramas
Letterbox panoramas are easily made on digital cameras using in-built image processing, without any technical knowledge.

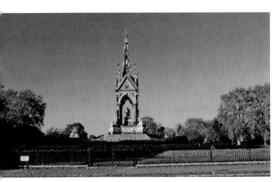

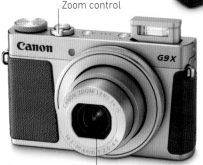

Zoom control

⌃ Point and shoot
Simple, entry-level digital cameras are useful for learning the basics and for taking reference shots for photographic projects.

« Canon Powershot G9 X
With a 20MP sensor and a 3x times optical zoom, this camera offers the convenience of a compact, with high-quality image capture.

Compact zoom lens

» Leica Q (Typ 116)
This premium quality, full-frame sensor camera is ideal for taking very high-quality images, which can be shared instantly using its built-in WiFi.

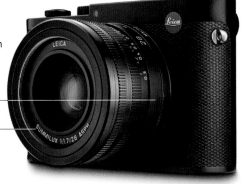

Macro setting ring

High-quality fixed-focal-length lens

Enthusiast photography

From the early days when the poor quality of digital cameras was ridiculed by enthusiast photographers who demanded the very best image results, digital cameras have developed to standards once thought impossible. Moonlight images with minimal noise artefacts, incredible standards of resolution and sharpness, exceptional handling of extreme lighting conditions – all these are possible with the best of today's cameras and have been miniaturized to fit into small bodies. In addition, today's cameras can capture video at high definition or better.

Travel photography

Digital cameras are ideal for travel photography thanks to their compact form, ability to capture thousands of images without having to reload film, and video capture abilities. However, their battery capacity is limited, so spares and chargers are needed for all but the briefest journeys.

Cameras offering lenses with extended zoom ranges, such as 24 to 300mm, enable you to cover every eventuality, from landscapes to portraits and wildlife. But, to keep long zoom lenses compact, their lens apertures are not large, which compromises their lowlight performance.

Exposure compensation dial

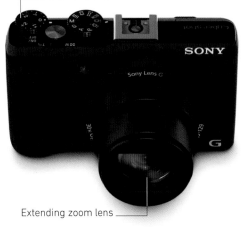

Extending zoom lens

>> Bridge camera
So-called because the design "bridges" the features of a compact camera with the more substantial handling of a larger camera. This allows faster, higher-quality lenses to be built in.

« Compact long zoom
Despite their small form, modern cameras can offer focal lengths ranging from very wide-angle to extreme telephoto, thanks to lenses that retract into the camera.

Larger body improves handling

Underwater photography

By fitting watertight housings or plastic cases, many normal cameras can be adapted to work underwater. However, it is generally best to use cameras specifically designed for the task, since they are more robust, reliable, and easier to use. Such cameras are a little bulkier than normal compacts, but they are resistant to shock from drops, and dustproof, yet capable of excellent results with both stills and video.

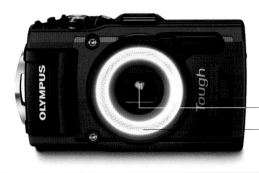

« Olympus Tough TG-4
Waterproof to 15m (50ft) and shockproof to over 2m (6ft), this camera is ideal for capturing more extreme adventures.

Waterproof lens

Flash unit

Advanced phone photography

Compact and inconspicuous, smartphone cameras are ideal for a wide range of photography. But their limited range of lenses – even in models with four built-in lenses – can limit their capacity to capture scenes. Supplementary lenses can be clipped on to enable close-up, wide-angle, and telephoto photography. These can increase the quality of smartphone images. Other accessories include waterproof or shockproof cases, auxiliary batteries, and attachments to improve handling when the phone is used for photography.

Lens holder

Carabiner

⌃ Olloclip lenses
This range of lenses, which includes macro, super-wide, and telephoto can be clipped onto a smartphone for a range of uses.

Accessory lenses

Advanced digital cameras

Today's entry-level digital cameras outperform professional-grade models of the late 1990s, some of which, at the time, cost more than the average family car. Not so long, ago these were the ultimate dream for amateur photographers, but now mid-range digital cameras are not only affordable, but can easily deliver professional-quality results with high specifications in every department, from low-light ability to focusing speeds and wireless communications. At the same time the quality of lenses has also improved significantly, while relative costs have fallen (*see p.132*).

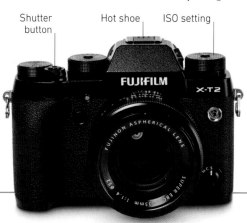

Shutter button   Hot shoe   ISO setting

» Fujifulm X-T2
Designed for professional use, this camera features a 24MP sensor and ultra-fast autofocusing, making it ideal for action photography.

Crop-sensor mirrorless digital camera

Cameras using sensors of about 27 x 22mm are called "crop" in comparison to full-frame sensors that measure 36 x 24mm. Smaller sensors enable smaller cameras and lenses to be made. Some models have permanently fixed lenses, some use interchangeable ones. Other cameras use the smaller 4/3 format of 21.6 x 17.3mm.

Mode dial   Optical viewfinder

Full-frame mirrorless digital camera

Using sensors the same size as 35mm film (36 x 24mm) enables cameras to make full use of legacy lenses for 35mm film cameras. The larger sensor also allows uncompromised image quality. However, while ultra wide-angle and large aperture lenses are easier to design than small sensors, the optics are also larger and heavier. The latest models can make studio-quality video recordings at ultra high-definition.

» Sony A7III
With a full-format sensor and lighter mirrorless design, this adaptable camera can be configured to suit many styles of photography.

Interchangeable lens

Single lens reflex camera

This type of digital camera uses a mirror to send the viewing image to an optical viewfinder. On exposure, the mirror flips out of the way and the shutter opens to expose the sensor. As the design directly updated the film-using SLR, it was the dominant type in the first years of digital photography. Cameras tend to be larger and bulkier than mirrorless equivalents. Some models use APS-C or similar cropped sensor sizes, others use full-frame sensors. Lenses designed for APS-C do not cover full-frame sensors.

☑ **Control cluster**
Controls arranged around the shutter button, such as power on/off, make for excellent handling.

Pop-up flash

Metal body

High-resolution digital camera

For the highest-quality demands – in advertising, fashion, museums, or industry – the medium-format camera is essential. With large sensors – about 44 x 33mm – resolutions as high as 400 megapixels, and some of the most fully corrected commercially available optics, they can capture extreme detail with high colour fidelity and richness.

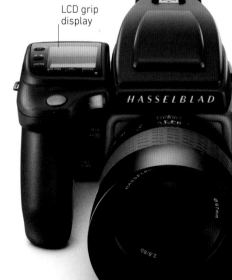

LCD grip display

⌅ **Quality first**
Large, heavy, and comparatively slow, high-resolution cameras are designed for highest-quality capture, with emphasis on no-compromise fixed-focal-length lenses.

≫ DIGITAL CAMERAS FOR VIDEO RECORDING

All modern digital cameras are capable of capturing video, some to ultra high-definition or better, some to studio quality. Lightweight compared to proper video cameras, stills cameras tend to produce very shaky footage however. Motorized stablizing gimbals that hold the camera steady are essential for filming on the move. Camera and lens must be specifically balanced on the mechanism.

⌅ **Affordable stabilizers**
Movie-making has been revolutionized by compact, hand-holdable gimbals that cost a fraction of professional film production equipment. They make it easy to produce smooth follow-action video.

Smartphone and ultra-compact cameras

Cameras in smartphones are powerful and more versatile than "proper" cameras in several ways. Their integration with the phone operating system allows apps to manipulate, annotate, and manage images. Their link to mobile and wireless communications allows images to be shared on social media networks, or sent to friends, clients, or agencies in an instant. In addition, all modern smartphones can capture video footage. The small camera modules inside them has also led to the development of ultra-compact cameras – so small they can even be strapped to a bird to record its flight.

Features of smartphone cameras

Packed into a tight space, smartphone cameras use tiny sensors and lenses set very close to the sensor. The lens or sensor may be set in a cradle that moves to stablize against camera shake during exposure or filming. Some cameras carry multiple lenses of different focal lengths that can be used together to give smooth zoom effects. A tiny flash unit supplies light in dark conditions.

☑ Opto-mechanical mastery

Modern smartphone cameras are miracles of miniaturization, precision manufacturing, and highly complicated electronics. They not only capture the image, but process it for depth of field, reduce camera shake to improve sharpness, and can even decide what kind of processing is best for a given subject.

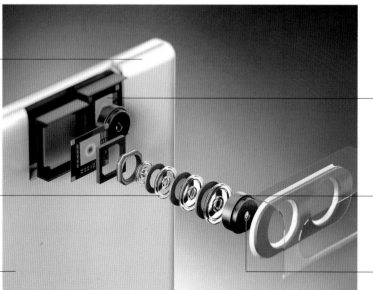

Splashproof, dust-tight casing

Multiple lens elements correct for aberrations

Camera software in the phone is vital to make the whole system operate: there are few mechanical parts

Secondary camera and lenses increase the focal-length range, effectively giving zoom effects

Image stabilisation cage compensates for camera shake to capture sharp images

Lens covers keep optics free of dust and water splashes but it is best to keep them spotlessly clean

Smartphone camera accessories

Smartphone camera lenses can be extended by accessories that clip on directly or mount on special adaptors. Close-up, wide-angle, and telephoto lenses are available, as well as adaptors to fit telescopes or microscopes. Auxiliary lights can also be fitted.

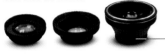

Lens attachments for macro, wide, and telephoto effects

Ring lighting gives pleasingly soft effects particularly suitable for portraiture

» Kenko Real Pro
Clipping over the camera of most smartphones, this manually focused lens gives up to 7x times magnification.

Sturdy clip secures to smartphone

Zoom ring to alter focal-length

Camera protection

One of the great advantages of a smartphone is that you have a camera with you at all times. But they are precision electronics, so it pays to protect them against bumps, falls, and water. Accessory cases can make smartphones shockproof, dustproof, and water-resistant to depths of 2m (6ft) or more, while retaining most functions.

« LifeProof case
Protective smartphone cases such as this allow images to be safely taken in more extreme situations.

Point-of-view camera

Ultra-compact cameras developed for smartphones and fitted in tough cases are ideal for point-of-view (POV) applications. Some are small enough to be harnessed to small animals, fitted to bicycle handlebars and helmets, or strapped onto a wrist. POV cameras can now capture ultra high-definition video, as well as stills of good quality.

▼ GoPro HERO7
With their rugged construction and advanced digital technology, POV cameras allow photography and film capture on the go.

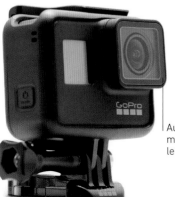

Autofocus and manual-focus lens

Point-of-view photography

Compact enough to be taken surfing, snowboarding, climbing, or on any adventure activity, POV cameras have created a whole new genre of action photography.

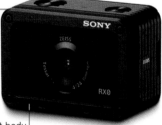

Sturdy, water-resistant body

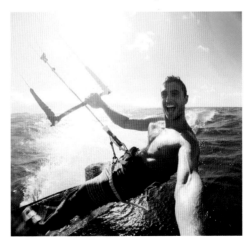

▲ Sony RX0
Extremely compact, this camera captures professional-quality images and 4K film, and can be controlled using smartphones and tablets.

« Capturing action
A "selfie" taken with a POV camera while parasailing captures the thrilling excitement of the moment.

Film-using cameras

From about 2005, major camera manufacturers gave up developing new film cameras in order to concentrate on digital models. Now that almost every photographer uses digital, there is a vast store of used or nearly-new film-using cameras. Apart from a handful of collectibles, many of these are of the highest pedigree, yet can be bought at a small fraction of their original cost. A few models remain in production: two or three at the very top end, and some brands at the other extreme of the scale prized for their quirky image defects. Instant-picture film cameras also live on.

Features of an SLR camera

Advanced SLR cameras offer a host of features, including multiple exposure controls, extensive shutter settings, autofocus modes to suit different subjects, and access to a wide range of interchangeable lenses. Some offer a built-in flash, but all can make use of extra flash units and studio flashes.

How an SLR camera works

In an SLR camera, light enters through the lens, is reflected onto a focusing screen, and, by means of a prism or system of mirrors, is relayed from there to the eyepiece, allowing the photographer to see exactly what the film will record. For exposure, the mirror flips out of the way just before the shutter opens – momentarily obscuring the photographer's view of the subject – to allow the light to reach the film.

The viewfinder on a modern SLR provides a wealth of information, such as aperture, shutter time, exposure compensation, and flash settings

Built-in flash is a convenient way of adding light, but it should never be relied on as the main source of light

The exposure mode dials on modern SLR cameras offer numerous settings. Using the manual setting allows you to experiment with exposure times

No matter what type of lens you attach, an SLR gives the same accuracy of framing. Autofocus is less effective with wide-angle lenses and those with a small maximum aperture

Light path

The exposure compensation dial is used to fine-tune the exposure reading in order to obtain the desired result

DX code sensors automatically set the film speed. This helps to avoid errors if you frequently change between film speeds. However, it is useful to be able to override the setting, for example, to "push" films to a different speed

A motor winder loads, winds on, and rewinds film. Using the serial or sequential mode, you can shoot several frames in quick succession just by holding down the shutter release button

Types of film-using camera

Use of film cameras is largely dictated by the availability of film in the sizes you need. It is possible to source everything from instant film through to large format film, but choice is limited. Of the cameras available, the largest variety takes 35mm film. Roll-film or medium-format cameras can also be bought secondhand.

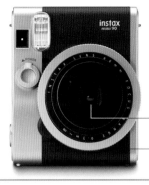

≪ Fujifilm Instax Mini 90
Combining digital image capture with instant film printing, this camera is only suitable for fun photography.

Simple optics for economy

Retro-styling suits film revival

Simple camera

Cameras with bodies and lenses made of plastic are inexpensive and find favour for their image quality, which ranges from soft and blurry to dream-like and distorted. These cameras are a fun introduction to film photography, yet have been adopted by exhibiting artists. They offer rudimentary exposure control, while focusing is by guesswork.

Manual film winding knob

Simple viewfinder

≫ Holga 120N
Originally designed for the Chinese working classes, this basic camera has found popularity in the West for its simple design and quirky image quality.

Advanced SLR camera

Professional-quality SLR cameras are extremely good value and a joy to use. The additional expense buys a camera that will last a lifetime, survive harsh conditions, and work reliably, while producing pictures of superb quality. They are largely independent of battery power, so are ideal for use in remote or challenging conditions.

Pentaprism viewfinder

≪ Pentax MZ-M
Compact and relatively lightweight, this inexpensive camera is ideal for the beginner.

Interchangeable lens

Hood for large reversed viewfinder

Manual film-winding knob

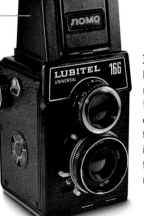

≫ Lomo Lubitel 166
First designed in the 1940s, this camera provides an inexpensive entry to medium-format photography. Modern reproductions are also available.

Medium-format camera

Modern medium-format cameras that use roll film have an image area – approximately 55 x 55mm – much larger than the 35mm format of 36 x 24mm. This ensures that quality is close to the best possible for a portable camera. There is a large secondhand market offering basic to first-class equipment, and inexpensive new models are also available.

Lenses

The camera lens determines the image quality possible on the camera. In general, the more expensive the lens, the better its image quality and reliability. Not being able to change lens or zoom will not necessarily limit the success of your photography. Some great photographers choose to work with just one focal length. Matching the lens to a task is, however, extremely satisfying.

Types of lens

The most common photographic lens is the zoom, which enables you to continuously vary focal length. It is used almost universally on compact autofocus cameras. Mirrorless and SLR system cameras use both zoom and fixed-focal-length lenses. Modern zoom lenses produce excellent images and are convenient to use. Generally, the more conservative the zoom range, the higher the image quality. Fixed-focal-length, or prime, lenses tend to give superior quality to zoom lenses for relatively lower costs. They best suit those with specific needs, such as close-up, portrait, or street photography.

Anatomy of a lens

A lens comprises precision mechanics holding a number of optical elements. Some elements are moved to adjust the focus or, on zoom lenses, to change focal length. A bayonet mount fits the lens to the camera.

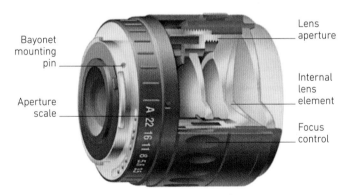

Bayonet mounting pin

Aperture scale

Lens aperture

Internal lens element

Focus control

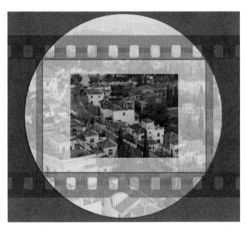

⌃ **Sensor size and field of view**
35mm format lenses can be used on sensors that are smaller than full-frame. This reduces the field of view, increasing both the effective focal length and depth of field of the lens.

Standard lens

Lenses with focal lengths of between 40 and 55mm give a natural, unforced view of the subject. They are the most versatile options for a wide range of situations, from portraiture to landscapes.

» **50mm**
Standard lenses – or their equivalent for smaller sensors – such as this give the best combination of low cost, large maximum aperture, and high image quality.

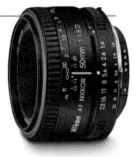

Fixed wide-angle lens

Prime lenses (those with a single focal length) for wide-angle views ensure superlative image quality with minimal distortion, even illumination across the image field, and high contrast.

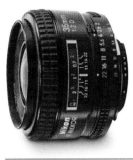

《 35mm
Lenses like this can produce crisp, detailed images that are relatively free of distortion and can control internal reflections.

Fixed macro lens

Macro lenses are designed for close-up work and produce life-size or magnified images of a subject. They are very highly corrected optics that give the highest resolution and contrast.

》 90mm and 50mm macro
90mm lenses are good for nature subjects, while 50mm macro lenses are more suitable for copying documents or art objects.

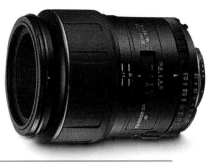

Wide-angle zoom lens

Ideal for landscape and travel photography, both of which often require wide-angle views, these powerful lenses combine versatility and convenience.

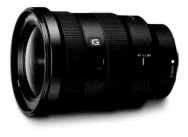

《 16–35mm
A lens with this range covering ultra-wide to moderate wide-angle views is an invaluable tool for the modern photographer.

Portrait lens

Portrait lenses with focal lengths of around 75 to 105mm give sharp images with out-of-focus backgrounds that flatter faces and skin tones.

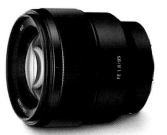

《 85mm
This is a popular focal length for portraiture as a face can fill a vertically oriented frame from a comfortable working distance.

Telephoto zoom lens

Zoom lenses covering ranges from moderate telephoto (suitable for portraits) to ultra-long (suitable for wildlife photography) are versatile, but are heavy and need support on a tripod for best results.

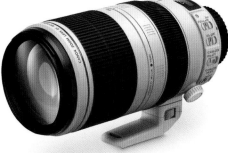

⌃ 100–400mm
This zoom range can replace several single-focal-length lenses, yet still produce excellent images.

》 LENS FILTERS

Filters are screwed onto a lens to alter the light entering the camera in order to confer subtle tints, change colour dramatically, or alter the image for special effects. The polarizing filter darkens blue skies and gives an effect that cannot be replicated with any digital technique. A plain or ultra-violet (UV) absorbing filter is useful for protecting the lens' front element.

》 Square filters
Systems of square filters that mount on holders and can be moved to vary their effect on the image are highly versatile. For example, this is the best way to use graduated filters.

Camera accessories

A bewildering array of accessories is on the market. While these can make tasks easier, they also mean having more to carry, more to set up, and more to go wrong. Start with a need, then look for the cost-effective and practical way to meet it. In general, the more expensive an item, such as a tripod or flash unit, the more likely it is to be of higher quality and more reliable.

The essential accessories

The key photographic accessories are those that support, protect, and light. Using a tripod encourages careful composition and ensures that images are sharp. Indeed, tripods can be the single best way to improve the quality of your photographs. Camera bags or cases help protect your valuable equipment from water, dust, and shock ensuring it continues to work efficiently. Finally, since photography is all about working with light, the other essential accessories are for supplementing and controlling light.

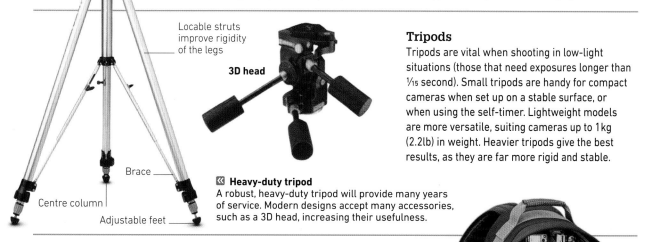

Locable struts improve rigidity of the legs

3D head

Brace

Centre column

Adjustable feet

Tripods

Tripods are vital when shooting in low-light situations (those that need exposures longer than $\frac{1}{15}$ second). Small tripods are handy for compact cameras when set up on a stable surface, or when using the self-timer. Lightweight models are more versatile, suiting cameras up to 1kg (2.2lb) in weight. Heavier tripods give the best results, as they are far more rigid and stable.

« Heavy-duty tripod
A robust, heavy-duty tripod will provide many years of service. Modern designs accept many accessories, such as a 3D head, increasing their usefulness.

Camera bags

As there is no such thing as a perfect camera bag for all occasions, many professionals own as many as a dozen models. Lightweight bags are good for urban use, but their minimal padding confers limited shock protection. Heavily padded bags are best for expeditions and travel, but are weighty and bulky.

» Bag types
Backpack designs are comfortable to carry but make reaching gear awkward. Shoulder-bag designs are less comfortable but easier to use.

Shoulder bag   **Backpack**

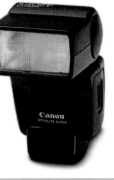

Flash units

The key lighting accessory is a separate, hotshoe-mounted flash unit. Modern units are amazingly powerful and offer extremely efficient automatic-exposure functions. They enable you to fill shadows in full sunshine, as well as work in complete darkness.

« Hotshoe-mount flash
The best flash units are those that swivel so the flash can be pointed upwards and sideways to control the direction of lighting.

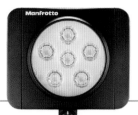

LED lighting

Light-emitting diodes (LEDs) can produce enough light for video or stills photography using modern digital cameras. LED arrays can be lightweight and provide softer light than flash units. Their continuous lighting is easier to work with.

» LED lighting
LED lamps provide stable colour but their high-frequency flickering may be picked up by some types of sensor or capture modes. Test before buying.

Lighting accessories

Reflectors throw light into shadows to brighten them. Diffusers or light shapers soften lighting. Use these accessories to help create the effects that best suit your photography and subject.

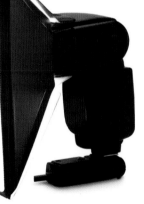

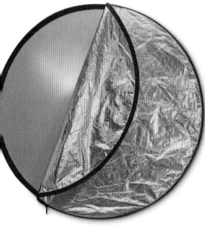

« Light shapers
Compact light boxes that unfold and attach to compact flash units can greatly improve lighting quality, but can unbalance the flash and disrupt handling.

« Portaflash reflector
Metallic fabric reflectors on a flexible frame make a dramatic impact on lighting as they fill shadows, and can add warmth.

Wireless control

Many digital cameras can communicate wirelessly through WiFi, Bluetooth, or infrared. Radio receivers can be connected to cameras, too. These abilities allow cameras to be remotely controlled to adjust focus, exposure metering, and shutter release from a distance or with automatic tripping devices. It is also possible to synchronize multiple flash units with the same controller.

» Wireless controllers
Detachable wireless controllers offer increased flexibility, allowing the camera to be controlled at a distance, and shots to be composed on a larger remote screen, such as a tablet.

Film and formats

Modern colour photographic films are made up of as many as 20 individual layers: even black-and-white film can comprise four or more. Each layer is thinner than the width of a human hair and carries a precisely-controlled suspension containing minute crystals of light-sensitive silver salts – typically silver iodide and silver bromide – and light-absorbing dyes. These need to be carefully balanced with one another in order to record colours accurately. Modern films can consistently capture a wealth of tonal and spatial information using wonderfully rich and true-to-life colours.

The basics of film

All films respond to colours, but they are made to record in black and white or colour. Fundamentally, all types of film record in negative but can be processed either to deliver a negative or a positive image. In both black-and-white and colour films, negatives are the end product. The transparency or slide, however, is delivered in positive.

Film speed

The amount of light needed for a good-quality image is measured by the film's speed. Throughout the industry, this is measured against a standard processing and the result is given as the ISO number. A low ISO number, for example 100/21°, indicates a film that needs more light (is slower) than one with a larger ISO number, say 400/27°. A comparable standard has been established for digital cameras, also quoted as ISO.

Colour palette

Different makes of film respond to light and colour in their own characteristic ways. A film such as Fuji Velvia is often chosen for its rich and vividly coloured palette. Softer, less brilliant colours can be obtained by using a film such as Kodak Elite. It is best to try out several films to see which one you prefer.

Film formats

Photographic film is trimmed to various sizes to suit different cameras and purposes. Smaller film formats are compact and more convenient but they do not offer the same potential for image quality as larger formats.

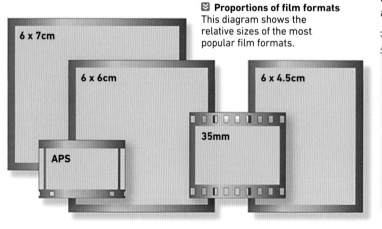

☑ **Proportions of film formats**
This diagram shows the relative sizes of the most popular film formats.

6 x 7cm

6 x 6cm

6 x 4.5cm

35mm

APS

⟫ HOW A NEGATIVE WORKS

The term "negative" means that the subject's tone values (bright and dark) – and colours (hues) – are reversed in the record. For example, where the subject looks bright, in the negative it appears dark due to the greater density of dyes (or silver, in the case of black-and-white film). When working in colour, the hue is also reversed. For example a red car will appear green on the negative, while a blue car will appear orange. When printed the colours revert back to the original.

Types of film

There are two main types of colour film. Tungsten is used with indoor lighting while daylight film is suitable for natural light. There are also two types of black-and-white film. Panchromatic uses developed-out silver to disperse light to form the image. This can easily be developed at home (*see p.140*). Chromogenic film uses clouds of neutral dye to absorb, rather than disperse, light in order to form the image, and is developed in the same way as colour negative film.

Colour negative film

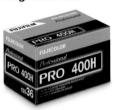

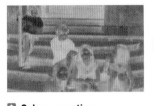

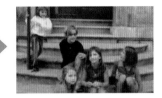

⌃ **Colour negative**
A well-processed film looks low in contrast, with weak and reversed colours.

⌃ **Colour print**
When printed, colours are brilliant, with normal contrast and densities.

Colour slide film

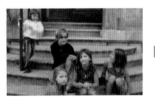

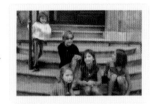

⌃ **Colour slide**
A slide (or transparency) should be perfect as further adjustments are difficult.

⌃ **Mounted slide**
For protection, the slide is usually mounted in a plastic or cardboard frame.

Panchromatic film

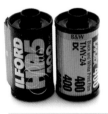

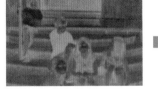

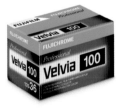

⌃ **Panchromatic negative**
Negative film can vary in appearance depending on how you process it.

⌃ **Panchromatic print**
The quality of print obtained depends on the appearance of the negative.

Chromogenic film

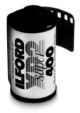

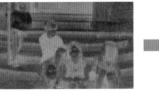

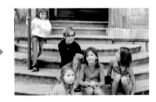

⌃ **Chromogenic negative**
These black-and-white films are low contrast like their colour negative counterparts.

⌃ **Chromogenic print**
Chromogenic negatives can be printed on normal black-and-white or colour paper.

Setting up a darkroom

With all the excitement over digital photography, it is easy to forget how satisfying it is to develop your own film, and have total control over the end product. Processing colour film at home is a specialist activity, but if you are working in black and white you can set up a darkroom for surprisingly little. Doing it yourself is one of the most gratifying of photographic experiences.

Equipping a darkroom

The illustrations show the basic set-ups for developing either films or prints (*below*) and for making black-and-white prints by enlargement (*opposite*). The equipment may look low-tech, but it can produce the very highest image quality. At the same time, the process is deeply rewarding, if rather time-consuming.

The wet bench

The wet bench is an area of the darkroom exclusively used for any "wet processes", such as mixing up and preparing chemicals, developing films, and developing and washing enlarged prints. A safelight can be used for print development, but not for film processing (*see p.140*).

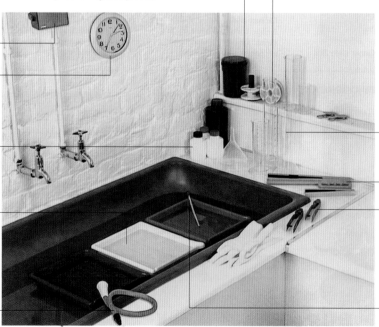

The developing tank should be cleaned and dried after use

Spirals should only be left out while drying

The safelight gives a "safe" red light

A timer is vital for accurate results

Chemicals should be stored in coded bottles

Processing trays may be colour-coded for different chemicals

The hose attachment is used to direct the flow of water

One measuring cylinder is used for each chemical

Squeegees help prevent drying marks

Processing tongs should always be used

A thermometer helps to ensure that a constant temperature is maintained

The dry bench

The dry section of the darkroom is where negatives are prepared and print enlargements made. This area is also where any electrical equipment, such as the enlarger, is kept, so it is vital that the area is kept dry.

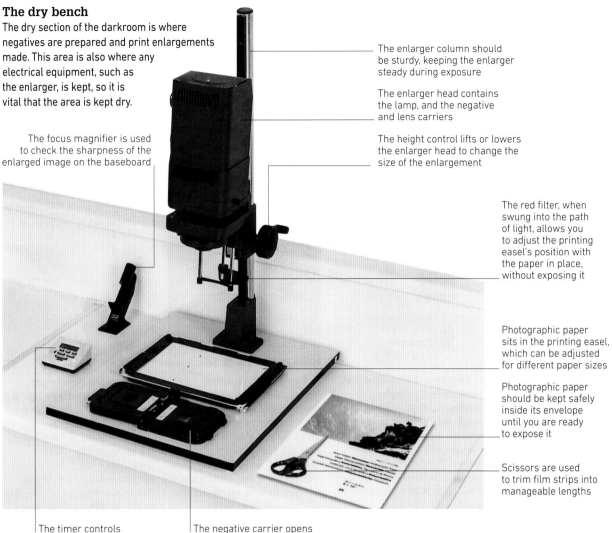

The focus magnifier is used to check the sharpness of the enlarged image on the baseboard

The enlarger column should be sturdy, keeping the enlarger steady during exposure

The enlarger head contains the lamp, and the negative and lens carriers

The height control lifts or lowers the enlarger head to change the size of the enlargement

The red filter, when swung into the path of light, allows you to adjust the printing easel's position with the paper in place, without exposing it

Photographic paper sits in the printing easel, which can be adjusted for different paper sizes

Photographic paper should be kept safely inside its envelope until you are ready to expose it

Scissors are used to trim film strips into manageable lengths

The timer controls the length of the print's exposure

The negative carrier opens up to allow the negative to be carefully positioned

>> WORKING IN THE DARKROOM

You need to work systematically to produce exhibition-quality work in your darkroom. For the best results, time all processes carefully and consistently. Develop prints for the manufacturer's recommended time and not a second more or less, and always develop film at 20°C (68°F). Similarly, time your enlargements with utmost precision and make a note of the timings and settings. This way, when you produce a satisfactory result, you can easily make another print equally as good by repeating the same steps. If you are disappointed with your results, you could try slightly different development times for your prints and films to see if they improve. If they do, you can adopt them as your standard. For example, you might decide that some prints need richer blacks or a greater contrast, and may benefit from an extra 30 seconds of development. Colour film and prints can also be processed at home, but costly equipment, which works at higher temperatures, is needed.

Black-and-white processing

One of the great attractions of working with black-and-white film is that you need just a few pieces of simple, low-tech equipment to process it. Furthermore, for developing black-and-white film you do not even need a dedicated darkroom or even running water (although both are an advantage); the chemicals are inexpensive; and careful work can deliver results of the highest quality.

How to process a film

The key to successful film development is meticulous preparation. Make up the three chemicals – developer, stop, and fix – following instructions to the letter, ensuring volumes and concentrations are as precise as possible. In particular, the developer should be at the correct temperature when it comes into contact with the film. If you are unused to working in the dark, especially when loading the film onto the spiral (step 2, right), it is a good idea to practise by using an old film in the light with your eyes closed until you are confident. For reliable results, it is vital that the timing of each step is consistent.

» **Working in the negative**
Subjects such as this architectural scene taken in Auckland, New Zealand, work best in the negative. The reversal of tones accentuates the bones and structure of the image. This effect can be achieved either by photographing the negative against a bright light, or by using the positive print in the same way as you would use a negative.

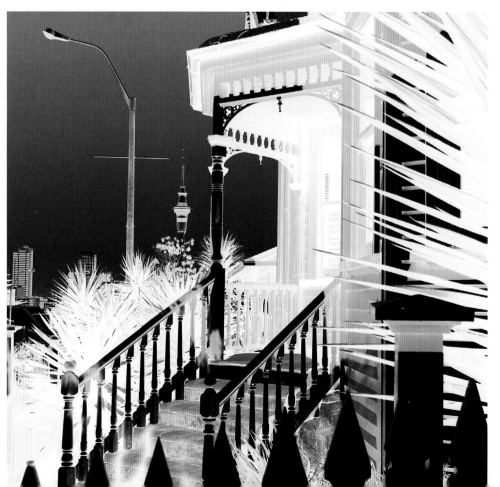

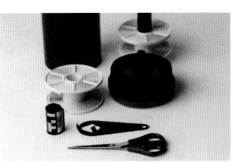

⌃ 1. Organize the equipment
Assemble a light-tight developing tank with a spiral (some tanks hold two or more spirals), a pair of blunt-ended scissors, and a film canister opener. Everything, including your hands, must be bone dry. It will help if all equipment is at room temperature.

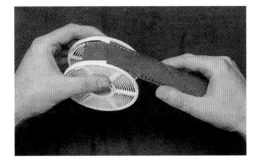

⌃ 2. Load the film spiral
In total darkness, open the canister and use the scissors to trim the end of the roll of film and round the corners. Then feed the film into the entry slot and inch it in by twisting each side of the spiral alternately. If the film becomes jammed, do not force it; start again.

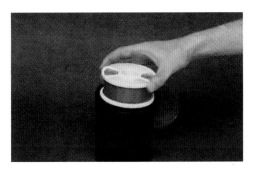

⌃ 3. Load the tank
Cut the spool from the film, then drop the spiral into the developing tank and close the lid firmly. Recheck that the temperature of the developer is 20°C (68°F). If not, you will need to adjust development times by referring to the manufacturer's charts.

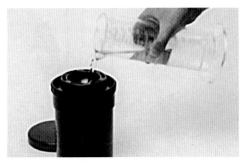

⌃ 4. Add developer
Pour all the developer into the tank and start the timer. Knock the tank sharply against the wet bench to dislodge any bubbles from the film, put the cap on and agitate (by turning the tank over and back) for one minute. Continue agitating according to the manufacturer's instructions.

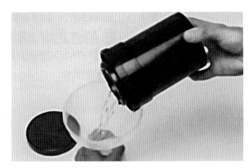

⌃ 5. End development and fix
When the development period is over, immediately pour out the developer. Pour in the stop bath. Agitate for 30 seconds, then pour the stop bath back into its bottle. Pour in the fix, agitate, and follow the manufacturer's instructions. At the end of the fix time, return the fix to its bottle.

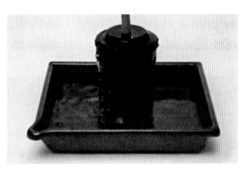

⌃ 6. Wash the film
Wash the fix off the film in clean water. If there is no running water, fill the tank with water, close it, invert it 10 times and dispose of the water. Repeat a further nine times. Add a drop of wetting agent to the final batch, agitate for 15 seconds, remove the film and hang it up to drip dry.

Black-and-white printing

Making a black-and-white print mirrors the photographic process of creating the original negative. By projecting a negative image onto the printing paper, the resulting image is positive. The construction of the paper means that the more light that reaches it, the darker it becomes. Unlike a digital print, which is created line by line, the image emerges onto the paper as a whole during development.

How to print

To be most efficient, select the images beforehand, then visualize how you wish to print each image. Do you want a high, low, or average contrast? The printing process itself is reassuringly low-tech and easy. First, you need to prepare the chemicals; developer, stop, and fix. Always use fresh developer. Blow dust off the negative using a puffer or can of compressed air – never use your breath. Turn off the room light and turn on the safelight to begin.

» 1. Load the negative carrier
Make sure your film is cut into convenient lengths. Place the chosen frame emulsion-side down and upside down on the carrier.

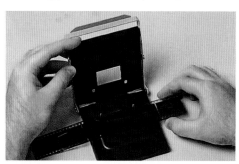

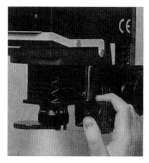

« 2. Set height
Raise or lower the enlarger head to vary the enlargement size of the image.

» 3. Frame the image
Set the enlarger lens to full aperture (to give the brightest image possible), and keep the image roughly in focus while you readjust the height of the enlarger as necessary. Arrange the image neatly within the frame area that you wish to use, and square it up so that no unsightly edges are visible.

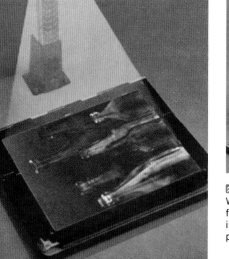

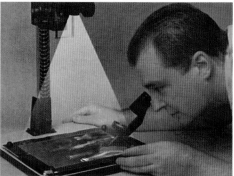

⌃ 4. Focus the image
With the lens still set to full aperture to facilitate focusing, use a focus magnifier to examine the image's grain. This is critical to ensure detail is printed sharp and clear.

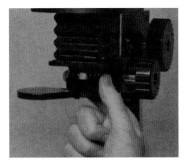

5. Stop down
To improve the quality of the image, set the lens to a smaller aperture, such as f/5.6.

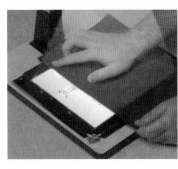

6. Make a test strip
Incrementally increase the exposure to a strip of paper using a mask, then develop.

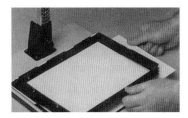

7. Expose the paper
Examine the test strip to choose the best exposure. Then place new printing paper in the easel, ensuring you do not accidentally change its position. Next, turn on the enlarger light and expose for the time determined by the test strip.

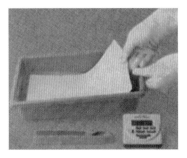

8. Develop the print
Slip the exposed sheet emulsion-side down into the developer and gently rock the tray. Use gloves or tongs to lift the paper by the corner to turn it over to check development.

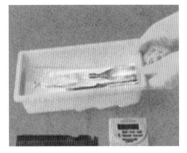

9. Stop development
Following the manufacturer's instructions for development time, lift the paper from the developing dish by its corner, drain, and slip into the stop bath to stop development.

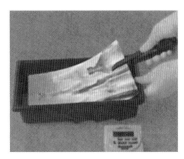

10. Fix the print
After just 30 seconds in the stop bath, lift the print by its corner, drain, and slip into the fix bath. Follow the instructions and do not exceed the recommended fix time.

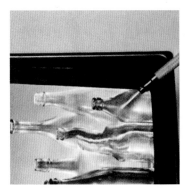

11. Wash the print
When the print is fixed, rinse off the chemicals with copious amounts of running water. Again, follow manu-facturer's instructions. Some papers are sufficiently washed in less than five minutes, others may need more time.

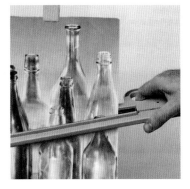

12. Dry the print
Modern PE (polyethylene) papers will dry flat by themselves, and need only to have excess water squeegeed off. Fibre-based papers tend to curl, so attach clip-on weights or pegs while drying.

TYPES OF PHOTOGRAPHIC PAPER

There are two main types of black-and-white printing paper. Fibre-based types use a paper core with a baryta (barium oxide) layer to carry the silver. These give the best results and deliver superior archival qualities, but they take longer to process. Polyethylene (PE) papers, also erroneously referred to as RC (resin-coated), have plastic layers over the paper core to reduce chemical absorption. This shortens processing. Modern papers are "variable contrast" and have a range of grades to match negatives of different contrasts built into the paper. The contrast is chosen by adjusting the printing light using filters, or through a setting on the enlarger head.

Analyzing a black-and-white print

When examining a scene your eyes continually adjust to the brightness. When looking at a dark area, your pupils open up to let in more light, and when looking at a bright area, they close down to shut out light. When making a print, you will need to make similar compensations to avoid dark parts of the picture becoming too black, and bright parts becoming burnt out. This is done by exposing different areas of the print paper to different amounts of light.

Burning-in and dodging

To correct the balance of tones in a print you can make over-bright areas darker by "burning-in", and hold back shadow areas to stop them becoming too dark by "dodging". You can do this with your hands, but you can also buy or make tools for the task. A burning-in tool is simply a piece of card with a hole in the centre that allows light to pass through. By positioning this between the enlarger lens and the paper you can increase the exposure time for selected areas to make them darker. A dodging tool is a stiff wire with a piece of card attached. The principle for dodging is the same as for burning-in, but in reverse. You need to keep the tools moving to prevent obvious lines from appearing.

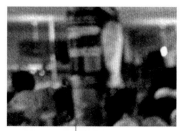

» Background blur
As the background is blurred, it does not need to hold much detail, but it should be neither too dark nor too light.

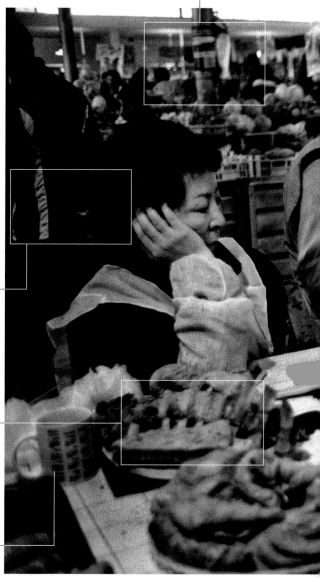

» Dodging the shadows
Without dodging, this area would have been uniformly black, losing the distinction between the woman's head and the jacket behind her.

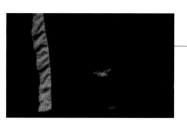

» Mid-tone detail
The key to black-and-white images is the mid-tone detail. Here it was lightened a little with dodging tools to ensure that the shadows were not too dark.

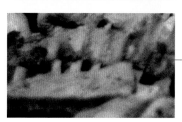

The use of a moderate wide-angle lens (35mm on 35mm film) meant that objects at the edge of the frame, such as this mug, are slightly distorted. A little dodging blurs the outline to disguise the effect.

Dodging facial tones

In the unmanipulated shot, the lower part of this woman's face was in shadow. A dodging tool was used to limit the amount of light in order to lighten the face.

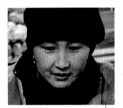

THE ORIGINAL IMAGE

This image of women playing chess while selling tripe in a market in Bishkek, Kyrgyzstan, was taken using ISO 400/27° film. A few spots of light were provided by overhead lamps and the background was bright, but overall, the available light was very low.

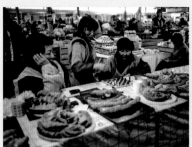

Assessing the image

The image is acceptable printed "straight" with no manipulation (left), but with a little burning-in and dodging it is far superior, as seen in the main image (below).

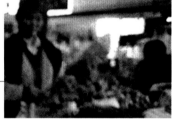

Avoiding overburn

Do not burn-in highlights next to mid-tones or you will make the mid-tones too dark.

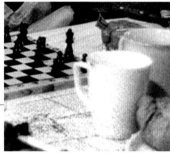

Burning-in highlights

The brightest parts of the foreground were the cups lit by an overhead lamp. It was necessary to burn-in to bring out shape in the mug. (Compare with the original image above.)

The foreground was burned-in – although it was already dark – to help frame the main subject.

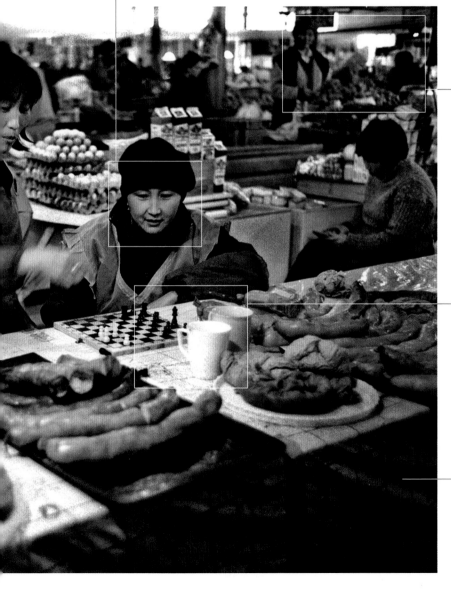

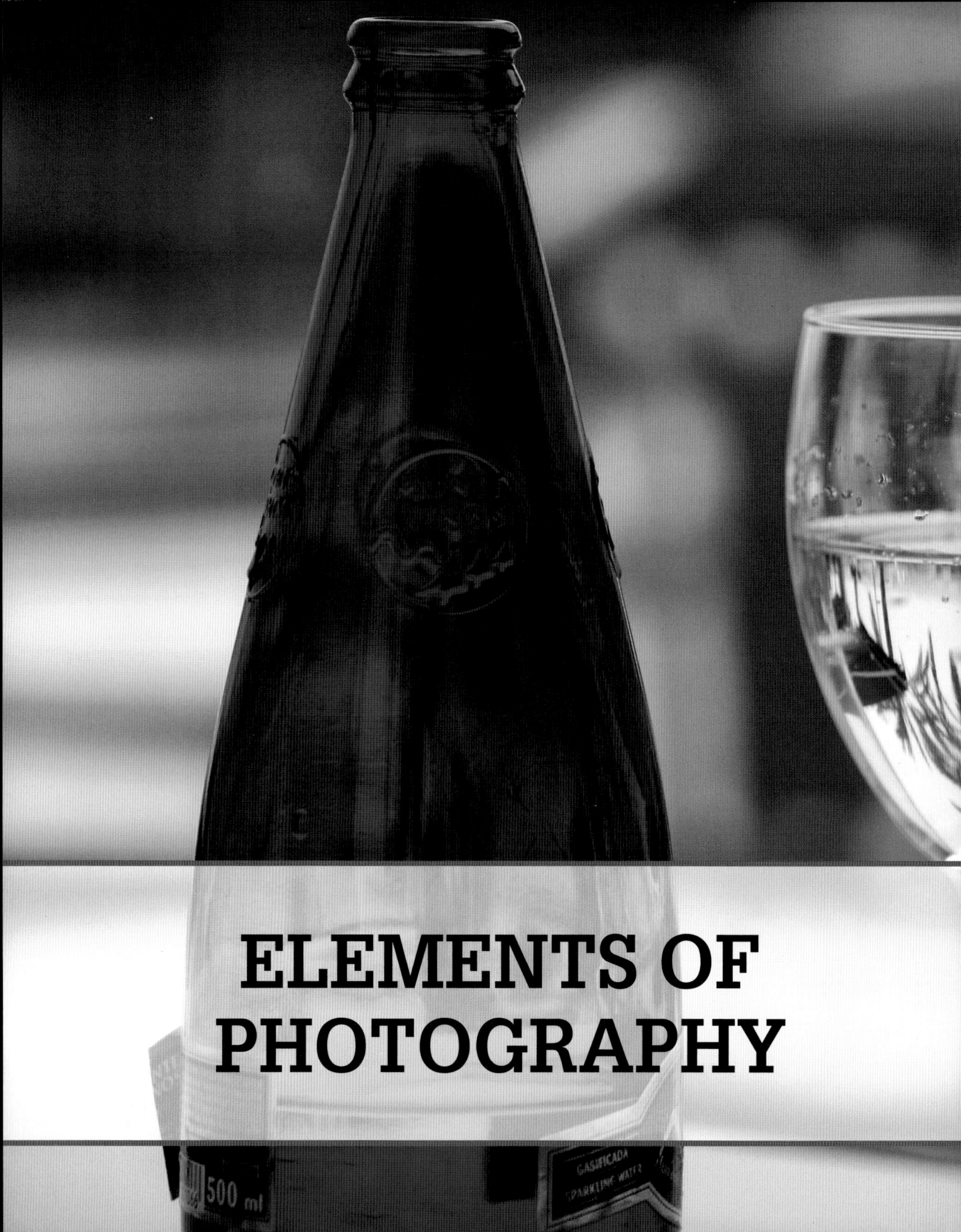

ELEMENTS OF PHOTOGRAPHY

GASIFICADA
SPARKLING WATER

500 ml

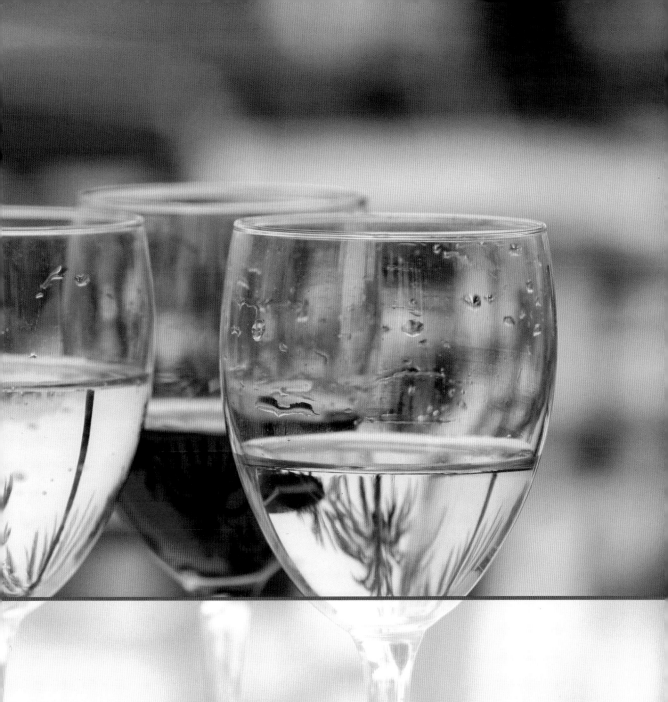

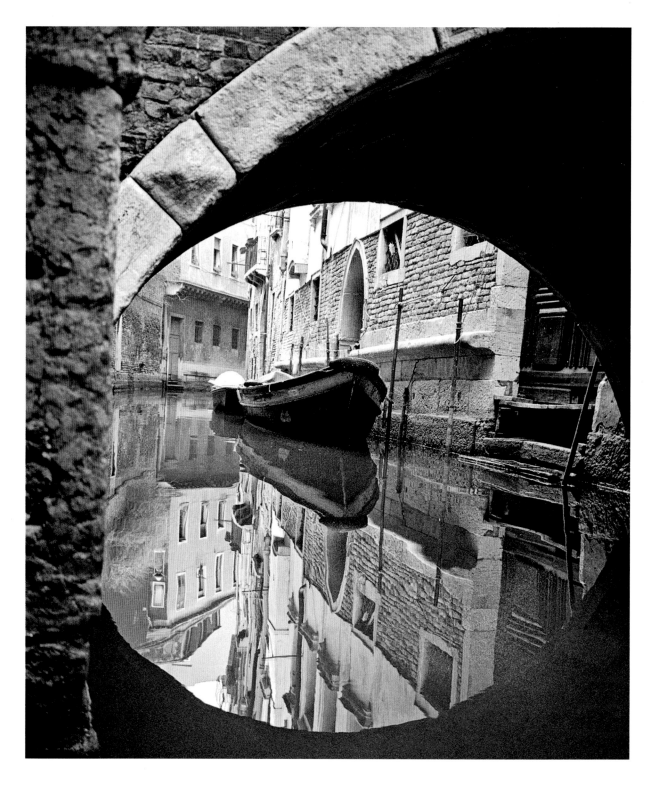

The foundation of any image is its technical quality. While the legendary photojournalist Eugene Smith cautioned "What is the use of adequate depth of field if there is not adequate depth of feeling?" it is equally true that a picture of poor quality has to work harder to communicate.

Technical quality in images is a complex combination of the elements of focus, exposure, composition, tone, and noise. Focus can be pin-sharp or blurred to give different artistic effects. Exposure sets the overall brightness of the image. Composition describes the way in which different parts of the image are arranged in relation to each other. Tone defines the way in which bright areas through to dark areas in the subject are represented in the image. The level of "noise" or unwanted information, such as the grain of film or digital artefacts, determines its visibility in the image.

The most successful images are those in which all these elements line up. It occurs when perfect composition partners with precise focus and appropriate depth of field, accurate exposure, and appropriately rendered tones supported by clean, clear reproduction.

If one of these elements is seriously defective, or causes the composition to be unbalanced, the image could be ruined. Perhaps the single element that can do the most damage is exposure. It can wreck perfect composition and focusing, and distort the overall brightness and accuracy of tones. Similarly, every other element could be in perfect balance, but if the noise or grain is excessive, details may be obscured and subtlety in tonal values destroyed.

◀ **Perfect composition**
The bridge and its reflection in the canal are used to frame the image. This draws the eye into the centre of the scene.

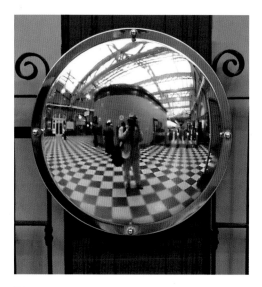

▲ **Sharp focus**
Accurate focusing was important for this image, making it sharp throughout.

This chapter contains simple techniques for improving your command of these basic elements. But if you try to remember every technique, you may lose the ability to take in your surroundings, or worse, suffer from shutter-finger paralysis. To help you, follow the "Three Ps" of Photography – Practise, Pre-visualize, and Project.

Practise using your camera and equipment regularly, as you would if you were learning a musical instrument or sport. Use the dials and controls until it becomes second nature. Learn which way to turn controls to set the options or modes you use most often.

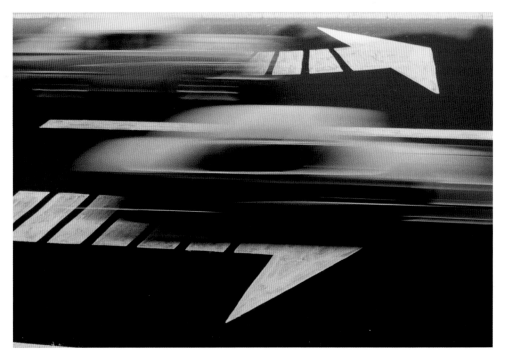

» Time exposure
An understanding of the photographic process will enable you to create images not available to any other visual art form. For this picture, Ernst Haas (*see pp.44–45*) set a long exposure that allows the moving cars to be "smeared" across the film, while static elements remain sharp.

Pre-visualize the result. Imagine the picture you want to make, such as a tonally rich landscape or a softly luminous portrait. Having a vision will help you coordinate your actions with your thoughts, which will help you master the photographic process.

Finally, choose a photographic project or idea to help shape the way you go about your photography. It could be as simple as showing off your garden, or exploring local history. Whatever your project, you will find it useful to have a target at which to direct your efforts.

⌄ Subtle tones
This image shows a good eye for colour and composition. The blues and greys complement each other and the tones are well balanced.

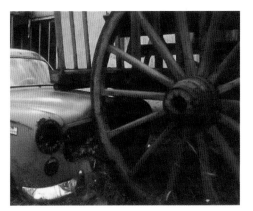

⌄ Visual tricks
It is fun to experiment with compositions – here Raghubir Singh (1942–99) creates an interesting image by framing through a car windscreen.

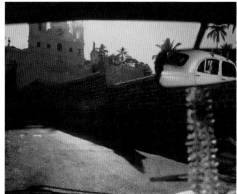

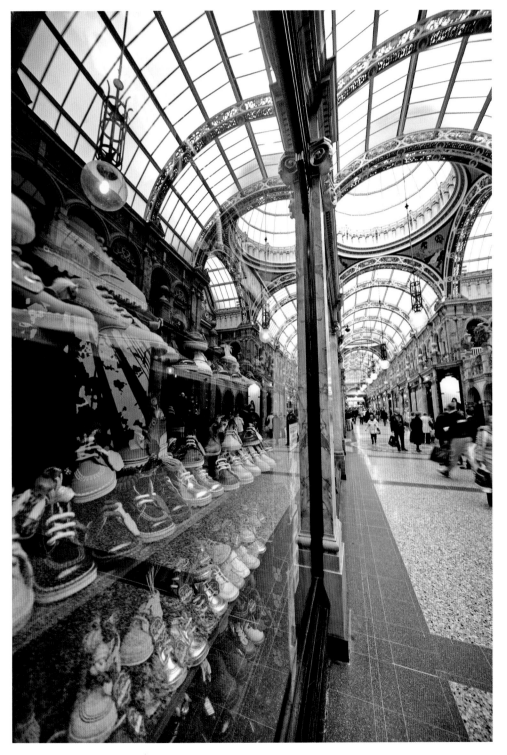

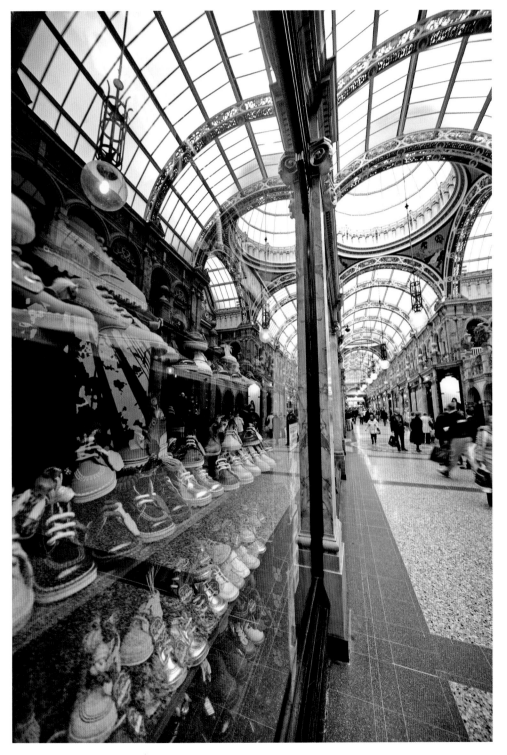 **Reflected view**
Photography
encourages
experimentation
with viewpoint
– this shopping
arcade is revealed
through a reflection.

The art of composition

It is easy to let worries about composition inhibit your photography rather than inform it. The problem is that the art of composition is often presented as a set of rules, which implies that unless you follow them your photographs are doomed to failure. The truth is, in fact, the opposite. Slavish adherence to rules will suppress your personal and creative response to what you see and experience.

Understanding structure

If you analyze the structure of a photograph or painting that you find appealing, you will discover that it will conform broadly to one of a number of basic, simple patterns. These organize the picture into static elements that have a stabilizing effect, and active elements that suggest movement or tension. A successful composition often arises from the interplay between the static and active elements in the picture. But there are no hard-and-fast rules that guarantee successful composition. It is best to be guided by your instincts.

Balancing the elements

Successful compositions organize the visual elements coherently. An effective compositional structure is the golden section or phi grid. In this, key elements lie on dividing lines, either horizontal, vertical, or both, in which the ratio of the larger section to the smaller section is the same as the ratio of the whole dimension to the larger section. This has been recognized to give harmonious, but off-centred arrangements, which are neither too static nor too energetic. The popular rule of thirds is a simplification of the golden section, but can lead to more rigid and formulaic structures.

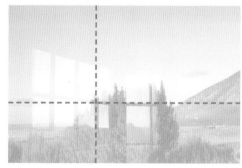

⌃ Golden section
This landscape made through a window reflecting other windows has its main lines lying on the golden section, both vertically and horizontally.

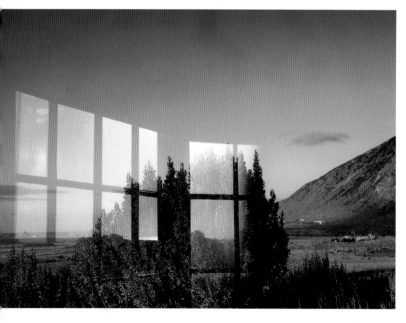

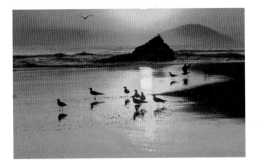

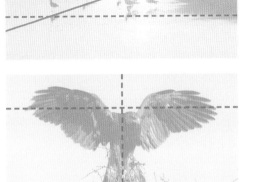

Diagonals
The diagonal line running from the lower left corner to the upper right forms the basic structure of this dawn image. Underlying the diagonal structure is a composition based on horizontal thirds.

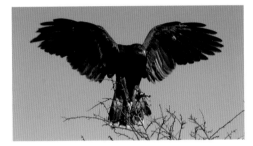

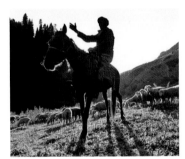

Symmetrical
A symmetrical subject such as this bird of prey provides a simple but effective image. Compositions such as this usually work better when the subject is centred in the frame so that the space around it offers a balanced dynamic.

HOW THE MASTERS WORK

Subtlety, depth, and visual surprise are the defining qualities of many great photographs, and the hallmarks of superb photographers such as Marc Riboud (1923–2016). The way in which a picture is composed is an important contributing factor to the success of an image and Riboud was one of the greatest masters of photojournalistic composition.

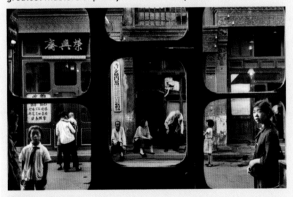

Marc Riboud
French photographer Marc Riboud framed what he found with matchless accuracy. You know, however, that nothing has been altered; everything has been quietly and patiently waited for. This image, titled *Window* (1965), was taken from inside an antique dealer's shop in Beijing. It is breathtakingly simple in composition, taking the regular grid of the window as its structure. Yet it remains peerless in the rightness of its timing, with its precise capture of every element perfectly positioned. Even the empty spaces feel alive.

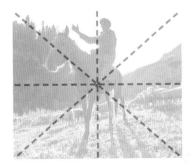

Radial
This shot of a friendly Kyrgyz shepherd posing against the setting sun offers an excellent example of a radial composition. All the lines in the picture – of the hillside, tree-line, ground, and shadows – neatly converge on a single point, giving the photograph structure and movement at the same time.

Composition in practice

Henri Cartier-Bresson (*see pp.38–39*) prescribed a demanding regime, saying that "Composition should be a constant preoccupation, being a simultaneous coalition – an organic coordination of visual elements." By allowing pictorial composition to be a "constant preoccupation", you will soon discover that it becomes an integral part of your visual experience. Then, you can make the transition from taking snapshots to capturing great photographs.

Analyzing a composition

After a little practice, good composition will become second nature. While travelling on the road to Essaouira, in Morocco, my eye was drawn to a stray dog. It disappeared for a while but when it emerged on the roof of a shop, it became clear that there was a picture in the making. Just as I was framing up the photograph, a boy on a donkey came round the corner and it was obvious that a better picture was going to walk into the frame. The exposure was already correct so it was then just a case of ensuring the image was in focus and judging just the right moment to release the shutter.

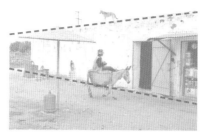

⌃ Diagonal lines
The diagonal line is a popular compositional device, and is often considered more dynamic than horizontal or vertical lines. Here the converging pair of diagonals lead the eye across the picture.

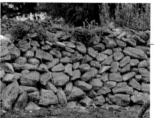

» Distant subjects
Features that are visible but not the main focus of the image, such as this wall, help to define space and distance. They form what is known as the active padding of a composition.

Empty space can help to hold the main subject, like the earth and walls in this image.

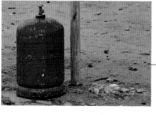

» Colour contrast
The red gas cyclinder provides a strong colour contrast with the blue door. This works well because it is balanced by the muted red earth colours.

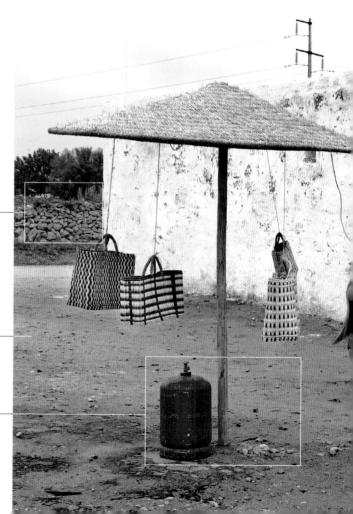

⟫ COMPOSITION AS ARTICULATION

On his approach to composition, Don McCullin (*see p.55*) tells us "I try to compose my pictures – even in the moment of battle and the moment of crisis – not so much in an artistic way, but to make them seem right, to make them come across structurally." It is the "coming across" that is important. Pictures, like words, are all about communication. In much the same way, they can be composed, or articulated, either well or badly. It is worth taking the time to make sure the image in your viewfinder is composed well. As with language, it is enough at first simply to be clear. With practice, you can aim for the poetic.

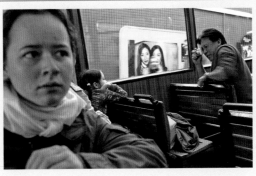

◀◀ Drawing the eye
While the central action in this shot taken on a tram in Hong Kong is the father taking a picture of his daughter, the near figure demands attention, especially her hand. The poster in the window then draws the eye. Although one's eye is pulled in many directions, the strong lines and repetitive shapes of the tram's interior hold all the elements together.

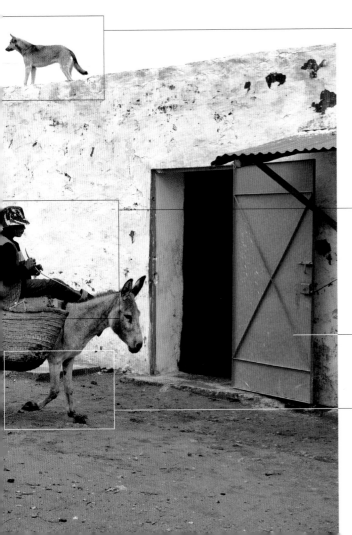

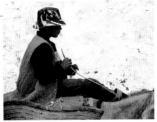

⌃ Counter-subject
The dog enlivens an otherwise empty sky. He was the original focus of the picture, but the arrival of the donkey turned him into the counter-subject – one that balances the main subject.

◀◀ Clear shapes
The profiles of rider and donkey are cleanly presented, without distractions. A shot that was taken one-third of a second later, with the donkey's face in the door frame, was clearly inferior.

Three strong rectangles here create a composition within a composition.

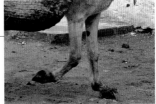

◀◀ Timing
Even the most tranquil composition can depend on perfect timing. Here, the position of the donkey's foot gives the viewer a sense of a leisurely pace of life.

Experimenting with viewpoints

The image you see through the lens is not just affected by your position, where you look, and your choice of focal length. These factors all play their part, but viewpoint is also about your outlook, your frame of mind at that time, and what your eye picks out from the scene in front of you. Vision and understanding – and sometimes a little luck – will guide your eye as well as your feet. Keep your wits about you, be attentive, and keep looking.

Using your feet

What you see depends on where you are located. This may seem obvious, yet it is often forgotten. While some photographers rely on lenses with "perspective control" features, many more mistakenly believe that altering zoom settings changes the perspective of a scene. As Ernst Haas (*see p.44*) put it, "the best zoom lens is your feet", advocating changing position to improve the composition of a photograph, in preference to simply changing the zoom setting.

Exploring perspectives

There is a historical reason why the perspective in most photographs is at eye level. Early cameras were so large and unwieldy, with exposure times so long, that they had to be fixed onto a stand (later a tripod). It was only with the introduction of what were then called "ultra-miniature" cameras such as the Leica, and compact roll-film cameras such as the Rolleiflex (which did not require the use of a stand) that photographers began to fully explore perspectives deviating from the standard position. The first master of the "unconventional" perspective was Alexandr Rodchenko (*see p.61*), although his work had perhaps its most immediate effect not on photographers, but on cinematographers such as Sergei Eisenstein.

These days, with ultra-compact cameras – not to mention high-quality mobile phone cameras – there is no reason for remaining stationary while you photograph. In addition, modern digital cameras with swivelling LCD screens give even greater freedom. Even at arm's length it is easy to monitor the framing of the shot. With these technological advances, there are no excuses for not fully exploring perspective.

☑ Shadows
The obvious framing here would be of the tree, with the sun behind it. Instead this view engages with the tree's shadows, which contrast with the road markings and texture of tarmac, creating an intriguing perspective on an obvious subject.

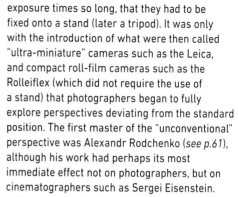

☑ Reflections
Perspective is given another dimension by reflections, because you view not only the scene that is reflected, but also the reflective surface. Here, the red car body helps to frame the photograph.

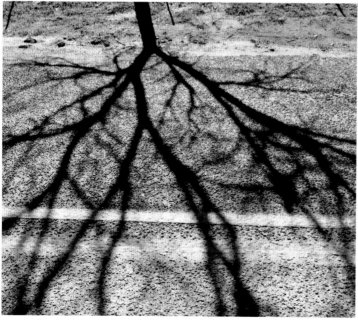

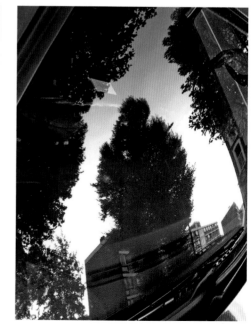

》 HOW THE MASTERS WORKED

One of India's greatest photographers, Raghubir Singh (1942–99) was a guru of photographic composition. Like his fellow countryman, Raghu Rai (see pp.58–59), he concentrated his work on India, publishing numerous celebrated collections of picture essays. One of his best-known projects was based on the simple idea of photographing his country from an Ambassador, a car that is ubiquitous in India. He used all his photographic skill to fully exploit the possibilities offered by the curves of his car, and the changes in shape obtained, for example, by opening the door to different extents. Using the doors, windows, and mirrors of the car as framing devices, Singh delivered a virtuoso exercise in unconventional viewpoints and photographic framing. A testament to his love of India, this project was, sadly, to be his last major work before he died.

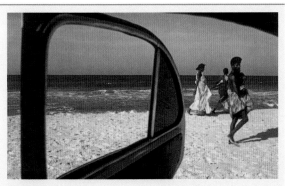

⌃ Raghubir Singh
A Way into India, taken in Rameshwaram, Tamil Nadu, is essentially a straightforward beach scene, which anyone could have photographed. It is, however, transformed into a formalist play of line, colour, and shape by the imaginative step of taking the picture from within the car.

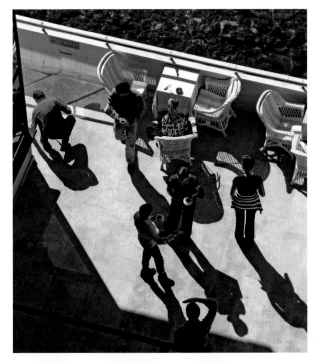

⟪ Overhead perspective
This viewpoint disorientates by changing familiar objects into more abstract shapes, with the effect of making the ordinary extraordinary. At coffee-cup level, this scene would be prosaic. However, viewed from above, it turns into a ballet of shadows, which perform parallel to, yet somehow independent of, the movements of the people.

⌄ Keep shooting
In a complex scene made up of moving elements, you cannot always capture the image perfectly first time. Do what the professionals do: keep waiting, keep looking, and keep shooting.

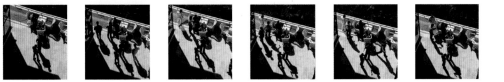

Taveuni, Fiji
The usual view of this scene would take in the whole of the girl, but the best picture was really at her feet, with the texture of the rocks and the contrast between the yellow leaf and blue water.

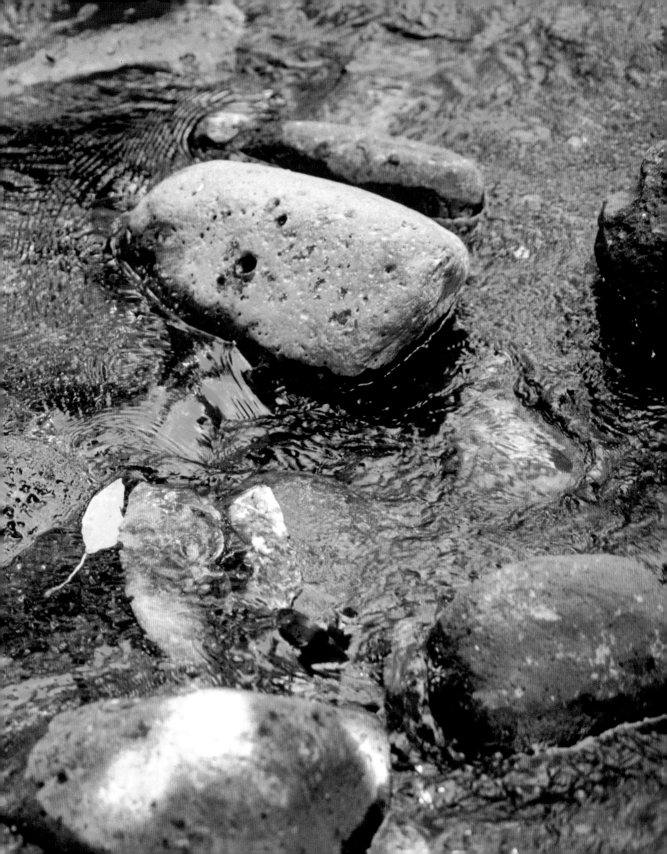

Using colour

"Colour is joy... One does not think joy. One is carried by it", taught Ernst Haas (*see p.44*). As such, colour is integral to the way we experience a subject. It directly evokes the mood and atmosphere of a scene, and dramatically affects our emotional responses to it. Vibrant, brilliant colours can create drama and excitement; while muted pastel shades are more likely to instil a sense of peace and calm. Success in colour photography is a matter of personal taste that calls on sensitivity and intuition.

##》 HOW THE MASTERS WORK

A poet among nature photographers, US-based Jim Brandenburg has done more than anyone to help give us an understanding and appreciation of the wolf. He has spent countless days in freezing conditions photographing these enigmatic animals. Using ultra-wide-angle lenses and the longest of telephoto lenses, Brandenburg eschews elaborate apparatus and allows nature's beauty to reach out through the medium of his work.

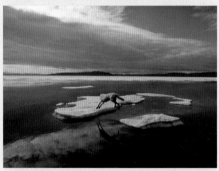

⌃ Jim Brandenburg
In *White Wolf*, the multiple symmetries of reflections and the strong diagonal line of the cloud formation superbly frame the leap of the white wolf, which is placed almost exactly in the centre of the picture. Here, Brandenburg skilfully weaves together the few colours of this austere Arctic landscape by relying on tonal differences to shape the image.

Colour and photography

Three independent factors come into play with colour photography. The first is the true colour, or hue, of the subject. Next is the illuminating light, which may contribute its own tint. Finally, there is the viewer, who either perceives the colour (if a human), or records the colour (if a sensory device). The result is that the colour we capture in a photograph may not be the same as the subject's colours, and what we see with our eyes may be different again.

Knowing your materials

Whatever kind of recording surface you use – colour film, instant print, or photo-sensor – the way it reproduces colour depends on the individual technical properties of the capture surface. The final product involves compromises between what is technically feasible, what is affordable, and what is acceptable.

If you recognize both the good and the bad points of the tools of your trade, you can learn how best to use their strengths and avoid their weaknesses. For example, in the days of film usage, photographers tried to match what they photographed with the character of the film they used. Films producing strong reds were good for autumn colours but not for a garden in springtime.

In the digital era, specific differences between sensors are not so apparent, and are generally evened out by image manipulation applications. Nonetheless, it is worth keeping in mind that in digital images highlights may appear blank, and mid-tones do not offer the richness that film can render, while shadows may be marred by noise and poor detail.

Balancing colours

The colour wheel is a common way to represent the relationships between different colours. Colours that offer the greatest visual contrast are located opposite each other on the wheel, while colours perceived to be more similar are closer together. However, it is not a wholly accurate model of colour perception, as it gives equal weight to colours that may not be seen in the same way. Blues, for example, would usually appear much darker and stronger than yellows.

The most harmonious, and often the most effective, colour schemes use colours adjacent to each other on the wheel, thus using a limited range of colours. Desert landscapes are effective because of the serene blend of sandy, yellow, and rusty colours. Strong contrasts such as blues against reds or purples against greens are less pleasing because there can be too many distractions for the eye to find a focal point. When photographing contrasting colours, ensure the image is not too busy. Aim instead for a graphic shot – a detail of some flowers, for example, rather than an entire flower bed.

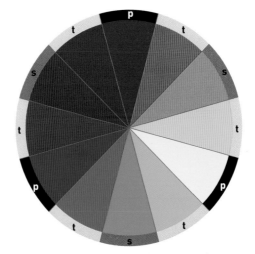

p = primary   s = secondary   t = tertiary

≪ The colour wheel
The wheel diagram is probably the earliest model of colour perception – its precursors appeared in China in the 6th century – and it is certainly the most intuitive. It is the basis for all subsequent colour models.

≫ Adjacent colours
In this snapshot of friends chatting, the emotional warmth of the scene is matched by the warm, earthy tones that dominate the colour palette, accented by the red New Mexican chillies. There is just enough contrast from the blue jeans and purple top to balance the picture

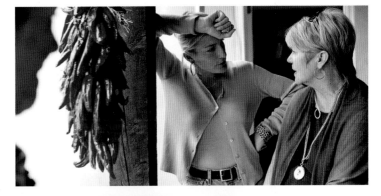

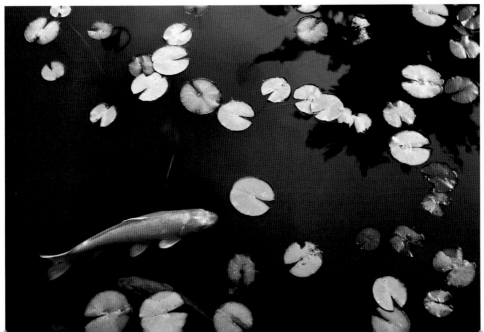

≪ Contrasting colours
The contrasts, not only of colour, but also of shape and distribution, as well as the reflections on the water's surface could make this seem an unpromising subject. However, increasing the contrast and deepening colour saturation can help to bring out out all the elements, which are offset against a neutral background.

Working with colours

The basic discrimination in colours is that of hue, which is the name we associate with a particular range of wavelengths of light, such as magenta, purple, and so on. Within a hue, there are different shades. For example, the same red can be described as light, brownish, or deep. This is a result of variations in qualities such as colour richness or saturation. In photography and printing the range of colours that can be recorded is greatly restricted. A key skill when working with colour is to look at the scene with the photographic process in mind, so that you can visualize how it will render the colours you see.

Exposing for colour

The myriad colours and broad range of scene luminance deliver a dazzlingly rich array of colours in this shot, taken from a herb shop in Marrakech, Morocco. The main problem is that the only colours in the image that will be reproduced accurately (where the brightness of the recorded image directly relates or is proportional to the brightness of the scene as you see it) are those that fall within the exposure latitude of the film or sensor.

» Out of gamut
Colours that can be seen but that do not print accurately, such as deep purples and blues, are said to be 'out of gamut' for the printer's colour space.

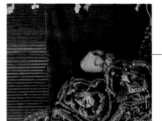

Areas in the full sun are overexposed and drained of nearly all colour.

» Skin tones
In general, it is best to set skin tones to the mid-point. In this image, skin tones were a shade over-exposed in an attempt to get enough exposure to show some detail inside the shop.

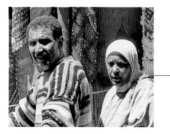

☑ Mid-tone colours
Colours that fall in the middle of the brightness range are likely to be the most accurately recorded, as well as being the most saturated.

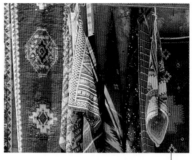

Underexposed areas may create silhouettes whose dark colours help to frame active areas.

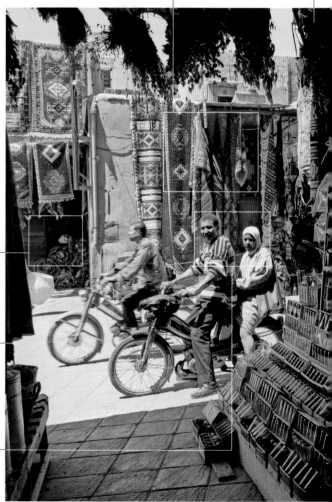

⟩⟩ DESCRIBING COLOUR DIGITALLY

Before digital photography, colour was described in terms of hue, saturation, and brightness. Now, colours are usually separated into sets, for example, red, green, and blue, and then defined by measuring the proportions of each. In digital photography, colours are defined by the separation primaries of red, green, and blue. These "pure" colours are good for describing sources that emit colour, with 0 representing the weakest colour, and 255 the strongest. So, pure blue would be notated as 0:0:255 (zero red and green, maximum blue). When printing images, it is common to employ the set of three subtractive primaries: cyan (blue-green), magenta (blue-red), and yellow, plus black.

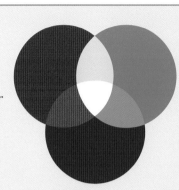

《 Primary colour mixing
Colour perception is based on mixing light of red, green, and blue in different strengths to give the entire visual spectrum, from pure colours to white and, in the absence of any light, black.

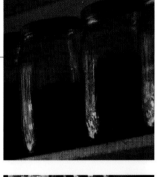

《 Dark colours
In shadow areas containing detail, there is little colour discrimination, only hints of the hue, but that is all that is needed to provide structure and some visual interest.

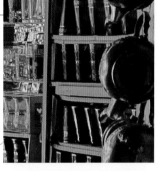

《 Contrasting colours
Where the scene presents us with lively lighting contrasts and colours in small areas, colour accuracy becomes less important. With digital photography, colour accuracy will be compromised by the difficulties in extracting accurate data from tiny areas.

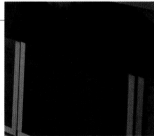

《 Maximum darkness
In very dark areas, no colour is recorded, although it may be visible to the eye. This means that trying to make the area lighter digitally will only produce greys.

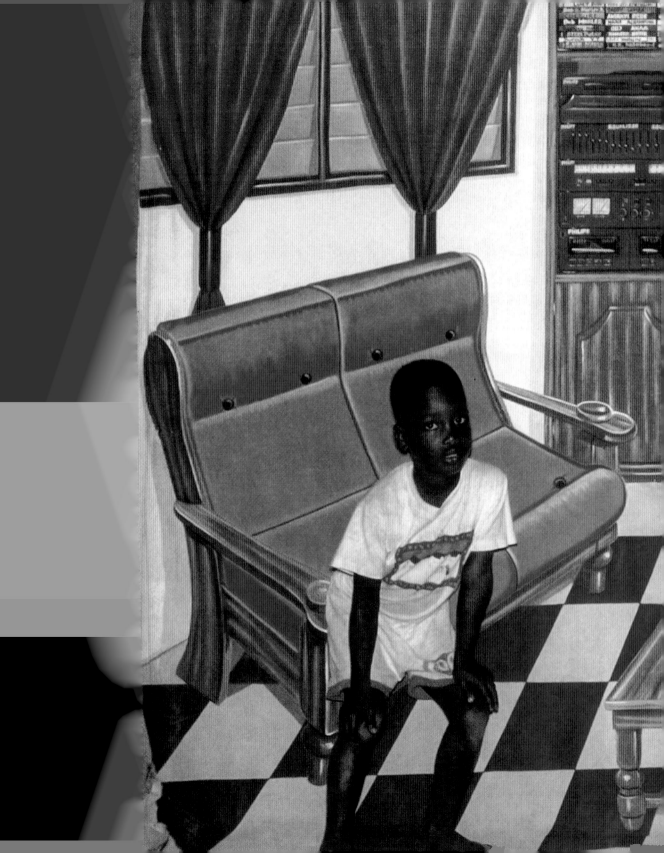

Portrait, 1996
Philip Kwame Apagya was born
in Ghana in 1958. His portrait
series, made in front of specially
painted backgrounds including
the image above, has become
immensely popular.

Working in black and white

Black and white is photography's basic way of recording an image, both on film and digitally. In digital photography, images are usually captured complete with colour information. You can discard this to achieve black and white – a map showing only the brightness distribution of the subject. Composition then becomes paramount as an exploration of tonal differences and spatial relationships.

>> **Shadowed landscape**
A colour image of this ruin would be dominated by the green grass and blue skies, but the greyscale image accentuates the shadow.

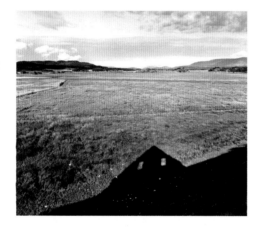

The power of black and white

One advantage of black-and-white film, is that it is much cheaper to run than colour. Another advantage is that black-and-white film will tolerate more exposure and developing error than colour. Furthermore, black-and-white prints – digital or otherwise – are longer-lasting than colour ones.

The chief attraction of black and white is, however, its aesthetic quality. Some photographers choose to work exclusively in this space because they value its abstract qualities and its ability to erase the distractions of colour. Also, in a world dominated by colour imagery, black-and-white pictures often stand out.

>> **Misty morning**
This woodland scene was full of pale greens and browns, but in black and white the quality of light becomes the main focus.

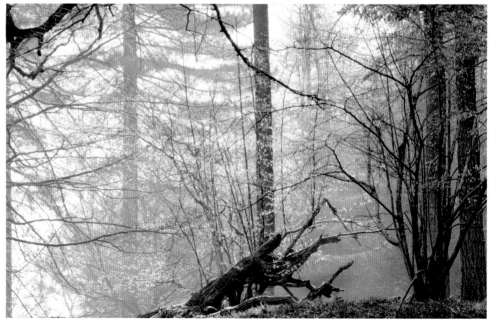

Brightness

A key term in black-and-white photography is "greyscale". This is the range of tones or "ramp" that climbs from black through mid-tones to white. The gradient of the ramp indicates the tonal quality. Rapid change from black to white makes a contrasty image. A more gentle ramp offers gradual tonal changes.

Monochrome

The terms "black-and-white" and "monochrome" are often used interchangeably. Taken literally, "monochrome" is a single colour, such as the tint taken by toned prints. The term also references the fact that when capturing colour images, you are reducing many colours to a single range. This is an important technicality, for what we see as different colours may be turned into identical brightness values. Red roses and their green leaves, for example, can become the same dark grey. For how to convert colour, see p.168.

Black-and-white film

The most common black-and-white film is the panchromatic type *(see p.137)*, which is sensitive to all visible wavelengths of light. However, black-and-white films are usually less sensitive to greens than blues, and more sensitive to blues than reds. That is why verdant landscapes may come out dark, and why deep blue skies may turn out brighter than expected. The grain of black-and-white film is a great attraction for some.

» CONTRAST IN BLACK AND WHITE

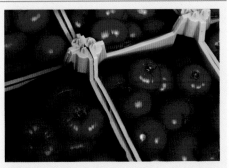

⌃ **Fruit box**
In a farmer's market display, boxes for tomatoes are specifically coloured green to contrast with the brilliant reds. A little violet lining paper complements the dominant colours.

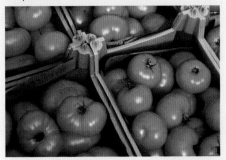

⌃ **Loss of contrast**
In black and white, the boxes of tomatoes are almost unrecognisable. Worse, the formerly strong contrast between red and green is eliminated by becoming identical greys.

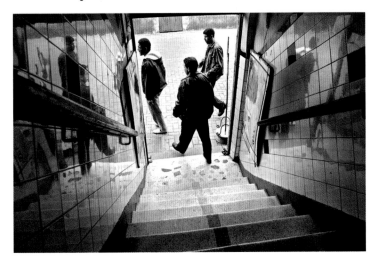

《 **Composition in black and white**
If the composition of a photograph is simple, as in this contrasty image of a restaurant entrance in Morocco, colour can be irrelevant at best, and a distraction at worst.

Digital toning

A partial solution to the lack of colour in the early years of photography was to tone a black-and-white print to give it an overall hue. The most popular colour in the late 19th century was a dark reddish-brown, known as sepia. Sepia toning lays claim to being the longest-lived photographic process. Even today a number of digital cameras offer a "sepia" mode.

Changing colour data

Traditional toning involves bleaching the image silver so that it becomes clear or pale, at which point it is chemically active and can be replaced by other metals or compounds that are coloured. This principle – bleach then colour – is also a key step in colour photography.

With digital photography, it is easier than ever to tone prints. One digital technique is to desaturate all colours. This reduces the strength of the colours, turning the image grey. Then, using the Colour Balance control (*see p.278*), you can add an overall coloured tone to the image by adjusting the colour levels. Another digital method is to use the Duotone mode, which is available in more advanced software.

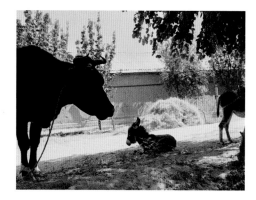

⏶ **Basic black-and-white image**
This pastoral scene in Samarkand, Uzbekistan, was photographed on black-and-white film and then scanned.

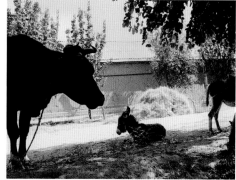

⏶ **Sepia image**
Many image manipulation applications offer a quick way of adding sepia tone to the image. Here it has been done using Photoshop.

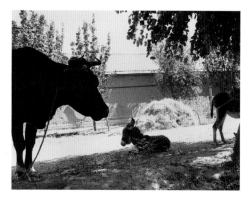

⏶ **Blue duotone image**
By printing the image using black and blue ink, the image is tinted overall in blue. Using software, you can control the relative weights of ink so that one is more intense in the shadows, while the other is heavier in the highlights.

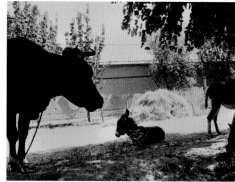

⏶ **Tritone image**
The tritone printing process uses three inks. Here, a blue ink was liberally applied to the highlights, tinting them heavily. A yellow ink was applied to the shadows, warming them. Black was added to provide weight to the tones.

Controlling greys

A colour image can be digitally converted to black and white in a number of ways. Desaturation mimics the principles of black-and-white film, whereby colours are treated equally and their brightness is translated directly into grey tones. With this method, a green, red, or bright blue might all translate into exactly the same grey tone. A more controlled method is to use the Channel Mixer found in advanced image manipulation software (*see p.272–273*), which creates a greyscale image by mimicking the effect of coloured filters. This is achieved by forcing one colour to be brighter than another. In this way, blue skies can be made to come out nearly black (imitating the effect of a red filter used with black-and-white film) or greens can be made to appear brighter than usual (which is what a yellow-green filter does for film).

Digital black and white

Producing digital images in black and white is not the contradiction it may seem and there are certain advantages in saving an image as a greyscale. First, a black-and-white or greyscale image is one-third of the file size of an equivalent colour image. This inevitably saves on memory card space and speeds up operations on a digital camera. It makes sense then, to capture in mono from the outset if you need only black-and-white images, for a newsletter, for example. Also, printing greyscale images gives generally much better quality than printing in colour.

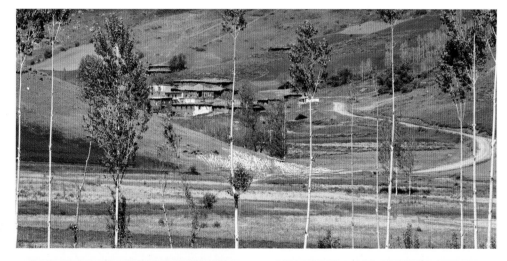

≪ Original image
This graceful landscape in northeastern Turkey is full of rich pastoral colours. The strong lines of the trees and the road suggest that it would work well in black and white.

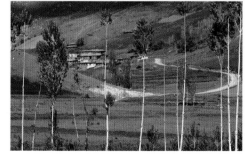

⌃ Simple black-and-white conversion
A simple desaturation of the colours to neutralize their colour values produces a very grey image. A conversion to greyscale preserves more differences in brightness but still results in a relatively flat image.

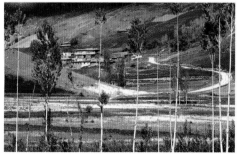

⌃ Channel mixer conversion
Using the channel mixer, the red was strongly boosted, and extra green added but the blue was reduced. The result is a very sharply contrasted landscape whose greyscale values closely mimic the original colour image.

Kashgar, Xinjiang, China
A black-and-white rendering helps the organization of this busy street scene into compositional elements described wholly in greyscale tones.

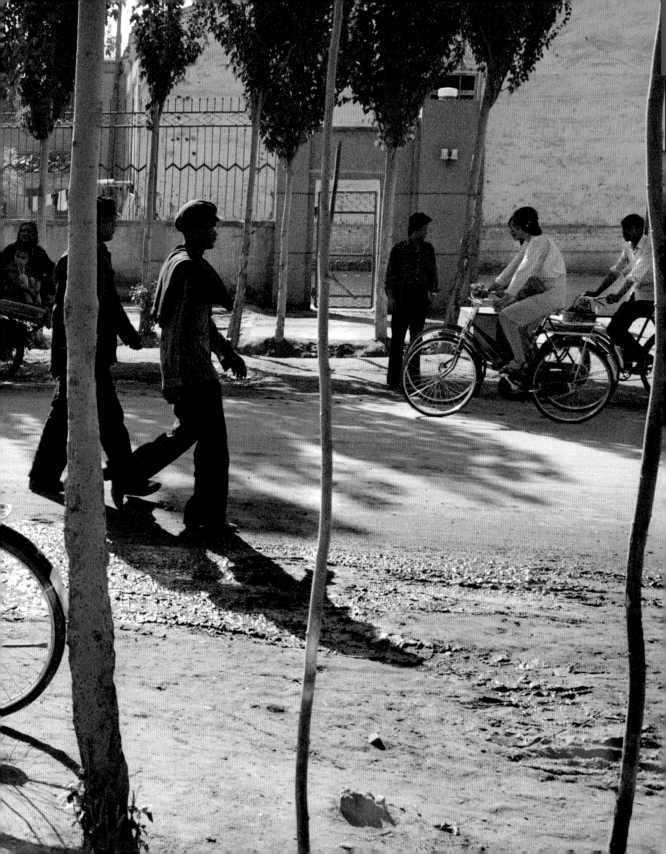

Working with light

"Wherever there is light, one can photograph", declared Alfred Stieglitz (*see p.63*). To which Ernst Haas (*see pp.44–45*) later added "All light is good light." Taken together, these two statements show that any light situation can be exploited for the purpose of making a photograph. Thanks to the high sensitivity of modern sensors, you can even photograph in dim moonlight. You are free, then, to exploit any available light to articulate your feeling for the subject, and give your image its emotional skin.

Extreme lighting
This atmospheric shot of the Sacre Coeur, Paris, was exposed for the portions of the scene lit directly by the sun, allowing the unlit spaces to remain dark.

Types of light
The issue is not what kind of light is good for photography – we know images can be captured in all kinds of lighting. However, some conditions are easier to handle than others. Lighting with a wide range between the darkest parts and brightest parts – "contrasty" lighting – can be tricky to expose accurately. But, while flat lighting – where the brighter parts are at similar luminance to the darker parts – is easier to expose accurately, it can make it more challenging to find effective compositions.

Contrasty light
When photographing an image that has strong contrasts between light and dark, it is easiest to ensure that the visually important parts of the image are correctly exposed. One effective strategy is to expose for the highlights: this creates richly coloured mid-tones and forces shadows to be very dark. If shadow information is needed, it is best to expose to just reveal a little shadow detail, then post-process the image to show up the highlights.

Brilliant light
Sunny days often inspire us to reach for our cameras, but the results often disappoint. Bright areas look washed out, while shadows appear too dark. This is because the range of luminance in the scene is too wide for a photographic sensor to cope with. In these situations capturing in raw format will help.

Flat light

On dull, flatly lit days, the cloud cover interposes between the sun and the subject, acting as a giant diffuser, so that the entire sky becomes the light source. Without the play of shadows, this may appear uninspiring, but it is in fact a gift to photographers. Its narrow luminance range reduces exposure problems, and improves the variety and subtlety of colours. Flat light generates a broad range of mid-tones, illuminating the scene without becoming part of the subject. This allows greater control over composition as there is no need to dance around to avoid shadows or bright patches.

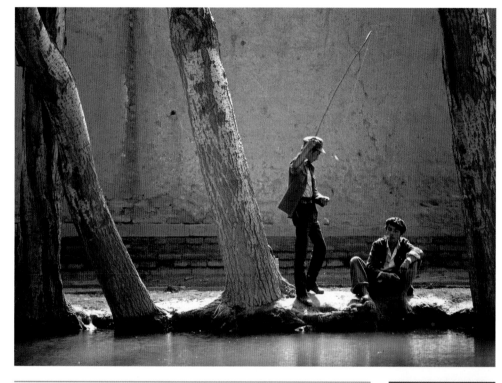

Low contrast
Outside, in flat lighting conditions, the entire sky illuminates the scene. As a result, contrast is soft and shadows are almost eliminated. Here, in Kashgar, China, the flat, soft lighting has erased nearly all moulding of forms and textures, so the image must rely on structure and composition for visual interest.

» HOW THE MASTERS WORK

The signature work of Alex Webb (1952–) glories in the extreme light contrasts of the tropical regions, which many photographers struggle to work with. By pitching his exposure at the highlights, Webb saturates the colours of people and objects in full light. This sends the unlit areas into the highest density, with barely any details. Webb's skill is in composing with the near-silhouettes of whatever lies in shadow.

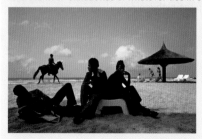

Alex Webb
Capturing a successful colour image of a tropical beach in full sun with dark-skinned subjects may seem a photographic impossibility. In *Ivory Coast* Webb shows how, if you work with what you have, you can create arresting images with rich gestures of light, colour, and form.

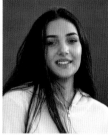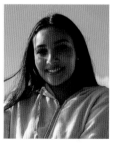

Soft and hard lighting
Soft lighting effects (*left*) are kind to skin textures: light comes from many angles, reducing the depth of shadows. With high-contrast lighting (*right*), light shines from one angle, so lit areas appear harshly bright while shadows remain dark – not so kind to faces.

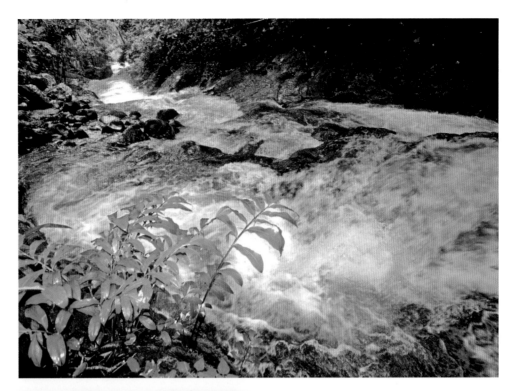

Lighting dark areas
Using too much flash here, in the poorly lit undergrowth of the Fijian rainforest, would have spoilt the photograph's dark, dank mood. Instead, a single beam of light aimed at the fern in the foreground lifts the image, without making it look unnatural.

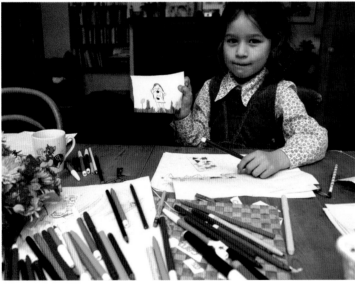

Balanced flash
Flash used indoors often results in bleached-out faces against a dark background. In this shot, colour and detail are retained by setting a wide aperture to capture maximum ambient light, while the flash adds to the available light.

Adding light

Substantial advances in photography were made when artificial lighting systems became readily available. There are three options for artificial lighting. A flash built into a camera is the most portable and convenient, but gives unsatisfactory results. A flash attached to, but held away from, the camera combines practicality with greatly improved results. Portable lighting units, producing either a flash or continuous light, give the utmost quality and control but the drawback here is cost and inconvenience.

Electronic flash

A built-in on-camera flash is a small light source. As they are necessarily placed very near the lens, they produce unflattering flat light that cannot sculpt the form of the subject. If the flash is mounted higher on the camera, or held out to one side, it can illuminate the form of a subject more clearly. However, the best approach is to add a diffuser to a flash unit: this softens the lighting and improves results even further.

≫ HOW THE MASTERS WORKED

Born in Albania and trained in the USA, Gjon Mili (1904–84) graduated from the Massachusetts Institute of Technology in 1927. Mili saw the artistic potential in the work of his classmate Harold Edgerton (*see p.97*) who invented the stroboscope, a device that gave out brief flashes of light rapidly repeated at short, regular intervals. Mili's brilliant innovation was to use the stroboscope to dissect the movements of a rapidly moving subject. With this, a golfer's swing or the rotation of helicopter blades could be examined at leisure and in detail.

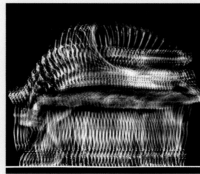

◄ Gjon Mili
This celebrated picture of the ballerina Alicia Alonso performing a *pas de bourrée couru* (a gliding, running movement on pointes made with many small steps) is typical of Mili's work, combining physical grace, artistic vision, and scientific analysis into a seamless whole.

Fill-in flash

Paradoxically, flash is very useful where ambient light is too bright. Used in this way, the flash adds supplementary light to the camera exposure that captures the overall scene. This light works on the shadows to bring out a little detail. You do not need to illuminate the shadow fully, only to prevent it from being black. This technique works well for taking shots at sunset or dawn when the foreground is often completely dark.

Red-eye

When the pupils of the subject's eyes are wide open and the flash is positioned close to, and pointing directly into, the eyes, red-eye is likely to occur. The flash lights the retina, which shows as a spot of red in the eye. The effect is especially marked in low light (when a subject's pupils are at their most dilated). The best way to avoid this

problem is to locate the flash well away from the camera. Another method is to fire small flashes close to the subject's pupils just before the main exposure, but this delays exposure so you may miss the moment. Image manipulation software is also very effective for removing red-eye.

Interior lighting

Portable lighting units, such as focusable Dedo lights, lamps, light stands, and light shapers (for example, barn doors), can be used to illuminate shots of interiors. They are invaluable for bringing light into dark corners and for balancing light and shade to produce the best effect.

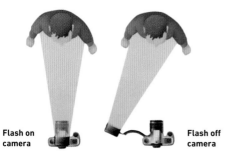

Flash on camera   **Flash off camera**

⌃ Distance of the flash
The further the flash is positioned from the lens, the less the risk of red-eye. Using an off-camera flash, held as little as 15cm (6in) away, will usually solve the problem.

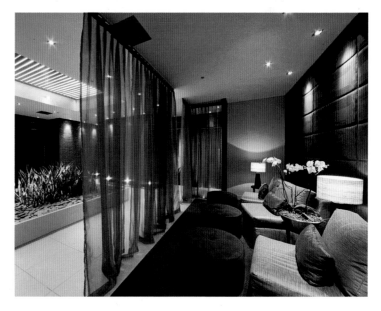

☑ Lifting Shadows
Three Dedo lights were used to supplement the existing light in this modern spa reception area.

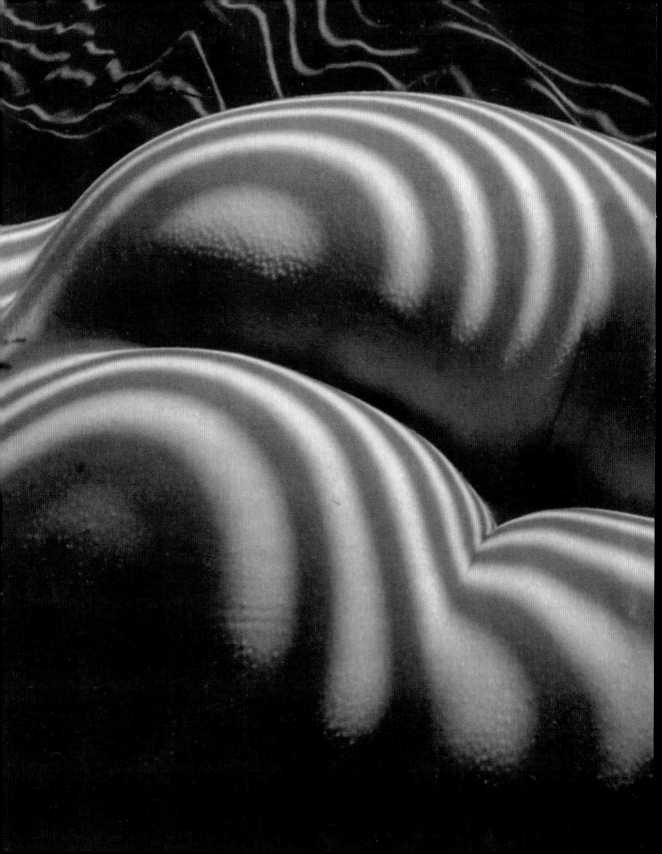

Blinds
Lucien Clergue, born in Arles, France in 1934, is the most celebrated of all photographers of the nude. This image is from a series that projected shadows on to the nude body.

Controlling exposure

Exposure control is one of the foundations of image quality. Setting the correct exposure can make or break an image. There is, however, no single rule that guarantees the correct exposure in all circumstances. Different situations require different approaches. Technical factors such as light levels and sensor sensitivity speed are part of the equation, but setting the right exposure depends above all on what you want your image to say.

Correct exposure

A working definition of correct exposure is: "the level of exposure giving you the desired result". In practice, this is usually the same as an average exposure that places the mid-tones in your subject (for example, grass) in the mid-greys of your image. Mid-grey is the tone that lies midway between deep darkness with a little detail and full brightness with some detail.

» Exposure for highlights and shadows
With strong lighting on the model, an exposure for the highlights (*right*) throws the unlit areas into shadow. Exposing for the unlit part of the face (*left*) gives a more natural result.

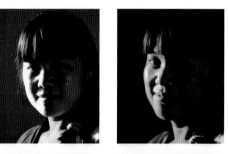

Setting the mid-tones

If you need to reveal detail in highlights or brighter areas, set the mid-tones lower than mid-grey. This gives a darker image overall with a loss of fine detail in the shadows. Conversely, if you wish to release more detail in the shadows, you will overexpose by setting the mid-tones lighter than mid-grey. This will give a brighter image in which fine detail in the highlights may be lost or hard to recover.

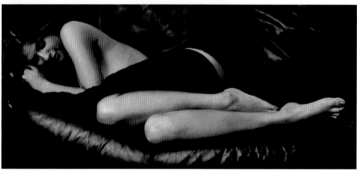

« Low-key exposure
As this image is essentially all about hints of exposed body, an underexposure of two stops brings out the sensuous lines of the model.

Exaggerated exposure

The technique of setting a non-standard exposure can be used creatively to vary the emphasis on colours or the composition of the scene. Try experimenting with strong underexposure and low light to produce low-key images for sombre or moody effects. Low-key results are overall very dark, with no tones lighter than mid-tone and colours, if present, will appear dark and rich.

Alternatively, try giving generous exposure to produce high-key results that appear bright and full of light. In a high-key image no tone is darker than mid-grey and colours, if present, appear light and translucent.

Bracketing exposure

A good technique for learning how exposure works is to make a series of different exposures of the same scene. This is bracketing: in addition to the camera-metered shot, make one with less and another with more exposure. Make a series of five images with extra overexposure and underexposure with each step. For learning purposes it is best to vary each image by one stop or more. When you review the results – best done on a desktop monitor – you will find that the camera's choice is not always the best. In contrasty light, the underexposed image may look more dramatic. In soft lighting, or with pale-toned subjects, the correct or overexposed image may be better.

》 HOW EXPOSURE WORKS

Camera exposure depends on the shutter setting (the duration of exposure) and the lens aperture setting (which controls the amount of light let in). Just as you can open a tap a little to fill a cup slowly (small aperture, long exposure), or open it fully to fill it quickly (large aperture, short exposure), a change in aperture matched by a balancing change in shutter time will give the same exposure i.e. if you increase one factor, you will need to reduce the other.

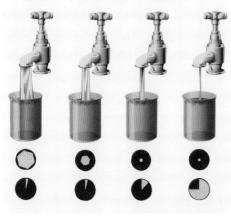

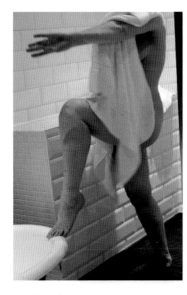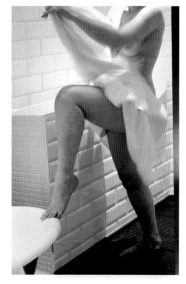

⌃ Adjusting exposure
A shot made using automatic settings (*above left*) is too dark. The whites appear murky and grey, so the skin tones look muddy. The yellow cast, typical of tungsten lighting, also reduces brilliance. Increased exposure (*above right*) gives a livelier result. The whites are white and the skin tones glow. The colour balance was also adjusted using image manipulation software (*see p.278*) to make the whites almost neutral without losing warmth.

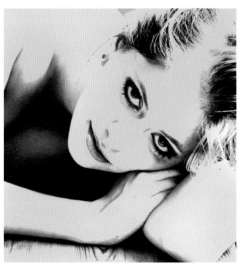

⌞ High-key exposure
With a forced overexposure of four extra stops, this portrait is given a modern, bright look and the colours in the shadows are revealed.

Exposure measurement

Modern automatic exposure metering systems analyze the scene against stored scenarios to work out the shutter setting and aperture to use. These "intelligent" or "evaluative" systems get it right most of the time. A good way to use them is to fine-tune the reading using the camera's exposure override controls to match your photographic vision.

Shooting against the sun

For this family portrait, a shot facing the sun gave the best background. However, the *contre jour* or "against the light" situation can confuse metering systems. The bright background makes the camera think there's a lot of light, so it sets a lower exposure. But that would make the faces too dark. The easiest method is to use the override control – which increases or decreases the camera's exposure – to increase the exposure by around 1.5 stops. A more precise method is to locate the important mid-tone e.g. the man's face, then aim the camera's central metering area at that. Hold or lock that reading by pressing the exposure lock button, then use it as the exposure setting for the whole scene.

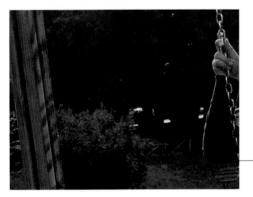

⌃ **Shadows with detail**
Important areas of colour should retain an indication of their hue. If not, the overall image will look too dark even if the exposure is technically correct. In difficult cases, you may have to introduce additional lighting or add colour with image manipulation software (*see pp.272–273*).

☒ **Burnt-out highlights**
The sky next to the sun will always be virtually white, no matter what the exposure setting.

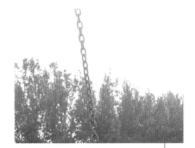

☒ **Veiling flare**
In this part of the image, the woman's face looks too light because of veiling flare – unwanted light on the image that is caused by internal reflections within the lens that reach the sensor as non-image-forming light.

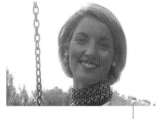

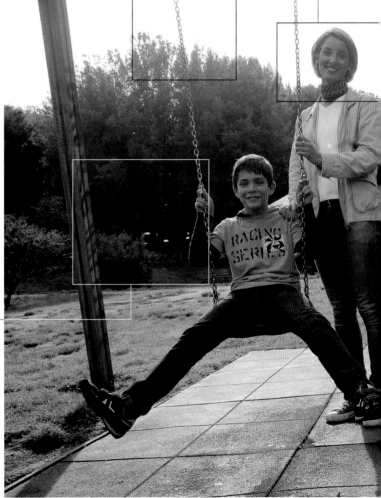

》 EXPOSURE VARIATIONS

An ideal way to learn about camera exposure is to analyze a scene by its luminance (or brightness) values. If you have a spot-meter mode in your camera (it measures from just a central three to five per cent of the image area), you can point it at different parts of your subject to get the correct exposure for each section. You will learn how just a small difference in exposure significantly affects the detail attained. This scene shows a difficult situation for exposure measurement because the sun facing the camera can upset the reading and cause underexposure.

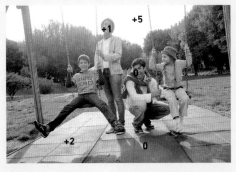

《 Analyzing the scene
The "0" here denotes the luminance in the scene that delivers the exposure for the image's mid-tone. Numbers indicate tones that are darker or lighter, in steps of one camera stop, according to the plus or minus signs.

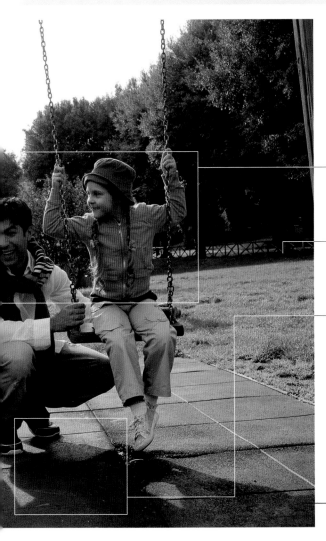

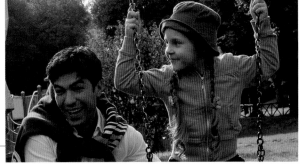

Normally, it is good practice to keep horizons level, but for informal shots, a little tilt is not only acceptable, it adds to the informality of the portrait.

⌃ Face tones
Exposure of any faces in the image will set the standard for the rest of the image. Other parts may be too dark or too light, but if the faces appear natural, the image will be acceptable overall.

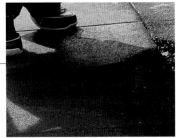

⌃ Reduced shadows
One of the effects of veiling flare (see opposite) is to reduce contrast by introducing light into shadows. Here, some of the shadows of the group are lightened by the flare so they appear unnaturally uneven.

In tricky lighting situations, locate a mid-tone grey, such as the ground here or the man's face, and set your exposure to that.

» Short exposure: road blur
Even the shortest shutter settings will not prevent motion blur in very fast-moving situations. In this image, taken from a moving car, a certain amount of blur is exploited to create ambience and interest.

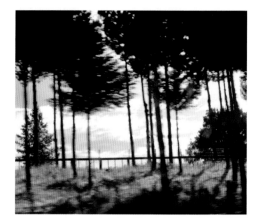

Using exposure time

If photography depicts a slice of life, then the shutter time determines the thickness of that slice. In the majority of situations, the main concern is that the combination of shutter time and aperture produces a well-exposed, focused image. Shutter setting, however, determines more than just the amount of light captured. It also controls the way in which we record motion and gives us the option to either freeze a moving subject or allow it to blur over the frame.

Capturing movement

In images, blur from motion is connected to the inter-relationship between speed of movement and exposure time. Long exposures capture normal movement as a blur. The effect is one of the medium's great contributions to visual language and imparts a realism to images. The faster the movement, or the longer the exposure, the more pronounced the blur. If you want a lot of blur, set a longer exposure, such as 1/15 second.

Short exposures, on the other hand, freeze the moment, giving sharply defined details. For minimal blur, set very brief exposure times, such as 1/2,000 second.

» Long exposure: in the rain
The camera was unintentionally set to a long exposure when these women rushed past in a heavy storm in Tajikistan. The effect successfully conveys the hurried atmosphere of people trying to get out of the rain.

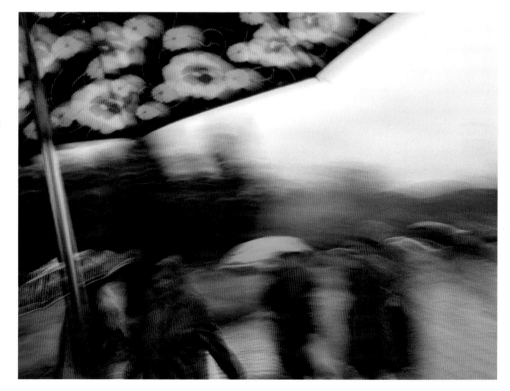

Setting priorities

All exposure calculations must balance the need for brief shutter times – to freeze movement and minimize camera shake and subject blur – with the need for an aperture setting that gives sufficient depth of field and optical correction. From this comes the notion of shutter priority and aperture priority. Shutter priority is generally chosen when short shutter times are needed to freeze action and the aperture can be as wide as necessary to give the correct exposure. Aperture priority is selected when greater depth of field is required and the shutter setting is not so critical.

⊠ Shutter time and distance
This diagram shows a train travelling at 161km/h (100mph). At a distance of 15m (50ft), a shutter time of 1/4,000 second or shorter is required to freeze its motion on film. At distances over 100m (300ft), the requirement drops to 1/500 second or shorter. If sharpness is critical, even shorter times should be set.

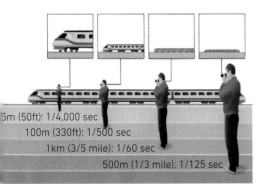

5m (50ft): 1/4,000 sec
100m (330ft): 1/500 sec
1km (3/5 mile): 1/60 sec
500m (1/3 mile): 1/125 sec

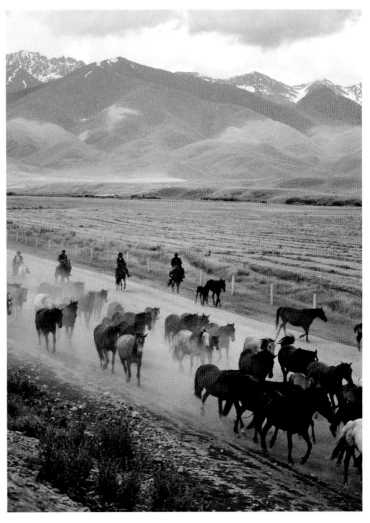

⚋ Long exposure time
While I was preparing for a landscape shot in Kyrgyzstan, these horses suddenly came thundering down the road towards the camera. A longish exposure gave greater depth of field at the expense of sharpness.

⚋ Freezing motion
If the photographic subject is moving fast, is near to you, and travelling across the field of view, you need to select the shortest shutter times – 1/2,000 second or shorter – to freeze motion. If the object is slower, further away, and travelling towards you, you can select longer shutter times of 1/125 second or longer. This table gives some indicative settings that you can experiment with.

» MOVING SUBJECTS

Subject	Direction of subject movement		
	Towards camera	Across frame (90° to camera)	Diagonally (45° to camera)
Pedestrian	1/30 sec	1/125 sec	1/60 sec
Jogger	1/60 sec	1/250 sec	1/125 sec
Cyclist	1/250 sec	1/1,000 sec	1/500 sec
Horse at gallop	1/500 sec	1/2,000 sec	1/1,000 sec
Car at 50km/h (30mph)	1/250 sec	1/1,000 sec	1/500 sec
Car at 160km/h (100mph)	1/1,000 sec	1/4,000 sec	1/2,000 sec

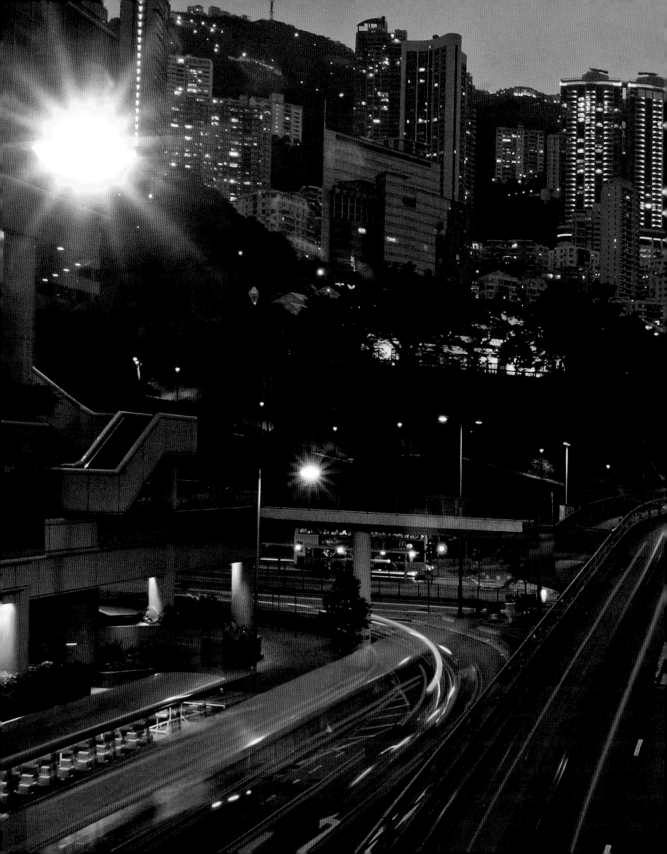

Time exposure
Photography can capture motion over time in a way that is unique to the medium. The flow of city traffic is dramatically recorded in this long exposure.

Using lenses

The lens is the eye of the camera. It translates what we see into a photograph and its qualities impact centrally on image capture. The lens we use affects our photographic vision, controlling how much of a scene we can capture, as well as what is in focus and its quality. Different focal lengths give us different views of the world and can limit, match, or expand our photographic intentions.

Understanding focal length

The focal length of a lens is the distance between the point from which the image is projected to the sharp image itself (at the focal plane), where the subject is at infinity.

A long focal-length lens magnifies a small portion of the view, while a short one shows more of the view. Imagine that you are looking through a hole in a fence. If you move close to the hole (short focal length), you can see lots beyond the fence, and it fills your view: that is a wide-angle image. If you move further away from the hole (long focal length), you see much less of the view. If that image is enlarged to fill your field of view, you obtain a magnified view: that is a long focal-length image.

Standard focal length

The standard lens for any format gives a neutral effect that is neither telephoto nor wide-angle. There was a time when all 35mm film cameras were sold with a standard 50mm lens. Now that zoom lenses, which have variable focal lengths, are the norm, the benefits of the 50mm have been forgotten. Using a 50mm lens offers excellent training, however. It concentrates the mind on composition, so that you look harder and move around instead of zooming in and out.

Comparison of views

A wide-angle or short focal-length lens has a radically different view of the world compared to a long focal-length lens. This is best seen by comparing views in which the main subject is kept at the same size. Try this: set your zoom to its widest setting and frame a subject so that it fits the height of the frame. Then set the longest setting and find the exact same framing: you will find you have to move a distance back from the subject to compose the second shot. This results in two very different perspectives. The dramatic changes in perspective as a result of using different focal lengths is why your choice of focal length has a huge impact on your compositions.

⊻ **Using a wide-angle lens**
With a short focal length (21mm), this lens makes the palace appear further away. The great depth of field of the wide-angle view is also evident in the relative sharpness of the whole image.

≫ **Using a telephoto lens**
A long focal-length or telephoto lens brings distant objects into the same picture plane as if they were relatively close. A 200mm lens makes the faraway building (Fontainbleau, France) appear closer to the sculpture than in real life. The building is out of focus because it falls outside the narrow depth of field.

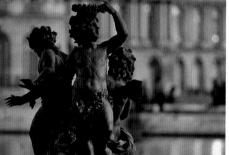

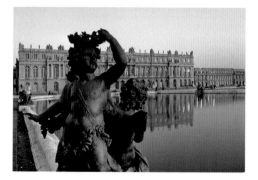

Field of view

The diagram below shows how fields of view alter with a change of focal length. As focal lengths increase, fields of view narrow, and vice versa – shorter focal lengths lead to wider fields of view for a given format. Note that the field of view is measured across the diagonal of the format and not the width, as you might expect. If you use single focal length (or prime) lenses such as 24mm, 50mm, or 180mm, then there are gaps or jumps in the changes in view. One advantage of using zoom lenses is that the changes in focal length are continuous, helping you with composition.

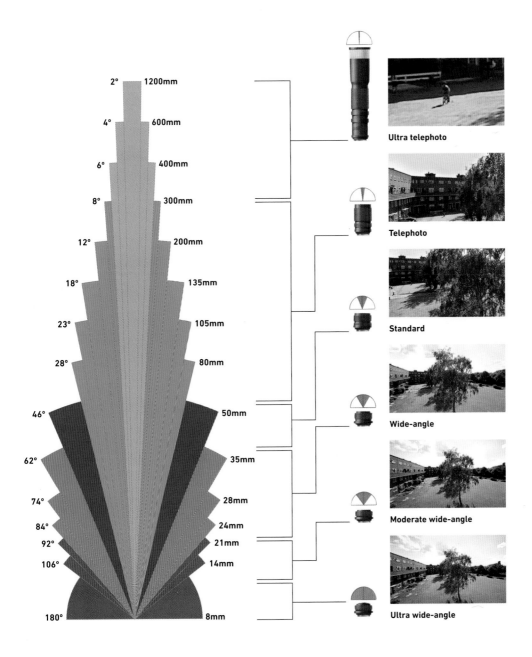

2°	1200mm
4°	600mm
6°	400mm
8°	300mm
12°	200mm
18°	135mm
23°	105mm
28°	80mm
46°	50mm
62°	35mm
74°	28mm
84°	24mm
92°	21mm
106°	14mm
180°	8mm

Ultra telephoto

Telephoto

Standard

Wide-angle

Moderate wide-angle

Ultra wide-angle

Focusing and depth of field

Depth of field fundamentally affects how a photograph reproduces a subject. While automatic focusing (AF) systems can focus far more rapidly and accurately than a photographer working manually, even the most advanced cameras cannot control depth of field. This requires high levels of creative input from the photographer as well as an understanding of lens aperture, focal length, working distance, and format size.

Focusing strategy

Auto-focusing systems work even in dim light, but they may select the wrong part of the scene to focus on. However, modern systems can automatically detect faces and eyes.

Manual focusing allows more control, but can be too slow, and also depends on good eyesight. You can combine auto-focus convenience and manual control by pointing the central focusing area at the element that needs to be sharp, initiate auto-focus, then hold or lock focus in order to reframe the image before exposing. As focal length increases, it is worth giving the system a little more time to focus accurately because depth of field is much reduced.

Camera shake

Movement of the lens during exposure will reduce sharpness. When using a lens set to a long focal length, image stabilisation built into the camera or lens can help ensure sharp images. Otherwise, use a tripod, or set a shutter time of 1/250 second or shorter for a focal length of 200mm.

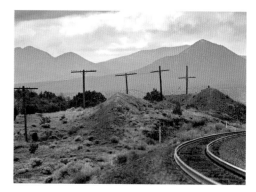

⌃ Distant depth of field
In images of distant subjects, the depth of field appears infinite, even with a long focal length. In this picture, made with a 400mm lens, the hills appear as sharp as the telegraph poles. These objects are said to be at infinity: changes in distance do not affect sharpness.

» Shallow depth of field
Using a full aperture and a long focal length throws the flowers in the foreground out of focus. This transforms them into a brilliant abstract blur of colour, which helps to frame the main subject of the photograph, a young bride in Uzbekistan.

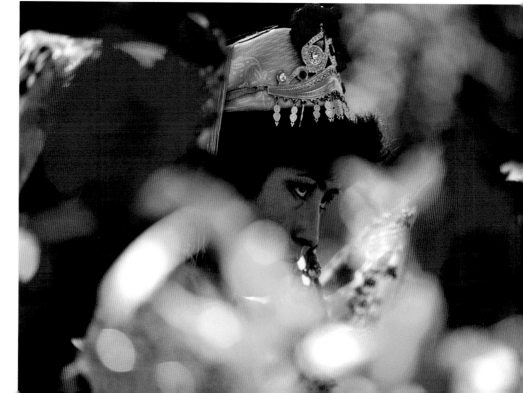

>> Varying depth of field

The three diagrams to the right illustrate how depth of field varies with aperture, how it changes with focused distance, and how it alters with focal length.

Understanding depth of field

Suppose you point your camera at someone approaching you from a great distance. You focus the lens on a point 5m (15ft) in front. The person will start off out of focus then become progressively sharp as they move towards the camera. There is a point at which they appear perfectly sharp, but as they approach even nearer, they will slip out of focus again. Having a shallow depth of field means that the zone in which the person appears sharp is shallow. Walking only a few steps is enough to lose sharpness.

Conversely, an extensive depth of field means that, once sharp, the person appears sharp while walking some distance. "Unsharpness" is, of course, subjective, depending as it does on how the image is viewed, how critical the viewer chooses to be, and what you wish to communicate in your image.

Controlling depth of field

The primary control of depth of field is the lens aperture. A smaller aperture gives greater depth of field, while a larger aperture reduces depth of field. Depth of field is also controlled by other factors and it can be maximized by increasing the focused distance (the space between focal plane and subject), shortening the focal length, and decreasing the format or sensor size. In short, to get more of a scene in focus, use a smaller aperture and distance yourself from the subject, or use a wide-angle lens. For less depth of field, use a wide aperture and get closer to the subject, or use a telephoto lens.

Changing the aperture (with 70mm lens focused at 10m)   depth of field ■

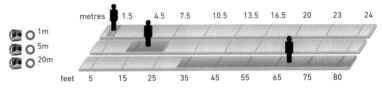

Changing the focused distance (with 70mm lens set at f/8)

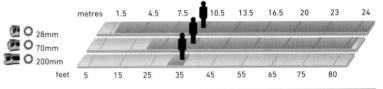

Changing the focal length (with aperture set at f/8 and focused at 10m)

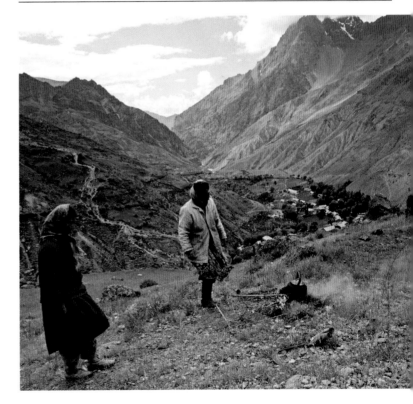

>> Extensive depth of field

With a wide-angle lens focused to medium distances and an average aperture, everything from blades of grass to distant peaks is sharp.

Filters and in-camera effects

Now image manipulation effects have become so easy to use, filters attached to the front of a lens may seem to be obsolete. However, in practice, filters remain essential for some effects, such as working with long exposures. In addition, many cameras offer built-in effects that avoid the need for software or even a computer, and allow you to check your results while you work.

Development of special effects

During the 1960s – a decade synonymous with adventurous artistic expression (see pp.96-99) – photographers began to look for new ways to diversify. The search to create photographs with a difference, using special effects or tricks to give visual impact, led to the invention of plastic filters offering numerous wild effects, including multi-coloured prisms (below right) that fit any lens combination.

⬇ Polarizing filter
This filter blocks strongly polarised sky light to darken the blues to almost black, offering strong contrast to the white clouds. Polarizing filters can be used for neutral density duties.

Using filters

While some effects, such as star-bursts and softening, remain easier to create with filters than with image software, filters are much less convenient. You have to buy separate filters and adaptors for different lens filter mounts, and then carry them around with you. However, two filter effects remain impossible for software to imitate with complete success. One is the polarizing filter (see p.133), which is mostly used to darken blue skies. Its effect is strongest when photographing a sky at right angles to the sun, and is minimal when pointed at the sun. The second useful

⬇ Coloured prisms
A flat prism filter and a rainbow filter were used to create this image of the Eiffel Tower. The prism splits the image into several parts that are each coloured by the filter.

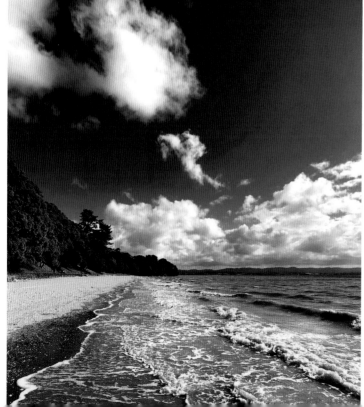

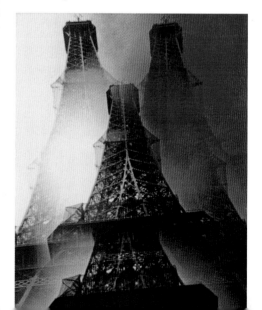

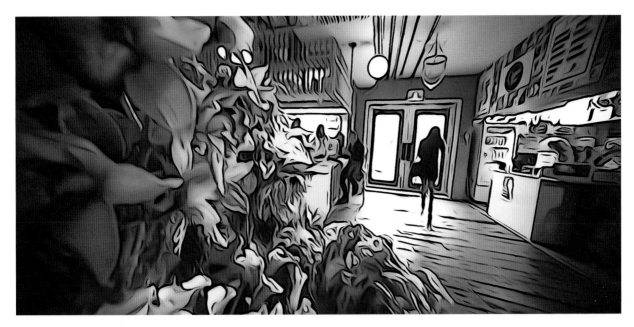

traditional filter is the Neutral Density (ND) filter, which blocks all colours of light equally. Using this, it is possible to set long exposures in bright conditions to blur movement of water or waves, for example (see below). ND filters also enable large aperture lenses to be used in bright light. Available in different strengths, ND filters may also be graduated, meaning they progress from clear to dark across their width. This allows a single exposure to cover both the sky and a darker foreground.

In-camera effects

Some effects can be created in-camera. You can change the zoom setting during a long exposure to make the image spread into converging streaks. Try long exposures so moving lights can "write" over the film. Many cameras and smartphones offer effects or "filters", such as paint strokes. They can also imitate toy cameras or produce facsimiles of dark-room processes. Some apply the effect directly to the captured file, while others save two versions: the original and the special effect.

⏶ **Paintbrush effect**
Exploiting "artistic" or painterly special effects can help turn prosaic snaps – such as this one of a shopping centre – into more interesting images.

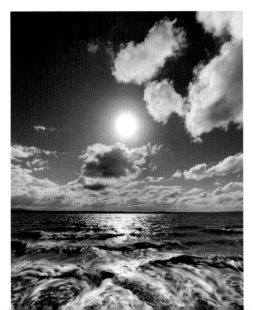

《 **Neutral density**
A longer-than-normal exposure to render the waves blurred would cause overexposure in the bright light. An ND filter reduces the light entering the lens to allow a long exposure time.

》 **Double exposure**
Some digital cameras can mimic the film technique of exposing one image on top of another. It can result in unpredictable, but creatively rewarding effects.

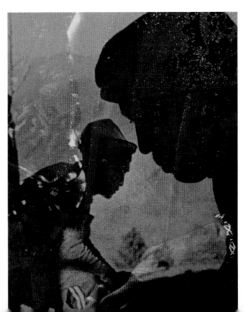

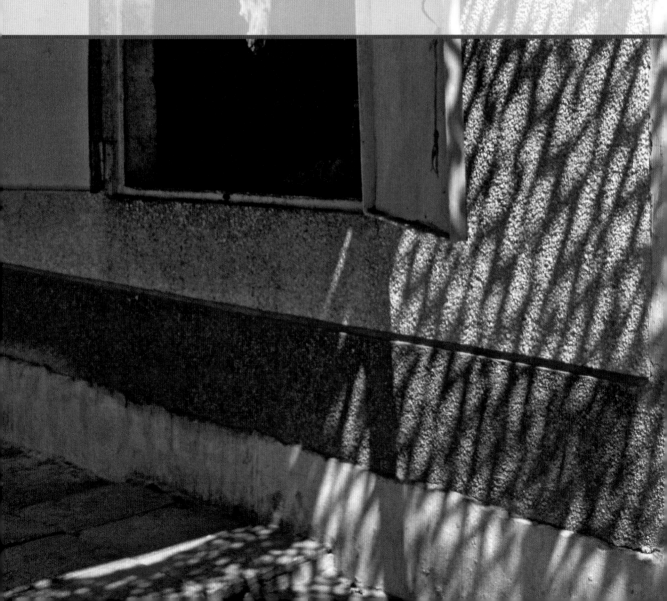

TAKING SUCCESSFUL
PHOTOGRAPHS

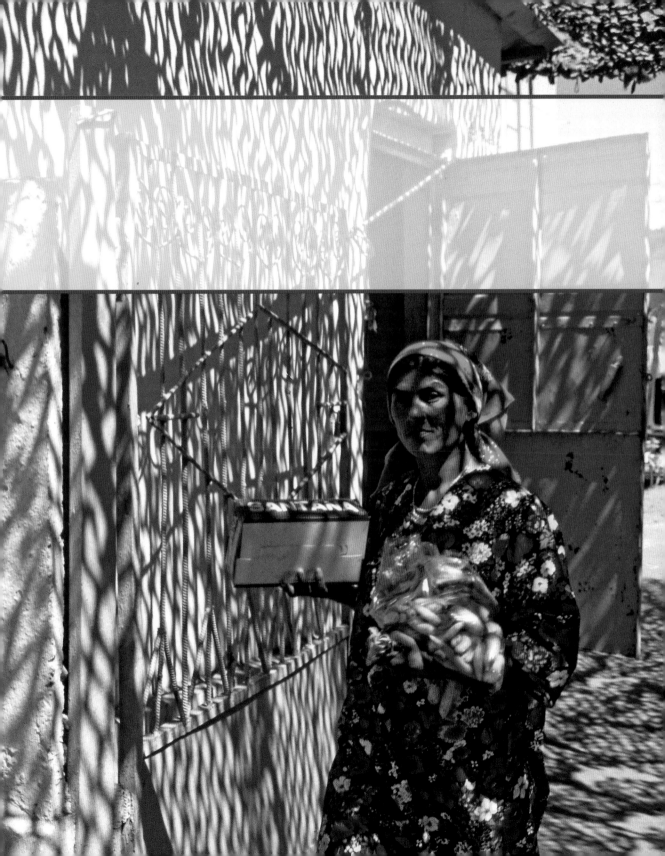

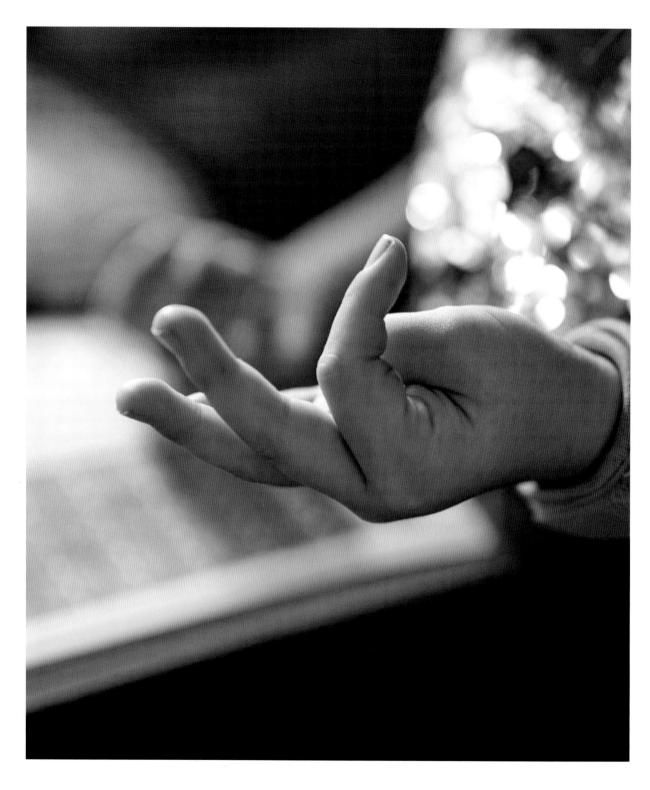

If there is a single formula for applying photographic techniques successfully, it is one shared by all of the world's great photographers. It is delightfully simple. Whether travelling the world or staying close to home, working in dangerous conditions, or in the safety of the studio, great photographers work hard.

That observant and witty photographer Robert Doisneau (1912–94) once pointed out: "If I knew how to take a good photograph, I'd do it every time." But great photographers do share a special mindset that ensures they are led – almost obsessed – by a vision. They seek the visual truth that communicates with perfect, inconvertible clarity. They know what they want and will not rest until they have seen it realized, and recorded it. The writer Mark Twain put it well: "You can't depend on your eyes if your imagination is out of focus."

To realize that vision in the form of a captured image, photographers are constantly observing and responding to the world around them. Photographers delight in all our world's beauty and even its sadness in the search for visual truth.

Thanks to the gift of light we can see the world, and great photographers use that gift with skill and persistence. Modern technology renders the mechanics of the photographic process straightforward: fast, accurate focusing can be carried out automatically, as can exposure-setting. Some cameras will even run off a series of pictures, and then select the best shot. What the cameras leave you are the obviously creative options. Once you have learnt and are confident with the right technique, you can deliberately use the "wrong" settings to create a particular effect.

There are still opportunities to discover new ways to photograph, none of which need cost anything to try. For example, you could take an accepted rule of composition and set out to break it. You could find a new way to look at popular subjects: for example, instead of the

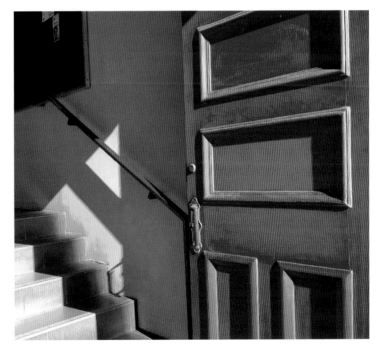

◪ **Combining shapes**
Using strong light and asymmetrical shapes with bold colours can create an interesting composition.

◧ **Child photography**
Instead of the usual portrait of a smiling infant, capturing a quiet moment of calculation can be as cute, and more memorable.

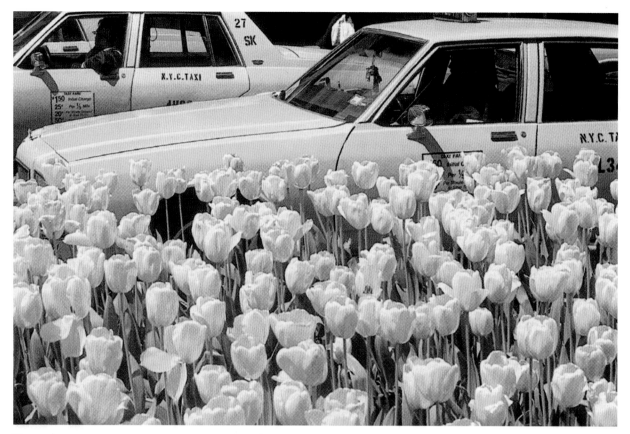

⌃ Colour splash
The bright yellow tulips are echoed in the passing taxis, emphasizing the juxtaposition between the natural and man-made world.

usual childhood snaps, try to record a child's inner life of learning and development. Instead of treating photographs as the final product, use them as intermediates by photographing prints placed on top of prints, or three-dimensional objects placed on prints.

As a photographer, you are totally free to find your own way forward. On the other hand, there is no inherent need for you to innovate in photography when the world is continually offering you new subjects, new debates, and new and exciting photographic opportunities. Nonetheless, whatever you choose to photograph there are steps you can take to make your images more your own. To do this, you will need some command over the basic techniques – just as musicians must know their instruments, be familiar with different styles of music and interpretations, and understand their music theory.

In photography, mastery of a technique, such as exploiting the effects of depth of field, is just

as valuable whether you are taking travel shots or portraits. Similarly, many of the skills (not all photographic) required for successful child photography are the same as the ones you need for photojournalism. If you are covering a wedding, you will employ the same skills of speed, observation and planning as you would for a major event such as a street carnival or a demonstration.

This section looks at a variety of photographic genres, concentrating on what you can do to get more out of the picture-making experience. Most importantly, these ideas do not need new equipment, only basic measures, such as getting up early, getting in to look more closely, waiting a little longer, or taking a few extra steps.

» Matemwe, Zanzibar
Cows taking a rest on a sunlit beach disrupt the accepted view of a tropical paradise, and create an amusing composition.

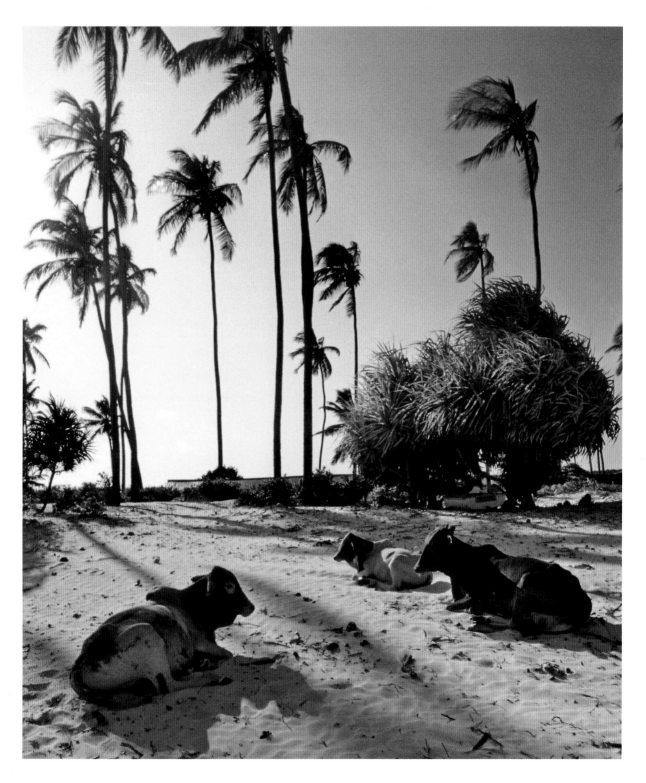

Portraits

The portrait is seldom a neutral record of a person. It almost always aims to communicate a personal response, or attempts to say something about someone. As a result, the portrait photograph usually has to strike a balance between truthful representation and subjective expression. Very often the skills needed to get the best out of a sometimes reluctant subject are more interpersonal and psychological than photographic.

» Matching background
Here the woman's patterned coat matches the background. The effect would be overpowering without the scarf that encircles her face. The vivid pink headband enlivens the whole image.

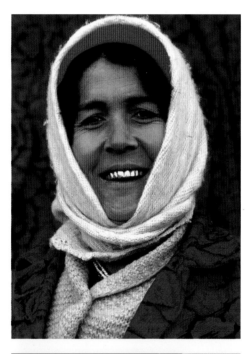

⌄ Using leading lines
A composition that makes use of converging parallel lines creates depth and stability, and draws the eye to the subject.

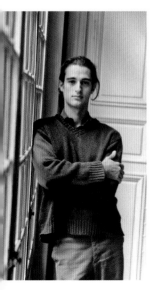

Setting up the shot

Portraits do not have to be set up in a formal way, and a model need not be conventionally beautiful. You may be inspired by a characterful face in a crowd. Then all you can do is approach the person and explain why you want to take their picture and what you will use it for. It helps if you have examples of previous work. Once you have their co-operation, the key elements of portraiture are background, lighting, and perspective, which will determine the lens you use.

Background

Generally the most versatile backgrounds for portraiture are those with some texture but without distracting details. For example, a rough stone wall is better than a brick wall with its hard straight lines. If an unattractive background is unavoidable, you can keep your subject in focus and blur the background by setting a large aperture to narrow the depth of field. Alternatively, you can adjust the image later using manipulation software.

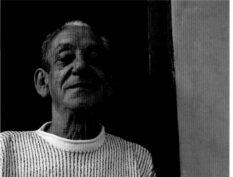

« Off-centre framing
Your subject need not always occupy the centre of the picture, and does not have to be looking straight ahead. Placing your subject off-centre can bring an otherwise inactive composition to life. The eyes cast down towards the camera add character.

Lighting

While soft lighting flatters skin tones, it is not the only way to light a portrait. In fact many types of lighting can be effective, so it is worth experimenting. A hard spotlight from behind the subject produces a rim or halo of brightness, creating an ethereal effect. A softer but still hard light can bleach out shadows reducing the face to an expanse of even tone. Lighting from the sides or above usually works well, but lighting from below is more difficult. If you are not very careful your portrait will look like a still from a horror movie. The only light guaranteed to give unattractive results is that from a flash mounted on a camera. This produces a hard light with hard shadows that seldom, if ever, flatters the subject.

» HOW THE MASTERS WORKED

The works of the great portrait photographers encompass a variety of styles and approaches. Madame Yevonde (1893–1975) was a pioneer of colour photography in the UK in the inter-war years. Working on advertisements for high-profile companies, she was also sought after by members of London's high society, who she satirized in her *Goddesses* series.

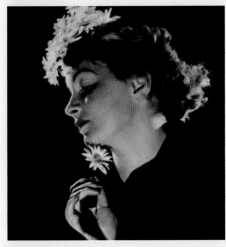

⌃ Madame Yevonde
Yevonde often used the Vivex tri-colour process. This gave her pictures a memorable artificiality, as in "Miss Susan Bligh as Calypso" (above), taken in 1935. She once famously remarked, "If we are going to have colour photographs, for heaven's sake, lets have a riot of colour, none of your wishy-washy hand-tinted effects."

Perspectives

Portraits can be taken from any perspective, from close-up to distant, depending on the effect you wish to create. However, most people tend to opt for standard head and shoulders shots. For these, focal lengths longer than normal (70mm–105mm for 35mm format or equivalent) give the best results.

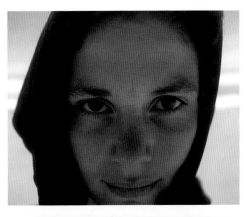

《 Focusing on the eyes
A most striking way of depicting a face is to zoom in on the eyes by framing tightly. By losing some of the face, you concentrate attention on the face's most arresting feature.

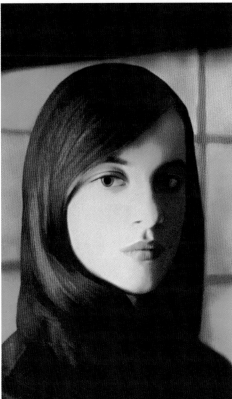

《 Digital manipulation
Skin tones and hair colour do not have to be naturalistic. Subtle use of image manipulation software can turn an average portrait into a visually striking, sophisticated image.

Analyzing a portrait

The most successful portraits are those that combine an accurate portrayal of the person being photographed with an interesting composition, attractive and appropriate lighting, and sharp focus. But your subject can also be your biggest problem. Many portrait sitters are either too willing to be photographed, with their own very definite ideas of how they want to look, or they are too unwilling, and may even refuse to sit still or show their face. This is where having highly developed people skills comes into play.

Building the relationship

When covering a national celebration in Kyrgyzstan, I approached this falconer with deference and was rewarded with his full co-operation. I was able to walk around him, asking him to turn this way and that until the harsh light fell in an attractive way. By taking care with the photography, I won the subject's trust and as he relaxed, his character was revealed. An unexpected bonus was the eagle stretching its wing to rest it in total confidence on the falconer's head. This touching gesture lasted only a few seconds. But by then, I was fully prepared to record this revealing moment.

☑ **Working with animals**
If portraits are tricky, working with animals is notoriously difficult. Here, a fetching turn of the head from the Golden Eagle, revealing a perfect beaked profile, lifts the portrait to a higher level.

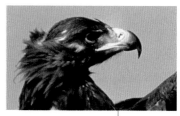

A neutral expression is best for portraits. It is easy for the subject to hold, natural, and unlikely to be exaggerated.

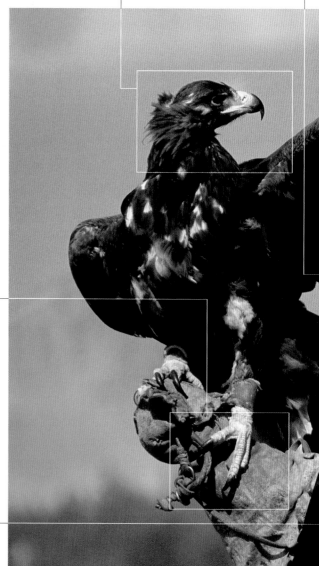

≫ **Retaining sharp details**
Although the main subject is the face, ensure that interesting details, such as the gloved hand and eagle's claw, are retained. This supports the image, showing the viewer more about the person.

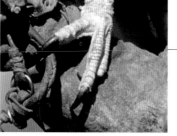

≫ **Including visual accents**
Small details can be very revealing. Here, a military service medal catches a glint of sunlight, rewarding the viewer with a hint at the background of the subject. It is worth waiting to catch a glimpse of visual accents such as this, as they add extra interest to the image.

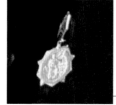

Avoiding overshadow

Shadows on the face are generally to be avoided, especially if the subject is in full sun. If you cannot avoid them, ensure they do not overshadow the eyes. Unfortunately, the bright sun made the subject half-close his eyes.

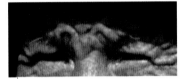

⟫ CHOOSING THE RIGHT ENVIRONMENT

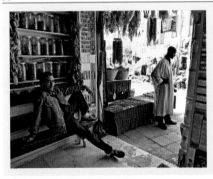

To make a great portrait, your sitter must be relaxed, so they need to feel that the setting is appropriate for them. Let your sitter choose the first location. Here a shopkeeper relaxes in his herb shop in Marrakech, Morocco. Do not be too preoccupied with lighting – great portraits have been made with a single bare bulb. By giving your sitter priority, you can work in tandem with them and share the portrait-making experience.

⟪ Double portrait

Portraits can include more than one person, and can also show the daily environment in which they live or work.

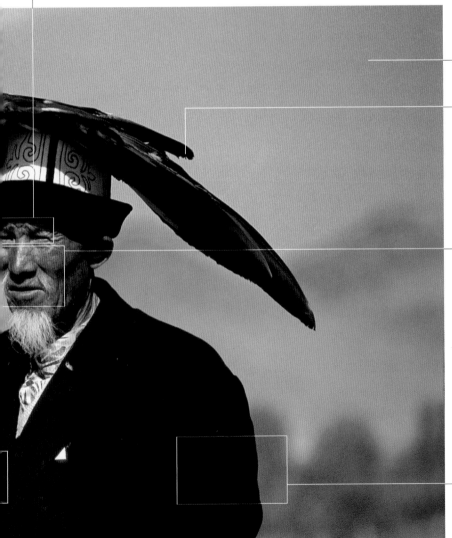

There is a little too much space to the right of the subject, but a large aperture and a long focal length on the zoom lens have put the background nicely out of focus so it offers no distraction.

A surprising wing gesture from the Golden Eagle creates an unusual composition.

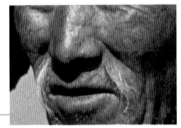

⌃ Classic nose shadow

The shadow of the nose helps to give shape to the nose without confusing the shape of the lips. Here, by careful observation, the face was photographed with just the right nose shadow – not quite touching the lips.

Enhancing shadow detail

Ensure that any large, dark areas retain some detail – enhance them through image manipulation if necessary. The amount of detail in dark areas will depend initially on the exposure that you set, which must be focused on the face.

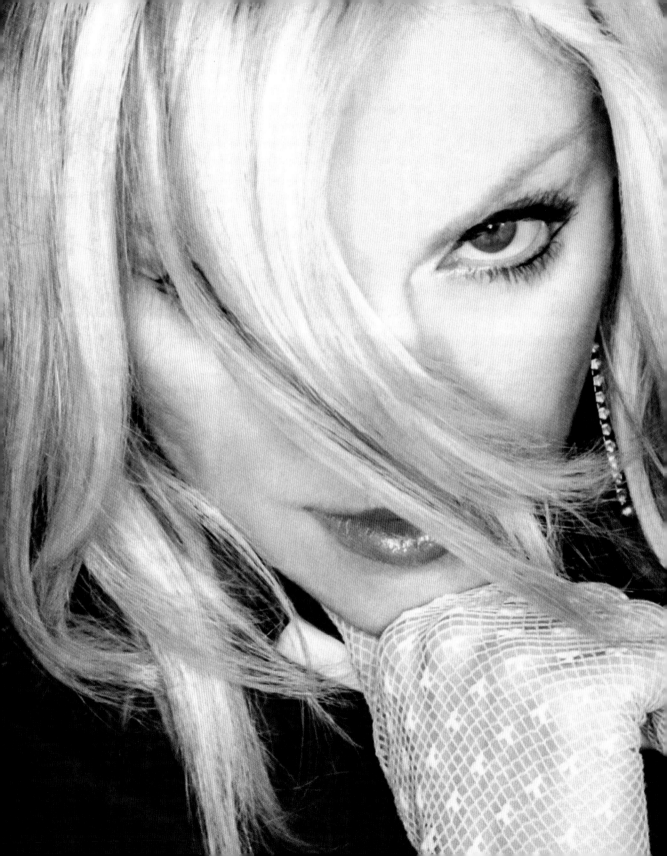

Animals

Animal photography is notoriously difficult because animals are constantly on the move, very shy, and easily panicked. But it can be immensely rewarding. Wildlife photographers spend much of their lives waiting days for their chosen animals to make an appearance, but such dedication is not a prerequisite. You can obtain rewarding images without venturing far from home.

Creatures close to home

Domestic animals are good subjects for photography, since you can draw close without startling them. If you have no pets, visit parks and zoos or seek out the wild animals that share your neighbourhood. You can find animals in most environments if you know where to look. Many cities have nature reserves, woods, and lakes. Areas such as cemeteries and playing fields often provide shelter for small animals as well.

The most visible urban creatures are birds, but mammals can also be found. A city fox is easier to spot than its countryside cousin, as it is less afraid of human beings. Learn about the habits of the animal. At dusk, most birds congregate prior to roosting, and mammals pass along favoured runs that can be identified by small gaps in hedges and fur caught in branches.

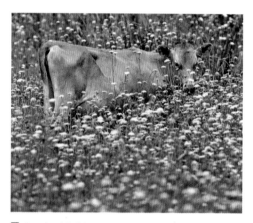

⌃ Depth of field
A narrow depth of field leads the eye from the out-of-focus flowers in the foreground towards the sharply focused face of the cow and beyond, where the flowers again become out of focus.

» Close-up photography
Digital cameras make it easy to approach very close to even minute creatures and insects. Depth of field is very limited: use small apertures and focus with great care.

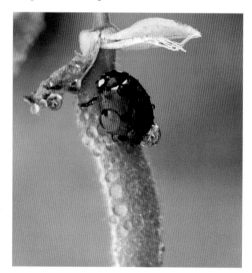

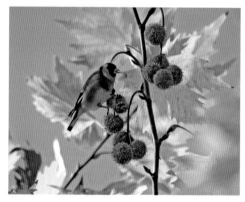

⌃ Waiting for the pose
To obtain a photograph of a bird busy at work, well posed and with good lighting, takes many attempts and much observation. This image was the best of over a dozen exposures.

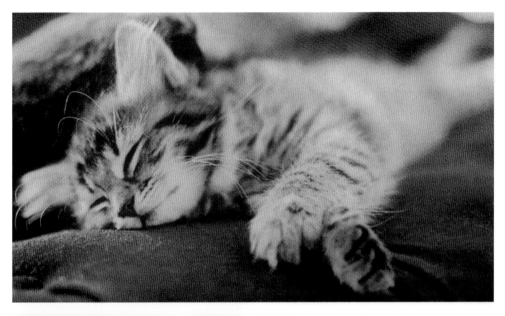

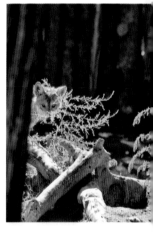

◀◀ Sleepy kitten
A sleeping pet is an easy target for animal photography. If you set up your camera and tripod at its favourite sleeping spot you will be able to make the most of the available light. The same principle applies if you are stalking wild animals. The more you know about them, the easier it is to catch them behaving naturally.

Visiting zoos and nature reserves

Many modern zoos and nature reserves are centres for research that help to save rare species from extinction. While it is no joy to watch a large mammal in confinement, your visit can support important conservation efforts.

Your photographs will be more effective if you compose your shots to minimize evidence of the artificial surroundings. As with photography in the wild, you may have to wait and watch for the animal to appear. Avoid visiting during school holidays as the animals can be disturbed by the increased number of visitors and may retreat into the depths of their enclosures.

Choosing the moment

Whether you are photographing your pet, an animal in the wild, or a creature at the zoo, you will need patience and perseverance to capture successful images. The best animal pictures show some of the character of the animal, in much the same way as a portrait of a person reflects their mood and personality. For this reason, it helps to have some empathy with the animal and a knowledge of its behaviour, so you can predict its movements and anticipate when you are likely to get the best shot. Unlike a human, an animal will not wait patiently while you set up the shot, so the trick is to follow its actions and take as many pictures as you can.

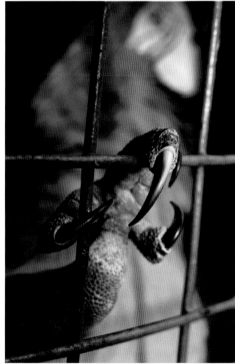

⌃ Different viewpoints
Use the close-up abilities of your camera to gain new insight into your subject by looking for unusual views and telling details, such as the feet of this macaw.

⌃ Showing character
A glimpse of an animal can reveal as much as a full view. Here a wolf appears wary even within its enclosure. Zooming close – 600mm – eliminates the surrounding wire fence.

On safari

One of the best ways to photograph animals is to take a wildlife safari. The game parks and nature reserves of Africa, North America, and elsewhere need and deserve the support of tourism. In return, they offer innumerable, unforgettable opportunities for photography. To make the most of the trip, it is worth making thorough preparations, such as ensuring you have the longest focal-length lens that you can afford, carry, and handle.

» **Selective cropping**
This bear was too far away to fill the frame. A tall, narrow crop that places the animal centrally in the frame makes the best of the image.

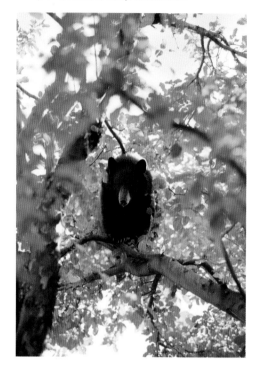

Choosing a camera

Digital cameras are ideal for photographing animals in the wild. Bridge and long-range zoom cameras are useable, but for best quality mirrorless cameras or SLRs offer an unbeatable combination of high image quality, rapid auto-focusing, and very rapid frame rate. Some mirrorless models offer totally silent image capture that can be a huge help in the wild.

Models using APS-C-sized sensors are an advantage as they combine compact build with a magnifying effect (a telephoto zoom of 70–200 mm is equivalent to a 105–300 mm: *see also p.133*). One weakness of digital cameras is a tendency to collect dust. Avoid changing lenses outdoors, as dust will settle on the sensor and make spots over every image.

Reflected image
The mirror-like reflection of the crocodile makes it clear that the water is still, reinforcing the stealthy nature of its movements.

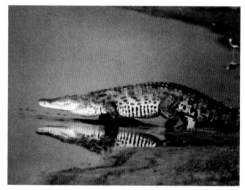

» COMPENSATING FOR CAMERA-SHAKE

Camera-shake increases in proportion to the effective focal length of the lens, and is a serious problem when shooting from a moving vehicle (common when on safari). Automatic image stablization is designed to counteract it, by either shifting optical cells within the lens, or moving the sensor itself.

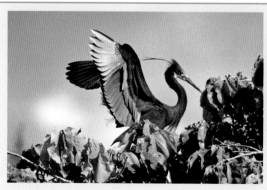

« Image stabilized from boat
While not perfect, this image would not have been possible with an unstabilized lens. It was taken from a canoe bobbing up and down on a choppy river.

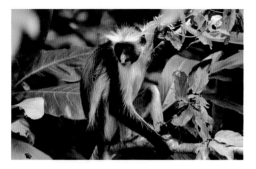

⌃ Approaching closely
Special reserves, such as the Jozani Nature
Reserve for the Red Colobus Monkey in Zanzibar,
are ideal for getting close to animals that are
normally too wary to be reached.

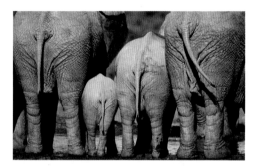

⌃ Unusual views
Photographing from unconventional viewpoints
or finding unfamiliar views of familiar subjects
is an effective way to create eye-catching, even
amusing, images.

Choosing a lens

Most of the time on safari you will be seeing
animals from a distance, so it is essential to use
a long focal-length lens to bridge the gap between
you and your subject. If you are photographing
large animals, such as elephants or giraffes, a lens
of 200mm can be satisfactory. But for smaller
animals or to cover great distances, a lens with
a focal length of at least 400mm is necessary.
Longer lenses offer greater magnification but
are heavy and expensive. Furthermore, dusty or
moisture-laden air limits the clarity of images
made over large distances. Modern long zoom
lenses covering a focal-length range of about
100–500 mm offer versatility and convenience
at the cost of only slightly reduced image quality
and lens speed.

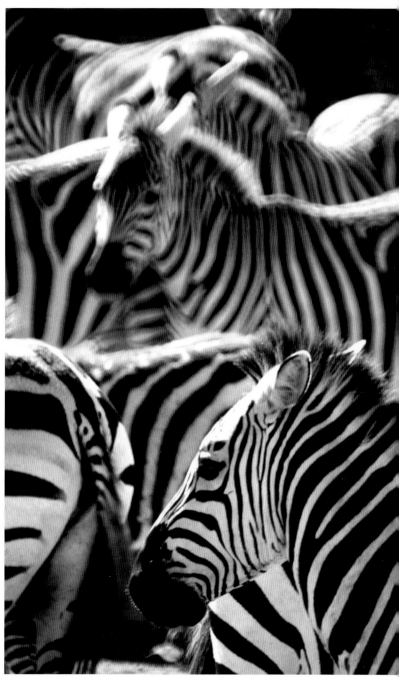

⌃ Capturing details
It is not necessary to show the whole
animal. Try concentrating on striking
features, such as these zebra stripes.

Events

Our lives are full of events, some of which we may wish to remember, and others we may prefer to forget. One of the greatest claims of photography is that it preserves our memories, but it is rare to find an image that reflects how we truly felt at the time. The challenge in photographing an event is to capture the action and the atmosphere through still images.

Choosing an approach

Your objective for photographing an event will shape the approach you take on the day. For example, if you wish to remember the people who played a special role at your birthday party, you will concentrate on taking portraits. Alternatively, if you wish to provide an objective record that is as complete as possible, you will photograph everything you can from every possible angle.

Deciding what to record

Start by deciding the purpose of your photographs. If you simply wish to capture interesting moments throughout the day, take some before-and-after shots, as well as the main event. If you want to tell a story, with a beginning, middle, and end, make sure your pictures include everyone involved, as people are usually central to a story. Use a smartphone camera freely: it may be less intimidating and less intrusive than a bigger camera and lens. As there is usually something happening all the time, do not review your pictures until the event ends.

☑ Starting the narrative
The first image shows guests queueing for a ride on a historical train. Long shadows draw the eye to the figures in the centre, balancing the shot.

☑ Setting the scene
The late-afternoon train ride carries guests through the countryside, so a picture is needed to represent the journey. By waiting for the right combination of the train's orientation to the sun and terrain, I was able to capture this image, with its attractive combination of light, shadow, and colours.

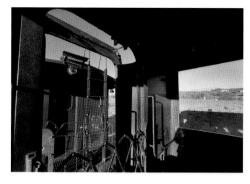

Selecting equipment

A zoom lens that ranges from moderate wide-angle to moderate telephoto (i.e. from 35mm to 80mm) is ideal for photographing events. Use very wide-angle lenses (focal lengths of shorter than 24mm for 35mm format) sparingly, as objects at the edge of the image appear distorted. This effect is particularly unwelcome when photographing people.

One of the most useful accessories for photographing an indoor event is a flash unit with a swivelling head, which can be attached to a camera hotshoe (a bracket with electrical contacts found on the top of most cameras). By swivelling the head, you can aim the flash at a nearby surface to bounce the light off and illuminate your subject. This provides a wider lighting coverage and softer light than flashing directly.

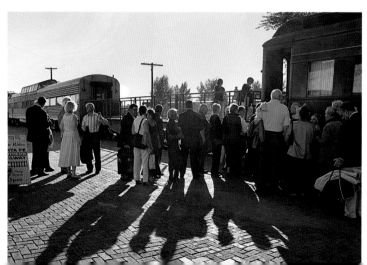

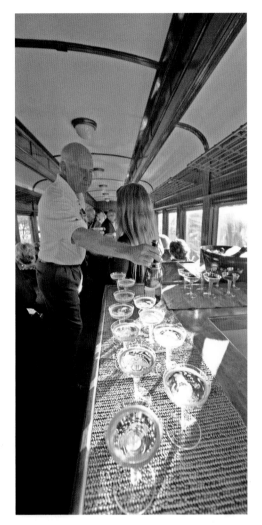

《 Showing the preparations
Others may while away the time as they wait for the event to get underway, but you have to watch and work. An extreme wide-angle view such as this distorts faces at the periphery, so frame your shot carefully.

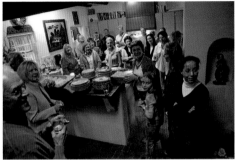

《 Depicting the main event
Once the train had reached its destination, the guests disembarked for a birthday party. To obtain the best shot, I set the camera to its widest angle setting (shortest focal length) and held it above my head to include as many people as possible.

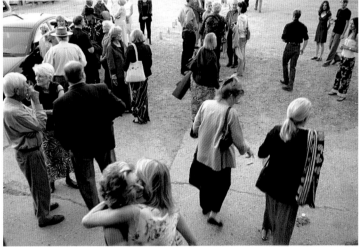

⌃ The end of the day
Sometimes you may feel you need to be in two places at once. At the end of the return journey, I had to choose between showing the guests descending from or leaving the train. I opted for the latter to obtain a high viewpoint.

》 HOW THE MASTERS WORK

Spaniard Cristina Garcia Rodero (1949–) documents the fiestas and religious festivals of her native country. Thanks to her detailed knowledge of the rituals and events, as well as repeated visits to major festivals, her work is unrivalled for its depth, extent, and humanity.

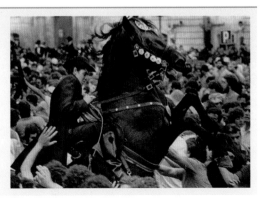

》 Cristina Garcia Rodero
Rodero works mainly in black and white, which is superb for cutting out the many distractions provided by colourful festivals.

Analyzing an event photograph

Family albums are full of photographs that record important events and milestones in life, such as birthdays, weddings, graduations, and other celebrations. A skilled photographer will ensure that, as well as compiling a collection of pictures that record each aspect of the event, there are also shots that encapsulate the event as a whole. It is essential to know when and where the key moments of the event will occur. Find out the running order of the day and plan where to be at what time, in order to get the best shots.

Finding the key shot

The secret to catching the key moment of an event is to keep working – never stop – and reduce checking of image previews to the barest minimum. If you wish to record an event well, you can forget about participating in it. You are there for the photography, not the fun. When reviewing the images that I took at a Hindu wedding, the picture below stood out. It contains all the vital elements of a key shot; it is colourful, and dynamic, showing the smiling bride at the centre surrounded by well-wishers. It encapsulates the joyful spirit of the event.

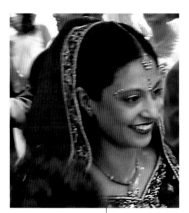

» Tracking the subject
By tracking the bride with the camera during exposure, I ensured that she is more in focus, while the others are blurred. This makes her the main focus of the image.

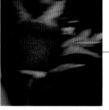

**» Capturing
visual accents**
Vivid spots of colour, such as the red rose buttonholes, help to enliven and structure the image. Here, the roses are repeated in an arc across the picture from left to far right.

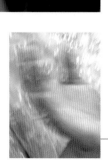

» Choosing depth of field
Camera exposure was set to maximize the depth of field, at the expense of a short shutter time. This resulted in blurring, such as the applauding hands. This is acceptable as long as the crucial details are sharp, and can add a sense of movement to the image.

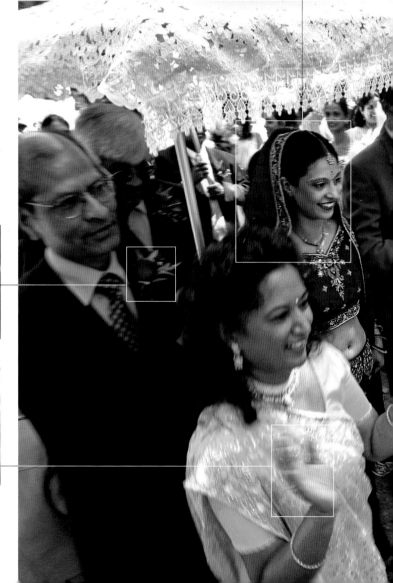

» GROUP PHOTOGRAPHS

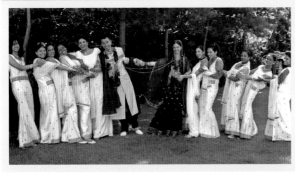

The group photograph is an obligatory part of recording major events such as weddings. But they do not need to be stiff, static, set pieces. Once you assemble the group, encourage frivolity such as jumping in the air, or tell a joke. Work quickly as the moment is easily lost.

« Tug of war
Rival "factions" try to pull the bride and groom apart, transforming a standard shot into a warm, amusing picture.

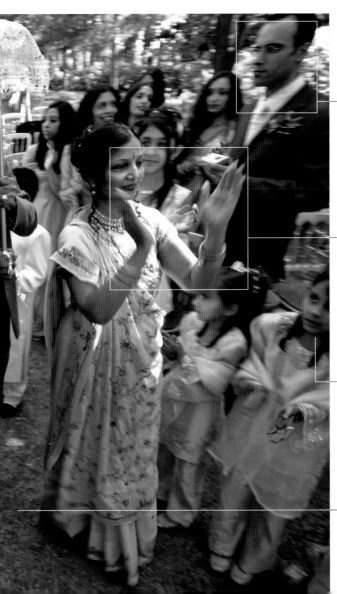

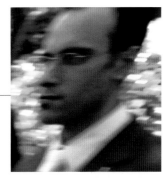

« Using a wide-angle lens
With wide-angle lenses, subjects at the periphery of the frame can be distorted. Here, a face has become egg-shaped. Where possible, place subjects away from the edges of the image.

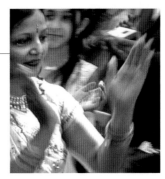

« Synchronizing your shot
Perfect timing is needed to catch rapid hand movements in their best position. The best technique is to anticipate movement, tripping the shutter just before the action.

Avoid cutting off a face at the edge of the frame unless there is a good reason. Here the crop was unfortunate and unplanned.

Quiet areas of an image are important for structure, but ensure they are not too large. If they are too dominant, you can reduce their impact by image manipulation, such as burning-in the corners to darken them.

Documentary

Central to photography's artistic and social development, the genre of documentary photography has evolved into many forms. It works in a variety of modes: from commercial photography, to investigative journalism, from mechanical record-keeping, to historically vital witnessing. At its heart, all documentary photography tries to do the same thing: present a true record – of real situations, real events, and real people.

Concerned photography

Social documentary, or concerned photography, is the best-known and most influential of all the forms of documentary work. Its subject is the human condition, the back stories to world affairs, and the lives of people. For some, the work should be ideologically motivated – speaking for the disenfranchised, exposing injustice. Such work tends to be long-term – creating picture series – and takes a lot of time to complete. Ethical standards are highest in this genre of photography: setting up, or any other manipulation of an image, is unacceptable.

Choosing a project

Inspiration is all around you. You do not need to travel far to find fascinating subjects. The key is not in uncovering an unknown, or even unusual, subject, but in interpreting any subject in an unusual or revealing way.

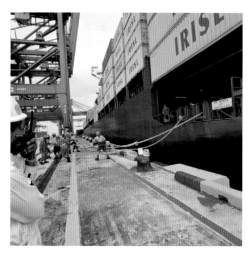

⌅ Creating tension
The tiny figures in the background and the large figure in the foreground offer a sense of scale.

⌄ Direct contact
Although hidden by sunglasses, it is clear the worker is looking straight into camera, and consenting to the photograph.

⌄ Ambiguous humour
Two workmen sheltering under a plastic sheet during a tropical downpour in Singapore appear to be surrendering to the elements,

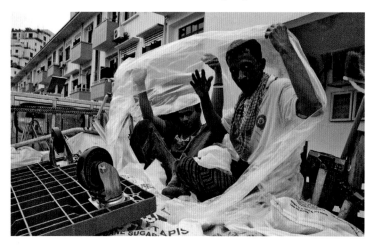

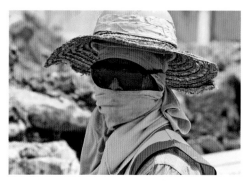

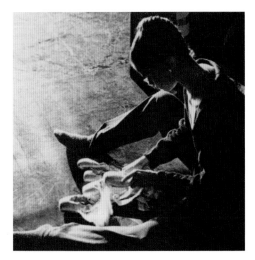

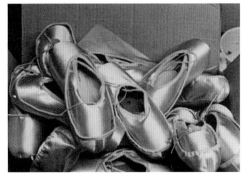

Telling details
At its best, documentary work does not need titles to identify its subject. This image says "ballet" more clearly than any words, and it does so in any language.

Chiaroscuro lighting
The advantages of black and white can be clearly seen in this striking backstage study of a ballerina. Combined with dramatic lighting, it reduces the image to shapes of light and dark.

Some of the best documentary works cast a fresh eye on everyday subjects, for example, the sheltering workers in Singapore on the opposite page. Others, such as the images on this page, look behind the scenes to shed light on familiar subjects.

The tools

While a handful of die-hards continue to use film for documentary photography, the vast majority of work originates on digital cameras. These offer high image quality, versatility in low light conditions, as well as discreet operation. Some mirrorless or interchangeable lens compact cameras can expose with total silence, and modern auto-focus systems can work in very dim light. Modern fast lenses, such as the 24mm f/1.4, 35mm f/1.4, and 50mm f/1, also encourage low-light work. On the other hand, compact cameras and lenses can also work well in normal lighting conditions.

A "proper" camera is not necessarily the best tool in some circumstances: smartphone cameras are more discreet and compact than conventional cameras, and may be less intimidating to subjects. They can offer entirely acceptable performance and image quality.

Being discreet
A prerequisite for documentary photography is the ability to work silently and inconspicuously. To capture the shot below the photographer had to take care not to distract the dancers.

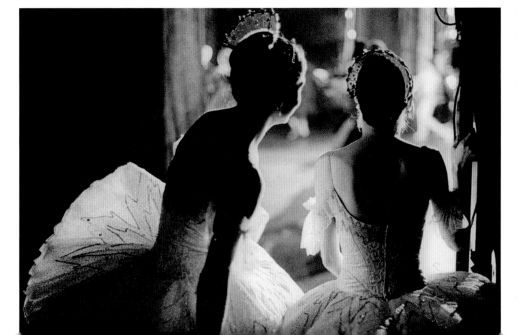

Principles of the narrative

Documentary photography's currency is the picture series or picture story. Aim for each image to add to the narrative, revealing new or surprising sides to the subject. When images work together – complementing or completing each other – they create a whole that conveys much more than separate frames. Nonetheless, aim to make each image as strong and visually arresting as you can.

Finding a story

Once you have decided on a subject area, you need to narrow down the choice of potential subjects until you have a specific theme. During a trip to Central Asia, I wanted to photograph the food of the region. I first chose to investigate the importance of meat in the area, and then sought "hooks" or stories beyond the mere act of meat-eating. A little research uncovered three potential hooks: the consumption of meat is a central part of festivities; working with animals is a substantial part of people's lives in the area; and the region may be consuming more meat than it can produce, which could cause a crisis that impacts rights across society. This final hook gave the best story as it brings together the role of meat in people's lives, which opens up the debate about how much is being consumed.

Covering the story

When you cover a story, ensure that you have photographed every aspect of it from every angle. For my coverage of food in Central Asia, this included people, animals, and the preparation and consumption of food.

Ensure that what you photograph is found, not constructed. Interfere with the subject as little as possible, but enter into people's lives without obstructing their work. Leave no footprint. No-one should realize you have been at work until they see your pictures.

☑ At the market
The first place I visited was a grand bazaar used for trading chickens. The resulting image has interesting elements but its contribution to the story is not clear. It was placed on reserve.

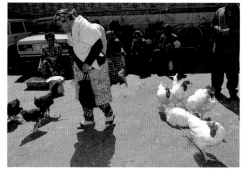

☑ Animal fair
More directly related to the story was an animal fair. I framed the shot in an unusual way, contrasting the woman selling the young cattle with the buyers, who literally appear as shadowy figures.

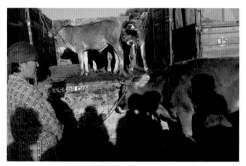

» Young shepherdess
The opening picture of the series should choose itself. It needs to sum up what the story is about – here, the relationship between the young population and its growing need for a diminishing food supply.

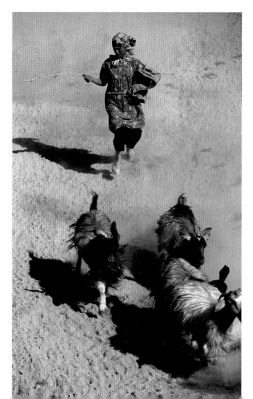

Food preparation
Although gruesome to Western eyes, the slaughter of animals is a part of everyday life here. The picture is completed by the dog who is struggling to maintain discipline.

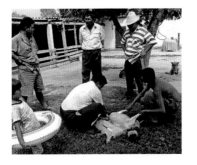

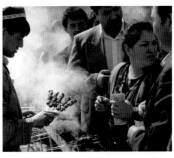

Barbecues
Smoke from "shashlik" barbecues is an attractive backdrop for photography. This shot was timed to show food being offered, but tension is evident in the subjects. It was left on reserve.

Wedding banquet
Eating is an important part of ceremonies in Central Asia. Here the village elders gave thanks for their food before settling down to a banquet at a traditional Islamic wedding.

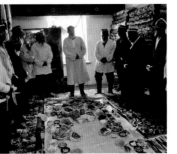

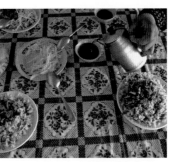

Simple meal
At this simple meal the food was served first and tea, an essential accompaniment, was poured. I tried to show details that are relevant to the story in their context.

Singing and eating
Not every image has to show food to be pertinent. A picture of the party in full swing can tell the reader what all the eating is about and provide a glimpse into people's lives. This was made using flash to supplement the main exposure, stopping the shadows from being too dark despite the very bright sunshine.

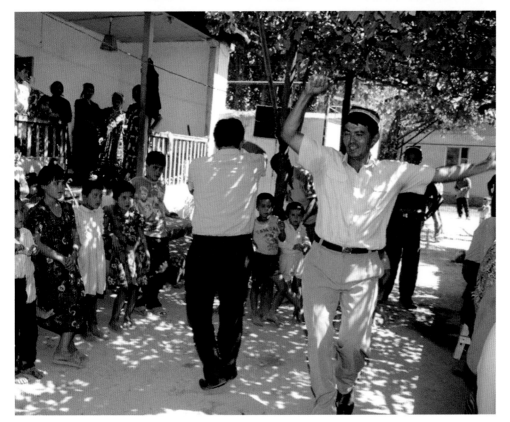

Innocence lost
Children search for scraps of wood in Kabul, Afghanistan. This image was taken by Chinese photographer Chien-Min Chung, who won the 2009 Award of Excellence from Pictures of the Year International for his documentary series "Afghan Child Labor".

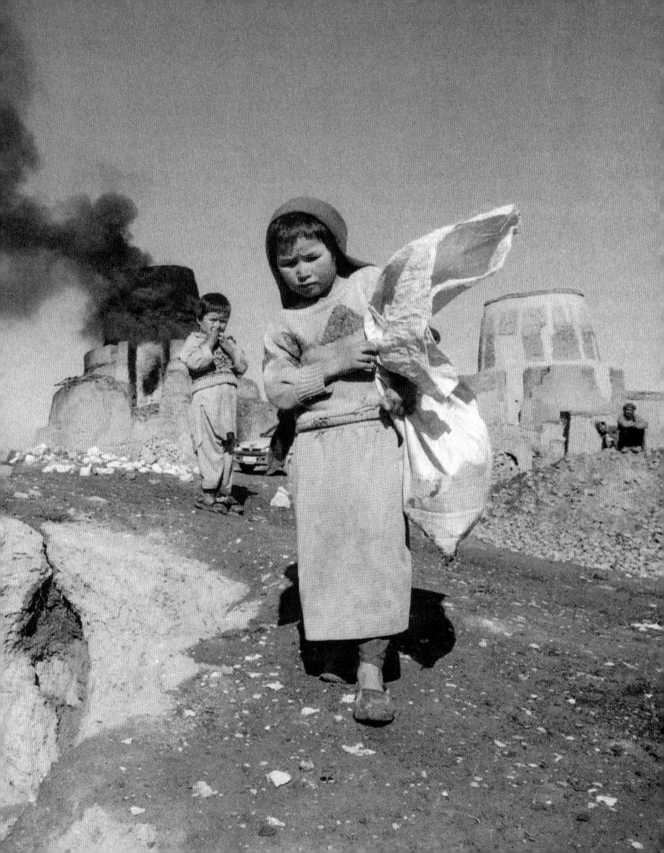

Children

In the earliest days, photographing children was all but impossible because no child would sit still for the long exposures needed. Today, children are one of the most popular and perennial subjects for photography. Responsive cameras and smartphone cameras have made the photographer's job far easier. However, as a subject, children still present a number of challenges.

Essential skills

Child photography is superb training for photojournalism. Trying to persuade an unwilling child to pose for a picture can be as difficult and stressful as trying to get past a police cordon. Children are easily distracted, and are often either too tired or too excitable to co-operate. The very qualities of a photojournalist – patience, understanding, quick reflexes, and great technique – are needed to be successful.

Settling your subject

A key technique of child photography is to exploit the subject's boredom threshold. After the child becomes used to the camera he or she will relax and behave naturally.

When you first bring out the camera the child may play up to you, in which case you should start taking pictures straight away. However, if the child is being shy or difficult you will need to win them over. Allow the child to look through the viewfinder and press a few buttons, even ask them to take a picture of you and show them the result. All these things help put children at ease and get them on your side.

You can take pictures freely with your digital camera or smartphone: just keep making images and review them only when you take a break or the child wanders off.

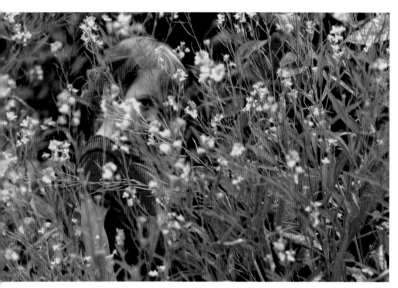

⌃ Capturing moods
A winning smile and a sunny mood are not pre-requisites for a great child photograph. Here, a sulk in the garden is captured perfectly in the tilt of the head and the accusing glance. The key to success of the image is the exact focus on the child's eye.

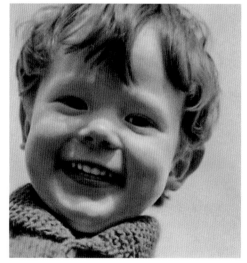

⌃ Child's eye view
We are used to seeing children from above, so a low perspective makes a refreshing change. Children love it when you get down to their level, so you should be rewarded with a big grin.

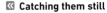

Capturing character

While studio photographs capture the likeness of a child, they rarely capture a child's true character. Spontaneity is the key to obtaining shots that show personality and individuality.

Children are the sternest test of auto-focus systems. One technique that works well is to set the lens manually and stay in focus by keeping at a constant distance by moving as if you are attached to the child by an invisible thread. If you wish to fill the frame, a long focal length (135mm or longer) works best. When using a zoom lens, keep in mind that using the full zoom may set a smaller maximum aperture, which calls for greater exposure, so it is best to work in shutter priority mode to ensure sharp results.

≫ HOW THE MASTERS WORKED

An influential figure in European photography, the Dutch photographer Emmy Andriesse (1914–53) studied photography between 1935 and 1937 at the Academy of Arts in The Hague. She went on to build a successful career working in child portraiture, fashion, advertising, and photojournalism. Being of Jewish descent, she went underground during the Nazi occupation, but recorded the Dutch famine of 1944, known as the "Hunger Winter", and the liberation of the Netherlands in 1945. Andriesse died of cancer when she was just 39 years old.

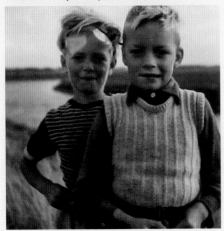

⌃ Emmy Andriesse
Best known for her extensive photography of children, which owes much to the traditions of August Sander, Andriesse's approach to photography was greatly changed by the events of World War II.

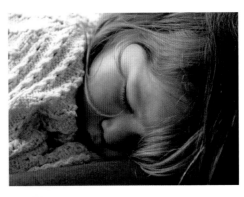

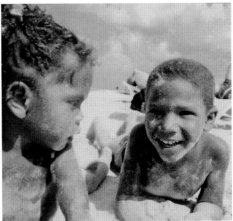

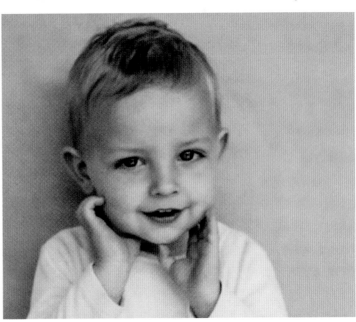

《 Catching them still
One of the most beautiful sights a family can enjoy is a child sleeping peacefully. It is usually best to set the longest focal length possible, then approach as close as you can.

《 Resting after play
If the children are too busy running about enjoying themselves for you to keep up with them, let them wear themselves out and catch them when they flop down for a rest.

⌄ Photographing shy children
Some children are unnerved by large cameras. Compact models are less likely to intimidate them. Here the child's uncertain expression and gestures add to the charm of the image.

Analyzing a child photograph

The perfect child photograph need not be an image that must appeal to people across the world. Rather, it can be an intimate study that holds meaning for just the subject and the photographer. It may be a private moment frozen in time; a flashback to the past that evokes everything loved about the child; it may bring together many elements whose totality references the spirit of childhood and happy memories; or it may simply bring out a feeling of tenderness.

Finding the picture

As with so much of photography, the key to taking great shots of children is to be constantly vigilant and have your camera with you at all times. When the moment arrives, all your photographic skills must come together to frame the image (give yourself plenty of room); to focus the lens (ensure the nearest eye is sharp); and to expose the shot correctly. In this picture a child waits for his turn during a parade in Bishkek, Kyrgyzstan. The obvious image is his portrait, taken close up. But the interplay of pinks between the balloon and his jacket, as well as the rose garden, suggest a wider view.

☑ Adding visible details
Details that become progressively sharper as they near the main subject help to draw attention to the face. Echoes of pink with the jacket also help the composition.

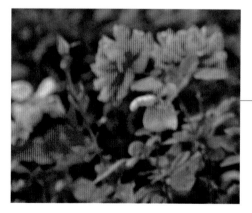

☑ Including focus blurs
Use a long focal length lens to throw background details out of focus, which accentuates the main subject.

☑ Correcting brightness
Exposing for the face renders the hat too white. Here it has been darkened digitally.

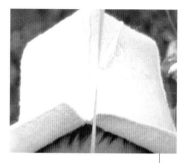

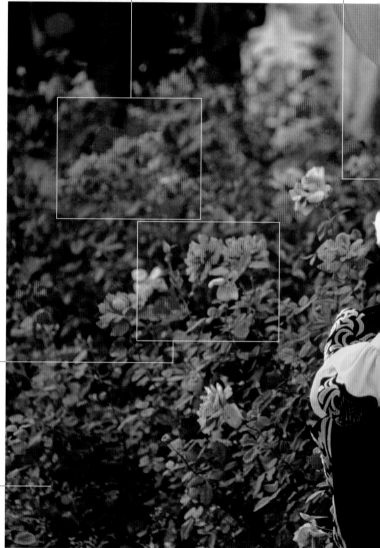

Try to include areas of low contrast and dark colour in your image, to give balance to a busy photograph.

⟫ UNCONVENTIONAL FRAMING

It is all too tempting – and entirely natural – to try to compose all pictures of children so that they occupy the centre of the frame. But other framings can be equally, if not more, arresting and can capture the character of a child by reflecting their unpredictable pattern of movements.

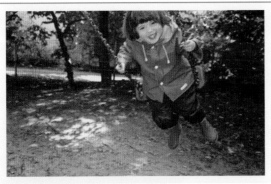

《 Swinging shot
A slight delay in the shutter run means that the child is almost out of frame, but it makes for a dynamic and fun image.

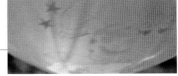

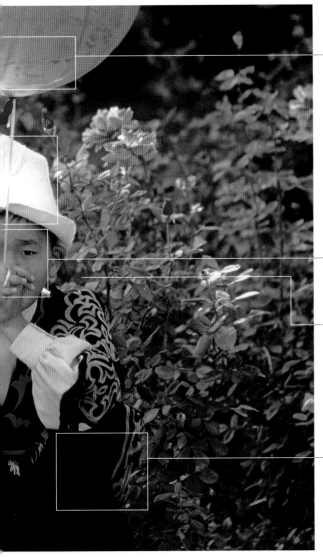

⌃ Centring the composition
The balloon was swaying slightly in the wind, so it was important for me to press the shutter when it was directly over the boy's head.

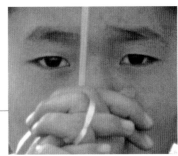

《 Achieving sharp eyes
Central to portraiture of any kind are the eyes. They should be focused as sharply as possible, unless you wish to produce a very specific effect.

Be careful not to allow light reflected from leaves to give the skin an unpleasant green cast.

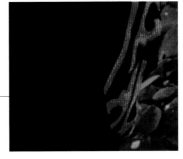

《 Using quiet areas
Exposure should be sufficient to deliver shadow detail, but the lack of detail in this small part of the image is not a problem. It is a quiet area in an otherwise busy image. We are only interested in the boy's face and clothes, and the roses.

The Wailing Wall, Jerusalem
Two girls watch male worshippers at the Western Wall in Jerusalem from a vantage point only open to them because of their youth – a fence on the right separates men from women. Taken by Micha Bar-Am in 1985.

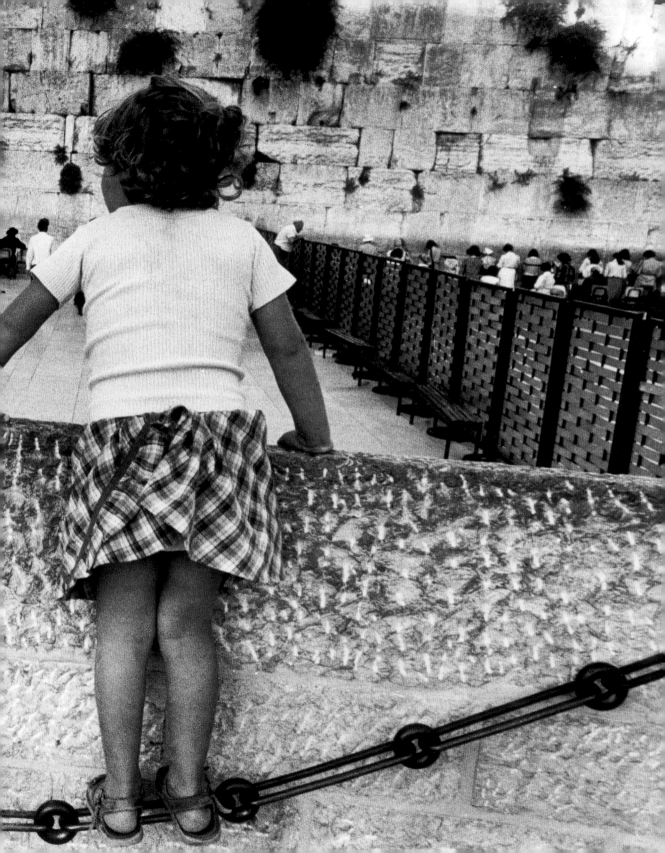

Travel

One area of photography in which amateur photographers dominate is travel. It is easy to see why – more people are going to more places and capturing more images than ever before. But successful travel photography requires more than merely watching a sunset with a camera in one hand and a dry martini in the other. Hard work is needed to ensure you are in the right place at the right time, and looking the right way to find distinctive images.

Original views

There are few destinations in the world that have not been photographed several times over. Most places are well known through multi-millions of images. The challenge of travel photography is to create original images, while coping with the tough conditions often encountered when travelling.

Idea of place

To create outstanding images, try to photograph not the place itself but an idea of the place, or your sense of it. Your goal is to encapsulate the whole place in an image or two. You do this primarily in the third person – as observer – perhaps by showing families enjoying a beach, a couple sharing a sunset, or a traveller shopping in an exotic bazaar. The spirit of travel, a sense of adventure, the joy of learning about our beautiful world – these are the key elements of travel photography. If you work to convey your deep feelings, rather than only snapping the visual candy, you will find that your travel photography improves.

◙ **Foreground interest**
By placing a colourful prow of a boat in the foreground instead of the stretch of beach, this image gives a greater sense of space and an involvement in the place.

» **Using scale**
This image taken in Uzbekistan has everything – a Timurid monument in the background; the social documentary of the weddings in the near background; and the boys in graceful poses in the foreground. All are dominated by the huge statue that disturbs the sense of scale.

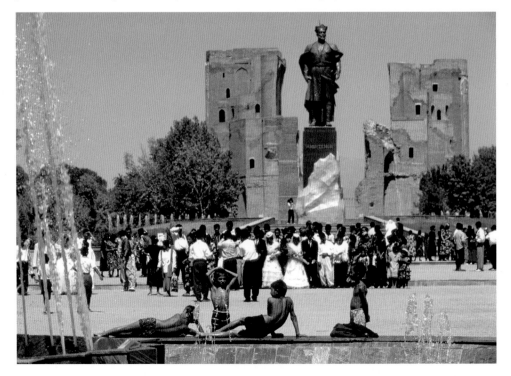

Caring for equipment

Check your equipment throughout the day, and clean each item whenever necessary. Keep lenses, particularly the front lens, clean and free of dust. If you use an interchangeable lens camera, keep your sensor clean by changing lenses in dust-free conditions where possible. Also use the camera's cleaning mode and the manufacturer's cleaning recommendations. Travel with ample memory cards so you never have to delete images to make space. Back up your images using a disk drive or a cloud service.

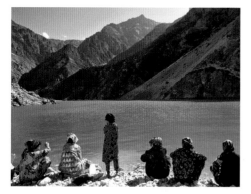

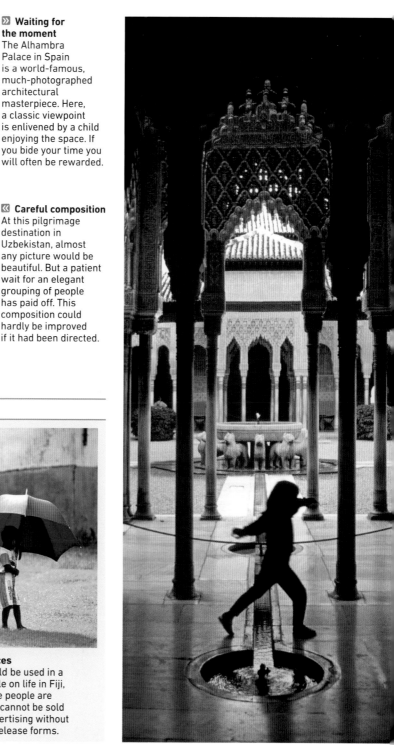

» Waiting for the moment
The Alhambra Palace in Spain is a world-famous, much-photographed architectural masterpiece. Here, a classic viewpoint is enlivened by a child enjoying the space. If you bide your time you will often be rewarded.

« Careful composition
At this pilgrimage destination in Uzbekistan, almost any picture would be beautiful. But a patient wait for an elegant grouping of people has paid off. This composition could hardly be improved if it had been directed.

» MODEL RELEASES

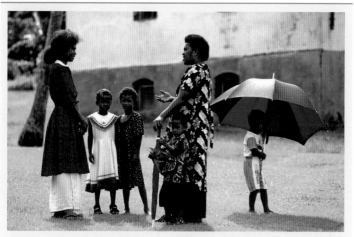

If you want to publish your images, you have a duty to any people depicted to be accurate and fair to them. If the pictures are used commercially, you must obtain model releases from each person (*see p. 303*) in the shot.

⌃ Showing faces
This image could be used in a magazine article on life in Fiji, but because the people are recognizable it cannot be sold or used for advertising without signed model release forms.

Analyzing a travel picture

Some travel pictures are simply stunning shots of a beautiful place, while others manage to inform, teach, or show the viewer something about life in another country. But since travel photography is one of the most oversubscribed forms of photography, a travel picture needs to stand out in order to create an impact. Merely being informative is not enough. Successful travel pictures are colourful and characterful, well timed, and, importantly, technically perfect.

Waiting for the moment

This photograph could easily be used to convey information about a way of life, or about what a visitor to Marrakech, Morocco, might expect to see. But the shot was also timed to capture an atmospheric light, and to show people going about their business and interacting with each other, which creates a more arresting image and a lasting impression. The zoom lens was set to a moderately wide angle so as not to distort figures on the periphery of the frame. Then it was a matter of waiting and watching people, until their positions and actions fell into a compositionally coherent pattern – the decisive moment in which independent elements add up to a meaningful whole.

Warm colours of the wall are adjacent to one another in the colour palette

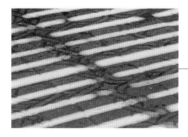

⌃ Sense of depth
The strong diagonal lines of light and shade lead the eye across the image and into the depths of the scene, creating a sense of a living space. The lively lighting also transforms the otherwise empty floor into something that contributes to the visual interest.

⌄ Capturing activity
The photograph shows activities typical of a Moroccan market – selling and buying.

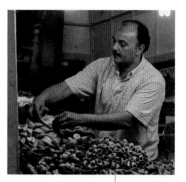

⌄ Delicious colours
The many colours of a Moroccan market are central to its appeal. Here the wide range of hues from reds through to greens provide an exotic visual feast.

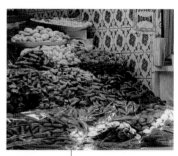

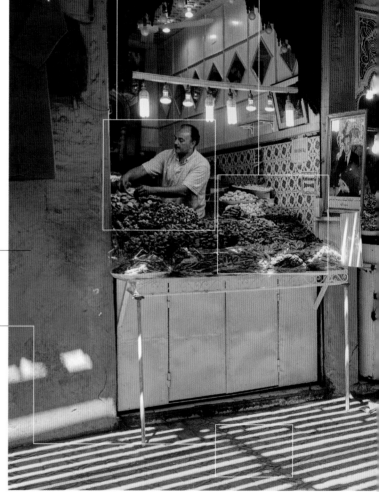

》 EYE CONTACT

Photographs of people you meet on your travels are more interesting if the photograph gives you eye contact with the subject. Direct eye contact will show that you have succeeded in creating a relationship with the person in the picture, rather than being merely an observer or, worse, an unwelcome interruption in their lives. This in turn helps make the viewer feel more comfortable about examining the image and creates a sense of involvement.

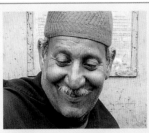

⌃ No eye contact
Although he is smiling, the lack of eye contact shows that the man is shy or uncomfortable about being photographed.

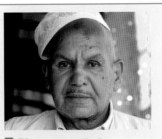

⌃ Direct eye contact
He may not be smiling, but the direct eye contact shows that he is aware of the photographer. He next broke into a broad grin.

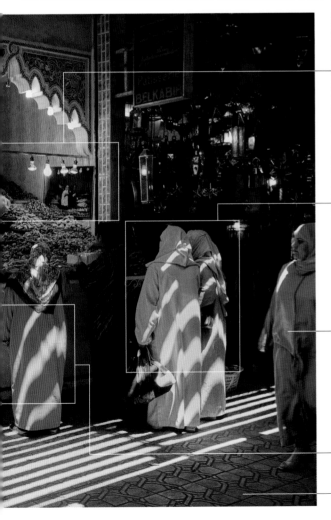

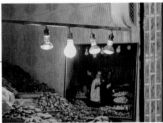

《 Perfect sharpness
As a measure of quality, sharpness is the first judgment made by any viewer, professional or not. If the image is not sharp it will be rejected, unless there is a very good reason to reconsider it.

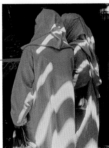

《 White balance
The standard bearers of accurate colour are the neutral tones. Here the whites and greys contain little other colour, which leads the eye to read all colours correctly.

Captured movement leads the viewer's eye into the scene

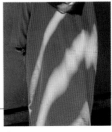

《 Tonal gradation
Smooth tonal transitions or gradations are a sure sign of correct exposure. Here the subtle changes in the pink tones are captured perfectly.

Precise exposure retains detail in the shadows

Zanzibar Island
An ultra-wide-angle lens captures both the man in the foreground as well as the distant ruins, and all with equal sharpness. As the lens was pointed down slightly, the ruined columns do not appear parallel to each other – as they should be – but converge a little downwards.

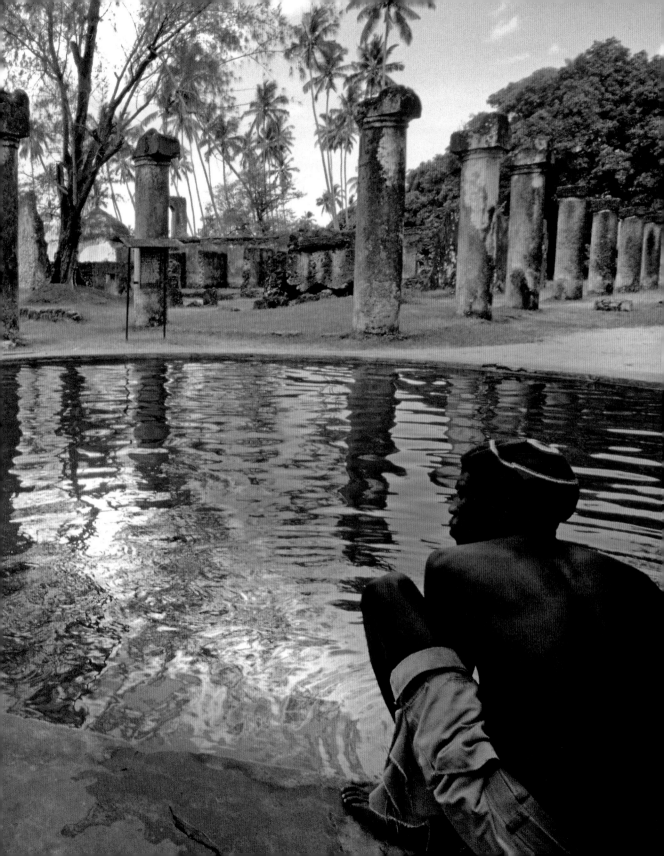

Landscapes

While the land may appear to be passively lying there awaiting your attention, in truth it is a capricious, challenging subject. Arriving at a destination, you may find terrain or vegetation preventing you from reaching a better viewpoint. Meanwhile, the light is changing rapidly. You may have to act quickly, or be prepared to wait. Landscape photography can range from an opportunistic, quick snapshot of whatever is on offer, to the reward of patient effort.

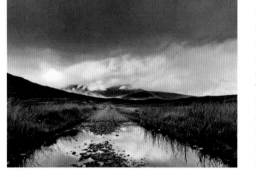

» Vanishing points
Converging parallel lines, such as the tracks of this path in the Scottish Highlands, are effective for conveying a sense of space and distance in the scene.

Working with light

Landscape photographers may seem to be at the mercy of the weather. Either the day is too cloudy and dull or it is too bright and sunny. But remember that all light is good light, and that a key part of photography is using it creatively. The great mountain photographer Galen Rowell (*see pp. 234–5*) put it simply: "I almost never set out to photograph a landscape... my first thought is always of light." In short, you can shoot landscapes in any light conditions. You just have to let the light lead you to the picture.

» Soaring heights
An outcrop of red sandstone near Issyk-Kul, Kyrgyzstan, has been photographed from below with a row of pine trees in silhouette to propel the energy of the image upwards, towards the blue sky. The composition falls into golden ratios (*see pp.152-3*), giving a sense of harmony.

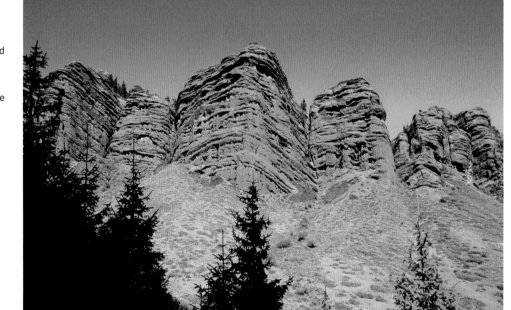

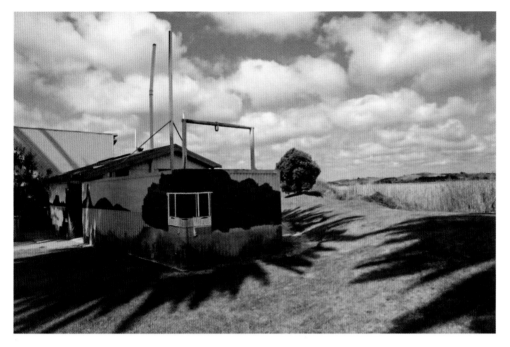

‹‹ Waiting for the right light
If you capture an image the first time you see a promising landscape, you may be disappointed with the result. Observe how changes in the light affect the scene. Here, the photographer waited until the shadows fell so that they appeared to emanate, rather intriguingly, from the building.

Harnessing the landscape

There are simple tricks you can use to improve your landscape photography. One is to exaggerate a format. For example, the panoramic shot (*see p.118*) is popular because it can make something unusual out of the ordinary. Another "trade secret" is to make use of reflections – these can provide visual interest in an otherwise unexceptional image. Remember too that landscape compositions do not have to be divided equally between the land and the sky. You might find the picture works best if you concentrate on the foreground and reduce the sky to a narrow strip, or you may want to create a dramatic effect by emphasizing the vastness of the sky.

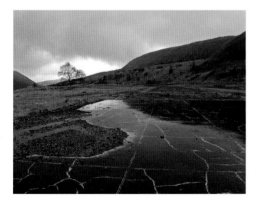

⌃ Cloud break
Here, the photographer waited until the clouds lifted in the distance, framing the tree on the horizon and allowing a reflection of light to creep over the foreground.

›› HOW THE MASTERS WORK

Artists have long been inspired by the glorious light and landscapes of the Mediterranean. Franco Fontana (1933–) is one of Italy's foremost photographers and his stunning images of his native land have been published and exhibited worldwide.

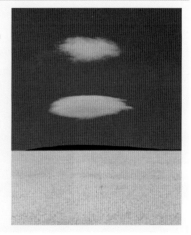

›› Franco Fontana
This classic landscape, taken in Italy in 1978, is characteristic of Fontana's clean, graphic, deceptively simple style. It also demonstrates a complete mastery over perspective, colour, light, and composition.

Analyzing a sunset photograph

Not surprisingly, sunsets were not a popular subject before the advent of colour photography, and even then they were difficult to capture because the lenses of the time were not well protected against flare from the sun. But with modern, multi-coated lenses, sunsets are an irresistible subject that appear easy to photograph. Yet results often disappoint because of the difficulty of exposing correctly for sunsets, which usually have a wide dynamic range.

Exposure and foreground

A common mistake when taking sunset photographs is to underexpose the image, which often results in areas of shadow appearing too dark, with little or no detail. To avoid this, measure the exposure at the part of the scene that is most important – often the area that is at right-angles to the setting sun. Then compose the shot to include features of interest in the foreground. These were the strategies for the sunset scene shown right, which I photographed in southern Wales. Exposure was metered on the golden sand in the foreground, and I took care to include details such as footprints and reflections in the wet sand, a small stream, rocks, crisp shadows, and seaweed.

Composing the image
The horizon has been placed in a classic position, roughly corresponding to the golden section, to give a balanced composition. It is important to ensure that the horizon is level.

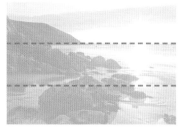

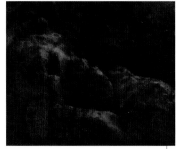

Adding shadow detail
Ensure that shadows hold detail. If necessary, enhance them with imaging software.

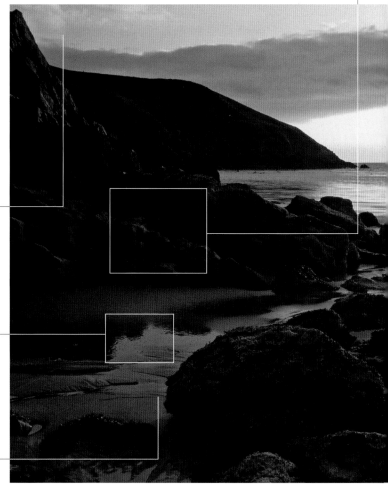

The sky may appear too light when exposure is set for the beach. Here, it was darkened during image manipulation.

Including off-centre interest
Ensure that there is an interesting play of light or some other effect even in "quiet" areas of your image.

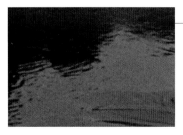

Note the diffused flare spot caused by internal reflections in the camera lens.

≫ USING GRADUATED FILTERS

An effective way to reduce the brightness of the sky without affecting the foreground prior to image manipulation is to use a graduated filter. This fades from maximum colour density at one edge to transparent around halfway across. Beware that the filter may cause lens flare from internal reflections if the sun is in view, and the gradient effect also varies with focal length and aperture.

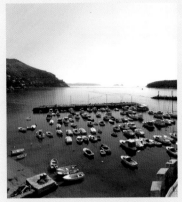

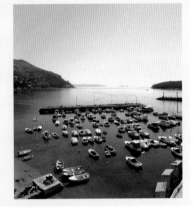

◁ No filter attached
This shot was taken with a wide-angle lens with no graduated filter. The sky appears too bright and lacks colour.

▷ Tobacco filter attached
A brown-coloured graduated filter introduces warm tones into the otherwise over-bright and pallid sky.

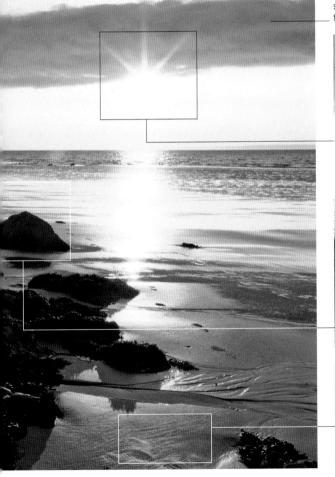

You can reduce the dynamic range of the scene with a graduated filter, to darken the sky without darkening the foreground.

◁ Working quickly
Even in slow-paced landscape work, timing is all-important. Here, exposure was timed to be just sufficient for the sun to appear past the cloud, but not enough for it to break through fully, as this would create too much flare.

◁ Selecting a position
The perspective of this shot was chosen to ensure that the silhouettes of the rocks in the middle of the image would appear sharp against a clean background.

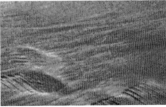

◁ Measuring exposure
The exposure was set so that the mid-tone colours are true to life and nicely saturated.

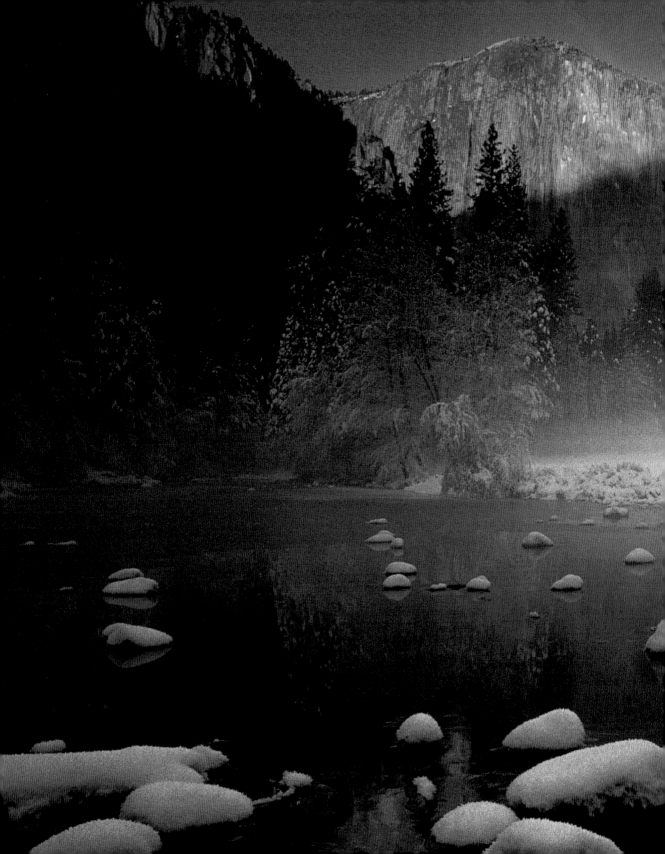

El Capitan and the Merced River in winter
In this striking image, taken by the
celebrated photographer Galen Rowell,
the sheer granite rockface of El Capitan
in Yosemite National Park, California, is
set ablaze by the light of the setting sun.
The reflected light spills into the inky
waters of the Merced River.

Plants and gardens

The natural world is one of the most popular subjects for photography, and it is no wonder. Plants, flowers, and gardens are inherently beautiful, and provide an unlimited variety of forms, colours, and compositions. But even such perfect material needs to be worked on, and the challenge for the photographer is to combine technical skill with imagination to create inspiring images.

Flowers and plants

A large part of the skill of plant photography lies in working with a narrow depth of field to focus on the crucial part of the image. But equally important is thinking creatively to create a distinctive image. Try experimenting with a variety of different viewpoints, compositions, and light conditions.

Working outside

While few things in life are more pleasant than walking around a beautiful garden in the sunshine in a cooling breeze, such conditions are less than ideal for plant photography. Bright sunlight causes lit areas to be very bright or "hot", while areas in shadow are dark. This high contrast is inimical to the accurate rendition of colours needed for the best plant photographs. In addition, the long exposure required for shots with an extended depth of field calls for the subject to stay absolutely still, which can only happen when there is not a breath of air. Partially overcast, still days are best for plant photography, but you can create beautiful images whatever the conditions.

» Using backlighting
Flowers with translucent petals look particularly beautiful when photographed from a very low angle against the light.

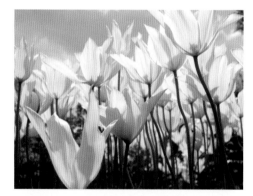

» Creating a painterly effect
Pictures of flowers need not always be pin-sharp. An impressionist view can give a sense of flowers swaying in the wind, moving in and out of focus.

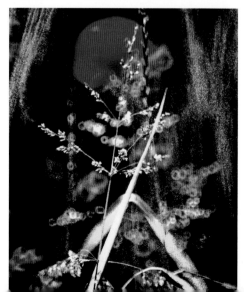

⌄ Highlighting texture
The strong sunlight catching these grasses almost burns out the detail and emphasizes their soft, furry texture.

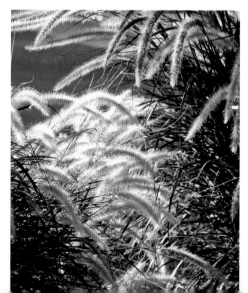

Working close up

Depth of field reduces rapidly the more closely
you focus and you may need to focus very near
a flower to fill the frame. Even with minimum
aperture set, depth of field may extend little
more than a finger's width. If you want as much
as possible sharp, use a short focal length, set
a small aperture, such as f/16, and high ISO to
shorten exposure time. Digital cameras using
small sensors are at an advantage here as
the small sensor may increase apparent depth of
field. For more reliable results, light the subject
with a flash that is aimed at a reflector to send
diffused light on to the flowers from one side.
For shadowless light, use a ring flash, in which
the flash surrounds the lens, to provide even
lighting that can be very flattering to flowers. For
the sharpest results, use specialist macro lenses.
Their focal-length range is from 24mm to 200mm.

Indoor studio

Because of the problems of photographing in the
open air, many professional flower photographers
prefer the controlled environment of the studio.
But you do not need an elaborate studio set-up to
make a success of flower photography. You need
only a table, a plain background, and a good source
of light, such as a large window. Indoors you have
the advantage of complete stillness so you can
make full use of a tripod to capture perfectly
sharp images.

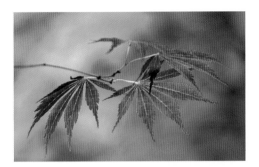

« Isolating details
The longest setting of a
zoom lens is excellent
for close-ups. This
image was taken on
a 100–400mm lens
set to 400mm.

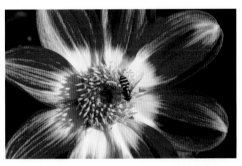

« Using a macro lens
Flowers are one of
the most rewarding
subjects for close-ups.
By using a macro lens
and a tripod you can
capture minute details.

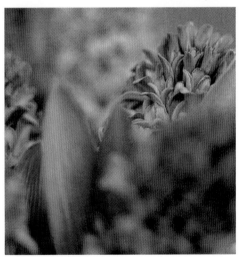

« Tight framing
By bringing a pot
of plants indoors
and setting it on
a table you can
frame the image
in ways that would
be difficult outdoors.

⊠ Making a study
Flowers arranged on plain white
card and photographed from above
make a simple and stylish image,
reminiscent of a botanical study.

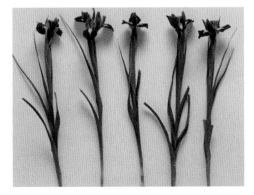

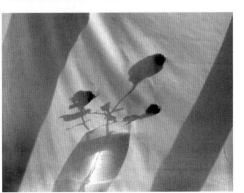

**« Trying a
different approach**
A sheet of muslin
hanging over a
window acts as
a back-projection
screen, giving an
unusual, abstract
view of roses in
a glass vase.

Capturing the spirit of a garden

Garden environments range from large, formal landscapes, which are organized with elements and views composed for the visitor, to private gardens, which are very often an unruly compromise between space and resources. The challenge of photographing a garden is not merely to record an attractive, accurate representation, but to find and capture viewpoints that will surprise and delight even someone who has intimate knowledge of the place.

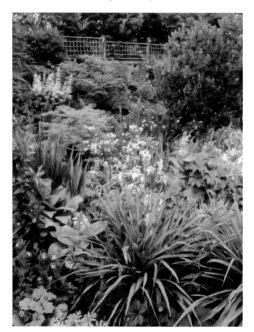

Different approaches

More than almost any other kind of location photography, a successful garden photograph should capture the unique *genius locii* – spirit of the place – that distinguishes it from all other gardens. This spirit may be evident only at certain times of the year, in certain lighting conditions, or when viewed from carefully chosen viewpoints. The trick, then, is to approach the garden with an open mind, walk through it slowly, looking at it from a variety of vantage points and perspectives. For some shots you may need to wait for later in the day to get the best lighting. Also try out different formats, the typical horizontal landscape format is not necessarily the best for every picture.

⊠ Formal garden
The garden of interior designer David Hicks merits a formal style of photography. The square format and neat hedges lead the eye to the central sculpture.

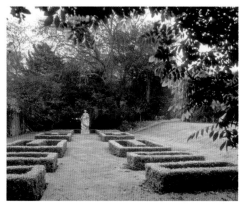

⊼ Informal garden
A slightly raised, wide-angle view, provides foreground interest and emphasizes the variety in this densely planted garden.

❱❱ PERMISSIONS AND ACCESS

As gardening has become a prosperous industry, owners of gardens have become aware of the monetary value of their properties. If you wish to publish your images or sell them as prints, you are operating in a commercial realm in which it is recommended that you obtain permission prior to photography. If you are not sure of your rights or obligations, you should seek expert advice.

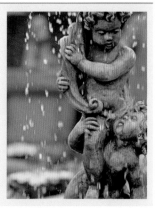

❱❱ Ornamental features
This image was taken at the Chelsea Flower Show in London, where amateur photography is permitted but commercial photography is restricted to those who have obtained permits.

Colour contrasts
You do not need to show the whole garden to give a flavour of its colourful character and architectural elements.

Sparse compositions
Some designs make a virtue of simplicity and modernism. This garden was photographed using the same approach.

Incidental patterns
With careful framing, details such as the pattern of stones in a path or the shape of steps, are also worth photographing.

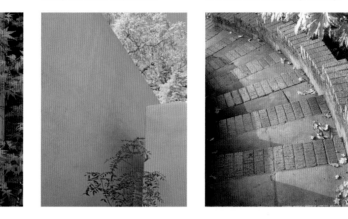

Exploring viewpoints

Garden design is all about offering attractive views, which is one reason why gardens are such a popular subject for photography. But simply snapping away at whatever presents itself is likely to produce disappointing results. Successful garden photography requires patience, consideration, and the ability to find unusual viewpoints. A view may be dull in one light but entrancing in another. And a small change in viewpoint – crouching down or standing on a bench – may make the difference between an average and a stunning composition. The very nature of a garden means that at times your viewpoint may be restricted. A zoom lens is ideal for garden photography, as it enables you to control what is in the frame. When composing a wide-angle shot that includes trees, keep the camera level – not tilted back or forward – to avoid converging parallels.

Shooting at night
A lamplit garden at night is transformed into a magical, mysterious place. Use a tripod and a long exposure to capture colours accurately.

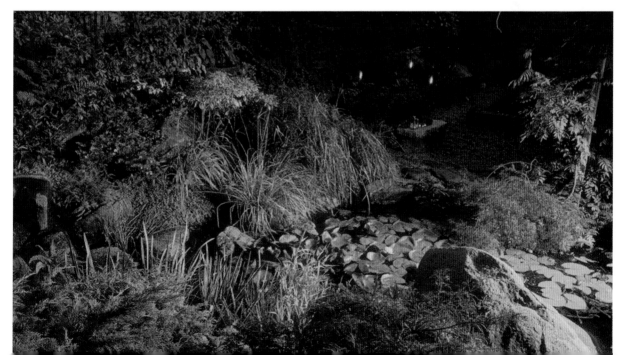

Garden symmetry
The elegant simplicity and spare lines of this garden, with its receding avenue of trees and mirror-like pool, is best represented by an equally refined and symmetrical view.

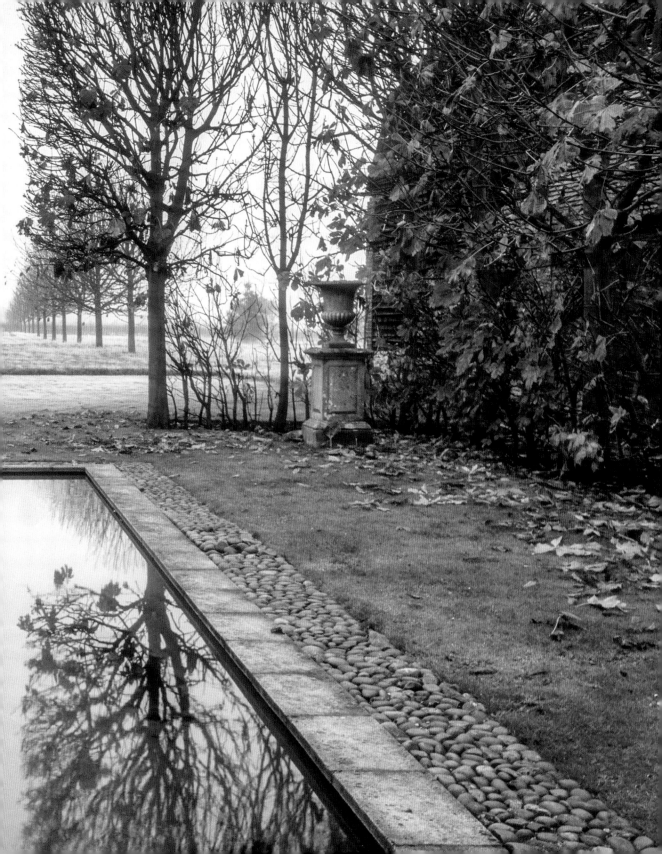

The nude

Much of photography is arguably the photography of beauty, and the human body – particularly the female form – has enjoyed a favoured, as well as tempestuous, relationship with the camera. There has never been a shortage of models, except in areas where there are legal restrictions on nude photography. A huge variety of approaches have been undertaken, yet the subject holds great potential for further development and innovation.

Lighting conditions

The best lighting for photographing the nude body is soft or diffused. This is because even a small amount of excess light will cause overexposure of the brighter parts of a light-skinned body. With darker skin, the situation is even more difficult to control. Shadows will lose detail while the curves of a body will reflect light, which over-exposes the image. As a result, the softest light with minimal shadows is the easiest to work with. However, photographers such as Lucien Clergue (*see pp. 176–7*) show that direct sunlight can be used – with results that are striking in proportion to the technical difficulty.

Composing the shot

While some photographers create successful images of the entire body, many of the best images limit the view to an almost abstract detail. It is easier to pose the model for a partial view, whereas many poses showing the whole body appear mannered or false.

If you are restricting the shot to just a part of the body it is best to use a medium-length telephoto lens (equivalent of about 70mm–135mm). This stops you getting too close to the model and so ensures that the parts of the body closest to you are not exaggerated.

Working together

Your model's comfort – both physical and emotional – is paramount. Explain what you want to achieve and allow them to position themselves. In so doing, you both work together to achieve the result you desire. You can also review the shots with your model. This is reassuring for them, and gives valuable feedback that will help them refine their pose.

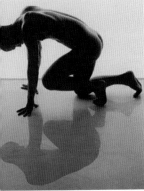

Formal study
The beauty of an athletic figure is shown best through simple outlines and lighting. The reflection adds dynamic drama to the pose.

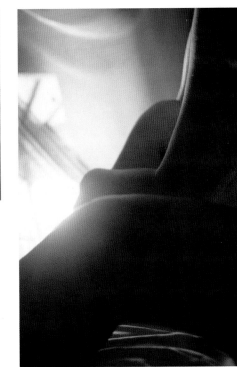

Backlit figure
The nude figure has been pushed to the periphery in this image, so that it is as much about light and mood as about the body.

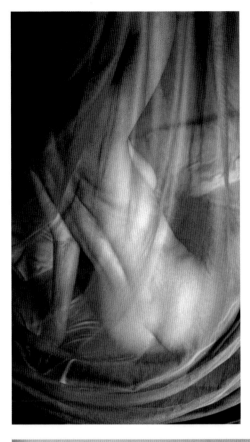

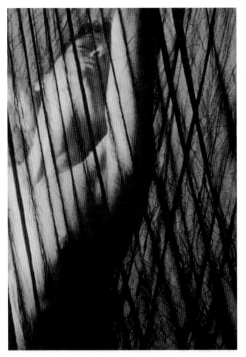

Dream-like effect
Here the same diffusion technique has been used, but the netting has been arranged to create strong diagonal lines across the body, giving the image an ethereal, abstract quality.

Blue diffusion
In this image, intense morning light is diffused by a blue mosquito net. The blue contrasts well with the skin tones, and by focusing past the netting, I created a soft haze over the body.

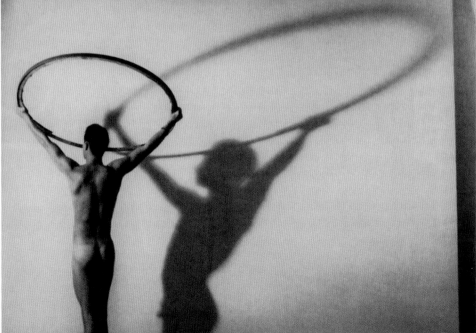

Using props
In this nude study, the subject is shown as much by the shadow as by the body itself. But the clever use of the hoop takes the image into the symbolic realm, suggesting the Olympics and athleticism with striking clarity. Props do not need to be elaborate to be effective.

Covering the shoot

On nude photoshoots the tiniest change in position or framing makes a big difference. It is best to ensure that you give yourself plenty of choice at the picture-editing stage (*see pp. 309–10*) by capturing as many images as possible. Once you create a working set-up, be sure to capture lots of images from different angles and positions to "cover" all possibilities.

Creating different effects

Use different lens settings to achieve different effects. Try varying the focal length, the point at which you focus, and the aperture setting. If your lighting is flat, experiment by overexposing, and if your lighting is more contrasty, try underexposing the shot, too. Alternatively, try out different white balance and picture profile settings to vary the colours. Use the highest quality settings on the camera. Skin tones always benefit from the best possible tonal quality, which demands high-resolution image capture, preferably in raw format. Another effective variant is to introduce deliberate blur or softness using soft-focus or diffusing filters. Finally, do not forget to shoot both vertical (portrait) format pictures as well as horizontal (landscape) format pictures – this will give you a range of choices when you come to select the most successful images.

☑ Preserving modesty

Many poses can be attractive without having to show more nudity than necessary, or more than is acceptable in many societies. You can still show sensual lines and skin textures.

» Using shadows
While faces are usually shown well lit, it can be effective to allow the face to fall partially or wholly into shadow. This simplifies features to their elegant outlines.

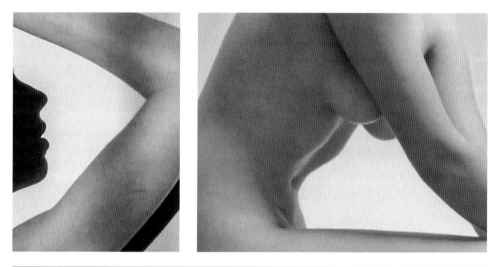

» STAYING WITHIN THE LAW

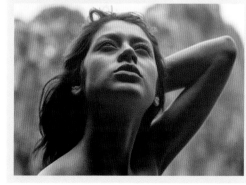

In some countries, nude photography is not permitted. Wherever you are in the world you need to be fully aware of local traditions and laws. Restrictions on nude photography may apply not only in public places such as beaches, however deserted, but also in your hotel room.

◀ Guarding your pictures

Do not keep a memory card with nude pictures in your camera when travelling through Customs or other inspection points. If anyone checks the camera's operation – routine when security levels are high – they may inadvertently see the pictures. At best it will be embarrassing, at worst you could face delays and questioning.

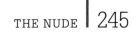

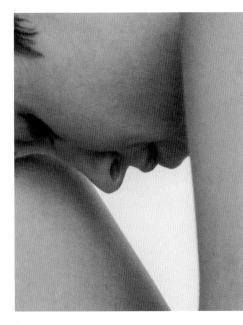

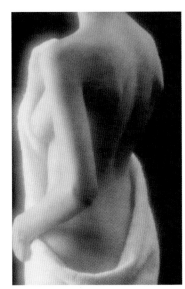

Backlit silhouettes
Models reluctant to reveal themselves fully can be photographed in silhouette against a strong light such as a window. The pose will need to show the shape of the body clearly.

Facial expressions
Inexperienced models may be tempted to smile too much for the camera, while professionals may not smile enough. The best expressions show that the model is relaxed and happy.

 Soft lighting
Low-contrast or soft lighting as well as the highest quality imaging is needed to render tonal gradations and subtle skin tones accurately.

Diffusion
Softening the image by using filters, special lenses, or image manipulation software imparts a hazy, romantic feel to your nude photography.

 Light and shade
Hard light is effective if you want to reveal shapes and lines – as here – rather than concentrating on tones and smooth transitions.

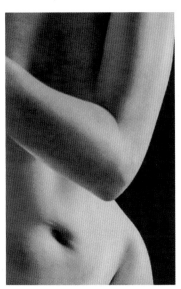

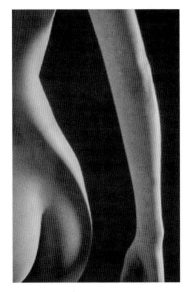

Reflected landscape
A magnificent landscape view of the Mungawai Heads, New Zealand, is reflected in a panoramic window while the model poses for the camera.

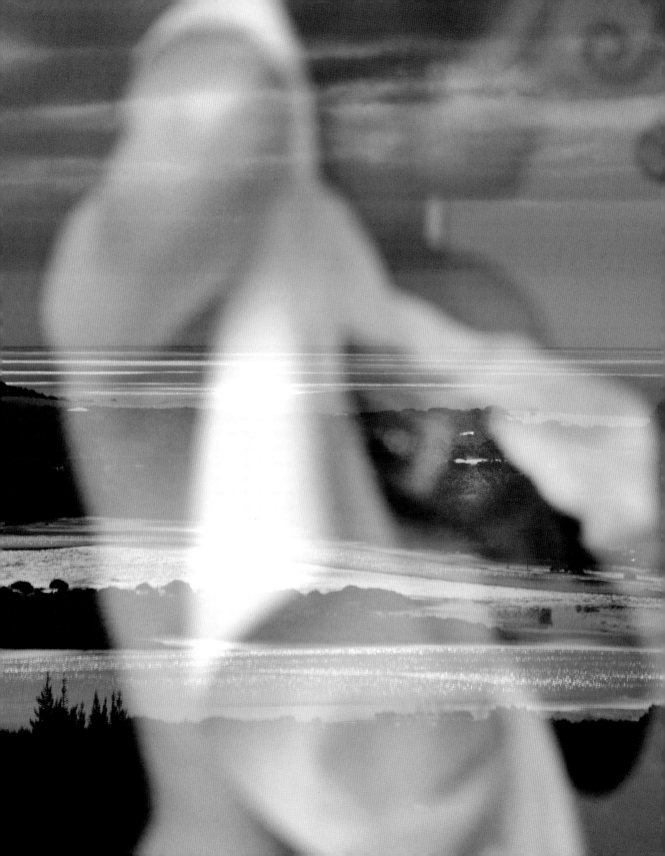

Architecture

Photographing buildings and interiors may seem to be straightforward because the subjects stay still. But it is technically demanding work that calls for precise framing and visual ingenuity. That said, photographing architecture is extremely rewarding. The challenge is to interpret the architect's vision using a two-dimensional medium to capture the essence of a complex three-dimensional space.

Portrait of a building

Your aim when photographing any building is to create a portrait, and it is as important to understand the architecture as it is to understand the sitter when capturing a human likeness. Whether you are photographing the interior or exterior of a building you should spend some time walking around to get a sense of scale, shape, and space. Two key aspects to successful architecture photography are lighting and spatial organization. Soft lighting, in the form of directional sunlight from a three-quarter angle, is best for capturing textures and form. You can also use the lines of walls and other structures to suggest depth and emphasize shape.

Finding a speciality

As your interest in photographing buildings grows, you are likely to develop a special interest. This could range from the gargoyles found on churches across Europe to the decorations on doors of homes in Africa, to the vernacular architecture of mountain regions. A specialist interest gives you the impetus to see more of and learn more about a site of architectural interest than the average tourist. Whatever your speciality, it is important to keep notes (these can be embedded into digital images using image management software). This way, as the collection grows, its value as a source of information will increase.

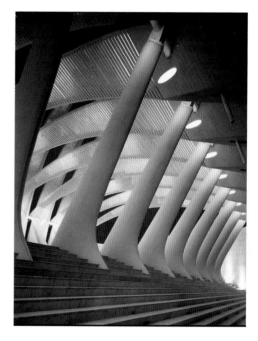

⌃ Linear composition
This Pavilion at the 2002 Seville Expo has been photographed to exploit the rhythmic repeating lines but the image lacks a sense of scale.

» Static composition
This photograph of the marina at Barcelona brings out its calm elegance. The linear composition and strong vertical lines emphasizes stability and static weight.

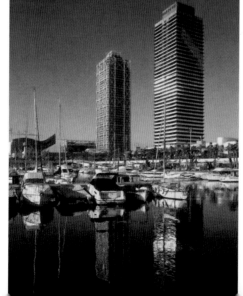

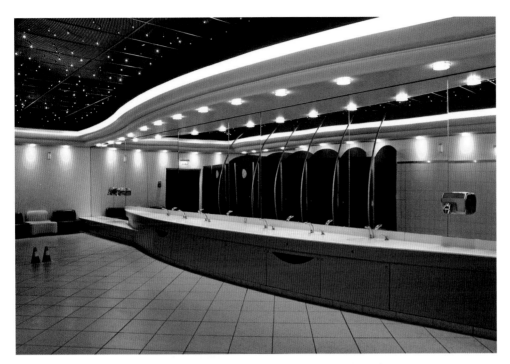

‹‹ Stylish interior
If modern interiors are your special interest, shut away your preconceptions. This public convenience in Normandy, France is a perfect example of an unexpected photo opportunity. A wide-angle view with the camera held level allows the space to speak for itself.

›› Using reflections
This shopping arcade has been shot from a low viewpoint that exploits the reflections of the glass ceiling in the shop windows to create a sense of light and space.

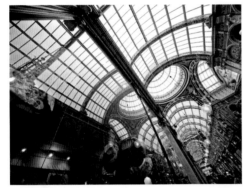

›› Symmetrical composition
The staircase at the British Museum is a perfect example of a strongly symmetrical shape. The picture is enlivened by the random positions of the small figures.

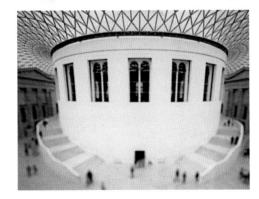

›› HOW THE MASTERS WORK

Modernist architecture provides endless scope for creating striking abstract images. The architectural photographer Richard Bryant elevates this approach to an art form. He has been awarded a fellowship of the Royal Institute of British Architects.

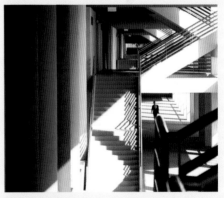

⌃ Richard Bryant
This image shows a masterful use of light, colour, and repeating graphic elements that draw the eye through overlapping spaces. The tiny figure on the stairs imparts a sense of scale.

Analyzing an architecture shot

A good way to judge an architecture shot is to consider whether the architect would be pleased with it. Does the image convey the architect's intentions? Does it accurately portray the style of the building? Does the fall of light show off textures and the articulation of space to their greatest advantage? The best architectural photography avoids exaggerated proportions and misleading spatial relationships, while capturing precise details.

Correcting converging verticals

When photographing buildings, such as this Spanish cathedral, a central issue is how to accurately represent the subject. Because of the size of most buildings, a key part of this is ensuring that vertical lines remain parallel. Tilting the camera upwards to take in the full height of the building will magnify the bottom of the image, which causes the building to "lean" backwards. This effect can be useful for emphasizing scale, but if you wish to avoid it you have two options. Technically, the best is to use a shift lens. This slides the lens upwards to "see" more of the upper part of the image. You can also use image manipulation software to return converging lines to parallel.

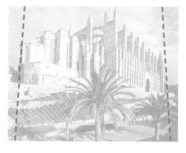

⌃ Sa Seu, Palma de Mallorca
Pointing the camera upwards caused the sides of the cathedral to converge. Digitally enlarging the upper part of the image corrects the convergence.

⌄ Exploiting sunlight
Light falling at an angle of 45° to the main face of the building is ideal as it enhances the textures of the walls. I chose a position to one side of the building to exploit the shadows and highlights to best effect.

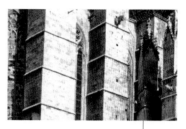

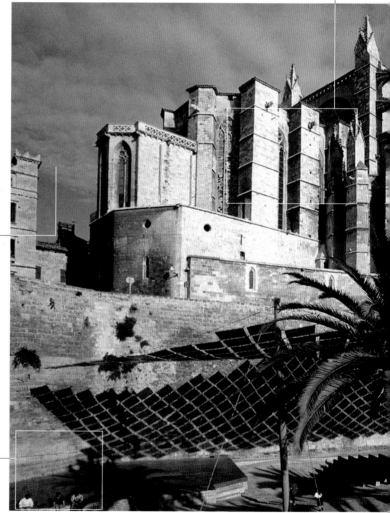

Thin cloud is excellent for architecture photography. Here the movement of clouds suggests a spreading away from the building.

⌄ Figures in the foreground
When composing a shot like this it is helpful to include people, to give a sense of scale.

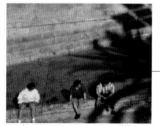

≫ RIGHTS AND ACCESS

Whether you are photographing an ancient monument or a modern shopping centre, always consider your right of access. If you are shooting at an ancient site, check with the relevant authorities to see if photography is permitted. In a shopping centre, restaurant, or gallery, remember that you are on private property owned by a commercial enterprise that has the right to ask you to leave. However, if you are discreet and do not cause an obstruction you are likely to be left alone.

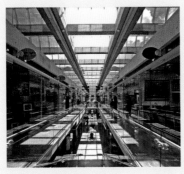

《 Photographing in a shopping centre
The clean lines, glass, metal structures, and symmetrical patterns of modern shopping centres are excellent for photography. Work swiftly and quietly but try not to look too secretive, and use a compact camera with a true wide-angle lens (equivalent of 28mm).

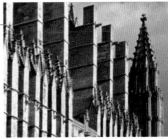

《 Space for composition
It is important to give a building space to "breathe" visually. Here, careless framing has lost the top of a spire.

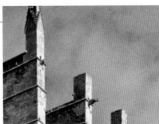

《 Choosing depth of field
Wide depth of field is the norm for architectural photography – I used a wide-angle lens set to a small aperture (f/11) to extend sharpness from the building to the nearest palm tree.

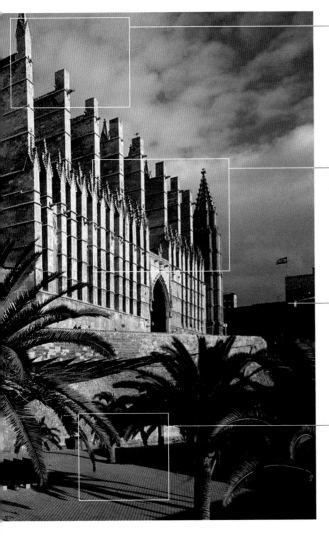

When working in bright sunlight, try to ensure that detail is present in any shadows. Otherwise, an area of black may disfigure the image.

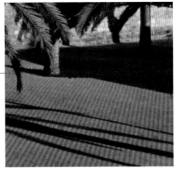

《 Avoiding moiré
When using a digital camera, try to avoid fine grid-like patterns such as stonework. This can interfere with the regular grid of the camera's sensor to cause distortion, known as the moiré effect.

Guggenheim, Bilbao
Framing with simplicity and eschewing all artifice, the photographer has fully exploited this magnificent modern structure's sweeping lines and reflective surfaces.

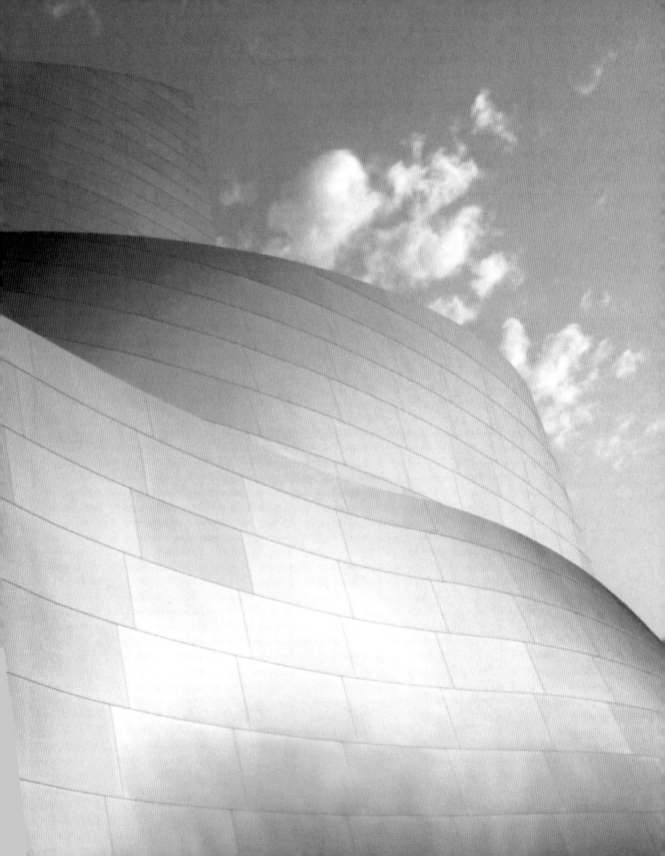

Art

For some, the term "art photography" is an oxymoron – a marriage of two contradictory terms. But photography can transcend its craft-based nature by combining innovation in vision with inventive use of materials. Art photography can be anything from a concept-driven image that seeks to articulate an art-critical position, to the simple pursuit of an abstract idea.

Qualities of art photographs

From fine-art prints to highly crafted collages, art photography covers a very broad spectrum. In general, work driven by ideas or concepts and that offers expressive values beyond the realms of aesthetics and technical perfection is more likely to be accepted as art than a purely observational or visually interesting shot. In addition, to be collectible, artworks must have traits such as permanence and uniqueness.

Finding a theme

A theme that resonates strongly within you can supply enough creative energy to last a lifetime. It could be as simple as memories of your childhood, portrayed through photographic montages of ephemera, or a place that is special to you, captured in different lights and at different times to convey different moods. Or the project could be more impersonal – investigating the way that light falling through your window can transform the

» Morning light
It is the content of a picture and the intentions of the photographer that define an image as art. In this image, daylight on a bed abstracts into a formalist composition.

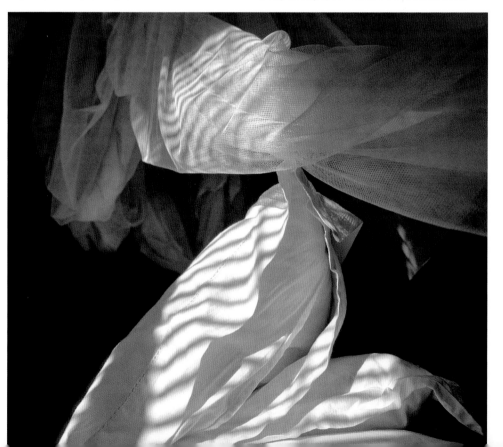

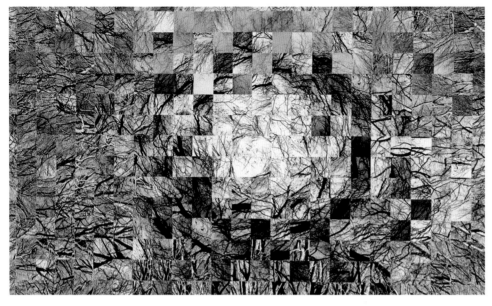

« Fine print montage
To create this piece, multiple pictures were taken of a tree and blue skies. The prints were cut into small squares, then reassembled to create a large collage that is a unique object.

appearance of objects in a room. Another approach is to play with scale and concepts of reality by combining three-dimensional objects with photographic images.

Creating an art object

Capturing an image is only the first step towards creating the final art object. If you are shooting a series, allow it to develop in form and content as your ideas change. If you are producing prints, you can make them unique by signing and numbering each one. Or you might modify the print by cutting and pasting. Some artists distress their prints by singeing them, spattering them with bleach, or leaving them in the rain.

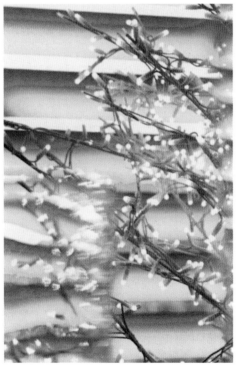

« Optical effects
With art photography you can afford to have fun and experiment. This image exploits the abstract and colourful distortion effects of Christmas lights seen through glassware.

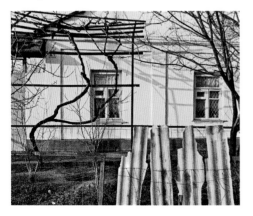

« Travel art
Art photography need not be confined to studio work. Here a scene in Uzbekistan superimposes non-localised, abstract patterns onto vernacular architecture.

Developing a series

Art photography as an institution carries established rules and ways of working. Central to this is the tradition of exhibiting a series of photographs that are linked by a theme. This comes from the past practice of publishing lithographs or engravings in groups of similar subjects, such as grand houses or fabled lands. Consequently, an exhibition of an artist's work is expected to be a coherent series, or thematically linked.

Pursuing a theme

Producing a series of images that are related to each other yet vary sufficiently to hold the viewer's interest requires considerable skill and commitment. First, you need to decide on a theme. It does not necessarily have to be original, but it should be something that you believe in. You can find inspiration all around you, in books, objects, people, and places. Be prepared to pursue your project through practical difficulties, such as access to subjects or limits of timing and budget, as well as conceptual traps. You must be flexible, yet guard the heart of the idea. For example, if you want to explore the emptiness of modern urban spaces, do you include people to counterpoint the soullessness of the space, or do you photograph the space entirely deserted? You may find it hard to depict the space because the only visible feature is the enclosure around it.

Selecting images

Picture editing is an important part of producing a series. One way to do this is to surround yourself with your images. Put them on every available surface, or repeatedly view them on your computer. Allow the pictures to choose themselves – you lose interest in some, but will keep coming back to others. The images on the following spreads were shot for a series exploring the notion that the shadow is as substantial as the physical object that casts it. But which images work best together and carry the idea forward?

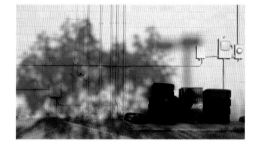

⌃ **Shadow and tyres**
The shadow on the wall is an attractive, soft silhouette that contrasts with the grime and detritus of the garage. This image is kept.

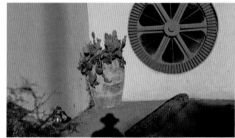

⌃ **Self-portrait shadow**
The human shadow is unique in this series and suggests that the photographer, rather than the shadow, is insubstantial. The image is rejected.

» **Shadow on porch**
The shadow of the tree across the door is so substantial it appears to physically obstruct the entrance. This image is kept.

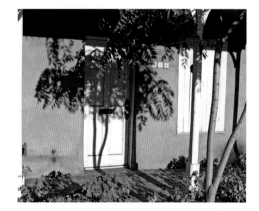

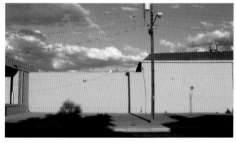

⌃ **Shadow on street**
The contrast of orange wall and blue sky is too good to lose, but the shadow is too insubstantial an element. This image is put on reserve.

》 PICTURE ORIENTATION

Which way to hold the camera – vertically for a portrait format, or horizontally for landscape format – is best guided by the subject, not set by convention. Landscape format offers the visual ground to show receding space, and emphasize the three-dimensionality of the subject. Vertical format tends to direct attention to the main subject rather than to the surroundings, which is why it is favoured for portrait images.

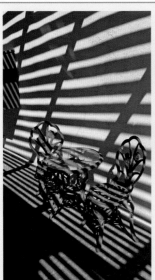
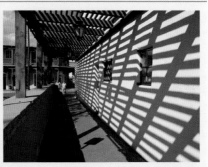

⌃ Horizontal format
Images taken with a horizontal main axis suggest space and movement. They are also good for cropping – removing much of the top and bottom can create a more dramatic image.

≪ Vertical format
Trying vertical shots as a variant on a landscape view can give surprisingly attractive results.

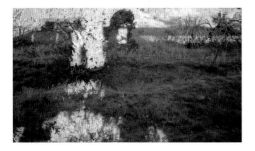

⌃ Shadow of train
A train ride at sunset provides a shadow of the train against the desert. The image is not visually arresting, its message unclear, so it is rejected.

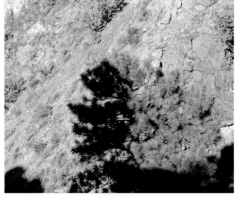

≪ Tree shadow
A shadow falling across a tree brings out its shape and makes it more substantial. But this is not the right concept. The image is rejected.

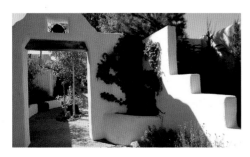

⌃ Shadows on mesa wall
This image with its white-washed walls and attractive lines, is unfortunately not about the substantiality of shadows. It is rejected.

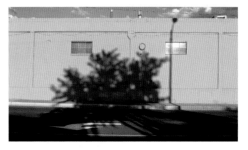

⌃ Shadow across street
With its dynamic shapes and colours, this strong image is clearly a front-runner for the project – it is accepted.

Ethereal landscape
The Japanese art photographer Hiroshi Nomura makes great use of strobe lighting in his work. Here, a sculpture of mirrored balls in a forest setting is illuminated with bursts of light. The image was then digitally enhanced.

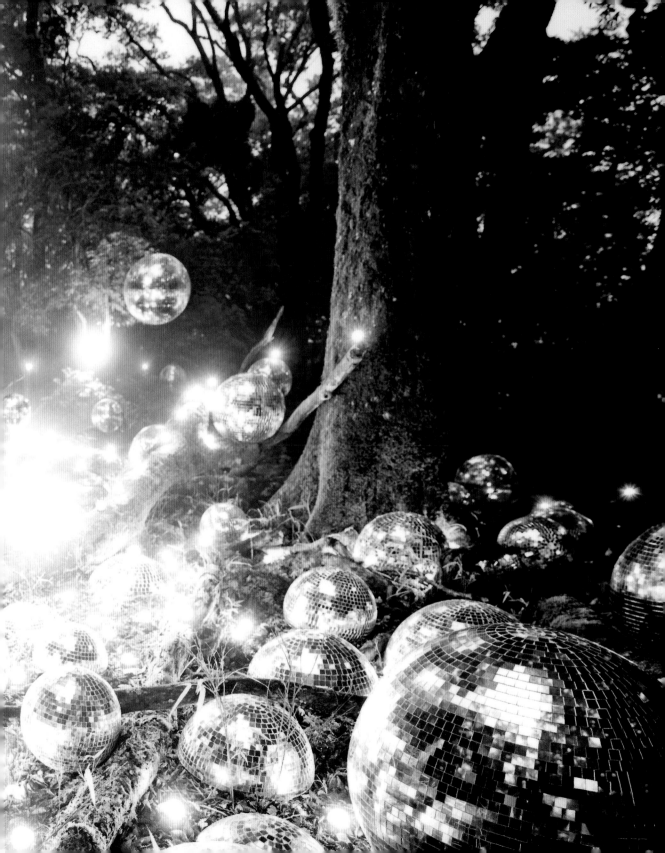

WORKING WITH
DIGITAL IMAGES

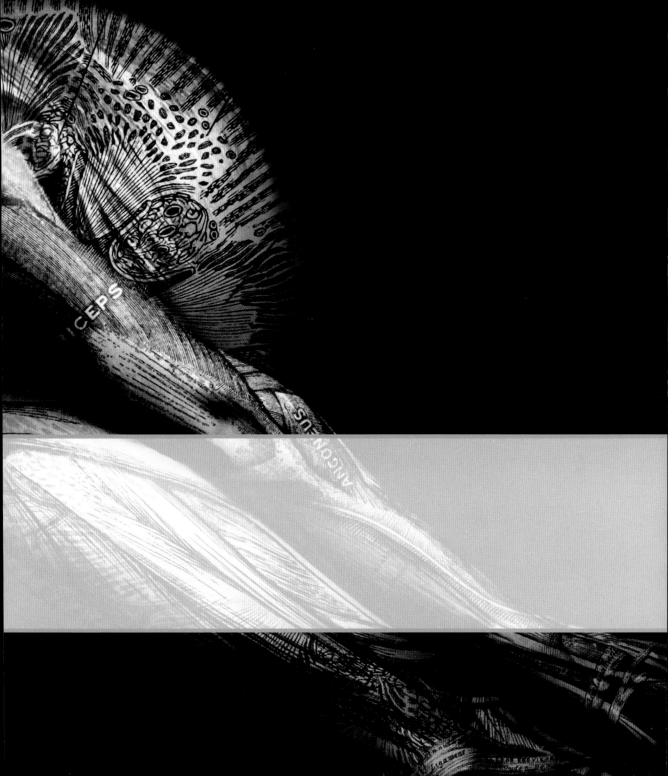

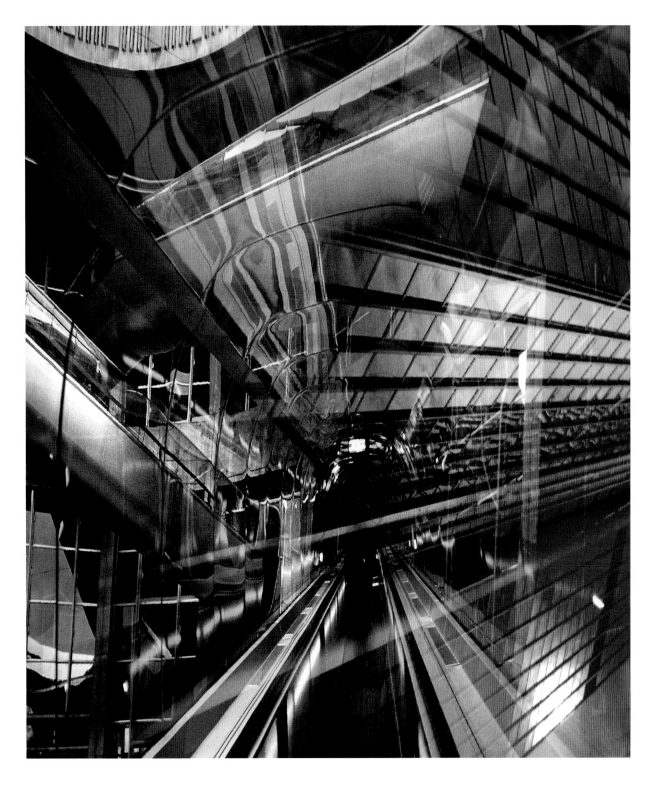

The technical demands of image manipulation are such that it was 1993 before the first truly practical software application, Adobe Photoshop version 2.5.1, was introduced. Even then, computers could barely keep up. Working with digital images could be extremely time-consuming and frustrating.

Today's computers can cope easily with image manipulation. They can make thousands of millions of calculations each second, and have tremendous processing power that can handle enormous amounts of data at any time. By the turn of the millennium, the software controlling computers – the operating systems – had become very stable and reliable.

If you are lucky enough to be learning image manipulation only now, you have been spared the agonies of those who worked at the cutting edge of digital photography development in the late 1990s. Back then, work was hindered by inexplicable crashes, illogical processes, incomplete features, and sluggish response – you really had to persevere to make any progress.

However, in the process of development and through competition, modern software has become loaded with numerous functions, some highly automated. Rather like modern cameras, which carry dozens of features in order to please as many people as possible, software developers aim to provide solutions for every user, from the amateur enthusiast to the busy professional.

The most frequently applied functions such as adjusting exposure, changing image size, correcting colour balance, and rotating the image are offered by every entry-level software program. More advanced programs

allow you to perform more elaborate tasks, such as fine control of tone reproduction, special effects, removing image defects, and working with layers of effects or images.

Learning to use even fairly elementary software can be a daunting task. But it is easier to master the software if you follow a few strategies. First, it is always good practice to experiment on a copy of the original file. Use small copies – less than 5MB or 8 megapixels – when you start learning a new software application. This will ensure rapid response and feedback. Work through the tools and menus systematically, making notes as you go. If you find a function that promises to be useful to you, make a note of it. Since the file is small, you can save it as a visual reference for the future, naming it after the command or filter.

Art effects
Manipulation such as the colour-pencil texture in this image can take photography close to fine art practice.

Double montage
The main effect – a double-exposure – was in fact done with film. But only digital image manipulation could have separated out some of the tonal details and enriched the colours which, in the original, were too dull.

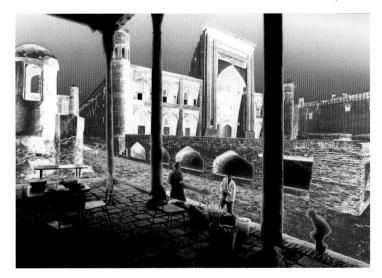

While software can make radical changes to images, photographers mostly use it to make minor enhancements to their pictures. The principal changes, which should be executed roughly in this order, are: control the size and proportions to ensure you have only as much data as you need, and to crop it to the required shape; adjust the exposure and tone to correct overall brightness and contrast; make sure the colours are accurate. At this stage you can make further adjustments by applying filters or special effects.

When preparing files for printing, you may need to increase the sharpness of the image as the final step. As a general rule, it is best to make your captured image as good as possible so it does not need much enhancement.

Image manipulation has come a long way in a relatively short time. It is now so sophisticated that it is often impossible to tell whether an image is original or not. Indeed, one of the keys to success is to use software to create a thoroughly convincing image that does not appear to have been manipulated.

⊠ Original image
The original image, of a sunset over Auckland, New Zealand, shows shadows that are too dark, contrasting strongly with the distant sun.

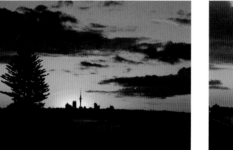

⊠ Shadows and highlight adjusted
By adjusting the shadows to increase detail, and the highlights to correct the colour, the image is closer to the view as seen.

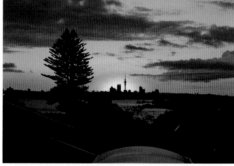

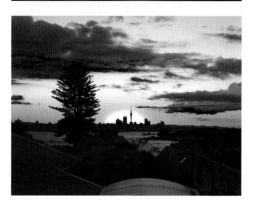

⊠ Sepia tone
The adjusted image has been sepia-tinted by turning all the colours to brown tones. This creates a romantic, mellow effect.

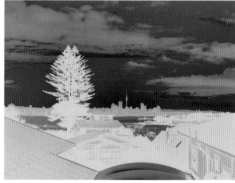

⊠ Extreme effect
A dramatic digital effect such as this can not only reverse the tones but also the colours. The effect is almost psychedelic.

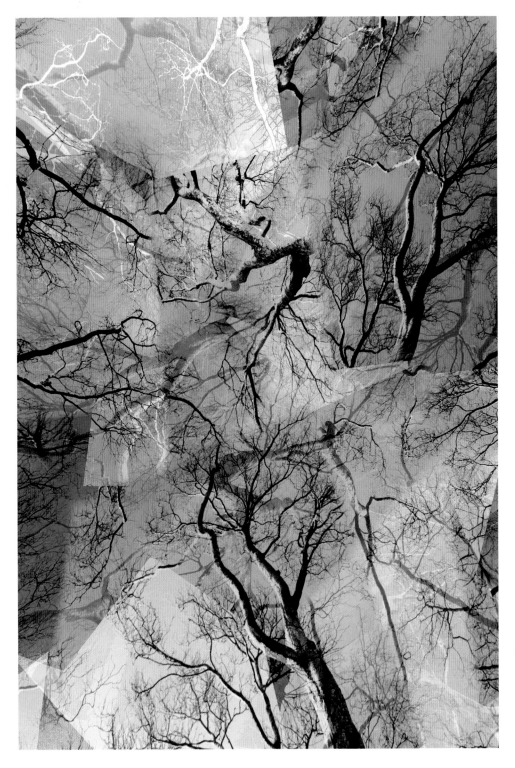

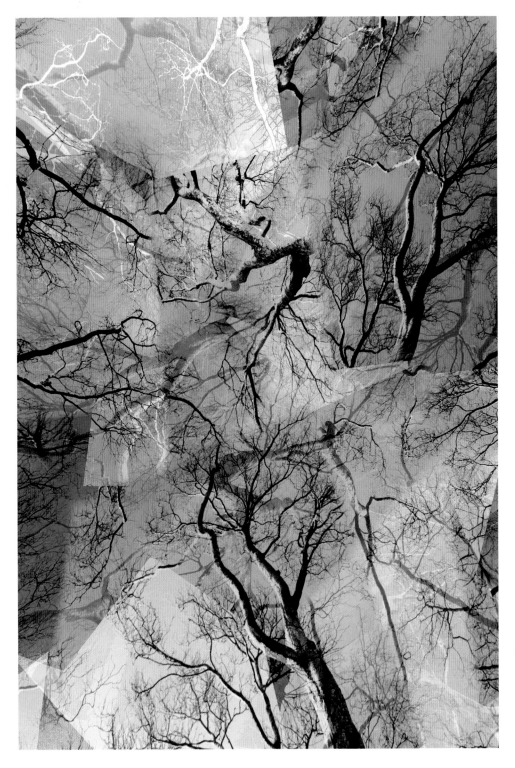 **Panoramic composite**
By creating a false panorama and overlaying images, a few shots of bare branches are transformed into a pleasing abstract image.

Digital workflow

It is tempting to dive straight into a fresh batch of images to find that prize-winning shot. But if you want to be able to find an image in a few years' time, you will find that getting organized at the beginning reaps many benefits in the future. If you photograph mainly for yourself, you can fine-tune one image at a time. But as your collection of images grows, so does the need to set a system that can support you.

Adapting to your needs

The fundamental strategy for efficient workflow is to ensure as much is correct as early as possible in the process. That starts with the quality of your capture: try to ensure your images can be used with minimal processing. As you photograph more it is worth investing in extra effort to add metadata and sort images early in their lifecycles. The flowchart on the next page sets out the basic steps of a typical workflow that you can adapt.

How to organize photos

Keep your images organized in folders using a naming convention that suits your work. Some photographers create a year folder within which are sub-folders for months. Within these, they put folders named after a country visited or subject. No single scheme for naming folders is ideal for all circumstances. That is why other ways of classifying images are useful. The most important technique is to use metadata to identify the subject matter of photographs.

Image metadata

Metadata is data about data – information that describes what is stored. The name of a file, for example, is a key piece of metadata as it distinguishes the data stored in one file from that in another. Metadata creates finer distinctions as well as connections between files. For example, you can add the label "apples" to all your images of apples around the world, while location metadata, such as "China", "Italy", or "New Zealand", distinguishes between different apples.

» KEEPING IMAGES SAFE

The key task after you have captured images is to ensure they are safe. Use the best-quality memory cards you can afford. Take great care of them. Do not delete images while out and about. Do not remove memory cards while the camera is on or showing any red lights. If you encounter any problems with a card, immediately swap it out for a spare card. Do not use the misbehaving card until you are sure it is good to go. As soon as you can, copy the contents of your cards to a computer or storage drive. At the same time, or as soon as you can after that, make a back-up copy to a separate drive or back up to a cloud drive. Always make a copy of the file before processing it if it is not in raw format: do not work on the original image file.

◄ Portable storage
Modern storage devices can copy from memory cards or upload images wirelessly direct from connected cameras without the need for a computer.

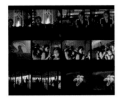

1. Ingest
Upload images into a new folder on your computer. Add metadata such as date, location, and copyright. Rename the images with sequential numbering (e.g. Malta001, Malta002). Back up to a secondary disk.

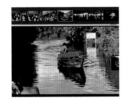

2. Inspect
Check a sample of images to ensure they are sharp, well-exposed with accurate white balance. If your camera does not turn portrait images upright, do it now. Do this during or immediately after a shoot.

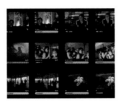

3. Evaluate
Examine your images to locate the firsts, seconds, and rejects: apply ratings to rank them. Use a calibrated monitor for a careful evaluation of colour, exposure, and overall quality.

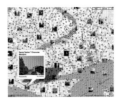

4. Apply metadata
Write and apply captions while you can remember all the details. Add other useful data, including geotags (geographical location data).

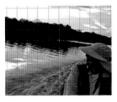

5. Set up
Create a new folder for files in process. Save images with new filenames if working destructively. If possible, use a storage device different from that holding the original image. Straighten, crop, or resize as required.

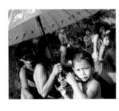

6. Enhance
Correct exposure and contrast to normalize the blacks and highlights (note, colour adjustments and sharpening may heighten contrast). At this stage apply drastic changes, such as conversion to monochrome or sepia.

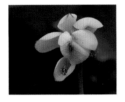

7. Soft proof
Check how the image will look when printed by reviewing proof colours: view with an applied output profile for your printer. Look for out-of-gamut colours and readjust as required.

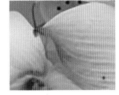

8. Clean the image
Examine the image closely and remove any flaws. Do not repair it before applying your adjustments, as increases in contrast, saturation, or sharpness may reveal clean-up efforts, and you will just have to do it again.

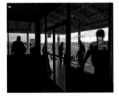

9. Final effects
Leave noise reduction to this step unless it was part of the raw processing. Apply sharpening, if required. Check the image to ensure no artefacts have been introduced, or local contrast is not too high for portraits.

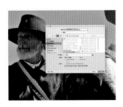

10. Prepare
If you used layers, use "Save As" to save a copy of the layered image under another name in case you wish to modify it later. Flatten the image, resize, and save it in the required format – JPEG is a safe choice if you are not sure.

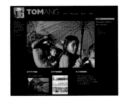

11. Use
If possible, export directly to the target destination, such as from Lightroom straight to your Facebook page, so you do not make any unnecessary copies of files. If you cannot export directly, create a project folder before exporting the files into it.

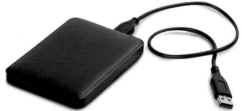

12. Archive and tidy
Store images on back-up media such as portable hard disk drives. Double-check that you have at least two copies of images on storage media, then you are good to format your memory cards in your camera.

Workplace set-up

The digital photography workroom can be any regular room in a home or office, with no extra expense needed to prepare it. You should follow a few basic steps to ensure your comfort and good viewing conditions. Perhaps the most important of these is invisible: the need to avoid working for long periods without a break. This is neither recommended for your health, or for the sustained quality of your work.

The environment

Computers, monitors, and other electrical equipment can get extremely warm when left running for hours at a time, so your chosen workroom should be well ventilated. Choose neutral coloured walls and fittings to avoid disturbing judgement of colour. If the room is sunny, use blinds or heavy curtains to reduce bright light. Ensure the room can be secured, for example, with a lockable door to keep valuable equipment and data files safe.

Setting up the workspace

The desk you work at should be stable and capable of supporting the weight of your equipment. It is also important that the desk is at the correct height. When you are seated at the keyboard, your forearms should be horizontal or slightly inclined down, and there should be ample space for your legs. Position the monitor so that the top of the screen is approximately at eye level. Ensure that your chair allows you to place your feet flat on the floor (or use a footrest) and that it supports your back. It may seem obvious, but make sure your desk is large enough, not just for the equipment, but so that you can use additional items such as books and notepads comfortably while you work.

Electrical arrangements

Most computer peripherals draw a relatively low current at low voltages compared to domestic appliances. This is fortunate as the peripherals for a modest workroom easily sprout a dozen power leads all needing electrical outlets to plug into. If in any doubt about electrical issues, seek advice from a qualified electrician. Do not be tempted to undertake electrical rewiring yourself.

Avoid wiring more than one appliance into a single plug or replacing a blown fuse with one of a higher rating. To avoid a loss of data or a computer crash, do not plug a device into a computer or other peripheral that is halfway through an operation. This is usually indicated by a flashing or lit light, or by noises indicating that it is running. To help protect your computers from electrical damage, use plug adaptors fitted with either surge protectors, which stop large rises in current, or spike suppressors, which stop sudden rises in voltage.

Lighting

To avoid glare and reflections, arrange desk-lamps so that they do not shine directly on to the monitor screen. Some lamps are specially designed to prevent this. Position the screen so that it does not face a light source, such as a window or lamp. If lighting is problematic, you can buy a hood, or make one from black card, to block out light.

Storage

Make sure you have safe storage for all your hard disks and memory cards. Any magnetic-based media such as hard disks are best stored at least 30cm (12in) from strong magnetic fields, such as those produced by loud speakers.

⟫ AVOIDING INJURY

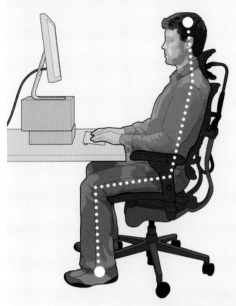

It is unlikely you will work the long hours that can lead to repetitive strain injury (RSI) from excessive typing or use of the mouse, but you should still be careful. Many computer users do, however, suffer from eyestrain and back pain so it is worth taking precautions. Monitor and listen to your body. If something starts to ache or feel uncomfortable while you are working, it is time to make adjustments or stop what you are doing.

• To avoid backache, do not work at the monitor for more than one hour at a time. Take a break, get up and walk around. After two hours' work, get up, stretch, and take a longer break.
• To avoid eyestrain, look out of the window at distant objects every hour or so. Do not take a break by watching television as this exacerbates eyestrain problems.
• Keep your equipment clean and well-maintained. Sticky mice and dirty monitor screens or keyboards can all add to stress and strain in a subtle way.

◀ Correct posture
When working at a computer for long periods, posture is very important. Make sure your chair and desk are set at the correct heights, and the screen and keyboard correctly positioned.

▽ Basic equipment
This image shows a simple digital photography workspace.

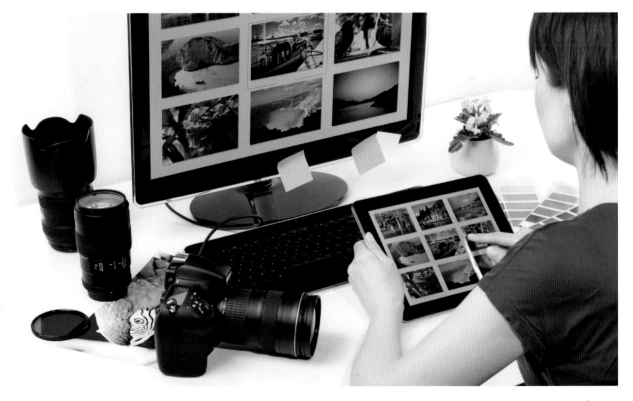

Digital transfer technology

The most revolutionary aspect of the digital image compared to the film-based image is that the digital form can be seen and used in millions of places at once. The process of digital transfer and storage is central to modern photography. You can transfer digital files wirelessly or using plug-in cables. Wireless transfer requires a network or pairing between data source and recipient to ensure a secure connection. Cable connection is generally interchangeable i.e. so long as the cables fit at both ends, data can be transferred. Industry standards for both wireless and cables are regularly updated, sometimes with a loss of compatibility. It is important to ensure that connections between your camera, card-reader, and computer are compatible. You may need to update your computer software to keep up with changes in cable or wireless technology. The other key issue is the transmission rate. Ensure the equipment you use can work with the large still and moving image files produced by today's digital cameras.

Connections and ports

The most widely used type of connection is USB (Universal Serial Bus). That said, there are at least ten different USB connector types, four versions and a number of proprietary designs. If you have a choice, for example, when choosing a hard disk drive, aim to use the latest version of USB – at time of writing – USB 3.1 gen 2, or USB-C (also known as Thunderbolt 3). Later versions transfer data at higher rates and use more reliable methods of connection.

» Different endings
Ensure that you use the correct ending for the socket on your device. With all but the USB-C there is a right way and a wrong way to insert the connector. Do not use force: if it will not insert snugly, it is probably the wrong one.

4 pin micro USB cable   **5 pin mini USB cable**   **USB A/B cable**   **USB male / female extension**

☑ USB adaptors
You can use adaptors to make USB leads compatible with different sockets.

☑ High-quality connector
Gold-plated connectors such as these are more reliable than standard types.

⌃ Hubs
Modern hubs enable you to work with different devices using different connectors.

» Card reader
Purchase card readers using the latest and fastest USB technology.

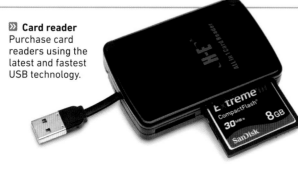

Memory card reader

A simple way of transferring images to a computer is by using a memory card reader. Many are specific to particular card types, while others will read different kinds of card. With these readers, the memory card can assist in transferring files between computers.

Mass storage drive

Rugged, dependable mass storage is essential for photography. RAID (Redundant Array of Independent Drives) devices offer the most security by doubling up data on separate disks. Even so, it is best practice to have backups to these drives.

Rugged exterior

Vents for hard-disk drives

« RAID drive
Compact, rugged drives with fast data speeds can quickly repay their initial high purchase costs.

Scanning images

Scanning is the way to import film-based images into the digital world. A scanner systematically examines the original image so that the colour and brightness information of the original is turned into data that can be used by image manipulation software. You can scan prints, colour transparencies, and colour and black-and-white negative films. Colour prints and transparencies fade over time, so it is best not to leave scanning until too late.

Glass flat bed

Control panel

Original to be placed face down

How to scan

Before scanning, ensure you work with clean originals by using special brushes or an air puffer to remove dust. If scanning prints, collect them into similar sizes to simplify operations. Align the original images carefully to avoid having to rotate them digitally after scanning. It is best to scan to the highest resolution, producing the largest file that the scanner can deliver. This is slower but saves work in the long run. Aim to obtain the best-looking scans direct from the scanner rather than rely on making extensive corrections later.

⌃ Flat-bed scanner
This type is designed to scan prints and solid originals, such as book or magazine pages. Typical of modern designs, this model can scan originals up to A4 in size to resolutions greater than 3,000 ppi (points per inch). It can also be used to scan film and transparencies.

⌄ Film scanner
Modern film scanners accept mounted and unmounted transparencies or individual strips of film, and offer resolutions of 4,000 ppi (points per inch) or more. Additionally, these scanners produce much better results than generic flat-bed scanners.

» STORING PICTURES ON THE WEB

One important innovation introduced by the Internet is remote data storage. This means that your valuable images do not have to reside on a hard disk on your premises; they can instead be stored in online systems that are secured against loss. Storing images on a website keeps them safe and releases space on your computer. Perhaps the most revolutionary aspect of this facility is that you can save new images or access old ones from anywhere in the world.

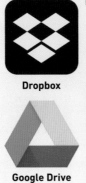

Dropbox

Google Drive

« Online services
Cloud services, such as Dropbox (top) and Google Drive (bottom) are excellent for backing up your media files – not only photos, but videos and music – provided your Internet connection offers good speeds. This is particularly important if you wish to access large files from cloud services. In selecting a cloud service, the low-cost options may prove tempting but you may suffer from lower reliability, less easy connection, and slower data transmission speeds. At any rate, it is sound policy to also keep copies on storage media in case you have no Internet access.

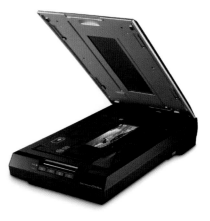

Image manipulation software

Central to digital photography, image manipulation software gives you almost total control over your images. However, before you can benefit from these programs, you need to master them. Start with a simple software package that covers the basics, including exposure, colour, and size adjustments, and a few special effects, before tackling more advanced programs.

Choosing software

With a choice of applications that range from the basic and free to the professional and costly, there is probably more than one that will meet your current needs and even grow with them. Some free software may offer professional features, and some expensive software may lack features that are essential for your work. The best way to select software is to take advantage of free trial periods.

Some types of available software only offer image manipulation features with no or limited cataloguing or management features. A few offer only cataloguing, while a growing number combine image management with manipulation.

Smart phone apps

In order to accommodate their relatively small touch-screens, image apps on smartphones emphasise ease of use, such as application of effects with a single click, with simplified adjustment options. Some apps are smartphone versions of desktop applications and offer a wide range of controls and manipulations. Many apps are free but paid apps usually offer more features, better interface design, and faster operation. Image manipulation may be built into some social media or picture-sharing applications, so there may be no need to move between different apps.

☑ Photo effects
Some apps, such as Hipstamatic, offer a wide range of image effects with additional paid-for effects, plus photo-sharing functions.

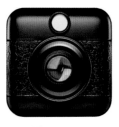

Hipstamatic

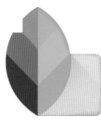

Snapseed

◙ Editing apps
Thanks to the computer power of smartphones, image editing apps can be very capable. Check out individual apps to see the quality of results as these can vary.

� Social media apps
Some apps, such as Instagram, are built for social media but also offer extensive built-in image tools, such as adjustments and filters, so you can edit within the app.

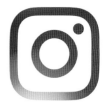

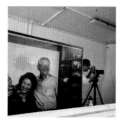

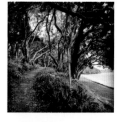

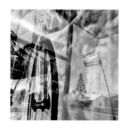

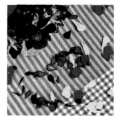

▲ @tomangphoto
Photographers who use photo-sharing sites to amass thousands of followers can achieve fame and fortune.

Basic software

Many photographers only need to make basic adjustments and organize small collections of images. Windows and Mac operating systems offer built-in photo applications. There are many other free applications you can install, some of which are very powerful. Or you can use free online applications that operate on your image through your standard web browser.

》 Built-in apps
Free, integrated into the operating system and easy to use: there are many good reasons for starting with the apps built into your computer.

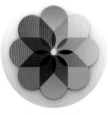

Microsoft Photos

Apple Photos

》 Intermediate apps
Applications such as PhotoPlus are easy to start using, yet offer more advanced tools that can be accessed when you are ready.

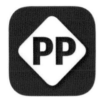

PhotoPlus

》 Online editors
You can edit images directly in your favourite web browser, but you will need to be online to operate most functions and response can be slow.

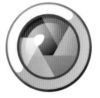

Pixlr

Enthusiast software

As your skills and needs develop, you may wish to progress to more powerful, fully featured software. Some applications give you speed previews of raw images. Others allow you to operate a camera from a laptop and organize professional shoots easily, or are packed with features that offer no obstacle to your artistry. Make full use of free trial periods to learn how suitable an application is for your purposes and budget.

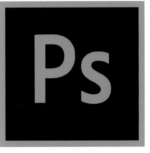

⌃ Adobe Photoshop
For many years, the de facto standard software. Still widely used and the standard by which others are judged. Photoshop is available only on subscription with cloud services.

⌃ GIMP
GNU Image Manipulation Program is a powerful image application. It is free, but requires time and effort to master.

》 UTILITY APPLICATIONS

Modern image files can be damaged by faults in memory cards, by accidental or regretted deletion, and by physical damage. Specialist data or image recovery software allows you to rebuild intact images even if deleted. The most important safeguard is to stop using a card as soon as you realize there is a problem. This avoids writing over old data with new, which makes recovery impossible.

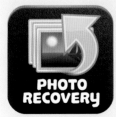

《 Deleted Photo Recovery
You will not need to use recovery software or apps often, but it pays to be familiar with one, such as this, in preparation for when you need it.

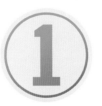

⌃ Capture One
This professional software controls a camera from a computer, and can process and also catalogue images. Powerful but tough to master.

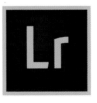

⌃ Adobe Lightroom
This powerful image management and processing program is widely used. It may be the only application a photographer needs.

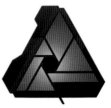

⌃ Affinity Photo
Many alternatives to Photoshop are available. They vary in capability, but apps such as Affinity Photo offer innovative tools not available in Photoshop, and at lower cost.

Frozen lake and herd
For this image, a winter landscape was reflected on itself and superimposed over an image of a building, then a herd of goats was added.

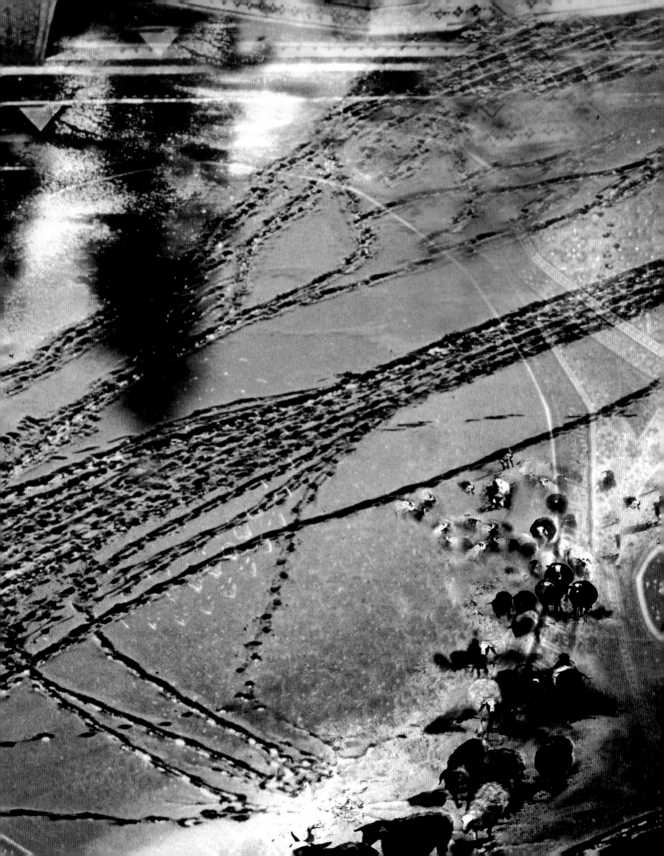

Adjusting brightness and contrast

Auto-exposure systems in modern cameras rarely make mistakes, and if they do, it is often easy to adjust image brightness in processing software. Automatic adjustments can give good results on an almost perfectly exposed image. For finer adjustments, the Levels control offers the best balance between ease of use and quality preservation.

What is the correct brightness?

The technically correct brightness of an image may not be the same as the visually correct one. Brightness affects not only the overall shade of the image, it also alters qualities such as colour and contrast. Darker images show richer colours, while lighter images offer softer, pastel shades.

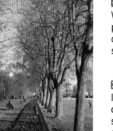

《 Original image
With correct exposure parts of the subject can be too dark and some too light.

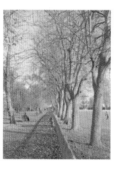

》 Brighter image
Increasing brightness overall renders shadows full of detail and makes highlights too light.

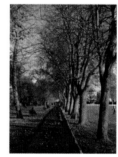

《 Darker image
Reducing brightness intensifies mid-tone colours but shadow details are lost.

Levels control

This control is centred on a display that shows how many pixels of a certain brightness are in the actual image. It monitors the levels of pixels, measuring their relative brightness. A peak to the left indicates a dark image, while a peak to the right indicates a bright image.

Colours can be adjusted separately or at the same time.

This pointer slides to the right to make pixels darker.

The Output Black is used to prevent pure blacks from being printed.

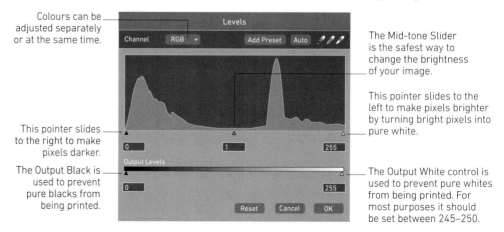

The Mid-tone Slider is the safest way to change the brightness of your image.

This pointer slides to the left to make pixels brighter by turning bright pixels into pure white.

The Output White control is used to prevent pure whites from being printed. For most purposes it should be set between 245–250.

Contrast

Contrast in an image measures how rapidly tones change from light to dark. If there are many intermediate tones, the image appears to be relatively low in contrast (below right). If there are few steps between light and dark, that is, the transition is rapid, the image looks high contrast (below, middle). The correct level of contrast is one that best suits the subject. Architectural forms may benefit from high contrast, whereas skin tones in portraiture or weddings generally work best with mid- to low-contrast. The majority of images work well with medium contrast (below left) but it is worth experimenting with other contrast values.

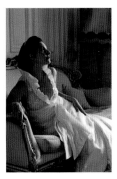

« Original image
You may need to correct the contrast of your raw images.

» High contrast
The difference between dark and light tones is marked, intensifying contours.

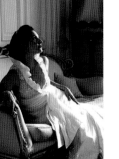

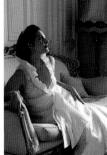

« Low contrast
Shadow tones are similar to mid-tones, giving a soft impression, and pastel colours.

High dynamic range

Modern digital cameras can record a wide range of light levels – from cloudy skies to shadows beside buildings – while capturing detail. However, some situations offer greater brightness or dynamic range. It is not possible for a single image to hold a large range of brightness. As a photographer, you may accept this limitation and work with it: this was the strategy for film-using photographers. Alternatively, you can manipulate the image so that bright tones become light mid-tone, while shadows are darker mid-tones: this is tone-mapping.

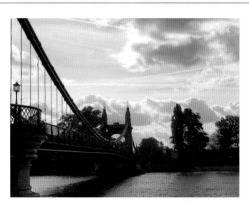

« Expose for highlights
The exposure for the sky brings out cloud detail at the expense of shadow detail, which is completely lost.

☒ Final image
After combining darker images with lighter images containing shadow detail, the result is one that is full of mid-tones, like a painting.

Tone mapping

This technique (often incorrectly called HDR or High Dynamic Range) involves making three or more exposures. One exposure registers bright tones as mid-tones, one is a normal exposure for mid-tones, while a third registers shadows as mid-tones. Using tone-mapping software, you can then superimpose the mid-tones of the images on top of each other. The result is that bright tones are mapped to light mid-tones, and dark tones are mapped to dark mid-tones around the basic mid-tone of the image. The result is typically quite painterly, with the tone-mapping software enhancing colours and contours.

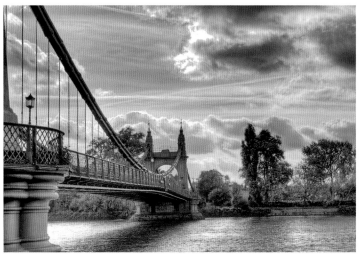

Controlling colour

Accurate rendering of colour could once only be achieved by highly skilled technicians using precise chemical processes. Now, in the digital era, colour processing is built into the circuitry of cameras, enabling them to work in varied conditions and still reproduce colours accurately. Any further colour modifications are then easy to make with image manipulation.

Adjusting colour

The Colour Balance control provides the easiest method of ensuring that colours are reproduced accurately. Digital cameras render whites untinted or pure, which, in turn, renders all colours accurately. This process is known as "adjusting the white balance". Some digital cameras allow you to use pre-set values but it is useful to be able to refine colour balance with software.

Colour balance

The best-known Colour Balance control is that of Adobe Photoshop, which is most effective for small adjustments. You must first assess the image carefully: does it have an unnatural colour cast, say green or cyan? One small movement of the slider can give an instant correction.

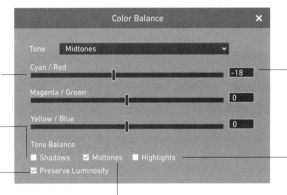

The colour adjustment slider moves between red, green, and blue and their complementary colours cyan, magenta, and yellow.

Shadows restricts changes to the important shadow tones. As these carry density, small changes can have a large effect.

The Preserve Luminosity option maintains overall brightness.

Primary hue bands have broad ranges, which are sufficient for most purposes.

Highlights restricts colour adjustments to the three-quarter or highlight tones. Light colours will not show much change in Colour Balance.

Midtones is selected by default, and restricts colour adjustments to the tones lying between highlights and shadows.

» Ambient light
Correction is often needed for a shot taken with indoor lighting. This image is almost acceptable but highlights are slightly yellow.

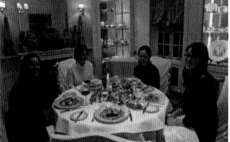

⊠ Ambient light corrected
By increasing the blue using Colour Balance and correcting brightness levels (see p.276), the yellow cast is largely removed.

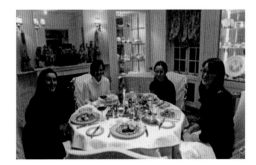

Changes in colour balance

Images with an overall tint or pale colour cast of any hue (but most commonly yellow or blue) may be made neutral though a correction of the colour balance. This is commonly achieved by ensuring that white, grey, or black areas are devoid of colour. Removing a tint from a grey patch, for instance in the metal utensils in the images below, automatically corrects the overall colour balance. Alternatively, you can change the colour balance in order to give your images a specific mood or feel. A red cast, for example, will add warmth.

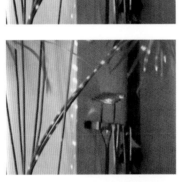

» Mixed light original
This interior is mainly lit by sunlight streaming through the window but there is also some additional light from indoor lamps.

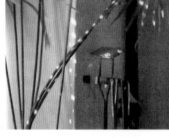

« Crossed correction
This image results from forcing the highlights to maximum blue, the shadows to maximum yellow, and mid-tones to slightly magenta.

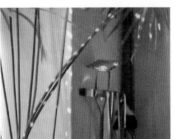

» Red cast
A slight red cast may make the image appear warm, but highlights will be pinkish while blue skies or leaves may appear a little dull.

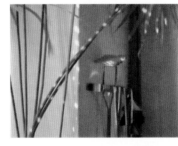

« Magenta cast
A common white-balance error leads to a magenta cast, which combines blue and red. This may dull a wide range of colours.

» Green cast
Even if only very subtle, a green cast is easily spotted. It is particularly unwanted with skin tones, tending to make them muddy.

« Yellow cast
A heavy yellow cast may look slightly unnatural but can still be attractive. Removing yellow may make the image look more dull.

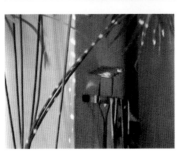

» Blue cast
A blue cast, while sometimes desirable, can make the image too cold. Removing a blue cast can also brighten the image.

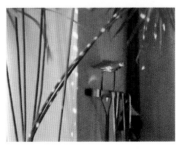

« Cyan cast
A slight cyan cast results in a dulling of warm colours. Just a small adjustment can make a significant improvement.

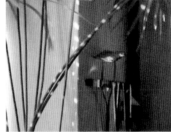

Adjusting sharpness

Until the advent of digital photography, each step of the photographic process tended to reduce the sharpness of detail in an image. In fact, a great deal of photographic practice was directed at minimizing this loss of detail. The arrival of image manipulation software has initiated significant advances, including the power to adjust an image to make it look sharper than it really is.

Sharpness and resolution

Photographic sharpness is dependent on the ability of a photographic system such as a camera, scanner, or enlarger to separate out detail so that it becomes visible. This ability is known as "resolving power" and there are defined methods for measuring it. The term "resolution", when used in connection with digital photography, is different to resolving power: it refers instead to the capacity of a camera or image to hold information or retain data. Resolving power and resolution are linked, in that more data is needed to record more detail. So, higher resolution cameras or files are needed to attain high resolving power.

Increasing sharpness

If a boundary is more defined, it appears sharper. The main control for increasing sharpness in image manipulation is the Unsharp Mask (USM) command. This works by searching for boundaries or edges and then slightly exaggerating the differences.

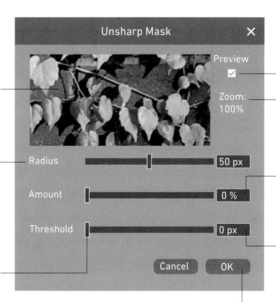

The preview window shows the result of applying the change. On some software, such as Adobe Photoshop, clicking on the window shows the unchanged state.

Set a small Radius (see opposite) if there is fine detail. Set a larger Radius if there are large areas of uniform tone. This parameter has a significant effect, so use it carefully. A very small Radius with a large Amount setting is often used to tidy up artefacts in digital camera images.

The slider is pulled to the left or right to set different amounts of change in each of the settings. Avoid using this to adjust Threshold as small changes can have large effects.

If the Preview option is ticked, it allows you to view the change to the image. This can slow down operations and is not strictly needed, so it can be turned off to speed up work.

View the image at 100 per cent for the best results. At other magnifications, the monitor image does not give such an accurate representation of the pixel structure.

Start with an Amount setting of between 50 and 150. A setting of 111 is simple to make, or use the slider to adjust.

The Threshold sets the difference in brightness between two pixels before the Unsharp Mask is applied. Increase this if the image is noisy (that is, has many specks or unwanted dots).

Clicking OK applies the changes. On large files, the change will take several seconds to complete.

Sharpness effects

Unsharp Mask should be used sparingly. Applying excessive sharpening to an image causes the edge contrast to be exaggerated into haloes, and defects or small details to become too prominent. When applied, sharpening should be only just sufficient to improve details. Some digital cameras apply their own automatic sharpening: turn this off if possible. For images with fine details set an average Amount and a small Radius. For images with hardly any fine detail set a low Amount and a larger Radius. Images used on the web may need a little more sharpening than those used in print.

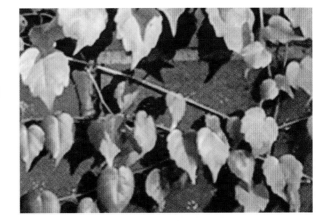

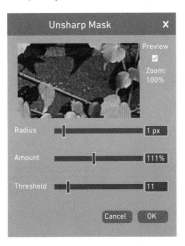
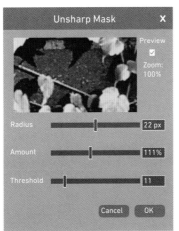
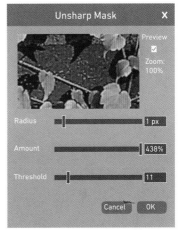

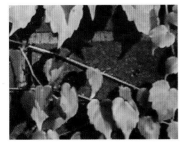
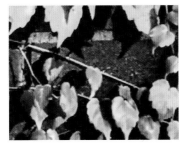
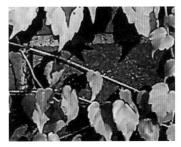

⌃ USM normal setting
With an Amount of 111, Radius of 1, and Threshold of 11, the Unsharp Mask command lifts the sharpness of the majority of scans and digital images. The Threshold setting can be lowered to increase the effect. This shows the image at 300 per cent enlargement.

⌃ USM large Radius setting
With a large Radius setting of 22, the sharpening effect has extended beyond the boundaries of the selection to include larger areas. This has the effect of increasing contrast overall and can be a way of improving the "sparkle" of an image.

⌃ USM large Amount setting
Using a large Amount setting with a small Radius is effective on this image as the contrast at the edges and boundaries is increased but limited to a small region, so it does not interfere with the fine detail.

Filter effects

Digital image manipulation is most dramatically demonstrated with the use of filters that can instantly transform any ordinary picture using fantastic colours and a plethora of distortions and textures. The best use of filter effects is, however, an exercise in balance. While some effects produce subtle changes, others can completely destroy the integrity of the original image.

Controlling filters

Have fun experimenting with the hundreds of variations of filter effects by first trying them out on small files to see the results. Subjects with very simple, clear shapes are the easiest to work with and the most likely to be successful. Filters are less effective with busy images, or those featuring people, since the results can be hard to read.

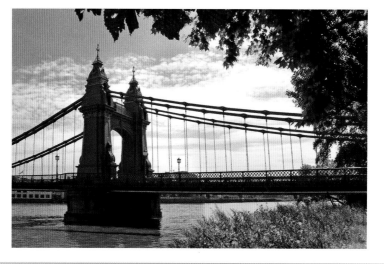

《 Original image of a bridge over a river
This simple but clear image of a bridge makes a great starting point for experimentation.

Distorting effects

Distortions do not change the colour or brightness of pixels. Instead, they change the shape and size of the image by effectively redistributing those pixels. Effects range from the wildly dramatic and complex to the subtle. They are particularly useful for correcting lens defects.

》 Spherize
Pixels are arranged as if they are wrapped around part of a sphere. This filter is used to adjust slight distortions. Here the bridge is straightened.

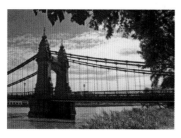

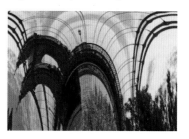

《 Polar Coordinates
When this filter is applied, the coordinates of pixels are rearranged to fit around a globe. It is fun to use because results are unpredictable.

Art materials

Mimicking the effect of crayons or oil paints, and the textures of different types of art paper, this filter is most useful when used in combination with other effects. It often requires correction of brightness and contrast.

» Coloured Pencil
Given a contrasty image with strong colours, the Coloured Pencil filter can produce passable imitations of pencil work.

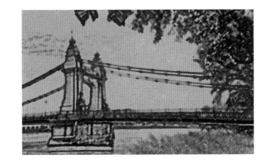

Stylizing effects

These techniques produce a miscellany of effects, which result in images that are only loosely based on the original. Shapes, colours, structures, and textures can all be manipulated and distorted beyond recognition. Stylizing effects are most commonly used to create abstract images.

» Extrude
Using this effect the photographer can quickly create graphic landscapes which are made up of extruded blocks or pyramids.

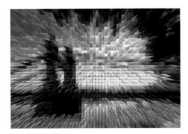

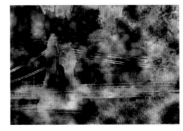

« Difference Clouds
An unpredictable filter, Difference Clouds overlays the image with a random pattern, then applies a Blend Mode (see p.288).

Texturizing and pixellation effects

By taking a group of pixels and treating them as one, pixellating or texturizing filters change the distribution of colours within the group, while retaining the broad outlines of the subject in the image. The main control is over the size of the group of pixels. Larger groups conceal more of the image's detail.

» Grain
This effect mimics film-based images of high sensitivity. It is useful for improving the results of lower-quality printers.

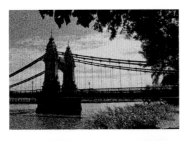

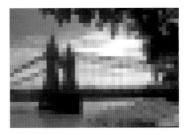

« Mosaic
Imitating and exaggerating the pixellation of an image, this filter is widely used in the media when someone's identity needs to be disguised.

» Colour halftone
This filter renders the image as it would appear if it were printed using halftone dots that are varied in size but not in strength.

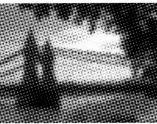

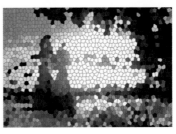

« Stained glass
Suited to colourful, graphic images, this effect is achieved by creating irregular patches of colour surrounded by a neutral border.

Selections and masks

Photographers have always sought to manipulate the photographic process in order to improve the captured image. The fundamentals of this procedure have not changed with digital photography, but the ease and accuracy of selecting parts of images in order to copy, cut, manipulate, or combine them with other images has taken a huge leap forward.

Making selections and masks
When parts of an image are selected, any subsequent digital effects or manipulations are confined to the pixels that are included in the selection. The most popular and widely used tool for making a selection is the Lasso, so-called because it "ropes in" an area of pixels. By making a selection in this way, you are also creating a mask, which restricts the area that the manipulation will affect. Masks and selections have, essentially, the same effect, but technically a mask is said to be a greyscale representation of a selection.

Degrees of selection
A pixel may be fully selected, partially selected, or not selected at all. The degree of selection at the periphery of a chosen area can be graded, or feathered, between full and partial selection. The practical effect of feathering is seen as a partial application of a change. A selection can accurately follow an outline with sharp angles only if feathering is set to a low or zero figure (measured in pixels). A large feathering value leads to loose selections, with rounded corners. This is shown in the selections on the right, made with the Lasso tool.

» Narrow feather
With a narrow area of feathering, the selection tends to be precise, accurately following even small details of the subject's outline.

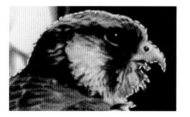
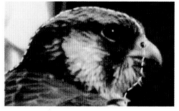

« Wide feather
With a wide area of feathering, the selection cannot be precise, so it may miss, or not fully select, areas with small, sharp boundaries.

Magic Wand
A Lasso tool gathers the parts of an image that you indicate, irrespective of the values of the pixels. The Magic Wand is an alternative selection tool. It searches for pixels that are similar to a sampled point on the image, that is, the pixel on which the tool is clicked. This tool is particularly useful for selecting large areas of the same colour, as in the black clothing in the image below.

» Contiguous selection
When the Magic Wand is used with contiguous selection, similar pixels are selected only if they are neighbouring those sampled.

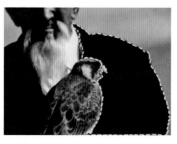
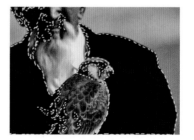

« Non-contiguous selection
With this option, the Magic Wand seeks out all pixels similar to those sampled, so any similar pixel in the image is selected.

Extract

One of the most common image manipulation tasks is the separation of a subject, typically a portrait sitter, from a distracting or unwanted background. The various specialist software programs all work on similar principles. The transitional edge or boundary of the subject must be defined by an outer margin and an inner margin before extraction can take place. The task is technically much more difficult if the subject has fine, blurred margins such as hair or fur. Semi-transparent objects such as glass bottles are also challenging photographic subjects.

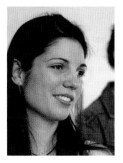

⌃ **Portrait before extraction**
You may want to remove the person in the background of this portrait since they draw the eye away from the main subject.

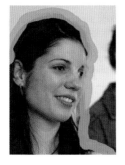

⌃ **Defining the edge**
The broad green line is the first stage in masking out the distracting background behind the main subject.

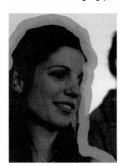

⌃ **Defining the area to be kept**
By filling in a contiguous area, you tell the software which area to keep, and which area to mask off.

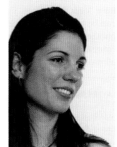

⌃ **Extraction**
When the subject is extracted, as above, it can then be placed on a different background (*see pp.288–89*).

Colour range

A close relative of the Magic Wand command is Colour Range, a quick, efficient, and powerful tool for making selections. It selects colours right across the image according either to a sampled colour (it then works in exactly the same way as Magic Wand) or a band of colour (which is chosen from a drop-down menu). The Fuzziness slider enables you to adjust how precisely similar the selected colours are to the sampled or chosen range.

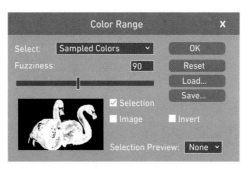

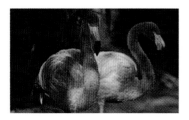

⌃ **Original image**
Assume we wish to extract these pink flamingoes from the background.

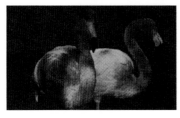

⌃ **Colour Range masked**
After applying the Colour Range control, you can mask the background (in blue).

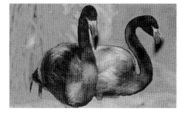

⌃ **Separating the elements**
With the image separated into two parts, you can apply different effects to each.

Sizing and saving for output

The image file size sets a limit on the quality of the output you can produce. As large files take longer to load or transmit, it is good practice to work with the file size that best suits the task. While modern cameras produce very large, high-quality files, at times even larger files are needed. Different methods of upscaling suit different kinds of image.

Image size and resolution

The pixel dimensions of a digital image sets its size. The file size of that image will depend on the file type and compression. The resolution of the image may refer to its pixel dimensions or to how densely pixels are packed into the output, such as print, e.g. 300 dpi, or screen, e.g. 96 dpi.

Image size

The Image Size dialogue is where changes to image size, output size, and resolution are made. The example below (from Adobe Photoshop) is typical. Avoid using this control to increase image size to more than double the original, as quality may disappoint.

This shows the uncompressed file size.

The original image size is measured either in pixels or as a percentage.

The Output Size is set to give the size of print you need.

Output Resolution determines the number of pixels required for printing (300 ppi is usually ample).

If this box is ticked, the file is interpolated to produce a different number of pixels.

If this box is ticked, the ratio of length to width of the image is automatically maintained.

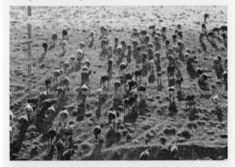

Image size

Image size	25MB
Dimensions	2508px x 3508px
Width	8	Inches
Height	11	Inches
Resolution	300	Pixels/inch
☑ Resample	Bicubic Sharper
☑ Constrain Proportions

Automatic
Bicubic Smoother
✓ Bicubic Sharper
Bicubic
Bilinear

The Interpolation Method is used to suit the image. Bicubic is best for photos.

» CROPPING IMAGES

If you want to change the shape or improve the composition of your image, cropping can remove unwanted areas. A crop can be a modest tidying or can create a radical change in composition. If you make a substantial crop, check that the image still has sufficient data for the size and type of print that you wish to produce.

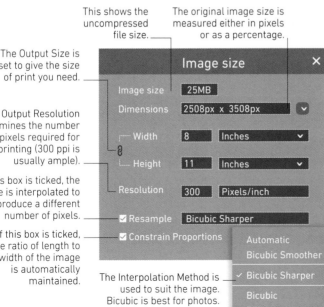

⌃ Original shot
The photograph of cattle in the late afternoon sun is full of strong horizontal lines. It is easy to miss the figure of the lone cattle-herder. A crop may show less but tell more.

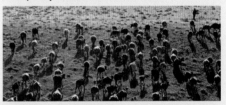

⌃ Letter-box crop
A severe crop of the original image helps to emphasize the lines of the hillside as the gradient changes. It also draws attention to the tiny figure of the cattle-herder in the top right.

Saving for output

Your camera might be able to capture large amounts of data, but it's no good unless you produce files good enough to use. The key element is to provide the sufficient number of pixels for the job at the resolution (dpi or dots per inch) specified by, for example, your printer, or when entering a photo competition. Also ensure that your file has no layers and is free of extras, such as masks or vectors.

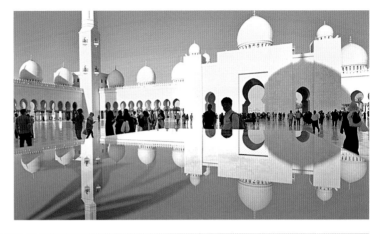

» Avoid enlargement
Images with a mix of sharp detail and delicate gradation are difficult to enlarge greatly with success.

Upscaling methods

In the early days of digital photography, image sizes were often too small for large prints or posters. A number of mathematical strategies or interpolation technologies developed to increase file size without losing details. These methods have lapsed in importance now that many cameras can produce image files of ample size for even poster-size prints. However, different techniques for increasing file size suit different kinds of image.

» CHECKING FILE SIZE

This table shows the average size of an open, uncompressed RGB file suitable for various sizes of print reproduction at 300 dots per inch (dpi). These file sizes are generous: if your file is smaller, it may still produce an acceptable print – make a test to confirm. Note that saved files may be smaller as a result of compression.

Size	mm	Approx inches	MB
A0	841 x 1,189	33⅛ x 46¾	400
A1	594 x 841	23⅜ x 33⅛	200
A2	420 x 594	16½ x 23⅜	100
A3	297 x 420	11¾ x 16½	50
A4	210 x 297	8¼ x 11¾	25
A5	148 x 210	5⅞ x 8¼	13
A6	105 x 148	4⅛ x 5⅞	8

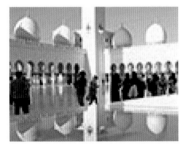

⌃ 72 dpi
This is the nominal resolution for sizing images for monitors and web pages.

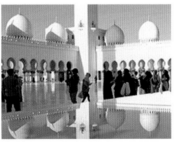

⌃ 150 dpi to 180 dpi
This range provides fair image quality for many purposes and creates files that are convenient to handle.

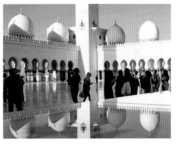

⌃ 300 dpi
Standardly used for the best-quality output, although usually more than necessary as 225 dpi is sufficient.

» Graphics enlargement
For enlarging graphic images, use nearest neighbour interpolation to preserve sharpness and avoid blurred edges.

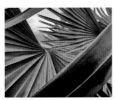

Original image

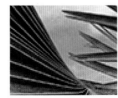

Nearest neighbour interpolation

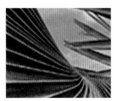

No interpolation

Layers and blends

One of the most creative techniques digital technology has given the photographer is the ability to work with layers of images blended in different ways. The number of image layers is limited only by your computer's memory and your artistic needs. The interactions between layers can be highly complex, visually intriguing, and artistically challenging.

The depth of an image

Before digital manipulation became commonplace, the depth of an image was rarely considered except in a metaphorical sense. Now, an image can have "depth" by virtue of layers. Images can be combined and laid over one another, and image manipulation can control how much of each image is allowed to show through. A high opacity shows little through from below, while low opacity reveals more. (The opposite measure – transparency – is also used sometimes.) Even combining just two layers can produce unexpected and interesting results, and contrasts, colours, and composition can be altered. Furthermore, a different blend mode can be applied to each layer.

Layers palette

The various layers of a photograph can be managed in the Layers Palette of an image manipulation application (the illustration below shows a number of the basic features). It should normally be possible to rearrange the order of layers by clicking on them and dragging them to a new position.

The Blend mode allows you to select the mode of blending or interaction between the selected layer and the layer immediately below it. (Difference is selected here).

Click here to reveal a number of options for customizing the display's features.

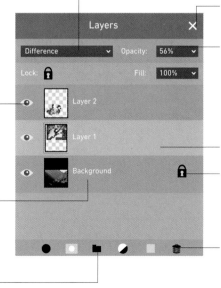

The eye indicates that the contents of the layer are visible, provided they are not hidden by an image on a layer above.

The background layer is usually locked and it is the base from which all layers are built. On completion, all layers should be "flattened" back to a single layer for output.

This window allows you to check or change the amount of opacity of the selected area.

The layer being worked on is indicated by shading. Any changes made will affect only the selected area.

The padlock icon indicates that a feature or characteristic is locked and cannot be changed.

Various options enable you to create new layers, sets of layers, and text effects.

Dragging an unwanted layer to the dustbin or trash deletes it and speeds up operations.

Blends

Control of the blending modes is invaluable for combining images because it gives you almost unlimited versatility with tonal effects. Choosing a blend mode can reveal details and visual interactions that would otherwise remain hidden.

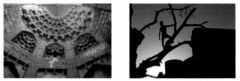

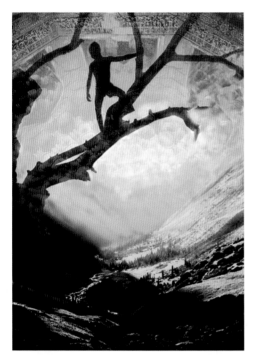

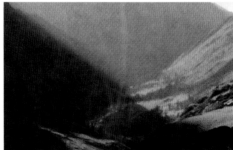

◄ Composite with blends
The main image (left) was created by combining the first two images in Exclusion mode, then merging the result with the bottom image.

☑ Blend normal
A normal blend (100 per cent opacity) reveals nothing. Here, the opacity is set at 50 per cent, so that both layers can be seen.

☑ Blend darken
Choosing this mode ensures that only the parts of the upper layer that are darker than the lower layer show through.

☑ Blend lighten
Here, only those parts of the upper layer that are brighter or lighter than the lower layer show through.

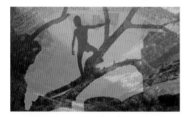

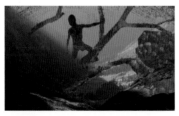

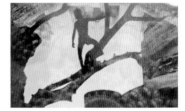

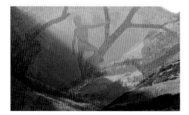

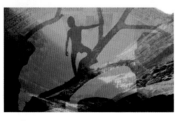

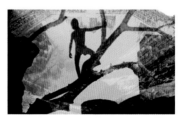

⌃ Blend color
Subtle colouring is possible when colour values for the top image are added to the grey-scale values of the lower layer.

⌃ Blend soft light
The effect here is similar to projecting two images onto each other. It imitates a traditional double exposure.

⌃ Blend vivid light
With overlapping dark areas made darker and bright areas made brighter, the effect is an overall increase in contrast.

Managing results

A perfect image – on screen or in print – is one that conveys your artistic message not only with good detail but also accurate colours. If you insist that a final print bears an absolute likeness to your original subject, or even to what you see on your monitor, you are likely to be disappointed as a perfect match is not possible. The key to making excellent prints lies in managing expectations.

Modern systems

Images obtained from modern digital cameras or scanners are likely to print out well on modern printers. They can also be used online with good to excellent results without modification. For the best results, use image manipulation software to match images to the output intended while assessing the image on a properly set-up monitor. It may take some experimentation to control and manage colour settings yourself for reliable results.

Colour management

Colour information can be translated from one device, such as a computer monitor, to another, such as a printer, to ensure that colour is output in a consistent way. Colour management is based on a common set of colours known as the "profile connection space". The way in which any particular device handles colour is defined by the differences between its own set of colours, which is called the colour space, and that of the profile connection space.

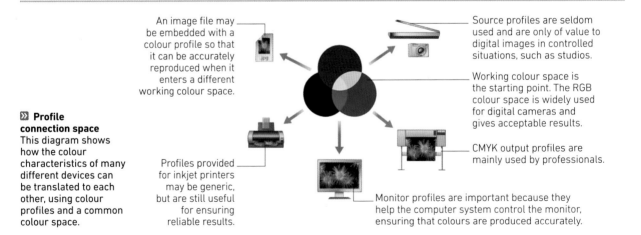

An image file may be embedded with a colour profile so that it can be accurately reproduced when it enters a different working colour space.

Source profiles are seldom used and are only of value to digital images in controlled situations, such as studios.

Working colour space is the starting point. The RGB colour space is widely used for digital cameras and gives acceptable results.

» Profile connection space
This diagram shows how the colour characteristics of many different devices can be translated to each other, using colour profiles and a common colour space.

Profiles provided for inkjet printers may be generic, but are still useful for ensuring reliable results.

CMYK output profiles are mainly used by professionals.

Monitor profiles are important because they help the computer system control the monitor, ensuring that colours are produced accurately.

Profiling the monitor

It is best to set your monitor up to meet industry standards (calibration) and know its colour behaviour profiling. For the most reliable, repeatable results, use hardware devices that measure the actual colour components of colours on your monitor. They use a sensor that faces the screen and is plugged into the computer. With the aid of an application that measures automatically, they both calibrate and profile your monitor. Using the measured monitor profile ensures accurate reproduction in prints and for the web.

Monitor settings

You assess your images by viewing them on your computer's monitor, so it is vital that your monitor displays your images with accurate colours, at the correct brightness and contrast. If, for example, your monitor image is too dark, you will tend to make your image brighter to compensate. This could result in your prints being too light. Common standard settings are shown below.

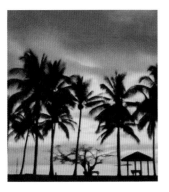

⌃ D50 white point
The D50 or 5,000K white point is a paper-white as seen under light from a bright tungsten-halogen lamp. This standard is used in the printing industry.

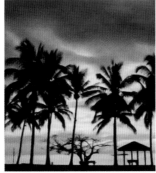

⌃ 9,300K white point
The 9,300K white point is used in TV sets and produces good colours but is a poor white point for checking colour accuracy.

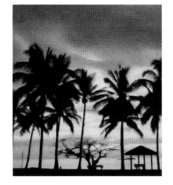

⌃ Gamma 2.2
The gamma of a screen measures the way the image is projected: the standard is 1.8 but a 2.2 gamma setting gives richer mid-tone colours.

Choosing paper

For good results with printing use the best paper you can afford. Those with weights greater than 180gsm (grams per square metre) are generally the best, although thinner papers with high-quality surfaces can give good results. Papers with glossy surfaces produce the greatest contrast between whites and blacks, and the most brilliant colours. Matt-surfaced papers give more subtle contrasts and colours.

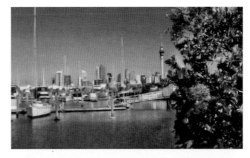

⌊ Printing even skies
If your printer cannot print large areas of even colour, such as the sky in this scene, try applying a little noise to the image by using a filter effect. This scatters ink-dots randomly, disguising unevenness in printing.

Printing hints

Check the document or print set-up before you print to ensure the image is at the output size required. Use the printer's highest quality or highest resolution and lowest printing speed settings for optimum results. It is also advisable to test the paper in your printer, even if it is from the same manufacturer, to ensure they are compatible.

» Printing a night scene
Printing dark images can consume large amounts of ink. By reducing the black output level, you not only reduce the amount of ink needed but also avoid the problem of ink "pooling" on the paper.

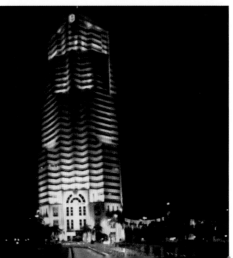

Hard output

The overwhelming proportion of images are seen digitally – on television, monitor, or smartphone screens. Yet a print on paper remains a thing of tactile and visual joy. Fortunately, one of the best-buy products of the digital era is the modern inkjet printer. Its relatively low price belies the fact that, in effect, an entire print factory can be sitting on your desk.

Types of printer and printer inks

In photography, there are two main types of printer. Dye sublimation types can be compact and portable. They use ribbons of dye to make postcard-size or smaller prints suitable for presents. The majority of printers use an inkjet technology. Here, reservoirs supply ink to nozzles that squirt extremely tiny drops of ink on to paper. Two main types of ink are used: dye for general prints and pigment ink for highest quality and permanence. The commonest inkjet printers print up to A4 size; other models print to A3 and larger. Some printers are able to print right up to the paper edge to make borderless prints.

If you intend to make many prints, choose a printer with separate colour cartridges rather than one that uses cartridges combining several colours. Printers may be relatively low cost for the high quality they produce, but ink can be costly. For best results, use the best papers you can afford.

Mid-range printer

A mid-range printer can produce photo-quality prints up to A4 size. Printers using six or more inks give better quality than those using only four inks. Many models offer a built-in scanner that can be used to scan originals or make photocopies. Models that connect wirelessly or that can print direct from the camera or a memory card are very convenient to use.

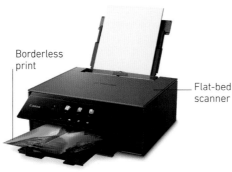

Borderless print

Flat-bed scanner

⌃ All-in-one
Modern machines offer six colour photo inks, a resolution of over 5,000 dpi, can print borderless photos, and even make scans or copies.

Online printing

Making prints at home is convenient if you have your own printer but only for ordinary-sized prints. If you need the occasional larger print for posters or exhibitions, it is best to use an online service. These are run by experienced printers who use their machines regularly and allow you to upload your image file to the service and order the size of print and type of paper you require from your desktop. Some services print on the highest quality archival papers, and others (below) print on specialist surfaces such as weather-proof vinyl or aluminium.

⌄ Outdoor exhibition
Online services can print to photo-quality on specialist materials suitable for an outdoor exhibition of poster-sized prints.

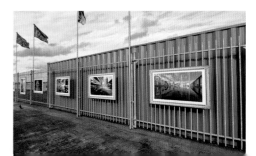

》 PRINTING IN BLACK AND WHITE

It may seem perverse to use colour technology to produce black-and-white prints but, thanks to the use of dark inks, inkjet printers can give superb results that easily rival silver-based prints. In fact, inkjet printers gave the photographer the first true blacks in prints, which were previously only obtainable with industrial-scale printing.

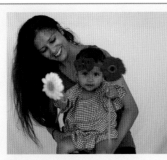

⌃ In colour
The strong colours worn by the models distract from their beauty and charm. Remove colour by adjusting the colour channels to turn into pure tonal values.

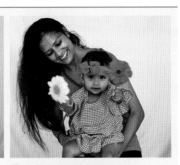

⌃ In black and white
Turned into a black-and-white image, the faces of the models come to the fore. Note especially how the gingham pattern is beneficially suppressed.

Online photo books

While many can make their own prints at home, hardly anyone can turn their prints into bound books. Online services using web-based apps give you the chance to produce your very own photo books. You design the layout, placing images where you want them, choose the type of paper and binding, and within days your book is delivered. You can make the process trouble-free with a little planning. First choose the look and design, and practise a few layouts to get used to how the design app works. All online apps offer templates that you can use for good results. Next gather all your images, preferably named in sequence or with the page number on which you want to put them. Check that the images are the correct size – not too big, not too small – for their intended use. Also ensure they look consistently exposed and sharp.

Edge-to-edge printing

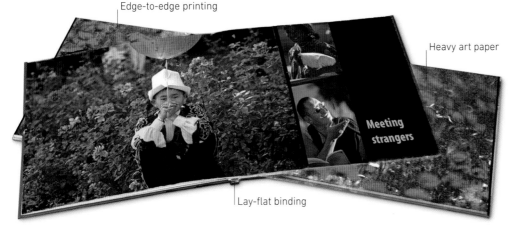

Heavy art paper

Lay-flat binding

Book quality

There are different ways to produce photo books to suit every budget. Low-cost options involve inexpensive bindings such as spiral wire, with lightweight papers. For higher quality, choose heavyweight art papers and more secure bindings, such as perfect (glue-based) binding. For the best presentation of photographs, choose borderless printing with lay-flat designs in which the pages lie almost without a "gutter" or dip in the middle.

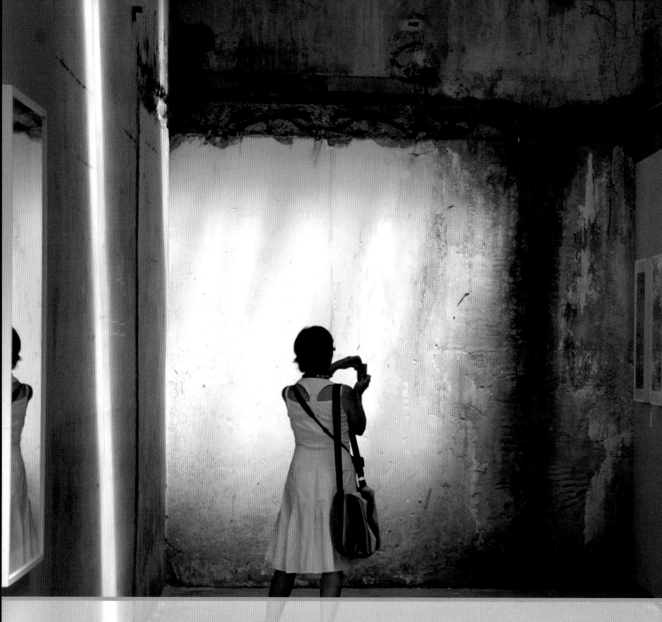

TAKING PHOTOGRAPHY
FURTHER

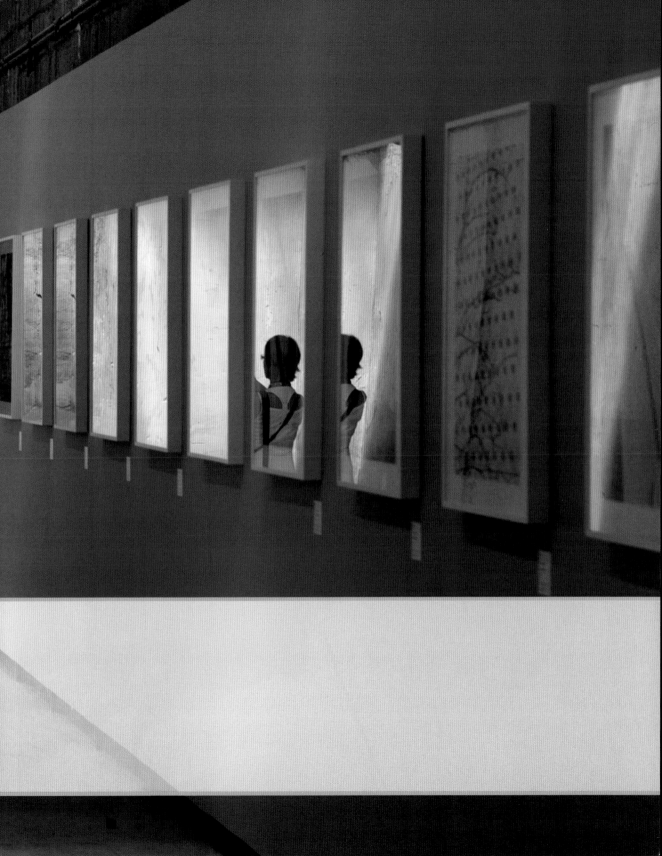

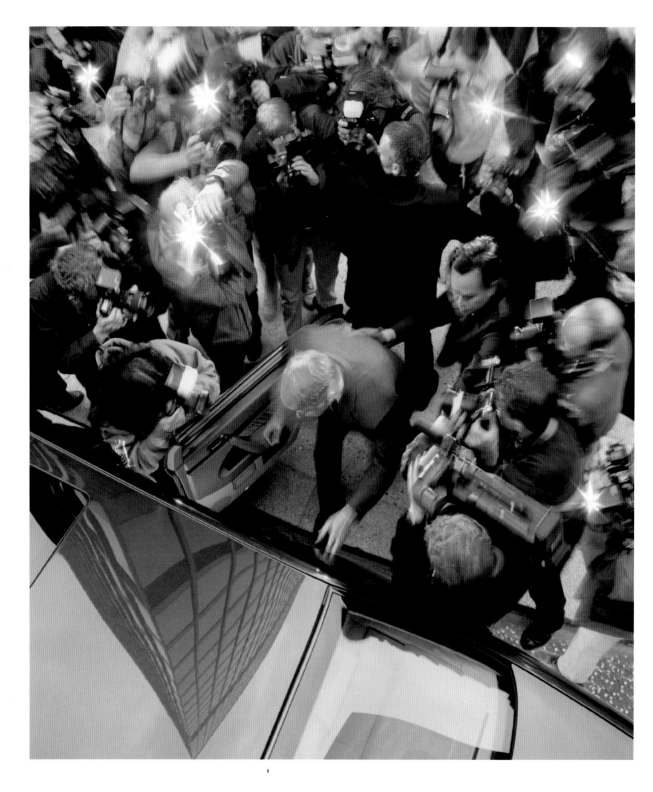

The breadth, depth, and variety of ways in which you can be involved in photography is one of its most attractive features. While the "frontline" work of photography is regarded as the most glamorous, it is also the most demanding and stressful. But there are many other ways to take your photography further.

There is no doubt that reaching the top in the world of photography calls for total dedication (if not obsession), hard work, true creative talent, plus a good dose of luck. But there are plenty of ways in which you can get more satisfaction out of your hobby that do not require quite the same level of endurance and investment in effort.

Although there is a wide variety of photographic jobs, from staff positions on newspapers and magazines to part-time freelance work for private and business clients, competition for all work is fierce. If you have a particular interest, such as sailing, archaeology, or theatre, you could try specializing in this area. However, while your images may have less competition, there will also be less demand.

Even if you do not wish to work full-time, you can still have a great deal of fun, gain much satisfaction, and even earn a little by working professionally. But before you are in a position to charge people for your services, you need to have confidence in your ability.

The best way to gain confidence is to take as many pictures as possible, as often as you can. You need to be constantly and continually framing the world, to view it as if through a lens. This will train you to see life with a photographic eye. You have probably had the experience of seeing something beautiful or humorous and wishing you had your camera with you. The more you think about, and take, pictures, the more you will start to notice much more prosaic things and appreciate their photographic potential, like the forgotten corner of a garden, a deserted alleyway, or the shadows on a wall.

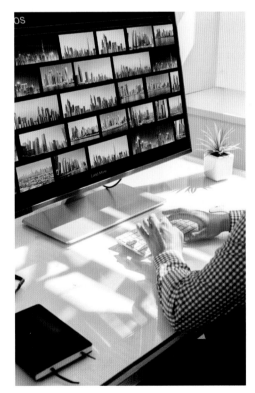

◀◀ **Press photography**
Although the paparazzi are perhaps the most well-known type of photographers, there is a huge variety of jobs in the profession.

◀◀ **Checking images**
Learning the technical aspects of photography is vital to improving your skills.

You can increase your confidence in your photography further by attending one of the numerous courses offered worldwide. These are often located in carefully chosen, inspirational settings. Many are taught by tutors who are top-rank practitioners themselves. However, it would be wishful thinking to believe that a course alone – even a university course lasting three or more years – is enough to make you a brilliant photographer.

Looking at pictures in depth is vital to your development as a photographer – never take an image at face value. You need to probe under the surface of an image and learn as much about it as possible. One useful technique is to avoid looking at the main subject first, but start at the edge and move slowly across. This is similar to the way in which musicians train themselves to listen for the bass line in a composition: you can always hear the melody over it, but if you listen only to the tune, you easily miss the bass. Working from the periphery gives you the structure of the image, then you can start to analyze it further, looking at technical features such as depth of field, the focal lens used, its tonal qualities, and colour.

As your experience in and understanding of photography grows, you will also realize the importance of seeking out, studying, and appreciating the work of the masters of photography. It is helpful to know the background of both the photographer and the subject of the photograph. Ask the standard journalistic questions of what, when, who, and why. What is the photograph about? When was it taken? Who took it and who may have influenced the photograph stylistically? Why might it have been taken in this particular way, and not in another way?

This chapter provides information to support you as you take your study of photography further. It is followed by a glossary of useful terms.

» Test-strips and prints
Printing test-strips and hanging them is a useful way to compare your prints. It also makes an attractive composition, becoming an image in its own right.

» Learning photography
Many photography workshops are held in country houses. Here photographer Ben Edwards discusses his own work.

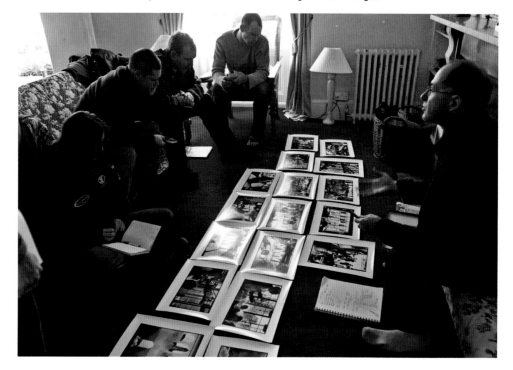

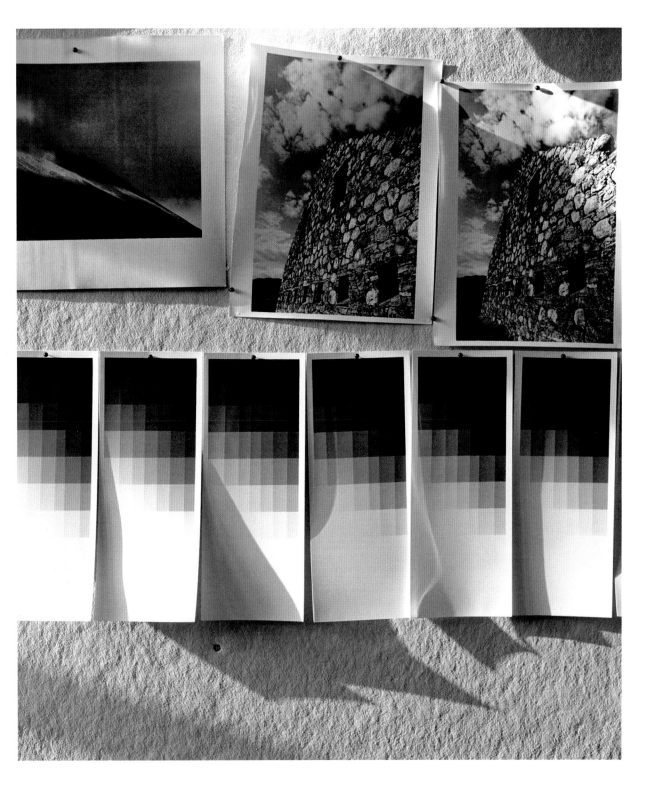

Turning professional

Working professionally in photography is one of the best jobs in the world. You are, after all, being paid to do something you love and enjoy. Not surprisingly, there are huge numbers of people looking for a career in photography – each year, colleges around the country train many hundreds more photography students than the market can accommodate. Whether this dismays you or whether it hardens your resolve will determine your future.

To study or not?

One of the key questions to ask yourself is whether you should train in photography at a college on a recognized course. In some countries you cannot call yourself a professional photographer unless you obtain a qualification. In others, it may be more efficient to learn through self-study to supplement working as an assistant to a professional photographer.

Studying photography

Courses that offer qualifications such as a degree or diploma will need a commitment of one to three or more years of sustained study. Be prepared to learn not only the practical aspects of photography but also about critical art theory. Degree courses generally concentrate on education (understanding photography) more than on training (actually taking photographs). Another option is to attend a residential course, often run as a summer school, in which you immerse yourself in a wholly photographic environment. Here, learning is highly accelerated. You concentrate on problem-solving, with experts on hand to offer guidance whenever you need it. To make the most of this type of "immersion teaching", you need to continue practising the skills you have learnt as soon as you return home. What is learnt quickly is also quickly forgotten. Intensive courses tend to be very specific – concentrating on landscapes or portraiture or image manipulation – so the resulting knowledge can be fragmentary. If you can afford to, and have the time, it is well worth attending a range of courses to broaden your knowledge.

Applying for study

To apply successfully to a course, it pays to plan ahead. Most courses only interview and select students at certain times of the year. Make sure that you meet any formal requirements such as educational qualifications. Next, prepare a portfolio to show your work. You will need to plan your finances very carefully – attending a course reduces your ability to earn and is itself a financial drain. Find out all you can about the course – the institution will be impressed if you can demonstrate that your own ambitions match those of the course. If it offers subjects you are not familiar with, for example, media theory, be sure before you apply that you are sufficiently interested in them to study them in depth.

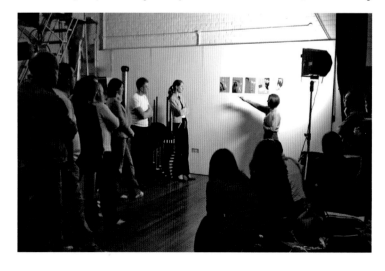

⊠ Critical review
Studying photography in a college environment brings you into contact with others, and also exposes your work to supportive but critical review from your peers.

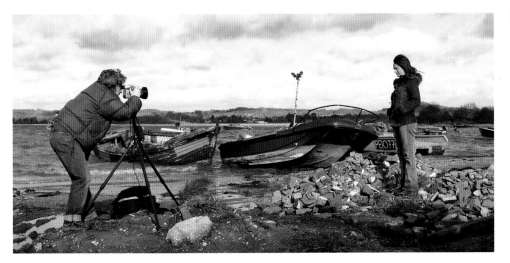

Working in all conditions
As a professional you will be expected to produce top-quality results whatever the situation or weather. In the above situation, it was freezing cold, blowing a gale, and the light changed constantly.

Learning as an assistant

The key requirement for a successful career in photography is the same as for finding work as a photographic assistant – versatility. If you have a wide range of skills – even if they are not fully developed – you will be in a better position than someone with only one highly developed skill. While working as an assistant you will improve your skills and progress much more quickly if you continually read instruction manuals, books, and magazines on photography, to supplement the practical experience you acquire. It will also help if you keep up to speed with contemporary culture of all kinds, not only visual.

You should be competent with using computers and standard software such as Adobe Photoshop. Many professional photographers rely heavily on their assistants for their ability to perform administrative and creative tasks on the computer.

Business skills

While working for a photographer, try to learn not only about the art of photography but also about the business aspect of photography: how to be a professional in a highly competitive world. Learn about working to the highest standards – both artistic and technical – to make extraordinary efforts for your clients. Learn to work honestly and to take your commitments seriously by being punctual for meetings, and ensure you maintain a constant flow of communication with your client, and keep to promised budgets and deadlines. The trust that you build up as a consequence of your professionalism will repay you in the form of re-commissions.

SELLING PRINTS

Selling a print is often an encouragement to take the step into professional photography. If someone wants to buy one of your pictures, you should offer them the highest-quality print you can. Use a professional laboratory for colour or black-and-white prints, unless you are highly proficient in the darkroom. Tell the laboratory that the prints are to be sold and ask for the longest-lasting materials. With digital images, you could make the print yourself with an inkjet printer. The best inkjet printers can produce long-lasting prints if you print on high-quality paper.

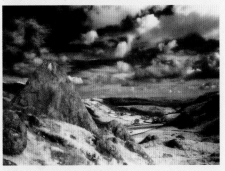

Atmospheric landscape
A landscape photograph such as the above could quite easily find interested buyers. It will also have a longer life – a monochrome print is less likely to fade than a colour version.

Commercial photography

There is a supply of pictures numbering tens of millions worldwide, available for anyone to buy for publications, websites, and even for making personal prints. While the market may seem to be saturated, the demand for images for use in everything from computer games to mobile phones, from computer "wallpaper" to greetings cards, continues to grow relentlessly.

Understanding stock photography

The term "stock photography" is used to describe pictures that are held by agencies or libraries, which sell picture-use rights to publishers, newspapers, television channels, and so on. Large picture agencies hold millions of images, and these collections are growing at the rate of hundreds of images each week. Some agencies hold images in a number of categories, from fashion to news and lifestyle. Others are more specialist, for example, offering only steam trains, gardens and flowers, or fine art reproductions.

Working with picture libraries

To place your work in a stock picture agency and to obtain a return, your pictures should be of the highest technical quality and must be appropriate to the library's visual style or subject matter. It is very difficult to join the top agencies unless your pictures are not only distinctive and original, but also feature subjects that are in demand. Try visiting the websites of some of the major picture agencies, such as Alamy, Getty, or National Geographic to gain an impression of the type of images that are used.

The system works in the following way. You submit a collection of, say, 100 top-quality images to the agency. If your work is suitable, a number of pictures may be selected (possibly as few as 15) and put into the collection. If and when reproduction rights for one of your images is sold, you will receive a portion of the fee (usually 50 per cent, or less if intermediate agencies are involved) when the agency itself is paid. The beauty of this system is that your pictures can be sold again and again, and the more the agency earns, the more you earn too.

Shooting for stock

Photographing for stock is a discipline in its own right. Technical quality is paramount (see also pp.304–305). Digital files will be accepted but may have to be at least 50MB in size and must meet very specific requirements. These requirements vary with different agencies.

To be a successful stock photographer you need to adopt a rigorous commercial approach to your image-making. The principle for the majority of images is to maximize their saleability and longevity. Images suitable for use in advertising earn very good returns. Alternatively, if it is an image that is repeatedly used (pictures of hand-shakes, for example, can be used to illustrate a range of subjects from advertising to corporate brochures) a fortune can be earned. A snap of a truck racing across a landscape may have more editorial value and more potential uses than a beautiful tropical landscape.

⊠ Multi-purpose picture
The subject may seem dull, but an image like this can be used for countless corporate purposes and earn a healthy return.

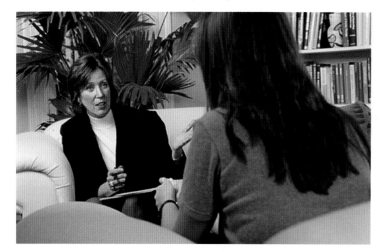

Image licensing

There are two types of image licensing – rights-managed (RM) and royalty-free (RF). For a rights-managed image, the client pays each time the image is used. As the photographer, you can also specify restrictions on the use of your image, such as no cropping. For royalty-free images, the client can pay a higher fee for a collection of pictures that can be used as many times as desired, without further payment for re-use. The market for such collections is now vast, with millions of images available covering thousands of subjects. It is possible to earn from supplying images to publishers of RF collections, but you will need to take large numbers of images, as your pictures will be purchased outright, and you may receive no further fee for their re-use.

Model release forms

A model release is a contract, usually in the form of a written agreement between you and the subject(s) of your picture, which allows you to use images of them, in return for a fee. In the modern, litigious, world, it has become increasingly necessary to obtain model releases if the person is easily identifiable in the picture. In fact, many agencies will only accept images that are fully model-released. However, if you have a crowd scene in which no-one is prominent, it is not usually necessary to obtain model releases.

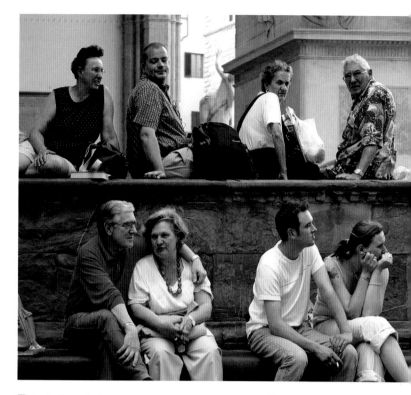

⌄ Typical stock pictures
All the images shown here are highly saleable. The main features they have in common are that they are bright, colourful, technically flawless, their subject matter is clear, and their message is international.

⌃ Public in Florence, Italy
In this picture of tourists relaxing in Florence, Italy, everyone is clearly identifiable. It was taken in a public space, with many different people involved so it was impractical to obtain model releases from everyone. However, if the image had been intended for a high-profile use, such as advertising an international credit card, it would have been advisable to obtain model releases in case of complaint.

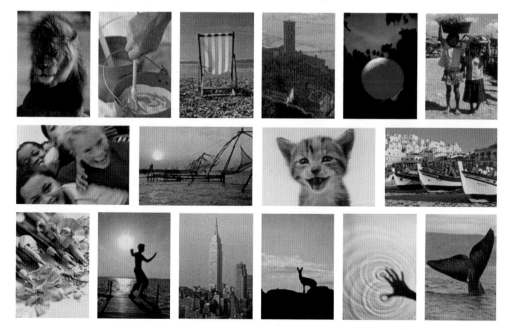

Assuring picture quality

You check a picture's quality – albeit often unconsciously – every time you look at it. We are confronted with hundreds of photographic images each day, and the process of judging the quality of an image has become so ingrained in all of us, it is almost automatic. But as your ambitions grow, a superficial assessment will no longer be enough. You will need to examine each image thoroughly, with a checklist of criteria to consider.

Quality criteria

The basic requirements for picture quality are surprisingly well-known to all visually literate people. Our frequent exposure to top-quality images in leaflets, magazines, and online has trained everyone to be highly critical of the images they view. An effective technique of analyzing your photographs in a deliberate, professional way is to scrutinize a picture from the edge and then work your way across the image. This focuses your attention on areas of the image that might otherwise be neglected.

To meet basic standards, the picture must be sharp. Important details should be clearly defined and not blurred or soft. Exposure should be accurate and neither too dark nor too light overall. Colours should be true-to-life and not exaggerated or too washed out. Neutral colours, such as greys or whites, should appear neutral. Finally, contrast should be accurate, with tonal changes appearing natural, and with smooth transitions between one shade and another.

》 BASIC IMAGE PROBLEMS

There are a number of basic problems that commonly affect picture quality. These should never be seen in a professionally produced image unless clearly and deliberately intended. You must learn how to avoid them if you are to be taken seriously as a photographer.

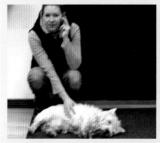

⌃ Camera movement
This fault causes the image to be unsharp or blurred. Avoid it by using a tripod or steadying your camera before shooting.

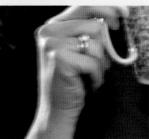

⌃ Subject movement
Movement in parts of the subject can cause blurring. Avoid it by posing your subject and using a shorter exposure time.

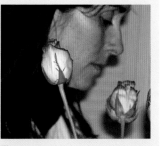

⌃ Poor focus
The subject is out of focus, while other details are sharp. This shows poor technical control – learn to focus accurately.

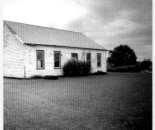

⌃ Light fall-off
Uneven distribution of brightness across the image suggests use of inferior-quality lenses or cameras.

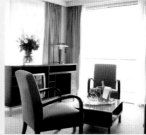

⌃ Burnt-out highlights
Exposure has been set for mid-tones without taking into account light from the window. This renders highlights too white.

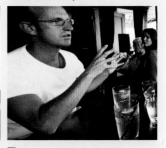

⌃ Wide-angle distortion
Objects with a recognizable shape, especially faces, should not be distorted. Avoid using a wide-angle lens.

"Pre-flighting" checks

In the space of a few years before the turn of the 21st century, the practice of delivering images in a digital form grew from rare to nearly universal. Many magazines, agencies, and internet-based operations will no longer accept prints or transparencies. Because of this, it is important to understand how to check or "pre-flight" digital files before delivering them. Ideally, you should ensure that the recipient of the files does not need to work at all on the files before putting them to use. Files of your final image should:

• be printable at 100 per cent size.
• be named consistently and helpfully, for example, corresponding to page number or order of appearance on a website.
• contain no more data than necessary, that is, contain no extraneous elements such as layers, paths, or spot-colours.
• be free of defects such as specks of dust.
• be in a format compatible with the systems in use. The most frequently used format is TIFF RGB saved in 24-bit, compressed.
• comply with colour-managed workflows to ensure colours reproduce accurately, that is, have an appropriate profile.

Including image information

Increasingly, when you supply your images to agencies and picture libraries, they will require you to include metadata in your image file. This is information about the image, rather than the image data itself. It needs to be embedded in the image file, and should include the following details:

• your name and contact details, including your telephone number with local and international dialling codes, email address, and website URL if applicable.
• captioning information, including the title of the image, the location and time of capture, the

occasion – for example, Mardi Gras – the names of anyone featured prominently, and keywords describing the image.
• other details, including a copyright notice, whether or not a model release has been obtained, and any restrictions on the image.

Automating functions

Adding information to a single image is tedious enough, but to do so to hundreds of images requires special software. Fortunately, digital asset management software, such as Fotoware Fotostation, Extensis Portfolio, or Adobe Bridge, can add a great deal of useful information to images at the touch of a button. For some purposes, such as news or current affairs photography, your metadata should comply with the IPTC (International Press Telecommunications Council) specifications. See www.iptc.org for full details.

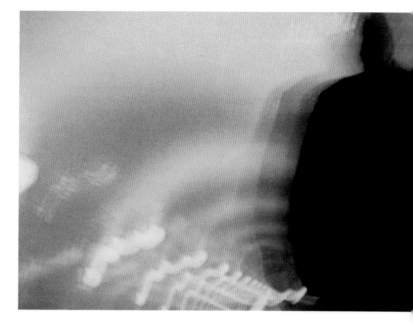

◢ Acceptable blur
Like all rules, technical requirements can be broken for specific purposes. Here, a professionally-created image exhibits severe blur from subject and camera movement, as well as poor focus. But instead of detracting from the image's appeal, these technical "problems" are used deliberately to create a sense of urban estrangement.

◀◀ Image caption information
Standard information such as this helps provide technical data, identify date and time of photography, as well as locating the file in the computer system.

File information						✕
Name:	DSC00239.jpg	Type:	JPEG	Size:	108.4x81.3cm	
Camera date:	13/04/2019	Pixels:	3072x2304	Colour:	RGB	
Modified date:	14/04/2019	Image size:	20.25 Mbyte			
File size:	2.74 Mbyte	Resolution:	72dpi			
Full path:	Volumes/Big Disk/Pictures/Sony P200					

Analyzing a saleable photograph

If someone needs a photograph and is willing to pay for it, that photograph is saleable. This means that just about any photograph can be sold – to the right person. The trick is to try to take pictures that satisfy as many categories of desirability as possible. The focus of an image's saleable qualities needs to be as accurate as its optical focus.

Flexible content

An attractive subject – such as this timeless scene of dhows returning to their harbour in Zanzibar – is a splendid foundation for a saleable image. But if, in addition, the image can be cropped into different formats and has individual graphic elements that can be exploited, then its commercial uses are greatly increased. The secret is to keep shooting – you can never be sure at the time which is the best, most versatile image. This scene provided many lovely shots. But this particular image, with its many ways of cropping, clean groupings, and bold shapes, can be used in many ways. If you have the time, bracket your exposures (*see p.179*) whether using a digital or film-using camera.

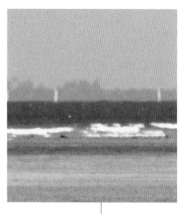

》 Using tone and colour
Deep blues or azure colours reproduce very well on a computer screen, but are much more difficult to print onto paper. However, the image does not rely on accurate colours. In fact, it would be equally effective in black-and-white, which is another advantage.

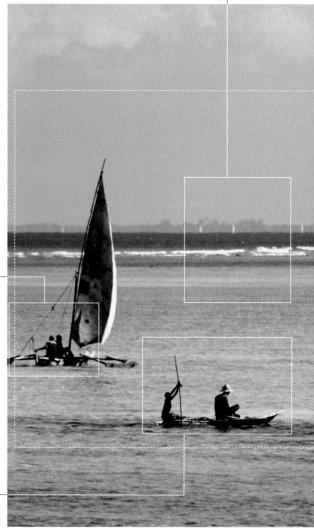

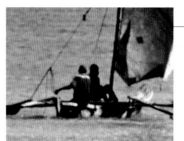

》 Compositional error
The photographer has accidentally framed this image to the right of the scene, leaving too much space to the right and cropping the edge of the boat on the left. It is important to frame generously to avoid such problems.

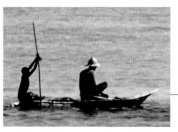

》 Peak of action
Good timing and a keen eye allow you to capture key moments. Here, the boy punting the boat imparts a sense of movement and energy to the image.

⟩⟩ TOP-QUALITY FILM FORMATS

The most frequently used image format for high-quality reproduction is medium format taken on 120 format roll-film, measuring from 6 x 4.5cm to 6 x 9cm (2¼ x 1¾in to 2¼ x 3½in). They are suitable for greetings cards and calendars, or double-page spreads of magazines. Larger formats such as 5 x 4in are even better. However, 35mm format pictures can be used for these purposes, but only if made with the greatest care.

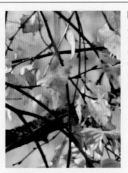

« Small Format
A scan of a 35mm format transparency, enlarged at the equivalent of 1m (40in) wide, shows inability to hold detail.

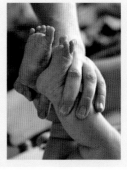

« Medium Format
A close-up of a medium-format image, enlarged at the equivalent of 1m (40in) wide, displays fine detail.

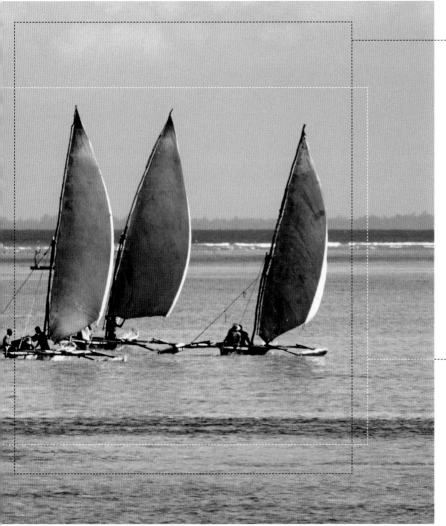

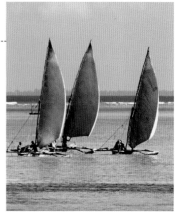

⌃ Vertical crop
This image also allows a vertical or portrait-format crop, which takes in the full height of the image and isolates the group of three dhows. The strong horizontal lines of the horizon and the band of deeper water help structure the crop.

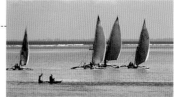

⌃ Letterbox crop
The letterbox crop – very wide and narrow – is popular for greetings cards and calendars. Images with the space to allow such a crop can be more useful than those with tight composition.

Creating a portfolio

A portfolio is a selection of your best work, which you present when seeking commissions or a position. A "selection" means just that. Do not merely collect your best shots, but bring together only those that meet the direct aim of obtaining work of the kind you wish to gain. Choosing pictures to meet a specific purpose is the art of picture editing.

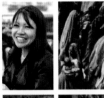

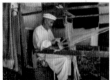
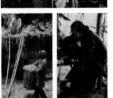
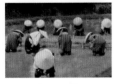

Original selection

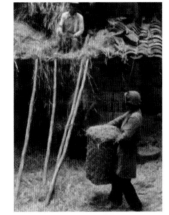

Men baling straw, Laos

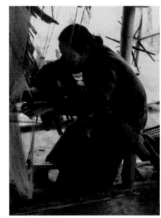

Weaver in Mung-Xai, Laos

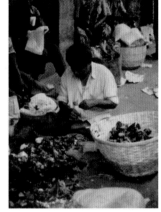

Flower seller in Mysore, India

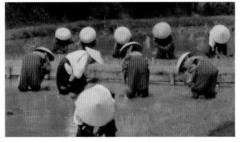

Women in paddy fields in Fushimi, Japan

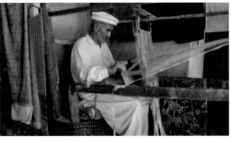

Weaver in Karimabad, Pakistan

Picture editing

A picture is the "best" only in relation to a specific use or purpose. Picture editing is the process of examining every picture to evaluate its suitability for the purpose that you have in mind.

Selecting images

Suppose you want to create a portfolio of travel photographs on a theme of people at work. Look through all your images and pull out the possibles, such as the images on the far left. At a second edit, remove any images that are not entirely relevant to the theme of people at work, such as the smiling girl and children among boats and colourful clothes. You may arrive at a selection such as the larger images above and to the left, from which you will then choose your final pictures.

Refining the selection

The process of picture editing is to weed out gradually the weaker pictures. With each edit, you will have fewer and fewer pictures, but those that remain will be a refined, strong set. At this point you should look at the overall impression of the images. Notice, for example, that the man on the loom (left) stands out as being very blue. You may need to change the colour balance so that he matches the others more closely. Then you may see that all the pictures are at similar distances, showing the full body, leading to a monotony of scale. So perhaps you need to look for shots that are more close-up – like that of the smiling girl (far left) – and some that are more distant. And it goes without saying that all the images should be technically perfect.

Presenting your portfolio

Your portfolio should include only the type of pictures that you want to be commissioned to take. There is no point showing flower studies if you want to work as a documentarist. Show enough pictures to demonstrate your talent but no more – too many reveals a lack of confidence. Explain the images only as much as you are invited to, and allow the person reviewing them to do so at their own pace. The way you present yourself is also important. Dress appropriately, and always be polite. Your work may be rejected today, but you may want to return at a future time with a different set of images, or approach another part of the company, so it is wise to make a good first impression. And always remember to leave your contact details.

》 METHODS OF PRESENTING YOUR PICTURES

Most portfolios are now digital and are viewed on a laptop or tablet, but you might need to present your work in different ways to suit the clients you visit. There is, unfortunately, no perfect way to show pictures for all occasions.

METHOD	ADVANTAGES	DISADVANTAGES
Laptop / tablet	Inexpensive if you already own a laptop, easy to manage and change to suit clients	Images may be compressed to save memory, so may not be shown at best quality
Hard drive / disk	Very inexpensive, large number of images can be shown, can be organized into presentations	Requires computer, can be quite slow, possible file incompatibility problems
Unmounted prints	Most flexible, convenient, least expensive, best view of prints	Prints are easily damaged, may appear too informal
Mounted prints	Presents prints well, helps protect prints if window-mounted, not too costly	Makes portfolio very heavy, impractical for large prints, clumsy to handle
Mounted slides	Inexpensive, lightweight; images can be grouped easily	Difficult to view without lightbox, needs loupe or magnifier to view detail
Plastic sleeves	Inexpensive, protects print	Prints can be hard to see clearly
Large format slides	Impressive and professional-looking, not too bulky	Very costly to produce, fragile unless window-mounted

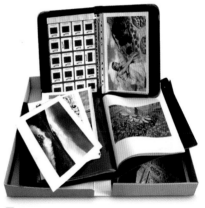

⌃ **Types of physical portfolio**
You can show bare prints from a box, enclose them in transparent sleeves, or display many slides on a single sheet. Use the method that best suits your work and the client.

Exhibiting photographs

As your collection of photographs grows, so too may the urge to share it beyond your immediate circle of friends. Even if you do not wish to approach agencies or organizations directly to seek commissions, there are other ways to show your pictures to a wider audience. You can hold exhibitions online, in galleries, schools, bars, and restaurants, and maybe even sell individual prints.

Planning your exhibition

How you put together a collection of pictures for exhibition will depend on the venue where they will be displayed and the overall effect you wish to create. The criteria for selecting images for public display is much the same as when you are creating a portfolio. Quality is of the utmost importance. Your pictures need not necessarily all follow a particular theme but you do need to think about how to arrange them to create impact and a strong narrative flow.

Forward planning

Approach your venue well ahead of time. Commercial galleries generally plan their schedules at least a year ahead, but venues such as a local library or school may show work at shorter notice. Find out about other local events, such as concerts or lectures, to see if your exhibition could be tied in. Be creative with your venue – any public space, such as a railway or bus station, or a corridor in a shopping centre could be used, and indeed may be more suitable for some kinds of work than a gallery. Remember that the presence of your photography alone can transform a location into a gallery.

Depending on where you are exhibiting you may need to consider how best to light your images. In an informal space, however, your options might be limited. It is best to create prints that are large enough to be viewed easily, even from a distance.

>> **Exhibition materials**
The majority of materials and tools needed to create an exhibition are inexpensive and widely available.

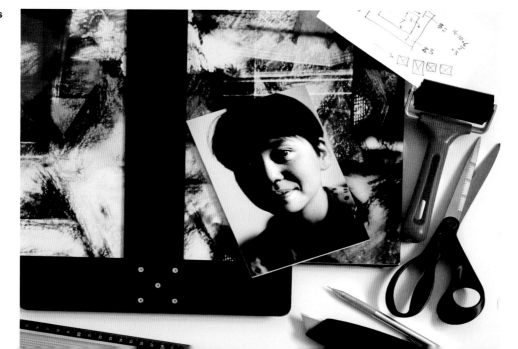

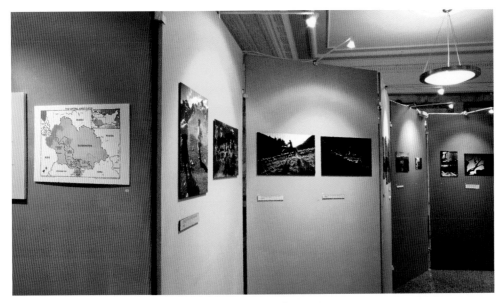

« **Converting space**
Non-gallery spaces, such as this entrance lobby, can be easily converted to house exhibitions by using inexpensive self-standing panels. For this show, the panels were colourfully painted to complement the Central Asian theme of the photographs.

Budgeting

The key to staying within budget is to put on the best show that you can afford, not one that costs more than you can manage. Make a comprehensive list of everything that you will need, and keep updating it. The largest expense is usually the cost of printing and mounting the photographs. But budget for additional costs, such as business cards, leaflets to publicize the show, catering for the opening night, and small "thank you" gifts for people who have given their time and help to make your show a success.

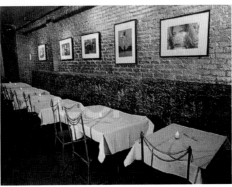

« **Restaurant gallery**
Bars and restaurants make excellent locations for showing photography. They are popular with diners, and it is possible to obtain good sales of prints from busy venues.

Sponsorship

To help with your finances, you may look for sponsorship. The best approach is to look for a partner, but sponsorships work only when benefits flow both ways. You need to answer the question "What will the sponsor get out of sponsoring me?" The pitch to a sponsor that starts "I can ensure your company gets lots of coverage in local newspapers" is more likely to succeed than one starting with "I need money for a great idea for photography." It is always easier to obtain services, such as printing materials, exhibition space, scanning, processing, and even refreshments than it is to obtain cash. Also, ensure that you ask in good time, because other people also have their own budgets to maintain.

Final steps

When you have a space booked, sketch the layout of the whole exhibition, and make thumbnail sketches of the prints in their hanging order. This helps you to plan the flow of the narrative. As the big day approaches, do not forget it is your chance to get your work and yourself known. Make full use of it; this is not a time to be diffident. Tell everyone you know and everyone else too. Circulate press releases to local newspapers, local radio or television stations, and specialist magazines, and spread the word on social media. At the opening and in a notice at the show, remember to say thank you. It is likely that the help you received from people was just as valuable as the help you received from your sponsors.

Creating a web presence

In today's interconnected world, the first time that most people will encounter your photographs will be on the internet. You control that interaction. Your pictures may appear on picture-sharing sites, on basic, automatically generated websites, or on professional-looking web pages that host your images to their best effect.

Automated or bespoke

If you have access to the internet, you can publish your pictures to the world. Many picture-sharing websites are free of charge and only ask that you register. But it is far more rewarding to create your own website to your own design that you manage yourself. Some image-manipulation software can automatically make web pages from your pictures. You choose the basic features, but the design may be quite basic and limited in scope.

☑ Organize materials
Prepare all your images, movie files etc. and collect them into one place to make it easy to build your website.

Creating your own site

Once you have bought a domain, you need to look into hosting your website. Some hosting services help you create your website using templates and basic design editors.

If you are skilled, you can create a site from scratch, but there are also many professional website developers out there who can take the technical challenges off your hands. Then you only have to decide on a design, template or theme for them to create, and populate the pages with your amazing content.

The key to success is to be clear what you want to achieve and stick to the plan. Extra features, such as e-commerce tools to enable visitors to order your prints or e-books, make creating your site more complicated. The fun part is compiling your pictures for the site.

Publicizing your site

Creating the site and populating it with images is only the end of the beginning. Now you have to ensure that everyone knows about it! Publicize the site on your social media pages, and encourage your followers and friends to share the content. Also, give all your friends, family, acquaintances, and business contacts the address of your website, and encourage them to show their friends, too. Word of mouth is a powerful tool! If you can, keep adding new content to the website to ensure it stays fresh and invites repeat visits. When you make a major change, such as add details about a new exhibition or complete a new project, circulate the news to everyone you know.

Value of activity

Given that there are millions of photography sites visited by hundreds of millions of keen photographers, the only way to attract attention is through regularly providing new and high-quality content. You can do that by simply posting new images frequently on picture-sharing sites. Some sites are regularly trawled by talent-scouts and picture buyers. It is possible to build up followings of many thousands this way.

Another way is to blog: make posts that combine pictures with news or information, either in text or video form. You can use your own website to hold the content, but it may be more effective to use widely available channels, such as YouTube or Vimeo, to host your videos.

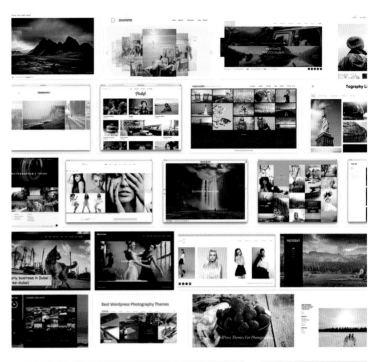

» Website themes

You do not have to be a skilled designer to create excellent websites as there are numerous professional design themes and templates available that you only have to populate with your images and text. Some services will even build and host your site for you, using "wizard" applications.

» PROTECTING COPYRIGHT

It is a fact that once your image enters the public domain, you lose a great deal of control over it. Unscrupulous photographers can copy your work and pretend it is theirs, or combine it with other images. The best protection is to use the lowest resolution, highest compression image compatible with good quality on your site. You may opt for a site design that does not use full-width images as these have to be relatively large. Another strategy is to apply watermarks to your images (as shown, right). These tend to be most effective when they most intrude on an image, so are not always ideal for showing off your work. On some kinds of image, such as landscapes, watermarks may offer no protection at all as they can be easily removed. Watermarks may also be hidden as tiny irregularities in the picture code. These can be retrieved by special reader applications. Invisible watermarks may be useful for establishing theft, but do not deter theft in the first place.

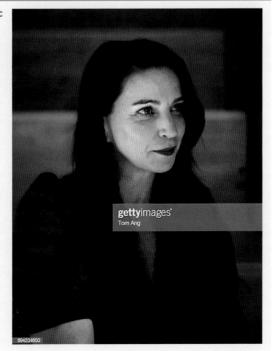

» Watermarked stock photo

Before a consumer purchases rights to use your work from a stock site, they will often only have access to a version covered with an imposing watermark and only be able to use it in low resolution.

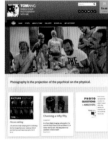

⌃ Home page

Your website home page should show your latest posts, any prints or goods that you have to offer, as well as quick ways to access all the deeper content.

Diagnosing problems

It is helpful to be able to diagnose image problems as the first step to finding a solution that either prevents, or lessens the likelihood of, the problem occurring again. The most common film problems are poor exposure or development, or a combination of both. Digital problems (*see pp.318–20*) vary a great deal in nature, while printing problems (*see p.321*) form a separate group.

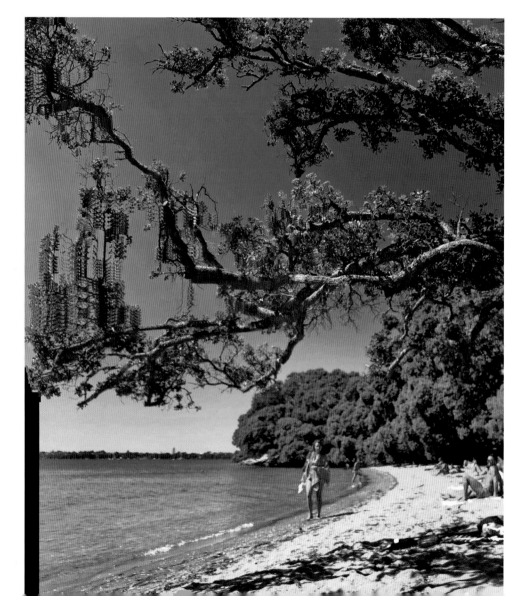

» **Deliberate error**
This image is full of artefacts and faults including the jitter in the tree's branches that were moving during the exposure.

⟩⟩ BLACK-AND-WHITE FILM

The first set of problems considered here are various combinations of exposure with development. Study them carefully and you will see that some problems can be turned to your advantage in certain circumstances. Other problems – from surge marks to light fog – are caused by poor handling, and should be avoided at all times.

PROBLEM	SYMPTOM	SOLUTION
Thin, flat negative	This negative is very thin, with little density even in bright areas (highlights) of the image. This is because of underexposure combined with underdevelopment, so that there is insufficient time for density to build up in the highlights.	Give full exposure, particularly if the subject contrast is low. If in doubt, expose for areas a little darker than mid-tone grey. Develop according to instructions, following directions for dilution, agitation, and temperature as accurately as possible.
Thin negative	The negative is thin, with little detail in the mid-tones, but highlight areas appear to have good density. This is caused by underexposure combined with correct or sufficient development.	Expose so that shadow areas with important detail are fully exposed. In this image, the bright background caused the girl's face to be underexposed. Extra development may rescue some shadow details.
Flat negative	Highlight densities appear correct but overall the image appears flat and low in contrast. This is caused by giving a correct exposure, followed with underdevelopment sufficient to build density in the highlights, but not to increase contrast.	Develop your negatives to give the contrast that you prefer to print with – the exact contrast is largely a matter of personal taste. A little underdevelopment can be used to reduce the contrast of negatives of high-contrast scenes.
Contrasty negative	Giving the image correct exposure at the time of capture but overdeveloping when processing results in a very contrasty negative. The highlights are blocked out to solid black and mid-tones are very heavy. It will be very difficult to make a good print.	Print on soft (low-contrast) paper or a low-contrast grade of paper to compensate for the high contrast of the film. To avoid the problem in future, slightly underdevelop a film exposed in a high-contrast situation, avoiding over-development at all costs.
Heavy negative	This image shows poor shadow details yet the overall density of the image is high – it appears a dark grey. The cause is underexposure, which failed to capture shadow details, combined with overdevelopment, which created density over the whole image.	It is best to give correct exposure and development, but underexposure may be necessary in poor lighting conditions. Extra development may be given to compensate, to create a usable negative. This is the basis of "push-processing".

⟫ BLACK-AND-WHITE FILM

PROBLEM	SYMPTOM	SOLUTION
Flat, heavy negative 	A negative that is relatively low in contrast or flat, but with normal or high density overall, is likely to result from overexposure and underdevelopment.	In highly contrasty lighting conditions, full development may not give the best print. Give extra exposure when photographing to allow for reduced development so that the contrast of the negative is reduced. This is the basis of "pull-processing".
Very dense negative 	Overexposure combined with overdevelopment will give rise to very dense negatives with high contrast. These negatives can be all but impossible to print. And they are also all but impossible to scan properly.	Avoid compounding overexposure by overdeveloping the negative. In extreme cases bleaching solutions may be applied to reduce overall density. Professional drum-scanning may also help to improve the quality of the image.
Surge marks 	There is increased density in this negative, in a pattern that corresponds to the holes in the film. These are caused by over-agitation that causes developer to rush through the sprocket holes of the film with great turbulence and give extra local development.	Reduce agitation or ensure that you invert the tank fully during agitation. Do not shake the tank from side to side. Alternatively, agitate by twirling the spirals or by stirring the developer.
Water marks 	Irregular crescent-shaped or round areas of lightness in a print are usually caused by lime deposits from droplets of hard (calciferous) water drying on the film.	When you have reached the end of film processing and have a clean film, soak it in a bath with wetting agent, gently shake off any excess water and hang it to dry. If possible, wipe off the water using a photographic squeegee.
X-ray marks 	This area of a black-and-white film should be clear but it carries patterns that repeat across the roll of film. It has been caused by x-rays used to check luggage kept in the cargo hold of an aircraft. These are much more powerful than those used for hand luggage.	Never place film in luggage that will be carried in the cargo hold. Do not use x-ray protective bags, as airport security will increase the power of the x-rays to penetrate the bags. Always carry unprocessed film – exposed or unexposed – in hand luggage.

》 BLACK-AND-WHITE FILM

PROBLEM	SYMPTOM	SOLUTION
Air bubbles	A small number of black or grey dots, sometimes with a darker centre, are scattered randomly over the film. Air bubbles were trapped when developer was poured in, slowing development at that point to cause a reduction in density in the negative.	Check that the lid is fastened tightly, then tap the developing tank firmly against the bench after developer has been added and the lid has been fastened. This dislodges any air bubbles that may be stuck on the side of the film.
Light fogging	Some parts of the image are white, right at the edge of the film. With colour film, there may be irregular bands of colour. The film has been "fogged" with light – light has been let in before development.	Ensure you load your camera away from direct light. If you are walking outdoors on a sunny day, turn your back to the sun to load the camera. Keep rolls of film away from direct light.

》 DIGITAL

Digital image problems fall into two broad categories. There are those that are caused by inappropriate action from the operator or a device, such as a scanner, and there are problems, known as artefacts, caused by the nature or limitations of the digital image itself, or its processing. Artefacts include moiré effects, blocked shadows, and posterization.

PROBLEM	SYMPTOM	SOLUTION
Soft scan	The scanned image appears unfocused and lacking in detail. Colours may also appear washed out and blended together. The scanner may not be properly focused on the original.	Focus manually if the scanner controls allow it. Or change the mount for the transparency to help it lie flat, and re-scan. If possible place the transparency between glass holders and re-scan.
Aliasing	Angled lines and details appear to be jagged or saw-toothed in profile. Details are lost and sharp edges in the image appear indistinct. The resolution of the image acquisition – either scanner or digital camera – is not sufficient to define the details fully.	Increase the resolution of the scan or your camera. If you obtained this result from making the file larger, you may have increased the file size by too much. If so, set a smaller increase.

» DIGITAL

PROBLEM	SYMPTOM	SOLUTION
Newton's rings	Multi-coloured concentric rings or patterns around a central core occur singly or there may be several. These are Newton's rings, caused by a small amount of air trapped between scanner and original behaving like a prism.	If scanning a slide, place it in a frame so that it does not touch the scanner glass. If scanning a film-strip, raise it off the glass with a sheet of paper with a window cut out of it. Ensuring the glass is perfectly dry may also help.
Print moiré	A new pattern of dots emerges when printed material is scanned. The pattern may disappear if the file is printed or viewed at a different size. There is a clash between the pattern of the printed material and that of the scanner.	Rotate the original by a small amount – five degrees, for example – and scan again. If the pattern persists, rotate a little more and re-scan. Alternatively, change the resolution and re-scan. There will be a setting at which the pattern disappears.
Noise in shadows	Dark areas of the scan or digital camera image appear speckled with darker and lighter spots. This is shadow noise, caused by the system's inability to represent dark areas accurately.	If the problem is a result of scanning you will need to upgrade your scanner to extract details from the shadows. If the problem originates in the digital camera, ensure you set the lowest sensitivity and highest quality, or use a better-quality digital camera.
Scanner jitter	Scans show jagged lines with the wrong colours or details, which appear to be out of position. This is visible only at high magnification and it is caused by irregular movement of the scanning head.	Re-scan with the original turned round and see if the problem is repeated. If it is, you may have a defective or, more likely, a poor-quality scanner. You will need to have the scanner repaired or use a superior-quality scanner.
JPEG artefacts	The image viewed in close-up appears to be arranged in blocks of similar colour, which obscure or break up details. These are the JPEG kernels or groups of pixels used to compress the image.	If you use JPEG compression to reduce your file size, you should set the highest quality that gives the size of file you wish to work with. Or set the highest compression that does not cause visible artefacting.

》 DIGITAL

PROBLEM	SYMPTOM	SOLUTION
Moiré from screen 	Irregular patterns such as concentric rings or wavy bars appear across the image. These patterns disappear at certain magnifications. They are caused by a clash between any grid-like pattern in the subject with the monitor's own grid.	No solution is needed if the final output is to print, as screen moiré has no effect on print. But if output is to screen, you may need to work at a different resolution. Try rotating the image by 5–15 degrees, or blur the image a little.
File error 	Images take longer than usual to open, thumbnail images do not correspond to the actual image or the images appear garbled, as shown here. The file is corrupted and data is missing or is unreadable.	This occurs when the medium storing the file, such as a hard-disk or memory card, is faulty. There may be incompatibilities between the memory card and the camera in which it is used. Back up all data and replace any card or disk that may be unreliable.
Poor data 	Images appear patchy, with uneven areas of colour. On manipulation, images do not appear as expected. This happens when there is not enough data for the image – there are many gaps and holes in the data.	If the image is a scan, re-scan the image at a higher resolution. If the image is a manipulated version derived from a digital camera, revert to the original image. If this is the original image, there is nothing you can do to increase the amount of data.
Over-sharpened 	Images may be nicely sharp but can also have light margins at the edges, known as haloes, and hard details, with little or no blurring. Small dots appear as sharply-defined squares. The image has been over-sharpened using Unsharp Mask.	Use Unsharp Mask sparingly to improve image sharpness, and only as the final step of image manipulation. If you are preparing images for use by a client, do not apply Unsharp Mask unless specifically asked to do so.
Posterization 	Transitions of tone or colour in the subject appear to be stepped or banded, with sudden changes in colour or density. There is insufficient image data to produce smooth changes, due to low resolution or excessive image manipulation.	Smooth skin tones need the highest resolution if realism is required. Capture or scan your image at the highest quality settings. Avoid excessive image manipulation such as extreme changes in contrast, exposure, or colour balance.

》 DIGITAL

PROBLEM	SYMPTOM	SOLUTION
Blown highlights	Bright areas are devoid of colour, white or nearly white. Attempts to darken the area leads to unsightly greys and no colour. Neighbouring areas also appear too pale and lacking in colour. The cause is overexposure due to direct sun or lighting.	Frame to avoid including the sun or bright sky in the shot. Record in raw format, and underexpose if you cannot avoid including the sun. Make corrections in software. If scene is static, use tone-mapping (HDR) techniques (see p.276–277).
Blocked shadows	Shadows appear to go black suddenly, with no transition zone of darker shadows. There is no detail in the shadows. This is caused by the way some basic scanners and digital cameras encode brightness information.	Give ample exposure to shadow regions while avoiding over-exposure in brighter parts. Use high-quality scanners or digital cameras. If possible, process digital camera images as RAW files instead of as JPEGs.

》 COMMON DIGITAL PRINTING PROBLEMS

Printer problems fall broadly into three categories. There are those that are caused by inadequate communications or other incompatibilities between the printer and computer or software, there are problems caused by printer faults, and finally, there may be incompatibilities between the printer and media used for printing.

PROBLEM	SYMPTOM	SOLUTION
Loss of coverage	The printer works well but suddenly prints uneven lines of ink, or the colour balance changes. The computer or printer may have run out of memory, one or more of the cartridges may have run out of ink, or some nozzles may have become blocked.	Avoid using the computer for other tasks while printing if you are working with large files or have many programs running. Run the cleaning program for the printer or replace the ink cartridges.
Ink pooling	The ink appears to lie on the surface of the paper, pools into puddles of ink, and will not dry. You are using an unsuitable paper or one that is not compatible with your printer.	Use only the manufacturer's recommended papers when you first use your printer. With experience, you can experiment with other papers. Photographic printing papers are generally unsuitable for inkjet printers.

》 COMMON DIGITAL PRINTING PROBLEMS

PROBLEM	SYMPTOM	SOLUTION
Gibberish text ±± └ü½U±T±±T±áσ+EQ‖·)§ ±]W■ü½ j]W■üU Tü½U±] ■ü½ Ñ·±★σTü½U±W ⌐ü½ T ±★┼(]W■ü½ W EÄÑUÄÑ+E]W■ü½ [·±±T■¦W±Tü½U± ±EÄÑT]W■ü½ YÄ%(]W■ü½ ·±áσ&]W■ü½ (]W■üU (] ■ü↲ T±·T±±E‖⌐σW² 4]W■ü	The printer outputs gibberish text that can go on for many pages. You may have sent the wrong type of file to the printer (the example shown is a facsimile). Or, the printer may have crashed and tried, unsuccessfully, to reconstruct an image.	Turn off the printer, wait a few seconds, and turn it back on. You may need to delete the spool file (see your printer instructions). You may also need to check that you are printing to the correct communications port.
Uneven coverage	Even areas of tone appear uneven, with gaps or streaks and visible lines. You are using a low-quality printer or one with blocked nozzles, poor-quality ink cartridges, or low-quality paper, or a combination of all three.	Set your printer to "quality" rather than "speed" printing, use matt or textured papers, use the manufacturer's own ink cartridges, and do not re-use ink cartridges. Introducing a little noise into the image can also improve results.
Dithered colours	The image appears to be made up of fine patterns of colours arranged into bands. The image is "dithered", that is, a few colours are used in patterns to simulate a greater range of colours.	Set the printer to print continuous tone, not dithered colours, and not graphics or poster colours.
Poor details	Fine details in the image appear blurred and hard to distinguish. Subtle changes in colour appear banded or sudden. The printer is set to a low resolution, the image size is too small for the output size, or you are using textured paper or printing onto the wrong side.	Use an image size adequate for the printed, output size. Set the printer to highest quality. Use paper with a smooth or glossy surface suitable for your printer, and ensure you use the correct side.

Glossary

Photography is full of terms describing everything from equipment to techniques. While you may not come across all of them, a knowledge of the language will help you to get the best from your photography.

24-bit Measure of the size or resolution of data that a computer program or component works with.

4/3 Four-thirds or 4:3: sensor format measuring 18 mm × 13.5 mm.

6500 White balance setting that corresponds to normal daylight. It appears warm compared to 9300.

9300 White balance setting that is close to bright daylight. It is used mainly for visual displays.

additive colour Combining or blending two or more coloured lights in order to simulate or give the sensation of another colour.

AE Abbreviation for Automatic Exposure.

AF Abbreviation for Auto-Focus.

aliased Appearance of jagged, broken or stepped tones that should be smooth or even, due to lack of image data or poor processing.

ambient light The available light that is not under the control of the photographer.

analogue A non-digital effect, representation, or record.

anti-aliasing A method of smoothing the diagonal lines in a digital image to avoid a "staircase" effect caused by the edges of individual pixels.

aperture The lens setting that controls the amount of light entering the lens of the camera.

aperture priority An automatic exposure mode that varies the shutter time as required.

APS-C Type of sensor format: approximately 25mm x 16.7mm.

artefact Any information on a digital image that is unwanted.

attachment A digital file that is attached to an email.

auto focus Camera systems that automatically focus the image.

background The bottom layer of a digital image; the base.

backlighting Lighting the subject from behind with the light source facing the camera.

banding Banded noise patterns seen in high-ISO images, particularly in shadow areas.

bicubic interpolation A type of interpolation in which the value of a new pixel is calculated from the values of the eight pixels that are adjacent to it.

bilinear interpolation A type of interpolation in which the value of a new pixel is calculated from the values of the four adjacent pixels on the left, right, top, and bottom.

black An area of an image with no colour or hue because it has absorbed most or all of the light.

bleed (1) A photograph or graphic object that extends off the page when printed. (2) The spread of ink into fibres of the paper, which causes dot gain – dots print larger than intended.

Bluetooth A standard for high-speed wireless radio connections between electronic devices, such as mobile phones, keyboards, and laptop computers.

blur (1) Unsharpness in the image, caused by focusing error, movement during exposure, or poor-quality lens. (2) Post-processing effect that reduces sharpness.

BMP (Bit MaP) A file format for image files native to Windows.

bokeh Quality or characteristics of unsharp parts of an image.

bracketing Taking a range of shots and deliberately under- and overexposing in order to find the best exposure.

brightness (1) A quality of visual perception that varies with the amount or intensity of light. (2) The brilliance of a colour related to hue or colour saturation.

brush An image-editing tool used to apply effects such as colour, blurring, burn, dodge, and so on.

burning-in A digital image-manipulation technique that mimics the darkroom technique of the same name. This method gives a selected part of the image extra exposure, making it appear darker.

calibration Process of matching characteristics or behaviour of a device to a standard.

camera exposure The quantity of light reaching the light-sensitive film or light sensor in a camera. It can be varied by adjusting the aperture of the lens and the duration of the exposure.

camera shake Unsharpness or blur in images caused by movement of camera/lens during exposure.

centre-weighted metering A type of metering that gives more importance to the central areas of an image.

channel A set of data used by image-manipulation software to define colour or mask.

clone To copy part of an image and paste it elsewhere on the same image or onto another image.

close-up lens An attachment lens used to enable normal lenses to work close-up.

CMYK (Cyan, Magenta, Yellow, Key black) The primary inks used in desktop and commercial printing that are used to simulate a range of colours.

ColorSync A proprietary colour-management software system that ensures the colours seen on the screen match those to be reproduced.

colour A quality of visual perception characterized by hue, saturation, and lightness.

colour balance The relative strengths of colours in an image.

colourize To add colour to a greyscale image without changing the original lightness values.

colour cast A tint of colour that covers an image evenly.

colour gamut The range of colours that can be produced by a device or reproduction system.

colour management A system of controlling the colour output of all devices in a production chain.

colour profile Description of colour characteristics of a device, such as a monitor, printer, or camera.

colour space Definition of a range of colours that can be reproduced by a device or that is enclosed by a standard e.g. Adobe RGB or sRGB.

colour temperature The measurement of the colour of light.

compositing A picture processing technique that combines one or more images with a basic image.

compression The process of reducing the size of a digital file by changing the way the data is coded.

Constructivism An abstract European art movement of the early 20th century focusing on architectural and machine-like forms.

continuous auto-focus Auto-focus mode in which adjustments are constantly made with changes in subject distance.

contrast A measure of the difference between the lightest and darkest parts of an image.

crop (1) To remove part of an image in order to improve composition, fit the image in the available format, or square up the image to the correct horizon. (2) To restrict a scan to the required part of an image.

crop sensor A sensor size smaller than full-frame, usually APS-C.

D50 Standard for white light suitable for viewing prints by tungsten lamps.

Dadaism An art movement founded in 1916 in Zurich by a group of poets, writers, and artists who sought to challenge what they saw as a smug art establishment.

DAM (Digital Asset Management) Systems and software applications for organizing files such as images and associated metadata.

D-SLR Abbreviation for Digital Single Lens Reflex.

definition Subjective assessment of the clarity and the quality of detail visible in an image.

depth of field The measurement of how much of an image is acceptably sharp, from the nearest point to the camera to the furthermost point.

diaphragm The apparatus in the lens that forms the aperture.

differential focusing Focusing on a subject and rendering some parts sharp, some parts unsharp.

diffuser An accessory that softens light or the image.

digital manipulation The process of changing the characteristics of a digital image using a computer and software.

digital watermark Image or information embedded in an image identifying copyright owner; may be visible or readable only by software.

direct vision finder Type of viewfinder in which the subject is observed directly, for example, through a hole or optical device.

display A device such as a monitor screen, LCD projector, or LCD panel on a camera that provides a temporary visual representation of data.

distortion Defect in lens performance that causes shape of subject to be different in image.

dodging Technique for controlling local contrast during printing by reducing selectively the amount of light reaching parts of the image that would otherwise print too dark. Also its digital equivalent.

dpi (dots per inch) The number of dots that can be addressed or printed by an output device; indicative of how much detail (or resolution) the device gives.

driver Software used by a computer to control or drive a peripheral device such as a scanner, printer, or removable media drive.

drop shadow Graphic effect in which an object appears to float above a surface, leaving an off-set fuzzy shadow below it.

duotone (1) Photo-mechanical printing process using two inks to increase tonal range. (2) Mode of working in image-manipulation software that simulates the printing of an image with two inks.

DVD (Digital Versatile Disc) An electronic storage medium, of which there are many variants.

electronic viewfinder An LCD screen, found under an eyepiece, showing the view through the camera lens.

enhancement A change made to one or more qualities of an image, for example, increasing the colour saturation or sharpness.

EPS (Encapsulated PostScript) A file format used for graphics.

EV (Exposure Value) A system for relating aperture and shutter settings to brightness values.

evaluative metering A type of metering system that divides a scene into a number of sections and measures the brightness in each in order to determine the final exposure.

EVF See *electronic viewfinder*

exposure Process of allowing light to reach light-sensitive material to create the image.

f/number Setting of lens diaphragm that determines amount of light transmitted by lens.

f-stop (f-number stop) The f/number or aperture setting.

feathering Blurring a border or bounding line by reducing the sharpness or suddenness of the change.

file format Method or structure of computer data.

fill in (1) To illuminate shadows cast by the main light by using another light source or reflector to bounce light from main source into shadows. (2) In image manipulation, to cover an area with colour using the bucket tool.

film speed The sensitivity of film to light, measured by the ISO number.

filter (1) Software that is used to convert one file format to another or to apply effects to the image. (2) Cover fitted to front of lens to alter the appearance of the image.

FireWire Proprietary name for IEEE 1394, the standard for high-speed cable connection between devices.

flare A non-image-forming light caused by internal reflections within the lens.

flash (1) To illuminate with a very brief burst of light. (2) Equipment used to provide a brief burst of light. (3) Type of electronic memory used in, for example, digital cameras.

flatten To combine multiple layers and other elements together into a single background layer.

focal length The distance from the centre of a lens to its point of focus on the film or digital sensor, when the lens is set to infinity. Usually measured in millimetres.

focus To bring an image into focus by adjusting the distance setting of the lens.

full frame Sensor sized approximately 36mm x 24mm, the same as a full frame of 35mm film.

gamma In monitors, a measure of the correction to the colour signal prior to its projection on screen. A high gamma gives a darker overall screen image.

GIF (Graphic Interchange Format) A highly compressed file format designed for use over the Internet.

graduated filter A type of filter that varies in strength from one side to the other.

grain Small particles of silver or colour that make up an image.

greyscale A measure of the number of distinct steps between black and white in an image.

HD (High definition) Images 1920 pixels wide. As HDTV: Video format of at least 1080 lines.

HDMI (High-Definition Multimedia Interface) Used for transmitting video data.

HDR (High Dynamic Range) Image or device reproducing wide range of tones. Usually applied to tone-mapped image in which highlights and shadows are made close to mid-tones.

HEIC (High Efficiency Image Format) Image format for high-quality compressed images.

highlights The brightest or lightest parts of an image.

hot-pluggable Connector or interface, such as USB or FireWire, that can be disconnected or connected while the computer is switched on.

hue Name for the visual perception of colour.

IEEE 1394 See *FireWire*

ILC (Interchangeable Lens Compact Camera) Mirrorless camera.

ILink Proprietary name for IEEE-1394, the standard for high-speed cable connection between devices.

image stabilization Mechanism in camera or lens used to compensate for camera shake to produce sharper images without using a tripod.

infinity Lens focus setting at which, for all practical purposes, the light rays enter the lens parallel to each other.

interpolation Method of inserting pixels into an existing digital image using existing data.

iris The hole created by the lens diaphragm to admit light into the camera.

ISO In photography, measure of amplification of light: larger numbers indicate greater amplification.

jaggies Appearance of stair-stepping artefacts or aliasing.

JPEG (Joint Photographic Expert Group) A data compression technique that reduces file sizes with loss of information. Most widely used type of image file.

Jugendbewegung (Youth Movement) Term used to describe a loosely coordinated network of youth groups active in Germany from around 1900 to the 1930s that shared a love of the outdoors.

k (1) A binary thousand, sometimes used to denote 1024 bytes. (2) Key ink in the CMYK process. (3) Degrees Kelvin, which measure colour temperature.

key tone The principal or most important tone in an image, usually the mid-tone between white and black.

layer A part of a digital image that lies over another part of the image.

layer mode Picture-processing or image-manipulation technique that determines the way that a layer in a multi-layer image combines or interacts with the layer below.

LCD (Liquid Crystal Display) A display using materials that can block light.

lens hood An accessory for the lens that shades it from light and protects it from rain.

light meter A device used to calculate camera settings in response to light.

lossless compression A computing routine, such as LZW, that reduces the size of a digital file without reducing the information.

lossy compression A computing routine, such as JPEG, that reduces the size of a digital file but loses some information or data in the process.

lpi (lines per inch) A measure of resolution used in photo-mechanical reproduction.

LUT (Look Up Table) Database relating various conditions to appropriate settings e.g. lighting conditions to camera exposure.

Macro Focusing in the close-up range but with the subject not magnified.

Manual exposure Setting the camera exposure by hand.

marquee Selection tool in image-manipulation and graphics software.

mask Selecting parts of an image to restrict the area that digital manipulation will affect.

megabyte One million bytes of data.

megapixel One million pixels. Used to describe a class of digital camera in terms of sensor resolutions.

memory card Small card able to store data without need for power.

mid-tone Areas of subject or image showing accurate colours, midway in brightness between lightest and darkest parts.

moiré A pattern of alternating light and dark bands or colours caused by interference between two or more superimposed patterns, which differ in phase, orientation, or frequency.

monochrome Photograph or image made up of black, white, and greys. May or may not be tinted.

ND (Neutral-Density) filter A filter used to reduce the amount of light entering the lens.

nearest neighbour A type of interpolation in which a new pixel's value is copied from the pixel nearest to it.

noise Irregularities in an image that reduce information content.

OLED (Organic Light Emitting Diode) Type of flat-panel display. Replacing LCD panels.

opacity A measure of how much of an image can be "seen" through a layer or layers.

optical viewfinder A type of viewfinder that shows the subject through an optical system, rather than via a monitor screen.

out-of-gamut Colours from one colour system that cannot be seen or reproduced in another.

output Hard-copy printout of a digital file.

paint To apply a colour, texture, or effect with a digital "brush".

palette (1) A set of tools, colours, or shapes. (2) A range or selection of colours in an image.

panoramic A view obtained by rotating a lens to see a wide area or by stitching images together.

partial metering Metering that measures from a part of the image, usually in the centre.

passive autofocus A type of autofocus in which the image is analyzed for sharpness.

peripheral A device such as a printer, monitor, scanner, or modem that is connected to a computer.

phase contrast auto-focus Auto-focus technique that compares light from different sides of the image to focus the lens.

photomechanical half-toning A technique that is used to represent continuous-tone originals, such as photographs, as a grid of dots of ink that vary in size.

photomontage A composite photographic image made from the combination of several other images.

Photo-Secession group An influential group of early 20th-century photographers led by Alfred Stieglitz, who aimed to elevate photography to a fine art.

pixel A picture element. It is the smallest unit of digital imaging.

pixellated The appearance of a digital image whose individual pixels are clearly discernible.

plug-in Application software that works in conjunction with a host program into which it is "plugged", so that it operates as if part of the program itself.

polarizer A type of filter that polarizes the light passing through it. Mainly used to darken sky or remove reflections from water.

posterization Representation of an image that results in a banded appearance and flat areas of colour.

post-processing Image manipulation or other effects applied to an image after it has been processed in the camera.

ppi (points per inch) The number of points seen or resolved by a scanning device per linear inch.

predictive autofocus A type of autofocus that calculates the speed of a moving subject in order to set the correct focus point for the moment of exposure.

prefocusing A technique of setting focus first before re-composing a photograph to take the shot.

pre-scan A quick view of the photograph or object to be scanned taken at a low resolution to allow re-cropping of the scan.

profile Process of determining colour characteristics of a device e.g. monitor, camera, or scanner.

program exposure A type of autoexposure control in which the camera sets both shutter time and aperture.

RAM (Random Access Memory) A computer component in which information can be stored or rapidly accessed.

raw Image file produced by camera with minimal processing, usually in format specific to the camera. Raw files need to be converted before they can be used.

read only Setting on file that allows data to be read, but not to be edited or changed.

reflected light reading The most common type of light reading, which measures the light reflected from the subject.

resizing Changing the resolution or file size of an image.

resolution A measure of how much detail an optical system can see.

retouching Changing an image using bleach, dyes, pigments, or software.

RGB (Red, Green, Blue) The colour model that defines colours in terms of relative amounts of red, green, and blue components.

scanning Process of turning an original into a digital facsimile, creating a digital file of specified size.

shutter priority A type of auto-exposure in which the user sets the shutter while the camera sets the aperture automatically.

shutter speed Exposure time: duration of light-gathering by sensor.

SLR (Single Lens Reflex) A type of camera where the photographer looks through the viewfinder to see exactly the same image that will be exposed onto the film or sensor.

stair-stepping Jagged, rough, or step-like reproduction of a line or boundary, which was originally smooth.

standard lens A lens of focal length roughly equal to the diagonal of the picture format.

stop (1) A step in processing that halts development. (2) A unit of exposure equal to a doubling or halving of the amount of light.

style Recipe or prepared settings for applying the same effects to a selection of image files.

subtractive primaries The three colours (cyan, magenta, yellow) that are used to create all other colours in photographic printing.

Suprematism An abstract art movement developed in the early 20th century in Russia by Kazimir Malevich extolling the supremacy of sensation and feeling in art.

Surrealism An art movement, founded in 1924 by André Breton that emphasized the role of the unconscious in creative activity.

system requirement The specification defining the minimum configuration of equipment and version of operating system needed to open and run particular application software or devices.

telephoto lens A type of lens with a focal length that is longer than the physical length of the lens. It is used to make distant objects appear larger.

tethering Controlling camera functions and uploading images from camera using computer software.

thumbnail A representation of an image as a small, low-resolution version.

TIFF A widely used digital image format.

tint (1) Colour that can be reproduced with process colours; a process colour. (2) An overall, usually light, colouring that tends to affect areas with density but not clear areas.

transparency adaptor Accessory light-source that enables a scanner to scan transparencies.

USB (Universal Serial Bus) The standard port design for connecting peripheral devices, such as a digital camera, printer, or telecommunications equipment, to a computer.

USM (UnSharp Mask) An image-processing technique that improves the apparent sharpness of an image.

UV filter (Ultra-Violet filter) A type of lens filter that stops ultra-violet rays passing through.

vignetting The technique of darkening the corners of an image through the obstruction of light rays.

warm colours Hues such as reds through oranges to yellows.

white balance A shade of white (warm, cold, neutral) used as a standard white.

wide-angle converter A lens accessory that increases the angle of view of the lens to which it is attached.

Zip Proprietary name for a data storage system. Also method of compressing files.

zoom lens A type of lens in which the focal length can be altered without changing focus.

Index

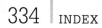

Acknowledgments

First Edition

Author's acknowledgments

To all the team at Dorling Kindersley, in particular Nicky Munro and Jenisa Patel, my very appreciative thanks for your hard work on a demanding project. Also thanks to picture researchers Carolyn Clerkin and Anna Bedewell for their dogged persistence, which enabled us to obtain the great photographs used in this book.

Many thanks to Alice Hunter, Cicely Ang, and Louise Ang for their contributions to the research. Thanks also to Ruth Silverman of Ruth Silverman Gallery, Berkeley, California, and Fifty One Fine Art Photography, Antwerp for their help with research.

And to Wendy, as always, my strength, support and inspiration – this book is as much hers as anyone else's.

Publisher's acknowledgments

Dorling Kindersley would like to thank the following people for their help in the preparation of this book:

Editorial: Corinne Asghar and Linda Martin
Design: Mark Cavanagh, Karen Self, and Karen Constanti
Illustrations: Patrick Mulrey
Proofreading: Constance Novis
Indexing: Chris Bernstein

The publisher would like to thank the following for their kind permission to use images of their products:

ACDSee, Adobe, Agfa, ArcSoft, Inc., Canon, Case Logic Europe, Corel, Cullmann, Epson, Extensis, Fuji Photo Film (UK) Ltd, Gossen, Hasselblad, ILFORD, Jessops, Konica Minolta, LaCie, Leica Camera Ltd, Lexar Media Inc., Linhof and Studio Ltd, Manfrotto/DayMen International, Microtek, Minox GmbH, Nikon UK Ltd, Olympus, Pentax, Ricoh, Roxio - a division of Sonic Solutions, SANYO Europe Ltd, Sony UK Ltd, Tamron Europe GmbH, Tatung (UK) Ltd

Second edition

Dorling Kindersley would like to thank:

Saffron Stocker for the original jacket concept and Vanessa Bird for indexing.

Picture credits

The publisher would like to thank the following for their kind permission to reproduce their photographs:

Abbreviations key: t-top, b-bottom, r-right, l-left, c-centre, a-above, f-far

8-9 Getty Images: Panoramic Images (t). **10** Magnum: Bruno Barbey (b). **11** Sotheby's Picture Library, London: (tc). **12** Magnum: Marc Riboud (tc). Science Photo Library: NASA (bc). **13** Malick Sidibe: Fifty One Fine Art Photography. **14** Getty Images: Ken Weingart. **16** Seapics.com: Doug Perrine. National Geographic Image Collection: Jerry Driendl Photography/Panoramic Images. **18-19** Corbis: Will Burgess/Reuters (b). **20** Corbis: Roger Ressmeyer. Getty: Photodisc Red/Geoff Manasse (tl runner). **21** Rex Features. **22** Magnum: Eve Arnold (bc). N.H.P.A: Stephen Dalton (tr). **23** Getty Images: Oscar Graubner/Time Life Pictures. **24** Corbis: Ansel Adams Publishing Rights Trust (b); Christopher Felver (tl). **25** Corbis: Ansel Adams Publishing Rights Trust (tl). Getty Images: Ansel Adams/National Archives/Time Life Pictures (cl). **26** Corbis: Keith Dannemiller (tl). The J. Paul Getty Museum, Los Angeles: Estate of Manuel Alvarez Bravo (b, cr). **27** The Estate of Diane Arbus, LLC (br). Fraenkel Gallery, SF: The Estate of Gary Winogrand (clb). Taka Ishii Gallery: (tl); Nobuyoshi Araki (cra). **28** Getty Images: Bernard Gotfryd (tl). Magnum: Eve Arnold (br, bl). **29** Dover Publications: (br). Réunion Des Musées Nationaux Agence Photographique: Felice Beato/Musée des arts asiatiques-Guimet,Paris (cra). **30-31** Estate of Guy Bourdin/Art & Commerce Anthology: Guy Bourdin. **32** Estate of Guy Bourdin/Art & Commerce Anthology: (b, crb, tl). **33** Corbis: Bettmann (tl). Getty Images: Margaret Bourke-White/Time Life Pictures (bl, br); Time & Life Pictures/Margaret Bourke White (cl). **34** Corbis: David Gallant (tl). Getty Images: Bill Brandt/Picture Post (clb, br). Réunion Des Musées Nationaux Agence Photographique: Bill Brandt Archive Ltd, London (cr). **35** Corbis: Stapleton Collection (bl, crb). Getty Images: Julia Margaret Cameron (tl). **36** Getty Images: Alfred Eisenstaedt/Time Life Pictures (tl). Magnum: Cornell Capa/Robert Capa (bl, br). **37** Magnum: Cornell Capa/Robert Capa. **38** Corbis: Reuters (tl). Magnum: Henri Cartier-Bresson (bl), (br). **39** Magnum: Collection HCB/FRM (bl); Henri Cartier-Bresson (cr, t). **40** Valdir Cruz: (cra). N.H.P.A: Elizabeth MacAndrew (clb); Stephen Dalton (bl). Throckmorton Fine Art, New York: (tl). **41** Reproduced with permission from Dupain's Beaches by Jill White (Chapter & Verse, Sydney, 1999): (br, clb). National Geographic Image Collection: (tl); David Doubilet (cra). **42** Corbis: Hulton-Deutsch Collection (tl). Getty Images: Alfred Eisenstaedt/Time Life Pictures (bc, cr). **43** Getty Images: Ernst Haas (tl). Magnum: Elliott Erwitt (bc, cra). **44** Corbis: Ted Streshinsky (tl). Getty Images: Ernst Haas (bl). **45** Getty Images: Ernst Haas (tr, tl, b). **46** akg-images: (tc); © DACS 2019 / © The Heartfield Community of Heirs / DACS 2019 (lc). FLPA - Images of Nature: David Hosking (clb); Eric Hosking (bl). **47** Eikoh Hosoe: Howard Greenberg Gallery, NYC (cra, tl). Graciela Iturbide: (br). Mauricio Rocha Iturbide: (clb). **48** Corbis: Andre Kertesz/Hulton-Deutsch Collection (bl); Andre Kertesz/Condé Nast Archive (cra); Peter Turnley (tl). **49** FLPA - Images of Nature: Frans Lanting (bl, br, cr). Frans Lanting Photography: (tl). **50-51** FLPA - Images of Nature: Frans Lanting/Minden Pictures. **52** Associated Press: John Froscauer (tl). Annie Leibovitz: nbpictures (bl, bcl). **53** Magnum: Herbert List (tr, br, tl). **54** Corbis: Leo Mason (b, cr). Leo Mason: (tl). **55** Corbis: Zen Icknow (tl). Don McCullin: (br). V&A Images: Don McCullin (bl). **56** Magnum: Rene Burri (tl); Steve McCurry (bl, br, cl). **57** Magnum: Susan Meiselas (bl, br, cr, tl). **58** Greenpeace: (tl). **58-59** Magnum: Raghu Rai. **59** Magnum: Raghu Rai (br, tr). **60** akg-images: (tl). www.bridgeman.co.uk: © DACS 2019 / © MAN RAY TRUST / ADAGP, Paris and DACS, London 2019 (br). Réunion Des Musées Nationaux Agence Photographique: © DACS 2019 / © MAN RAY TRUST / ADAGP, Paris and DACS, London 2019 (bl). **61** Magnum: Bruno Barbey (clb). Novosti (London): (tl). Sebastiao Salgado: Amazonas/nbpictures (br). Photo Scala, Florence: The Museum of Modern Art, New York / © DACS 2019 / © Rodchenko & Stepanova Archive, DACS, RAO 2019 (c). **62** Bildarchiv Preußischer Kulturbesitz, Berlin: (tl). Corbis: Philip Gould (clb). The J. Paul Getty Museum, Los Angeles: © DACS 2019 / © Die Photographische Sammlung / SK Stiftung Kultur - August Sander Archiv, Cologne / DACS 2019 (c). Magnum: W. Eugene Smith (bl). **63** Corbis: Bettmann (tl). The J. Paul Getty Museum, Los Angeles: Estate of Georgia O'Keeffe (cr). Science & Society Picture Library: (bl, br). **64** Corbis: Miroslav Zajíc (tl). Réunion Des Musées Nationaux Agence Photographique: CNAC/MNAM Dist. RMN/Adam Rzepka (bl, br). **65** Réunion Des Musées Nationaux Agence Photographique: Shoji Ueda (clb, clb, cr). Uniphoto: (tl). **66-67** Nederlands fotomuseum. **68** Getty Images: Andreas Feininger/Time Life Pictures. Stockbyte: (tl runner). **69** N.H.P.A: Stephen Dalton. **70** Archivi Alinari: Wanda Wulz (tr). Getty Images: Adri Berger (tl). Science & Society Picture Library: NMPFT - Kodak Collection (bc). **71** NASA: Goddard Space Flight Center. **72** Corbis: Bettmann (bc). **73** akg-images: Société Française de Photographie (c). Science & Society Picture Library: NMPFT (tl). **74** Science & Society Picture Library: NMPFT (br). Topfoto.co.uk: (ca). **75** Science & Society Picture Library: Science Museum Pictorial (tc, tr). Topfoto.co.uk: Harlingue/Roger-Viollet (bl). **76-77** Getty Images: William Grundy/ London Stereoscopic Company. **78** Harry Ransom Humanitites Research Center, The University of Texas at Austin: Gernsheim Collection (c). Science & Society Picture Library: Science Museum (tl). **79** akg-images: Archie Miles Collection, Coll. Archiv f. Kunst & Geschichte/Archie Miles. (bc). Corbis: Stapleton Collection/Peter Henry Emerson (t). **80** Science & Society Picture Library: NMPFT (t). akg-images: (bl). **81** Corbis: Samuel Bourne/Historical Picture Archive (tr). Science Photo Library: Eadweard Muybridge Collection/Kingston Museum (bl). **82-83** Corbis: Timothy H. O'Sullivan. **84** Mary Evans Picture Library: (b). popperfoto: (cl). **85** www.bridgeman.co.uk: Stapleton Collection, UK/Jacques Henri Lartigue © Ministere de la Culture - France/AAJHL (bc). Corbis: Bettmann (tr). Science & Society Picture Library: NMPFT - Kodak Collection (bl). **86** Corbis: Bettmann (b). Science & Society Picture Library: NMPFT (tr). **87** Corbis: Condé Nast Archive/Baron de Meyer (cr); Bettmann/Jacob August Riis (br). Getty Images: Lewis W. Hine/National Archives/Time Life Pictures (bl). **88-89** Archivi Alinari. **90** Oskar Barnack Archive/Leica Camera AG: (cr). Getty Images: Erich Salomon (b). **91** akg-images: Hedda Walther (tr). Corbis: Dorothea Lange (tl); Hulton-Deutsch Collection (tr). **92** www.bridgeman.co.uk: El Lissitzky (bc). Science & Society Picture Library: NMPFT (cl, tl). **93** Corbis: Bettmann (br). The J. Paul Getty Museum, Los Angeles: Edward Weston (tr). Science & Society Picture Library: NMPFT (bl). **94-95** Réunion Des Musées Nationaux Agence Photographique: Michele Bellot/Estate Brassai. **96** Getty Images: Michael Rougier/Time Life Pictures (bl). The Museum of Modern Art, New York: (tl). Magnum: Burt Glinn (br). **97** Getty Images: Weegee (Arthur Fellig)/International Centre of Photography (tr). Science Photo Library: Professor Harold Edgerton (br). **98** Magnum: David Hurn (bc). NASA (tl). popperfoto.com: (cr). **99** Getty Images: Larry Burrows/ Time Life Pictures (br); Ronald S. Haeberle/Time Life Pictures (tr). **100-101** Getty Images: Lambert. **103** Canon (UK) Ltd: (br). Corbis: Howard Sochurek (tl). NASA: Langley Research Center (bl). Science Photo Library: Edelmann (tr). **104** akg-images: Gruner & Jahr (tc). Getty Images: Neal Preston/Camera 5/Time Inc/Time & Life Pictures (tl); Tim Graham (bc). **105** Steve Cavalier: (tr). Cindy Sherman: (bl). Science Photo Library: Philippe Plailly (br). **106-107** Magnum: Abbas. **108** Apple: (tl). Getty Images: Andrew Wong (bl). **109** Magnum: Chris Steele-Perkins (tc). NASA: European Space Agency and H. E. Bond (br). **110** Corbis: Channel Island Picture Agency (tl). Getty Images: Chung Sung-Jun (b). **111** Heather Barnett: (tl, tr). Harry Borden: (bl). **112-113** Magnum: Ferdinando Scianna. **114-115** Getty Images: Joel Sartore (b). **116** Corbis: Lightscapes Photography, Inc. Alamy: Chris Ivin (tl). **118** Wendy Gray: (tr). **120** © Sony Corporation: (b). **121** Alamy Stock Photo: Cameras and photo equipment (bc). Dreamstime.com: Kawee Wateesatogkij (br). Getty Images: Digital Camera Magazine / Future (tr). **122** Getty Images: PhotoPlus Magazine / Future (bl). **124** © Canon: (cb). Getty Images: T3 Magazine / Future (cr). © 2019 Leica Camera AG: (bc). **125** Alamy Stock Photo: Hugh Threlfall (br). © Canon: (cra). The Olympus Tough! TG-4: (cb). © Sony Corporation: (cla). **126** Alamy Stock

Photo: Deyan Baric (c). © Sony Corporation: (br). **127** Getty Images: Digital Camera Magazine / Future (tr). Hasselblad.com: (bl). Shenzhen Zhishen Information Technology Co., Ltd.: Zhiyu n Crane Plus (br). **128** iStockphoto.com: adventtr (bc). **129** © 2019 BowerUSA: (cla, tc). Alamy Stock Photo: Design Pics Inc (bc); Mohd Zaidi Razak (bl). iStockphoto.com: skodonnell (cla/Lifeproof case). Kenko: REAL PRO CLIP LENS 7x Tele/http://www.kenkoglobal.com/photo/mobile_photo/lenses/7x_tele.html (tr). © Sony Corporation: (crb). **131** Alamy Stock Photo: incamerastock (cra). Dreamstime.com: Julitt (bl). Thanks to Fujifilm UK for supplying the images: (tc). **133** © Canon: (bl). © Sony Corporation: (cl, cr). **134** Pixabay: alexng / Alex Ng. from Hongkong (bc). **135** iStockphoto.com: ramzihachicho (c). Manfrotto www.manfrotto. com: (cra). © Sony Corporation: (br). **137** Alamy Stock Photo: Andrew Cheal (clb). Petar Milošević: https://commons.wikimedia.org/wiki/File:Ilford_XP2_super_400.jpg (bl). Thanks to Fujifilm UK for supplying the images: (cla, cl). **148** Andy Mitchell. Image Source: (tl runner). **150** Getty Images: Ernst Haas (t). Andy Mitchell: (bl). Succession Raghubir Singh: (br). **153** Magnum: Marc Riboud (bl). **157** Succession Raghubir Singh: (tr). **160** FLPA - Images of Nature: Jim Brandenburg/ Minden Pictures (bl). **164-165** P.K Apagya/Fifty One Fine Art Photography: apagya. **173** Magnum: Alex Webb (b). **176-177** Lucien Clergue. **198** Corbis: David H. Wells (bc). Getty: Photodisc Blue/Mel Curtis (bl). **199** Yevonde Portrait Archive: (bl). DK Images: Angus Beare Collection (tr). Photolibrary.com: Workbookstock.Com Co/Op Service/ Arwen Mills Roxann (br). **202-203** Corbis: Regan Cameron. **204** Corbis: Stuart Westmorland (bl). **205** Getty Images: David Maitland (bl). Andy Mitchell: (tl). **206** Getty Images: John Kelly (cl). **207** Alamy Images: Papilio/Robert Pickett (tr). Getty Images: Paul Souders (cl). **213** Jamie Jeeves: (tl, tr). Patrick Baldwin: (bc). **216-217** Panos Pictures: Chien-min Chung. **218** Zefa Visual Media: Masterfile/ David Muir (br). **219** Corbis: Tracy Kahn (bl). Prentenkabinet, University Library, University of Leiden, The Netherlands: Emmy Andriesse (bl). Zefa Visual Media: Grace (br). **221** Photolibrary.com: Plainpicture (tc). **222-223** Magnum: Micha Bar Am. **224** Getty Images: Tim Thompson (cl). **231** Franco Fontana: (br). **234-235** Corbis: Galen Rowell. **236** DK Images: Jacqui Hurst (cl). **237** Getty Images: Richard During (cr). **238** DK Images: Lindsey Stock (br). **239** DK Images: Jacqui Hurst (tr). **242** Corbis: Wartenberg/Picture Press (cl). **243** Corbis: Julie Dennis Brothers (b). Pixtal: Christopher Gray (tr). **244** Getty Images: Hans Neleman (b). Pixtal: Christopher Gray (cl, cr). **245** Pixtal: Christopher Gray (tl, tr, bc, bl, br). **248** Arcaid.co.uk: John Edward Linden (br). **249** Arcaid.co.uk: Richard Bryant (br). Millennium Images: Paul Freeman (bl). **252-253** Alamy Images: Ambient Images Inc/Larry Brownstein. **258-259** Getty Images: Hiroshi Nomura. **260-261** Catherine McIntyre: Catherine MacIntyre. **266** Dreamstime. com: Zzvet (bc). **267** Dreamstime.com: Anton Starikov (crb). **269** Alamy Stock Photo: Artur Marciniec (bl). **270** 123RF.com: Anatoly Fedotov (c/ USB A/B cable). Alamy Stock Photo: Freer Law (clb/USB plug); Studioshots (cb); studiomode (bl). Depositphotos Inc: artavet (clb/Type C male to micro USB female); kataklinger (c); pavelr (clb/Adapter USB, clb/USB to mini USB). Dreamstime.com: Akinshin (cr); Anmbph (cl). iStockphoto.com: Jarp (clb/conexion phone micro usb, clb/Mini usb black conexion); popovaphoto (clb/micro-jack to micro USB, clb, clb/ mini to micro USB). **271** Epson: 2019 Seiko Epson Corporation: (br). Getty Images: N-Photo Magazine / Future (cra). Rex by Shutterstock: Future / Joby Sessions (tc). **292** © Canon: (clb). **296** Getty Images: VCL/ Spencer Rowell. InMagine: Image100 (tl runner). **297** Alamy Stock Photo: Andriy Popov (tr). **302** Getty: Photodisc Green (bl). **303** DK Images: Jerry Young Collection (cbr). **305** Photolibrary.com: Plainpicture (tr). **311** Corbis: Kevin Fleming (cr).

All other images © Dorling Kindersley.
For further information see: www.dkimages.com